THE NOT-TWO

SHORT CIRCUITS

Mladen Dolar, Alenka Zupančič, and Slavoj Žižek, editors

The Puppet and the Dwarf: The Perverse Core of Christianity, by Slavoj Žižek

The Shortest Shadow: Nietzsche's Philosophy of the Two, by Alenka Zupančič

Is Oedipus Online? Siting Freud after Freud, by Jerry Aline Flieger

Interrogation Machine: Laibach and NSK, by Alexei Monroe

The Parallax View, by Slavoj Žižek

A Voice and Nothing More, by Mladen Dolar

Subjectivity and Otherness: A Philosophical Reading of Lacan, by Lorenzo Chiesa

The Odd One In: On Comedy, by Alenka Zupančič

The Monstrosity of Christ: Paradox or Dialectic? by Slavoj Žižek and John Milbank, edited by Creston Davis

Interface Fantasy: A Lacanian Cyborg Ontology, by André Nusselder

Lacan at the Scene, by Henry Bond

Laughter: Notes on a Passion, by Anca Parvulescu

All for Nothing: Hamlet's Negativity, by Andrew Cutrofello

The Trouble with Pleasure: Deleuze and Psychoanalysis, by Aaron Schuster

The Not-Two: Logic and God in Lacan, by Lorenzo Chiesa

THE NOT-TWO

LOGIC AND GOD IN LACAN

Lorenzo Chiesa

THE MIT PRESS   CAMBRIDGE, MASSACHUSETTS   LONDON, ENGLAND

© 2016 Massachusetts Institute of Technology

All rights reserved. No part of this book may be reproduced in any form by any electronic or mechanical means (including photocopying, recording, or information storage and retrieval) without permission in writing from the publisher.

This book was set in Joanna MT Pro by Toppan Best-set Premedia Limited.

Library of Congress Cataloging-in-Publication Data is available.

ISBN: 978-0-262-52903-7

Le monde, le monde est en décomposition, Dieu merci
(Seminar XX)

CONTENTS

Series Foreword ... IX
Preface: Toward Para-ontology ... XI

1   WOMAN AND THE NUMBER OF GOD ... 1

1.1   Of Strange Enjoyment and Being an Angel ... 1
1.2   From *other satisfaction* to *Other enjoyment* ... 6
1.3   Of Being the Other in the Most Radical Sense, and Matters of Cum ... 9
1.4   God: Between Feminine Enjoyment and Phallic Love ... 14

2   LOGIC AND BIOLOGY: AGAINST BIO-LOGY ... 23

2.1   There Are Two Sexes, but There Isn't a Second Sex ... 23
2.2   Biology Soul-Loves ... 29
2.3   From Libido to Drive ... 40
2.4   Potential Energy versus the Lamella ... 54
2.5   Less than Less than Nothing: In-difference ... 60

3   LOGIC, SCIENCE, WRITING ... 77

3.1   Sexuating the Explosion of Sexuality ... 77
3.2   Semblance and Truth ... 81
3.3   Beyond Aristotle and Frege ... 93

4	**THE LOGIC OF SEXUATION**	**105**
4.1	The Two Formulas of Sexuation: Essence and Existence	105
4.2	The Hysteric and the Father	117
4.3	The Four Formulas of Sexuation: Modality and Number	129
4.4	Logic: Producing a Necessity of Discourse	145
CONCLUSION: 0, 1, UNDECIDABILITY, AND THE VIRGIN		**161**
Notes		181
Index		239

SERIES FOREWORD

A short circuit occurs when there is a faulty connection in the network—faulty, of course, from the standpoint of the network's smooth functioning. Is not the shock of short-circuiting, therefore, one of the best metaphors for a critical reading? Is not one of the most effective critical procedures to cross wires that do not usually touch: to take a major classic (text, author, notion) and read it in a short-circuiting way, through the lens of a "minor" author, text, or conceptual apparatus ("minor" should be understood here in Deleuze's sense: not "of lesser quality," but marginalized, disavowed by the hegemonic ideology, or dealing with a "lower," less dignified topic)? If the minor reference is well chosen, such a procedure can lead to insights which completely shatter and undermine our common perceptions. This is what Marx, among others, did with philosophy and religion (short-circuiting philosophical speculation through the lens of political economy, that is to say, economic speculation); this is what Freud and Nietzsche did with morality (short-circuiting the highest ethical notions through the lens of the unconscious libidinal economy). What such a reading achieves is not a simple "desublimation," a reduction of the higher intellectual content to its lower economic or libidinal cause; the aim of such an approach is, rather, the inherent decentering of the interpreted text, which brings to light its "unthought," its disavowed presuppositions and consequences.

And this is what "Short Circuits" wants to do, again and again. The underlying premise of the series is that Lacanian psychoanalysis is a privileged instrument of such an approach, whose purpose is to illuminate a standard text or ideological formation, making it readable in a totally new way—the long history of Lacanian interventions in philosophy, religion, the arts (from the visual arts to the cinema, music, and literature), ideology, and politics justifies this premise. This, then, is not a new series of books on psychoanalysis, but a series of "connections in the Freudian field"—of short Lacanian interventions in art, philosophy, theology, and ideology. "Short Circuits" intends to revive a practice of reading which confronts a classic text, author, or notion with its own hidden presuppositions, and thus reveals its disavowed truth. The basic criterion for the texts that will be published is that they effectuate such a theoretical short circuit. After reading a book in this series, the reader should not simply have learned something new: the point is, rather, to make him or her aware of another—disturbing—side of something he or she knew all the time.

Slavoj Žižek

PREFACE

TOWARD PARA-ONTOLOGY

This book focuses on the treatment of logic and, secondarily, God in Lacan's later oeuvre. My emphasis will be for the most part on his Seminars of the early 1970s, as they revolve around a logical and critically onto-theo-logical investigation of the basic axiom "There is no sexual relationship." The latter is, for Lacan, empirically and historically circumscribed by the clinic of psychoanalysis, formalized by its theory, yet already self-evident in our everyday lives at the level of our love and sex misadventures. The present work should also be regarded as a related enquiry into the notion of truth, which tellingly Lacan defines as our "unfuckable partner."[1] If "There is no sexual relationship" marks both the ultimate deadlock and the origin of subjectivity and sexuation, so that there are nevertheless sexed liaisons, but they do not rely on a measure, or ratio [*rapport*], between the two sexes, then truth corresponds to the truth of incompleteness.

The same point can be approached numerically by means of what Lacan calls the "not-two" [*pas deux*].[2] For him, *Homo sapiens* as a speaking species is fundamentally characterized by difference. This difference is the sexual difference between the semblance of the One that defines those subjects who are sexed as "man" and the not-One that defines those subjects who are sexed as "woman," independently of anatomy. In other words, the not-two condenses the idea that our love and sex life is dictated by man's impossibility of fusing with the *heteros* of woman as an-other One, whereby a two-as-One would follow from the addition of One and One. Concrete sexed liaisons are sustained by a transcendental logic (the so-called phallic function) that attempts to suture this impossibility, and only partly succeeds in doing so, for woman remains not-all caught in the semblance of the One.

This composite field of research thus gives rise to the following major interrogations:

1. What is the precise functioning of the transcendental logic of sexuation/subjectivation that compensates for the truth of incompleteness by establishing phenomenally a semblance of the One, while also presenting incompleteness as a phenomenal impasse?[3]
2. Given the logical truth of incompleteness as the basis of the speaking animal's sexuation/subjectivation, can we ever constructively experience love, a "desire to be One,"[4] as a true phenomenon? Or is a true phenomenon nothing more than an oxymoron, which gives itself only negatively as a phenomenal dead end?
3. Given the logical truth of incompleteness, can we think onto-logically this truth in itself without turning incompleteness into another truth about truth, i.e., into yet another figure of God as absolute being?

Although logic, God, and love as a semblance are all discussed, this volume especially tackles the first query, while building the prerequisites for answering the others. I will address the issue of true love in a separate book. Here, however, I deem it appropriate to spend a few preliminary words on what I will call from now on, with reference to the third query, *para-onto-theology*, or *para-ontology*, since it delineates the outer limits of the current study.

Throughout the history of Western metaphysics, the question concerning the existence of God has undoubtedly been the ultimate question about truth. Lacan starts off from the assumption that, even after the "death of God," namely, the fact that the logical truth of incompleteness appears to us as conclusive, we still need to ask such a question precisely if we intend to develop a defensible form of materialist atheism. In Seminar XX, he puts forward what he calls "the God hypothesis": "As long as somebody says something, the God hypothesis will persist"; or also, "it is impossible to say anything without immediately making Him subsist in the form of the Other."[5] Saying immediately makes Him subsist as a *hypothesis*, the hypothesis of the Other as One. He subsists as a hypothesis that, as such, will persist as long as there is language. The God hypothesis is necessary for the symbolic order, or structure. It survives even the truth of incompleteness.

On the one hand, the necessity of the *logical* existence of the God *hypothesis* for each and every speaking animal is far from entailing the existence of an *ontological* divine essence. But, on the other hand, the very acknowledgment of the incompleteness of structure, or absence of a meta-language, cannot itself go without somehow tacitly positing that "there is no meta-language" is the truth about truth, and consequently that God *is* in such a fashion. A religious man believes, first and foremost, in the ultimate meaning of the world, in the world as "that which works,"[6] although he may well accept that "the world is in a state of decomposition."[7] This is why we should not renounce an exploration of the extrasymbolic dimension generated precisely by the materialist premises of Lacan's God hypothesis, by his attempt at "exorcizing the good old God" through it,[8] summoning him with words, and intentionally making *explicit* his implicit evocation as already inherent to speech as such.

So, is the hypothesis qua hypothesis real? Yes, to the extent that, as Lacan contends, structure is the real: "Structure is to be understood in the sense that it is that which is most real, it is the real itself [...] I stress that this is in no way a metaphor."[9] God is a structural hypothesis (i.e., structure's structural hypothesis) as well as the impossibility of proving it, i.e., the real of the fact that structure finally amounts to a flaw of structure.[10] And, beyond that, is God more than a hypothesis, i.e., a divine essence that would confirm the non-provable hypothesis? Lacan's answer seems to be: we cannot exclude it. Even though, after millennia of religious obscurantism, we are finally able to assume that "the universe is a flower of rhetoric,"[11] who knows? Yet what we know is that even if God were more than a real hypothesis, his nonhypothetical being could only be given to us as hypothetical. ...

Lacan's sporadic but incisive pronouncements on this topic point in the direction of agnosticism as the only coherent kind of atheism. In concluding, against Freud, that God and language are inextricable, he seems to move toward the by now widespread idea among cognitivists that transcendence is somehow favored by certain aspects of brain function, and thus amounts to a sort of inescapable illusion of our species.[12] Yet he also adopts this *critical* stance—which shatters the utopia of psychic freedom but is then often reduced in the life sciences to dull and fatalistic determinism—as the point of departure for a *meta-critical* orientation he delineates only with reluctance. Critically, God is the unfuckable partner who stands as an uninvited guest in all love-sexual liaisons, eavesdropping on us, so that our ordinary amorous predicaments inevitably amount to a *ménage à trois* with him.[13] In this regard, God is but a name for both the supposed consistency of the Other without which there would be no symbolic order nor biological perpetuation of *Homo sapiens* and, conversely, the fact that this supposition is a mere semblance, that there is no guarantor of language, no Other of the Other; thus the sexed Other herself vanishes, does not exist. We are here confronted with what I would label Lacan's deconstructive moment.

Having said this, meta-critically, the same oscillation between the Other as One and the Other as barred needs also to be taken in a serious way from a different, para-onto-theological angle, and challenged: How can we rule out the prospect that the unfuckable partner is precisely the ultimate One as not-One who fucks with us, or fools us—for primarily, he fools himself? Could what phenomeno-logically appears to us as the *oscillation* between the One and the not-One (as related but discrete) not eventually be in itself nothing else than an *equation* of the One with the not-One?

Lacan is very attentive to this matter. He appreciates that we should carefully listen to President Schreber's psychotic delusion according to which the order of God turns against any alleged rational order of the cosmos.[14] Psychotics as "non-stupid" do indeed err, Lacan claims, because of the certainty they grant to their *Weltanschauungen*, but these must not hurriedly be dismissed by meta-critical speculation. If the subject of the unconscious as the subject of psychoanalysis "extends" the subject of modern science,[15] and probably overcomes him by uncovering his constitutive contradictions, then we cannot underestimate Lacan's own admission that, starting with Descartes's liquidation of the evil genius, modern science works on the unwarranted a priori presupposition that God is not deceiving us.[16] In other words, any novel thought of being informed by Lacanian psychoanalysis needs to reassess the most extreme implications of the hyperbolic doubt: there could be "some evil spirit, supremely powerful and cunning"[17] who does not allow us to think correctly, because he is himself the truth and the *whole* truth of incompleteness, which is where his basic *inconsistency* lies. Contra popular versions of deconstruction and poststructuralism, a sympathetic reassessment of the fruitful impasses of the Cartesian cogito is called upon throughout Lacan's oeuvre.

What I am sketching here is a tentative way out of the current impasse afflicting some of the otherwise most compelling contemporary debates on realism and materialism aimed at showing that thought can access an "in-itself"—absolute contingency—that exists independently from thought. Taking Quentin Meillassoux's "speculative realism" as a privileged reference, I would claim that his philosophical enterprise fails as soon as he surreptitiously posits, in the guise of the "acausal universe,"[18] the truth of incompleteness as the truth about truth. He thus unintentionally promotes a form of religious atheism, precisely insofar as he does not measure himself against the eventuality of the "evil genius" as the truth of incompleteness. As an alternative to his "absolute necessity of everything's non-necessity"[19] I propose the following para-onto-theological binary *theorem*, which stems directly from Lacan's logical "God *hypothesis*" (in turn rooted in the empirical *axiom* "There is no sexual relationship"): either incompleteness is, and we can only *half-say* it as truth, for as soon as we say it we evoke completeness; or it is true that incompleteness is the complete truth of a deceivingly inconsistent God, an absolute being whom, by definition, we will never comprehend, for he is illogical. Either the absence of the sexual relationship is through us not only phenomeno-logical but also noumenal, or God, the unfuckable partner, cheats on us. Either the contingent in-itself that language is, i.e., the material "idizwadidiz" [*seskecé*],²⁰ *is* the truth, or this meaninglessness of truth has also at the same time an inconsistent *meaning*.

Such "either/or" is nonnegotiable,²¹ and the only way to protect the "either" from an unwanted religious absolutization of incompleteness is to keep both options open, stating that the acausal universe could hypothetically coincide, from the standpoint of outside the universe, with absolute necessity. On the contrary, overlooking such an outcome—as Meillassoux does— amounts to a supreme form of absolutization, *hic et nunc*, operated from inside the universe as if one were outside of it (i.e., as if one were God).²² Most importantly—and this point is crucial—thanks to a reversal of Pascal's wager, the undecidability at stake would in turn award us the freedom to act as though God did not exist (as a divine essence), for if he existed he could only be fooling us—without even knowing it, after all, since he would also be cheating on himself.²³

In Seminar XV, not surprisingly dedicated to the notion of the act, Lacan comes close to enunciating this practical maxim: "As long as this *or* is retained," that of the question of knowing whether God exists or does not exist, "he will always be there." While, as we have seen, the "God hypothesis" persists as long as somebody says something, "nevertheless [...] *we can act as if he were not there*,"²⁴ that is, assume his inconsistency. The hypothetical "evil genius" is not mentioned here, but surfaces in passages that profoundly resonate with this. For example, in Seminar XX, he features in his Judaic variant as the tyrannical being we must blindly obey, since he does not relate to man in a rational way as the most perfect to the less perfect, but rather insinuates the abyssal insight that what is, is "radically imperfect." Predictably, in this context, Lacan reaches a similar atheistic-agnostic conclusion: if, on the one hand, "that being *as such* may provoke hatred"—due to the botched world he has created—"cannot be ruled out," on the other, "one can no longer hate God" as soon as one acknowledges that "he himself knows nothing [...] of what is going on."²⁵

With the "death of God" we have buried the Aristotelian conception of being as that by which beings with less being participate in the highest of beings. Henceforth we must endure the possibility that, if there is a God as absolute being, he is such just as a "ferociously ignorant"²⁶ One that is not-One, and *para*-onto-theologically put this distinct idea *aside*, while also coexisting with it. As Felix Ensslin has lucidly argued, the final lesson of Lacanian psychoanalysis could well lie in an emphatic encouragement to dispose of the resentment associated with divine viciousness.²⁷ But, we should add, this must be considered a never-ending task if we are not to relapse into more benign figures of transcendence, masked as atheistic, among which we should no doubt include what, with regard to Meillassoux, Alenka Zupančič has effectively dubbed "a God guaranteeing that there is no God."²⁸

Persevering in convening the "evil genius" only to act as if he were not there is the most drastic step it takes to exorcize "the good old God."

***

In this book, para-onto-(theo-)logy will emerge at several points, and chiefly in the open conclusions of the different chapters. In so doing it will highlight the threshold where Lacan's transcendental logic of sexuation/subjectivation contravenes, if not collapses, his own antiphilosophical veto against enquiring into the origins of language. He explicitly brings it into play in a passage from Seminar XX where he allies psychoanalysis with a discourse on the *par-être*, a discourse on being as *para*-being, as "being beside" [*être à côté*].[29] Para-ontology is a *lateral* ontology concerned with the contingency and materiality of the signifier. As its name clearly indicates, it does not overcome, or sublate, philosophical ontology ("They speak about the end of metaphysics: in the name of what?"),[30] but rather unsutures its desire for totalization, namely, its supporting the m'être (the delusional belief of being the master [*maître*] of myself, of being-me-to-myself [*m'être à moi-même*]),[31] which always involves a thwarted attempt at mastering the uni-verse as One.

Apart from this eloquent yet isolated instance, which cannot alone ground a novel thought of being, para-ontology needs to be tracked down in its nascent form and, beyond Lacan, patiently invented using a scattered constellation of daring metaphysical assertions that are soon mitigated, or even retracted as inappropriate speculative temptations the psychoanalyst should eschew, if not as veritable slips of the tongue. The following passage epitomizes, in my view, Lacan's torn stance: "Discourse begins from the fact that here there is a gap. But we cannot remain at that, I mean that I reject any position of origin. But, after all, nothing prevents us from saying that it is because discourse begins that the gap is produced. It is a matter of complete indifference toward the result. What is certain is that discourse is implied in the gap and since there is no meta-language, it cannot get out of it."[32] Such vertiginous fluctuations bear witness to the (repressed) struggle of an antiphilosophical first philosophy in the making, accordingly often accompanied by a plethora of question marks, qui sait, il n'est pas exclu, il est bien possible. To give just a couple of significant examples: "It is well possible after all that $1+1+1+1$ does not make 4 [...] knowing whether that makes, three, four, or two is relatively secondary; it's God's business";[33] "Is there something of the One for the animal?";[34] "It cannot be ruled out, after all, that a swallow reads the tempest, but it is not terribly certain either. That is the whole question";[35] "That being as such may provoke hatred cannot be ruled out";[36] "No language of being. But is there being? [...] What I say is that there isn't. [...] Being is merely presumed in certain words [...] it is but a fact of what is said";[37]

"Who knows whether the fact that we can read the streams I saw over Siberia as the metaphorical trace of writing isn't linked [...] to something that goes beyond the effect of rain?"[38]

In order to penetrate this exceedingly abstract territory, which, with few remarkable but partial exceptions,[39] remains uncharted; in order, that is, to rescue, rehabilitate, and (why not?) squeeze Lacan's meta-critical "ontological brain"[40] against an all too common, both friendly and hostile, precipitous relegation of his cogitation to the domain of antiphilosophy;[41] in order finally to pose, as he does not fail to suggest, "the problem of which logical procedure [we should adopt] to approach nature," given that "nature presents itself as not being one,"[42] we first have to analyze in a systematic way this very presentation as laboriously mapped out by Lacan himself, namely, the phenomeno-logical absence of the sexual relationship, his own evacuating the vestiges of Aristotle from our brain.

In dealing above all with the *Il n'y a pas de rapport sexuel* and the way in which it is counterbalanced by the phallic function as a far from optimal transcendental logic of sexuation/subjectivation, this book remains primarily exegetical. By and large it limits its scope to thoroughly assessing Lacan's most comprehensive critique of traditional ontology—in short, of the tenet "it is necessary at all costs that the One is, and that Being is One"[43]—which he carries out, in parallel with the development of his so-called formulas of sexuation, starting from Seminar XVIII, and which finds its most courageous—albeit fragmented—expression in Seminar XX. The fact that I will here devote myself to interpreting and digesting Lacan, with as little forcing as possible, does not, however, in the least mean that the present volume has no ambitions toward originality. Not only is his entire oeuvre as an incessant work in progress notoriously difficult to unpack in a methodical manner, but most of the Seminars in question—which I favor over contemporaneous written texts precisely because of their stronger vacillations as prolific openings—have only very recently been published in French.[44] Moreover, quality secondary literature on the logic of sexuation and its intimidating mixture of formalization, classical philosophy, deviational Freudianism, and biology does not abound. Although studies dedicated to this period of Lacan's production are indeed available to the reader, even in English, they tend to be either cluttered with psychoanalytic jargon or unacceptably simplistic, if not plain incorrect (the latter is especially the case with regard to misleading applications of Seminar XX and the notion of feminine enjoyment to disciplines such as gender studies and literary theory).

Among the few authors who have successfully embarked on a careful, transparent, and nonparochial scrutiny of the logic of sexuation, I would single out the following names: on the one hand, on a more theoretical front, François Balmès and Monique David-Ménard; on the other, with a prevalently clinical inclination, Colette Soler and Geneviève Morel. Balmès excels at uncovering the axiomatic "antinomies of the sexual," whereby sexuality can be approached only through "a discourse of antitheses, oxymoron, and paradoxes," such as "sexual *jouissance* is not precisely sexual."[45] David-Ménard convincingly argues that incompleteness, the not-all, does not exempt Lacan from thinking the liaisons between the sexes in terms of the universal, and, more to the point, that the ensuing "constitutive paradoxes of sexuation" influence logic just as much as logic is needed to grasp sexual identity.[46] Soler is indispensable reading on the logic of feminine sexuation, for she distances it from a misogynous (Freudian) identification with hysteria, as well as powerfully restating the Lacanian tenet about the in-existence of woman, which should be seen not as a facile judgment of attribution presupposing a reference to a readymade substance/essence, but as a "conditional imputation" that unchains anatomy from destiny: "It is not because they are women that they are 'not all,' but if they arrange themselves on the side of the 'not all,' they can be defined as women."[47] In a similar vein, Morel provocatively contests the nowadays mandatory idea of "*gender*" by showing how it rests on an obsolete "Aristotelian logic of class and attribute," and thus naively takes for granted the notion of subjective identity.[48]

Last, but not least, I would also like to mention Slavoj Žižek. Although the commentaries he provides on the logic of sexuation are seldom sustained for more than a dozen pages,[49] and soon launch into a myriad of other related topics, they have influenced my understanding of Lacan since the very beginning of my involvement with psychoanalytically informed philosophy. These passages still remain unsurpassed in acumen, pace, and an enviable ability to decipher and dialecticize what initially appears deliberately inconclusive, as well as to mercilessly crush fallacious vulgarizations.[50]

Having acknowledged the authors above, it is then imperative to underline that they remain only tangential to my work. I do dialogue with them, but only for brief moments. Moreover, I do not dwell on my disagreements with their positions, which are, on some occasions, quite deep-seated.[51] More importantly, I believe that, by selectively focusing for the most part only on the Seminars in which the formulas of sexuation are developed, I attempt to provide a more thorough account of Lacan's striving to formalize sexual difference; for instance, I dedicate many pages to a genealogy of the formulas in Seminar XVIII—where Lacan fights his way through the basic theoretical assumptions of Frege's propositional logic in order to adapt it freely to the phallic function—which is overlooked by all these authors.[52]

My line of argument, intended to prepare the field for para-ontology, is also more manifestly onto-logical; that is, it takes at face value Lacan's programmatic invitation to resort to formalization for the purpose of "separating severely" the One from being.[53] At the border between critical and meta-critical perspectives, this eventually leads him to hint at a materialist "being of signifierness," of the *fact* of language, of its producing signifying meaning irrespective of any foundation of meaning—a being which is hence inextricable from the void, and from a "*jouissance* of the body" consonant with "There is no sexual relationship."[54] Such a separation of the One from being has at the same time vast repercussions for the notion of phenomeno-logical existence, which I also investigate in detail: as Lacan puts it, "*there exists* has a meaning," but "it is a precarious meaning," bound to in-existence and ex-sistence: "It is precisely as signifiers that you all exist. You certainly exist, but this does not go far."[55]

Unlike the authors referred to above, I equally reserve considerable space for Lacan's dismantling of sexuality as considered by mainstream bio-logical discourse: developing a new logic of sexuation based on incompleteness requires first the relinquishment of any alleged *logos* of life, and of whatever originated it, as a teleological "evolution." This, on the one hand, goes together with lending an ear to the life sciences' own contemporary endeavor to have done with what Lacan, tacitly following the medicine Nobel laureate Jacques Monod, defines as animism, namely, the persistent anthropocentric assumption that natural objects in the world think (as we do).[56] On the other hand, however, I remain firmly convinced that any future ontology derived from psychoanalysis should continue to endorse the question "What is a science that includes psychoanalysis?" as opposed to the—badly posed for Lacan—"Is psychoanalysis a science?," that is, avoid conforming psychoanalysis to science.[57] While I fully understand that materialist continental philosophy, especially if inspired by Freud and Lacan, can no longer neglect the life sciences and must dialectically be exposed to them, I am also wary of current attempts to establish the theoretical basis of a "Lacan-influenced neuro-psychoanalytic" science, or of a thought that would be ancillary to it.[58]

***

In chapter 1, I start by offering a new reading of Seminar XX. Although the present volume focuses especially on the phallic function as our transcendental logic of sexuation/subjectivation and on Lacan's formalization of it,[59] here I will also extensively tackle the notion of God on what I have earlier defined as the critical (or phenomeno-logical) level of his enquiry. Structure as the "God hypothesis" is neither simply One nor two, Lacan argues. It is the continuous alternation between One and not-One. Man unsuccessfully aims at totalizing structure by reifying the feminine Other, whom he can love only as the other One, and with whom he attempts to establish a fusional two-as-One that would obliterate woman's phallic incompleteness just as much as sexual difference.

I first confront Seminar XX because, while it is possibly the most complex of the Seminars revolving around the axiom "There is no sexual relationship," and perhaps the most inconclusive, it also undoubtedly remains to date the most commented-on and liable to misinterpretations (due often to a lack of involvement with earlier works). In short, such mistaken appraisals tend to share an identification of woman, who for Lacan emerges as a singular, non-universalizable *une femme*, with *The* Other. This view is especially confusing when voiced from allegedly feminist quarters: Woman as *The* Other supposedly irreducible to castration—namely, in the end, as the unity of substance of the classical metaphysical God—corresponds in fact for Lacan to nothing other than the illusory counterpart of the evanescent object through which *man* enjoys woman in his fundamental fantasy. We therefore need to interrupt this short circuit. The unbinding of *a* woman from *The* Other will also provide us with the right coordinates of feminine *nonphallic jouissance*, a supplementary enjoyment that is, however, linked to structure as its *not*-all, and thus does not prevent the Other sex from enjoying phallically.

Seminar XX is also the latest of the Seminars I have decided to analyze in detail. It closes what has convincingly been defined as Lacan's "phrasal trilogy,"[60] where he adopts and manipulates Frege's notion of function—or, as Miller pertinently called it, "the sentence with holes"[61]—for the purpose of pinning down the logic of sexuation as a phallic function that evidences "the capability of formalization paradoxically to capture its own limits with respect to whatever is thought to escape it,"[62] namely, the sexual relationship. Furthermore, if the phallic function can be shown to amount to a revision of his earlier theory of sexuation, whereby "the idea that there is only [the masculine] sex for speaking beings"—and that the phallus is what allows us to "construct two types of sexual position, and think the relation between the sexes"—is replaced with a "beyond of the phallus, which implies that we no longer think of feminine and masculine sexuality in terms of parallelism or symmetry,"[63] then the trilogy that Seminar XX concludes can rightly be regarded as a condensation of Lacan's entire teaching. What follows it in the mid- and late 1970s is difficult to categorize. Lacan abandons formalization in favor of an application of mathematical knot theory to psychoanalysis, whose cogency remains to be defended. In parallel, as Le Gaufey has observed, it is clear that after Seminar XX Lacan also privileges an understanding of human sexuality on the basis of "There *is* a nonrelationship," which has para-ontological implications that widely differ from those of the more famous "There is no sexual relationship," and which I do not intend to evaluate in this book.[64]

Embracing an antichronological order for these precise methodological reasons (the urgency of preemptively debunking the suspicious popularity of Seminar XX, and the fact that what follows it overall constitutes a theoretical dead end), in chapter 2 I then address how, in order to develop a formalization of *Homo sapiens*' transcendental logic of sexuation, Lacan needs to confront the biological notion of sex from a psychoanalytic perspective. Here again my arguments underlie a polemic against a naive mantra, common even among otherwise sophisticated readers: Lacan, the thinker of the sexual unconscious structured like a language, would not deal with biology; whenever he speaks about sexuality, this is not to be understood biologically.[65]

Certainly, his attack on the—more or less explicit—essentialist teleology of evolutionary theory, including that of the beginnings of molecular biology, is a constant throughout his oeuvre. For instance, the XX and XY chromosomes are not, according to him, a scientific writing of the way in which sexual difference generates the sexual relationship, but, rather, yet another reassertion of the mythical cosmic complementarity between matter and form, *yin* and *yang* as predicated in premodern times. However, when, in Seminar XIXB, he suggests that "There are two sexes" but "There is not a second sex,"[66] the two sexes at stake, where one, the feminine, is not symbolically a second sex, also have obvious biological undertones, albeit only with regard to what he calls "the little difference."[67] The asymmetry of sexuation both materially presupposes the anatomical little difference—which is perhaps so little, Lacan seems to imply, that as such it is initially indifferent to (sexual) difference—and symbolizes/differentiates it in a retroactive way as the inexistence of the second sex.

In other words, in chapter 2 it is important for me to show that the discussion of the real of structure or "God hypothesis" as neither One nor two also entails a treatment of sex as a natural fact, for it is inextricable from sexuation. If the semblance of the One invariably unearths the absence of the relationship between the first sex and the Other sex as not-One, then the ensuing not-two should be taken as much as a phenomeno-logical impasse as an onto-logical anchoring. Number is here the real in a double sense; the not-two as the number of *in-difference* stands both for the signifierness of the (differentiality of the) symbolic qua limit of structure and, as such, for our only real grasp of nature (as indifferent yet modifiable through language, particularly by means of science).

In chapter 2, I equally intend to highlight the way in which this very stance on the real of sex as also natural both criticizes the fusional bias of biology's take on sex, but also, in light of recent development in the life sciences, suggests a possible dialogue with them. Ignoring the clinical and everyday evidence of "There is no sexual relationship," biology continues for the most part to take for granted a cosmic harmony between the sexes, the two-as-One, and thus reduces itself to what I will call a "psycho-erotology." Yet psychoanalysis cannot overlook the fact that cutting-edge research in behavioral neuroscience also contrasts this stance, and goes as far as defining sex as a set of "symptoms" that only successively allow for a "diagnosis" of male and female.

Advocating a vigilant exchange between Lacanian psychoanalysis and the life sciences will then lead me to dissect Lacan's own attempt at constructing, as early as Seminar XI, a psychoanalytically informed understanding of the nature of Homo sapiens' sex through a deconstruction of the Freudian notion of the drive. I argue that while for the most part he succeeds in dismissing the idea of libido as a free-floating but ultimately unifying sexual energy (Eros), an overall "substratum [substrat] of the transformations of the drive"[68] which thus amounts to a logos qua order of life, at a certain point the conclusions he draws fall short on the basis of his own antisubstantialist yet naturalist premises. The story of the so-called "lamella," of what was lost with the advent of sex in the cosmos—to be seen as more than an innocuous myth—seems in fact to end up anthropomorphically projecting the absence of the sexual relationship and the concomitant not-all of the phallic function onto sexual reproduction itself as independent from language.

Such hesitations with respect to the onto-logical value of sexual difference as natural will finally permit me to show how Lacan outlines incompatible philosophies of nature, measure them against the more explicitly philosophical proposals advanced by contemporary Lacanians such as Žižek and Johnston, and sketch my own para-ontological position on these matters.

Chapters 3, 4, and the conclusion discuss the main topic of this book. I will summarize them here only very generally, so as not to compromise the patient step-by-step reasoning process they required. In short, for Lacan, the phallic function stands for the transcendental logic of Homo sapiens' sexuation and subjectivation—where there is no sexuation without subjectivation, and vice versa. His theoretical aim is to formalize this function. First and foremost, it will therefore be a matter of seeing how such a transcendental logic specifically works, and why a correct understanding of it demands formalization. This will also involve, on different occasions, challenging Lacan's reticence in speaking about the phallic function's origins and the scope of its applicability.

Focusing especially on Seminars XVIII, XIX, and XIXB, in the second half of the book I will thus unfold what, for the most part, Seminar XX takes for granted and critics very often ignore, if not misinterpret. That is, the fact that the absence of the sexual relationship, as such inextricable from language, nonetheless paves the way for the establishment of sexual liaisons; that man and woman emerge retroactively only thanks to these liaisons as, respectively, "all phallic" and "not-all phallic"; that such definitions, along with others, require a certain kind of formal writing, thanks to which the phallic function is written as the impossibility of writing the sexual relationship; that this writing demonstrates that, paradoxically, as Lacan puts it, "a good fuck" does not in the least refute "There is no sexual relationship."[69]

Chapter 3 spells out that the phallic function is, albeit subversively, a function in the sense inaugurated by Frege's modern predicate logic, one whose argument corresponds to *Homo sapiens* as an undetermined x. Chapter 4 details how the phallic function functions—as a logical circulation between the so-called formulas of sexuation—while also reproposing the absence of the sexual relationship on another—phenomeno-logical—level. The conclusion shows that—against Frege and logical positivism, and perhaps in a yet to be examined anticipation of Badiou—the phallic function as a transcendental logic of sexuation/subjectivation is nonetheless, for Lacan, second to an onto-logical primacy of *number* over logic. The real of structure is numerical; it corresponds to two numbers, the zero and the one, or better, the oscillation between them as the "bifidity of the one"; this bifidity opens onto an extra-logical "impossibility of numbering," or infinity, which is enjoyed by woman as not-all phallic, and thus phallically undecidable.

CHAPTER 1

WOMAN AND THE NUMBER OF GOD

1.1 OF STRANGE ENJOYMENT AND BEING AN ANGEL

According to a well-established interpretation, which gained considerable consensus during the 1980s and 1990s in the context of debates concerning the relationship between feminism and psychoanalysis, the role of the divine in Lacan's late work should be identified with that of feminine enjoyment/*jouissance*.[1] I am going to challenge this reading and explain why, in Seminar XX, Lacan claims, rather, that feminine *jouissance* constitutes the basis of *one* face of God—that is, of "one face of the Other."[2] In other words, the divine of the "God hypothesis" implied by structure cannot be confined to woman alone: feminine *jouissance* is not the exclusive God face of the Other.[3]

Certainly, this Seminar advances clearly the idea of an enjoyment that is "beyond the phallus"[4]—this "beyond" will itself have to be examined closely, following Lacan's repeated warning that the "supplementary" or "additional" [*supplémentaire*] value, the "*en plus*" it entails, should by no means be seen as a transcendence[5]—and articulates it with reference to the experience of female Christian mystics such as Hadewijch of Antwerp and Saint Teresa. Yet the issue at stake is far more complex. First, Lacan specifies that mysticism can also at times embrace phallic *jouissance*—he cites in passing, without giving any more detail, the example of Angelus Silesius—just as feminine mystical *jouissance* can equally be felt by biologically male mystics (such as John of the Cross).[6] Secondly, and most importantly, only a few lines after maintaining that one of the divine faces of the Other is supported by feminine *jouissance*, he also concludes that while the connection between sexual difference and the divine "doesn't make two God [...] it doesn't make just one either" [*ça ne fait pas deux Dieu* [...] *ça ne fait pas non plus un seul*].[7]

It is my intention to unravel this decisive and underestimated formula, which will inevitably also lead me to an investigation of the role of number in

Seminar XX, as well as of the closely related notion of love. In a nutshell, my main argument is as follows: for Lacan, there are two faces of God as the two faces of structure or "God hypothesis." Structure is not simply one, because of its oscillation between the (masculine) One and the (feminine) not-One. But, for the same reason, neither is it two, since the oscillation between the One and that which is Other than One produces a not-two.

To begin with, let us examine how Lacan understands *jouissance* in Seminar XX. Right at the opening, he introduces it in a particularly dense but enlightening lesson. His arguments presuppose here a line of enquiry he had been pursuing at least since Seminar XVII and its theory of discourses:[8] psychoanalytic discourse—and its novel historical determination of the status of other discourses—starts off from fully assuming the empirical evidence, already intuitively experienced in our everyday lives, that human sexuality is inextricably entwined with the absence of the sexual relationship [*rapport*]. In short, the speaking being cannot symbolically represent sex as such, which hence remains a logical impossibility: the absence of the sexual relationship amounts to the absence of sexual meaning, that is, to the absence of a *measure*, or *ratio* [*rapport*], where sex is concerned. As Lacan already claims in Seminar XI, "in the psyche, there is nothing by which the subject may situate himself as a male or female being"; such a sexual localization can be achieved only in a complex, incomplete, and precarious manner by means of culturally mediated "equivalents" (i.e., as we will soon see, the so-called phallic function).[9]

More precisely, psychoanalysis acknowledges that it is impossible to enunciate this relationship as a One/All, whereby one sex could relate to the Other sex as an-other One, thus achieving a unified couple, or two-as-One. Consequently, Lacan contends, the sexual relationship as One, which *would be the* "*jouissance* of the body as such," can be supposed only in terms of the *asexual* being One of the body.[10] Psychoanalysis accepts the logical necessity of the supposition of the One, but refuses to grant it any essence. In doing so, it claims to break with all classical philosophical discourses revolving around an ontology of substance,[11] in order to focus, in its theory and practice, exclusively on the *sexual enjoyment* involved in the partial liaisons (*les relations* which are not a *rapport*) between sexed human beings as beings of language.

The impossibility of establishing the sexual relationship as One follows from the fact that, although there are two sexes, *sexual jouissance* can be mediated symbolically—for both men and women—only by the contingent bodily inscription of the signifier in the image of the male sexual organ, or phallus. As Lacan has it, "woman's sex does not say anything" to man, or better, for him, "nothing distinguishes woman as a sexed being, but sex," the phallic bodily enjoyment he obtains from her during intercourse.[12] Of crucial importance, here, is the specification that sex—bluntly put, in the sense of "having sex"—ultimately differentiates woman as a *sexed* being there where the lack of an independent feminine symbol that would linguistically mediate her biological sexual characteristics fails to accomplish this.[13] Lacan's argument is not that woman is less sexed than man—nor that she is even without sex, leaving aside the symbolic dominance of the phallus and man's having sex with her—as a precipitate reading of these pages could suggest ("nothing distinguishes woman as a sexed being" ...), but rather that, given the asymmetry of the phallic signifier, her sexuation—her sex as a sexed being of language—and following this, her *jouissance* of man, is "strange" [*étrange*].[14] In other words, *l'étrange* must not by any means be confused with *l'être-ange*, "being-an-angel," although the two terms are homophonous.[15] *L'être-ange* in fact points to a projection onto woman of *asexual jouissance*, which Lacan resolutely denounces as the structural illusion connected to the being-One of a chimerical body, or, we may add, to the basic fantasy of man, that of totalizing *jouissance*.

Not surprisingly, Lacan also states that *jouissance* insofar as it is sexual can only be phallic, for both men and women: "Analytic experience attests precisely that everything revolves around phallic *jouissance*."[16] Having said this, at the same time, "woman is defined by a position that I have indicated as 'not-all' [*pas tout*] with respect to phallic *jouissance*."[17] So, if on the one hand the sex of woman says something to man only through his *jouissance* of her body, on the other, since she is not entirely contained within phallic *jouissance*, the latter will also be "the obstacle owing to which man does not come to enjoy woman's body": what he enjoys is, rather, the "*jouissance* of the organ."[18] That is to say, to the extent that *jouissance* is sexual, and hence phallic, it is marked for man by a hole; man never relates to Woman as a universal, which is why Lacan bars the definite article, the "*La*," of "*La femme*."

Moving from this premise, it is now a question of seeing how this fault [*faille*] or gap [*béance*] within *jouissance* is confronted, or alternatively avoided, by a woman.[19] In the first lesson of Seminar XX, Lacan seems to provide two answers: it can either be realized as a *phallic jouissance* that is *étrange* in comparison with that of man, in the sense that it deals with the nontotalizability of *jouissance* (with its structural being deficient, or "in default") differently than masculine *jouissance*, or be evaded to attempt to achieve the totalization of *jouissance* by positing precisely what is lacking as the enjoyment of an asexual *être-ange*, that is, by using the impasse of phallic *jouissance* as an alibi for a mythical—and ultimately man-oriented—desexualization. Woman can as such ex-sist as a *singular* being that does not exist as a universal, and sexual difference consequently be maintained, only if she *confronts* the fault within *jouissance* in her own way.

Note that up to this point Lacan has not yet invoked what, in later lessons, he will call "Other *jouissance*," a feminine *jouissance* that is neither phallic (it famously lies beyond the phallus, and hence cannot be considered as sexual) nor angelical (and thus totalized) but, as we shall analyze shortly, mystical. By way of anticipation, it can therefore be advanced that Seminar XX is concerned with four different kinds of *jouissance*: (a) masculine phallic *jouissance*, which in attempting to totalize enjoyment uncovers its very nontotalizability; (b) feminine phallic *jouissance*, or *jouissance étrange*, which is the nontotalization inherent *and* immanent to the thwarted process of totalizing enjoyment, as well as mutually dependent on it; (c) *asexual* and mythical *jouissance être-ange*, which is the fantasy of masculine phallic *jouissance* as totalized (projected onto woman or adopted by her, as we shall see); (d) nonsexual but really existing feminine *jouissance stricto sensu*, which is a mystical supplement of phallic *jouissance*. In order to refrain from locating it on a transcendent level, we could also call it "nontotalizability"; feminine *jouissance stricto sensu* is, for Lacan, beyond the phallus (and its inherent nontotalization), but this beyond does not ex-sist without referring to the phallus.[20]

Let us now dwell on feminine *phallic* enjoyment, the *jouissance étrange*. As Lacan has it, woman phallically "possesses" man just as much as man "possesses" woman; she is far from being indifferent to the phallus (i.e., in common parlance, to "her man"). Or, more accurately, "it is not because she is not-wholly in the phallic function that she is not there at all." Being not-all in the phallic function involves, rather than excludes, being "not not at all there," to the extent of being "in full" in it where sexual *jouissance* is concerned. In other words, as I have already observed, woman—her *pas-toute*—is not less sexed, i.e., phallically engaged, than man.[21]

What, then, is so "strange" about feminine phallic *jouissance*? In a few words, woman approaches, and sustains, the phallus in her own way; she complies with the "requirement of the One" [*l'exigence de l'Un*], which is inseparable from phallic *jouissance*, but replaces the "One of universal fusion" that underlies masculine phallic *jouissance* with a singular "one by one" [*une par une*].[22] For woman, the masculine sex is phallically the one by which she makes herself be taken, but only one by one, not universally. To put it simply, woman is, at the same time, infinite and countable, or better, she becomes countable precisely insofar as she exposes the count as nontotalizable.[23] Lacan gives an example to explain this: the myth of Don Juan. He has women one by one; as long as he knows their names, he can list them and hence count them. Yet if, at a given point in time, he has possessed, say, one-thousand-and-three women, this is just the one-thousand-and-third instance—and obviously not the last—he again counts woman as one. This different form of counting, which inherently hinders the semblance of successful totalization, explains why Lacan unexpectedly calls Don Juan a "*feminine* myth."[24] The singular one-by-one as opposed to the attempted fusional One of masculine phallic totalization, albeit entwined with it, is a feminine—but nonetheless phallic—counting that shows "what the other sex, the masculine sex, is for women": it is the sex that always has to count one more woman.[25]

We now need to take a step back and ask ourselves: Why does phallic *jouissance*—as the only possible sexual *jouissance*—underlie the "requirement of the One"—or its "one-by-one" feminine variation—in the first place? Lacan explains this underrated yet fundamental issue right at the beginning of Seminar XX. Phallic *jouissance* depends on love as "the desire to be One"; *jouissance* is not a "sign of love," but it remains nevertheless "secondary," i.e., epiphenomenal, with respect to it.[26] The body of man and woman as beings of language is certainly sexed symbolically (in an asymmetrical way), but the sexual *jouissance* obtained from the body of the Other "remains a question, because the answer it may constitute is not necessary. We can take this further still: it is not a sufficient answer either, because love demands love. It never stops demanding it. It demands it ... *again* [*encore*]."[27] Thus, against common readings of the title of Seminar XX, "*encore*" does not primarily refer to the "I want it all and I want it now!" of masculine phallic *jouissance*, or to the "!!!" of feminine/mystical *jouissance* beyond the phallus,[28] but to the "I want more!" of love.

The following argument should by now be clear: human sexuality issues from the primacy of the absence of the sexual relationship, from a real impossibility of representing sex, and *jouissance* should consequently be seen, first and foremost, as a "negative instance," which "serves no purpose."[29] That is to say, it is the demand for love as a—thwarted, "impotent"[30]—desire to be One that in the end sustains human sexuality—and thus, indirectly, reproduction and the preservation of the species—as based on a relationship that is not One between the sexes. In other words, as Lacan claims later in Seminar XX in a passage that should be read together with the one above, and equally refers to necessity, we eventually even manage "to give a shadow of life to the feeling known as love. This is *necessary, really necessary*; it is necessary that this goes on [*ça dure encore*]. It is necessary that, with the help of this feeling, this leads, in the end [...] to the reproduction of bodies."[31] In short, as beings of language, we do not primarily make love because sex is instinctively "fun." Rather, we (strive to) have sex because we love, whatever our polymorphously perverse motivations for sleeping with the other may be. *Jouissance* is no more than a by-product of the impossibility of the One necessarily desired by love.

Here, we should pay particular attention to the fact that Lacan obliges us to thoroughly rethink the opposition between love and desire—on which he had insisted throughout his early Seminars—in the more general terms of an interaction, if not of a non-eliminable presence of desire within love. Love can well be, as a passion, as the desire to *be* One, the "ignorance of desire," yet this does not in any sense involve a weakening of the *desire* to be One.[32] Lacan's question "Is love about making one?," which at first sight seems to be redundant in a context that defines love as the desire to be One, cannot simply be answered affirmatively:[33] love as the *desire* to be One always goes together with the "again!" of the demand for love, hence it would be misleading to identify its aim with a final "making one." Love desires to be One, and fabricates in the process a fragile semblance of the One. In other words, the capitalized One at stake in love—as *desire* to be One—does not lead us back to what is allegedly a primordial unity, the "earliest of con-fusions." Rather, it evidences the fissure of the One (the One of the enunciation "Y a d' l'Un," "There's such a thing as One") as the "essence of the signifier," a differential gap which alone allows us to propose a discourse on *jouissance* and being.[34] If Lacan concludes the first lesson of Seminar XX by returning to the irreconcilability of "being absolute" with "being sexed," this is not just a reminder of the fact that angelical *jouissance*, the supposed being-One without fissure of a totalized body, would necessarily be asexual, but that we can finally think the existence of God—which as a hypothesis implicitly upholds all of our enunciations—as *insubstantial*, as a nonangelical One with a fissure, only on the basis of *sexual jouissance* and its nonphallic feminine supplement.

1.2 FROM *OTHER SATISFACTION* TO *OTHER ENJOYMENT*

It would not be an exaggeration to suggest that, in Seminar XX, Lacan goes so far as positioning love and desire on the side of the satisfaction of needs, as opposed to—albeit inseparable from—what he names the "other satisfaction" of—the uselessness of—phallic (masculine and feminine) *jouissance*. This topic is extensively covered in the fifth lesson. The sixth lesson then introduces feminine *jouissance* as "beyond the phallus." Keeping in mind that, contrary to what has been proposed by several critics, Lacan's efforts are aimed overall here at *distinguishing* "l'autre satisfaction," i.e., phallic (masculine and feminine) *jouissance*, from *l'Autre jouissance* (or, as it is also referred to, *la jouissance de l'Autre* and *jouissance radicalement Autre*),[35] i.e., an exclusively feminine nonphallic *jouissance*,[36] it is now a matter of investigating how the discussion of precisely these two notions paves the way for his conclusion that while this differentiation "doesn't make two God [...] it doesn't make just one either"—a topic I will analyze in the final section of this chapter.

The fifth lesson revolves around the contrast between the satisfaction of needs and "another satisfaction." In particular, against any naturalist-reductivist reading, the satisfaction of needs in the human being can be grasped only indirectly as what does not fulfill this other satisfaction, which "supports itself from language" and can be defined as "*jouissance*."[37] This specification thus entails an elaboration of the previous assumption according to which *jouissance* is epiphenomenal with regard to love-desire and their indirect fulfillment of the sexual biological function; to put it simply, (a) love-desire makes reproduction possible, and (b) *jouissance* is a by-product of their interaction with (sexual) need, if not a replacement of it, yet, nevertheless, (c) (sexual) need as such, its "non-other" satisfaction (i.e., satisfaction *tout court*; compliance with the pleasure principle), can be approached only in a roundabout way by means of the other—unsatisfied—satisfaction of *jouissance*.

Moving from this interweaving of need, love-desire, and *jouissance*, how should we decipher Lacan's crucial claim that other satisfaction "supports itself from language"? In a few words, this simply means that *jouissance* does not precede the institution of human reality as a linguistic reality.[38] Or, at least, that any discourse about an alleged prediscursive human reality, and an associated *jouissance* which would not be deficient, is automatically mythical because being a "man" or a "woman" does not per se denote anything like a prediscursive reality; that "men [and] women [...] are but signifiers."[39] More generally, there is no such thing as a "human species" at the level of prediscursive reality; the species—and its sexual *jouissance*—is made possible only "thanks to a certain number of conventions, prohibitions, and inhibitions that are the effect of language."[40] From this perspective, *jouissance*, love, and desire all equally follow from *Homo sapiens'* rupture from—what appears to be—the immanence of animal need. Such a predicament is scientifically accountable in terms of the premature birth that characterizes the speaking being, which is itself responsible for a prematuration of sexuality that goes together with (sexual) neoteny, the retention of infantile traits in adult individuals—a series of intricate points Lacan reiterates in passing even in the very lesson of Seminar XX that we are scrutinizing, thus confirming that his treatment of *jouissance* still depends on the biological theses he discussed in his Seminars of the 1950s.[41]

This being said, the very fact that *jouissance* sustains itself only from language, that is, from the absence of the sexual relationship that determines human *sexuality* as deprived of essence, necessarily entails the supposition of a mythical substance that enjoys itself absolutely. On the one hand, there is "*jouissance* of a body" [*jouir d'un corps*]—in the subjective and objective sense—only insofar as this very body is symbolized—or insofar as the "signifier is the cause of *jouissance*."[42] On the other hand, psychoanalysis presents itself as a discourse on how discourse as such is founded on an inevitable supposing of substance. Lacan also attempts to move beyond this fluctuation between the absence of the sexual relationship and the mythical substance by introducing a "new form of substance," a "*substance jouissante*"[43] through which both the myth of absolute *jouissance* and the *jouissance* of the symbolized body could dialectically be thought anew.[44] While with respect to substance as really existing body, and as such symbolized, *jouissance* can be enjoyed only in part, given that there is no sexual relationship as One ("One can only enjoy a part of the Other's body [...] one has never seen a body completely wrap itself around the Other's body [...] We must confine ourselves to simply giving it a little squeeze, like that, taking a forearm or anything else—ouch!"),[45] with regard to substance as supposed by language, the logical necessity to posit it involves the positing of an imaginary absolute *jouissance*, the *jouissance* of the body as One.

But, as Lacan has it, here necessity goes together with impossibility, or better, that which is necessary in logic qua the founding exception to the rule is impossible in reality.[46] We thus have to conceive of one mythical man, the Father (of the horde), for whom the phallic function that decrees the partiality of *jouissance*—that is, the fact that there is no sexual relationship, or—which amounts to the same thing—that human sexuality equals the absence of the sexual relationship as One—is not valid. To put it differently, we have to think of an absolutely self-enjoying and hence ultimately asexual substance that embodies "the correlate of the fact that there's no such thing as a sexual relationship":[47] Lacan calls it "the substantial aspect of the phallic function" and then proceeds to formalize it as $\exists x . \overline{\Phi x}$ (there exists an x, the Father, for which Φx, the phallic function, is negated) in his so-called formulas of sexuation.[48]

As will become apparent in chapters 3 and 4, in the early 1970s Lacan puts forward strong arguments to deny any essence to the purely symbolic existence of the Father, that is, to detach the exceptional one which does not abide by the phallic function from its imaginary embodiment. And yet, in Seminar XX, he decides to ambiguously characterize such exception as the *substantial* aspect of the phallic function. We could argue that "Father," and his substantiality, stand here for the imaginary/phantasmatic reification into One of the logical existence of the one, where the latter is actually inextricable from its movement toward the not-One. This reading could be supported by Lacan's recurrent distinction between the living/self-enjoying God of religion and the God hypothesis of metaphysics. However, the broader issue at stake cannot be settled so easily: for instance, is the embryonic theory of *substance jouissante* sufficient to reconcile the apparently antinomical claims for which "psychoanalytic discourse [...] is lent support [...] by the fact that it *never resorts to any substance*, never refers to any being" (and thus unmasks the substantial aspect of the phallic function as an imaginary mirage), yet "*the substance of the body*, on the condition that it is defined only as that which enjoys itself, [is] precisely what psychoanalytic experience assumes"?[49] Should these two statements be read together as (1) "psychoanalytic discourse is lent support by the fact that it never resorts to any substance, never refers to any being" *as the being One of the body*, but, at the same time, (2) "the substance of the body, on condition that it is defined only as that which enjoys itself" *sexually*, that is, on condition that *the enjoying body is not One*, "is precisely what psychoanalytic experience assumes"?

The apparent contradiction could in this way be explained, yet, given that Lacan never expands on *substance jouissante*,[50] a more general tension remains: to put it bluntly, is there substance in the real, or is there not? Is Lacan trying to sketch the para-ontology of a human corporeal *substance without essence* as not-One, which would be graspable *aside* from the logical existence of the God hypothesis, that is, of the oscillation between the one/One and the not-One? Should this be the case, does he successfully manage not to entail here any being as the being One of the body? What seems certain at this stage is that the very interpretation I am advancing is a palpable instantiation of the fact that, as Lacan acknowledges, to speak about *jouissance* puts more than ever "this the Other [*ce l'Autre*]," i.e., the symbolic order as such, into question.[51] In brief, it is precisely an enquiry into substance from the standpoint of enjoyment that indicates how the really existing Other as not-One (always mediated through "the Other sex," i.e., woman) can ultimately be thought only against the background of an absolute mythical One and, vice versa, how any cogitation about the symbolic-imaginary phallic whole goes hand in hand with the nontotalizability of linguistic reality.

1.3 OF BEING THE OTHER IN THE MOST RADICAL SENSE, AND MATTERS OF CUM

Before returning in the next section to this oscillation by analyzing the number of God, I intend now to focus on feminine *nonphallic jouissance* as a different way of calling the consistency of the Other into question. Instead of challenging it by means of language—that is, by uncovering the logical co-dependence between the one/One and the not-One in the symbolic order, as phallic (masculine and feminine) *jouissance* does—feminine nonphallic *jouissance*, rather, indicates that this order is as such not entirely sayable. While the "other satisfaction" of phallic *jouissance* ultimately amounts always to a *jouissance* of speech,[52] in the sense that it supports itself from language and can even be regarded as an (always deficient) satisfaction of the "blah-blah,"[53] all that women can say about their *jouissance* beyond the phallus—as exemplified by the "sporadic" writings of mystics—is that "they feel it, but know nothing about it."[54]

This contrasting reference to speech clearly corroborates the view that Lacan distinguishes *l'autre satisfaction* from *l'Autre jouissance*. To sum up, we could suggest that not only is there a satisfaction which is other with respect to the satisfaction of needs, but that this very "other satisfaction," phallic *jouissance*, has its Other. First and foremost, we should resist the temptation to turn this other otherness into a transcendent feeling. The "supplementary" nature of unspeakable feminine *jouissance* should, rather, be understood as that which, in "escaping" symbolization, nonetheless refers to it qua symbolization's inherent impasse, as the not-all of symbolization.[55] Conversely, woman's "beyond the phallus" or "*en plus*"—"Be careful with this 'more,' beware of taking it too far too quickly," Lacan warns us[56]—that is, her being not entirely contained within the phallic function, should also be considered as a precondition for the symbolic as such, since the latter is also not-One, and can propose itself as a one/One only on this basis.

The best way to understand the nontranscendence of feminine *jouissance* with regard to the symbolic is by closely analyzing its positioning with respect to sexual difference. Again, Lacan does not hesitate to state that *jouissance*, insofar as it is sexual, is phallic.[57] If feminine *jouissance* lies "beyond the phallus," it inevitably follows that it must be seen as somehow nonsexual, i.e., as not subjected to the *jouissance* of the organ. Yet for this very reason, it is not asexual, i.e., it does not partake of the *jouissance* of the organ's structural mirage of a *jouissance* of the body as One. Rather, feminine *jouissance* is nonsexual within the sexual relationship (that is not One). Lacan says that feminine *jouissance* derives from woman's "being the Other, in the most radical sense, *in the sexual relationship*" (as a liaison that is not a rapport). "Woman is that which has a relationship to *that* Other"; or also, woman is that which has a relationship to herself as Other in the most radical sense.[58] In other words, feminine *jouissance* is the consequence of woman's unique opening onto the Other as barred, as not-One; or—better—onto the barred Other insofar as it is barred only as marked by the signifier: "Woman has a relation to the signifier of that Other, insofar as, qua Other, it can but remain forever Other. I can only assume here that you will recall my statement that there is no Other of the Other. The Other, that is, the locus in which everything that can be articulated on the basis of the signifier comes to be inscribed, is, in its foundation, the Other in the most radical sense. That is why the signifier [...] marks the Other as barred: S($\bcancel{A}$)."[59] Woman's relation with the "most radical" Other when she experiences feminine *jouissance* is thus far from coinciding with the attainment of the alleged primordial unity of substance, that is, with the mythical end of sexual difference—and of the symbolic order along with it—which is instead evoked by the image of the *être-ange* qua the purely *asexual* enjoyment of the body as One, fictitiously situated outside of the Other (or before/after it).

L'être-ange (being-an-angel) as a deceitful mirage of onto-totological reconciliation that would eliminate sexual difference through the body as One must, therefore, be opposed to both phallic *and* nonphallic feminine *jouissance*, both the *jouissance étrange* (strange enjoyment) through which woman relates to man by making herself be taken/counted "one by one" *and* the silent impulses of fervor and passion experienced by the mystics, which man cannot relate to. Furthermore, not only is the feminine mystic's expressing *one* of the faces of God (or "one face of the Other"—an expression we still need to unravel fully) not enough to turn her into an angel, but the ineffectiveness of the angel can be obliquely materialized in the far less edifying body of the hysteric, in her paralyzing refusal to come to terms with sexual difference. Lacan advances this point concisely but effectively when he claims that hysteria aims at the "outsidesex" [horsexe], and for this reason stands for a "playing the part of man" [faire l'homme]. As Lacan puns, the hysteric is a "hommosexuelle"—i.e., a "man-sexual" rather than a homosexual woman [homosexuelle]—in the sense that she attempts to embody the epitome of the masculine-phallic fantasy of overcoming sexual difference in an asexual being as corporeal being One.[60] In the end, the hysterical angel intends to occupy the mythical place of the desexualized partner of the noncastrated and hence fully enjoying Father, who would thus be himself asexual: in not facing an Other sex, in having all women as The angelical/hysterical woman, his sexuality—which can only be differential—would remain in fact undetermined.[61]

How should we then understand more precisely the nonsexual linking of feminine/mystical jouissance to the concreteness of human sexuality—characterized as it is by the absence of the sexual relation and the hegemony of the phallic function? Lacan answers this question in passing when he criticizes the medical notion of frigidity, as well as the contiguous distinction—endorsed, in the wake of Freud, by many psychoanalysts, especially women—between clitoral and vaginal jouissance (whereby one of the two, depending on the theory, could be deemed a physiological condition, an orgasm, that would be at least in part independent from the male organ, or its surrogates, and intercourse). These issues are badly articulated, Lacan contends, since what is at stake in feminine jouissance as such has nothing to do with sex, with "matters of cum [affaire de foutre]."[62] If, as he suggests, woman experiences feminine jouissance without being able to talk about it, then "frigidity" could represent nothing other than man's incapacity to grasp this feeling—i.e., his reduction of a jouissance that is not sexual to an absence of jouissance tout court.[63] Similarly, the distinction between clitoral and vaginal jouissance would remain after all internal to sexual, i.e., phallic, jouissance, and therefore render the endeavor to establish which is more "feminine" meaningless.

Much of what we have been discussing so far can be recapitulated by means of Seminar XX's diagram of sexuation (see below).[64] If we focus on its center, we can see that woman—as schematized in the right half—is passively implicated in masculine sexuality—i.e., the left half—as a, the object a in the relation $\$$ (barred subject) $\rightarrow a$, which is to say that she stands as the object-cause of man's desire in fantasy. Lacan observes that, from the perspective of the masculine side of sexual identification, the object a is that which "is put in the place of what cannot be glimpsed of the Other";[65] that is, the fact that jouissance, qua sexual, is phallic ultimately means that man "is not related to the Other as such."[66] More precisely, "it is inasmuch as object a plays the role somewhere—from a point of departure, a single one, the male one—of that which takes the place of the missing partner, that what we are used to seeing emerge in the place of the real, namely, fantasy, is constituted."[67] Fantasy is a masculine phallic way—man's only way—to relate to woman sexually; it is a replacement for the fact that, in the case of human beings as beings of language, there is no sexual relationship as One. In this sense, fantasy emerges at the place of the missing partner as real, and creates a semblance of the One out of it. Fantasy articulates the noncorrelation of subject and object in the case of *Homo sapiens*, it adjusts the otherwise defective desire of the former for the latter. In other words, the object can be such only as object of desire in fantasy, where it supports the masculine subject as vanishing $, as a sexed existence that is split and alienated in language.

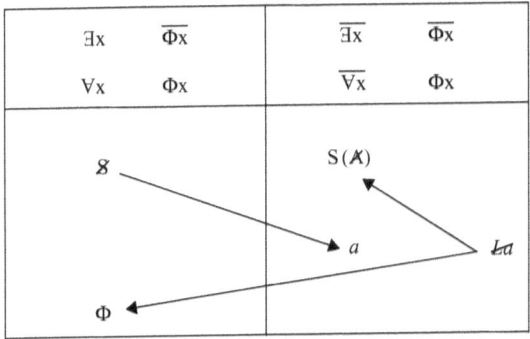

Can *woman* ever enter (phallic) sexuality qua the fantasy $ → a by taking up an *active* role in it? Lacan seems to categorically exclude this option when he maintains that "for woman [...] something other than object a is at stake in what comes to make up for [suppléer] the sexual relationship that does not exist"[68]—a point which is clearly reinforced by the diagram of sexuation: $ lies exclusively on the masculine side, while a lies exclusively on the feminine side qua *object* of $. There is, however, a passage in the third lesson of Seminar XX which deeply problematizes this assumption. In it, Lacan speaks of the *mother* and unequivocally claims that "woman's jouissance is based on a supplementation for this not-all [une suppléance de ce pas-toute]" inasmuch as "she finds the cork for this jouissance [based on the fact] that she is not-all [...] in the a constituted by her child."[69] While this argument about woman as *phallic mother* is a consolidated idea which Lacan already advanced in the 1950s, it directly contradicts the former passage: here woman (as mother) clearly *does* make up for [suppléer] the sexual relationship that does not exist with nothing other than *her child as object a*.

In the third lesson, Lacan also claims that "woman serves a function in the sexual relationship only qua mother."[70] This can straightforwardly be read from man's perspective: masculine phallic sexuality as the fantasy $ → a ultimately revolves around an attempted reduction of the not-all of woman to object a, namely, to a (castrated and unconscious) resumption in adult sexual life of the Oedipal dialectics between child, mother, and the imaginary phallus.[71] But it should also be understood from the stance of woman's own subjectivity: again, woman as mother compensates phallically for the absence of the sexual relationship with her child as object a. Does this mean, then, that woman as mother occupies the position of $\$$ whenever she relates to her child as object a? Would this statement not inevitably lead us to conclude that either woman as mother is, in the sense of sexuation (which is symbolical, not biological), a "man," or that, against the diagram of sexuation, $\$$ (the subject alienated by language who partly separates himself from this alienation, and thus relates himself to his object, only thanks to phallic sexuality in fantasy) is not a prerogative of man?[72]

We can attempt to solve these paradoxes by admitting that Lacan might have added to his diagram the vector $\cancel{La} \to a$, that of woman qua mother. *Mutatis mutandis*, i.e., against the background of the premise that, unlike man, woman is not entirely contained by the phallic function, $\cancel{La}$ could even be conceived as a feminine $\$$, which in the case of the mother relates to object a. This is to say, once more, that woman is herself as alienated and sexed in and by language as man; we have seen how her being beyond the phallus nonetheless involves being "in full" in the phallic function where sexuality is concerned. Woman as phallic mother therefore implies a redoubling of a, which should now also be located on the masculine side of the diagram.[73] Let us not forget that, for Lacan, woman qua phallic mother does indeed endeavor to overcome sexual difference incestuously, that is, put an end to it by assimilating/phagocytizing her child. Consequently, the statement "woman serves a function in the sexual relationship only qua mother," which Lacan seems to understand primarily in the sense of "*from man's perspective*, woman serves a function in the sexual relationship only qua mother"—i.e., in their post-Oedipal, "mature" relationships with women, all men tend to re-create the relationship with the mother[74]—conceals another, more troubling statement: as soon as, *from woman's perspective*, woman starts to serve a function in the sexual relationship only as mother, sexual difference, and the symbolic order with it, are at risk.

We are now in a position to shed further light on the intricate claim that "woman's *jouissance* is based on a supplementation for this not-all [*une suppléance de ce pas-toute*]" inasmuch as "she finds the cork for this *jouissance* [based on the fact] that she is not-all [...] in the a constituted by her child." What still remains to be explained is why that which works as a supplementation [*suppléance*]—or replacement, substitute, stand-in—for a non-totalization is presented in terms of a cork, whose primary use is to prevent something excessive from overflowing. I believe that Lacan is trying here to think the *supplémentaire*, that is, "additional" aspect of feminine *jouissance* (its "beyond," or "extra"—*en plus*—characteristic) together with the *suppléance*, that is, the supplementation (which makes up for a deficiency)—itself a *jouissance*—provided by the child/object *a* as a "cork." On closer inspection, in the sentence in question, he is clearly using the term *jouissance* in two different ways: feminine *jouissance*, the *jouissance* of the not-all as such, is corked or contained by means of a child qua the object *a*, which, as a supplementation to the negatively additional character of feminine *jouissance*,[75] produces itself a form of phallic *jouissance*.

Thus the maternal vector $\cancel{La} \to a$ comes in the place of the mystical vector $\cancel{La} \to S(\cancel{A})$, but if the latter is completely foreclosed by the former, this leads to the disappearance of woman's very presence in the phallic function (the vector $\cancel{La} \to \Phi$) qua *woman*—and not simply qua the phantasmatic object *a* of masculine desire—as well as eventually to the disappearance of sexual difference (and the human species) as such. In other words, $\cancel{La}$, that is, the fact that there is no universal for woman, no *The* woman; $\cancel{La} \to S(\cancel{A})$, that is, her privileged relation to the nontotalizability of the symbolic order, which is precisely that which prevents us from obtaining a universal for woman; and $\cancel{La} \to \Phi$, that is, woman's own nonmasculine way of engaging in the phallic function as a nonuniversal, are all mutually dependent and could not be obtained in isolation. As for the maternal function, on the one hand, it seals this state of affairs (as "good mother" one is tempted to add) through reproduction; on the other, it may also destabilize such a precarious balance. At its purest, woman's serving a function in the sexual relationship *only* qua mother is that which would turn $\cancel{La}$ into *La*, transform woman into a universal Mother, only after she has incestuously assimilated her children.

1.4 GOD: BETWEEN FEMININE ENJOYMENT AND PHALLIC LOVE

Let us now consider in more depth Lacan's claim that "for woman, something other than object *a* is at stake in what comes to make up for the sexual relationship that does not exist." We should be able to grasp that this refers to the *feminine phallic* vector of sexuation, depicted as $\cancel{La} \to \Phi$ in the diagram: woman as a nonuniversal in relation to the symbolic Phallus. We have already encountered it in the guise of the "one-by-one" by means of which woman symbolizes the masculine sex as a Don Juan. Just as man does not relate sexually—i.e., phallically—to the feminine Other, that is to say, there is no $\cancel{S} \to \cancel{La}$ vector but, rather, the phantasmatic vector $\cancel{S} \to a$, so too does woman not relate sexually—i.e., phallically—to the masculine Other, that is to say, there is no $\cancel{La} \to \cancel{S}$ vector but, rather, the $\cancel{La} \to \Phi$ vector. In other words, just as, for man, woman is only an object-cause of desire, so too, for woman, man is man only through the symbolic Phallus Φ, namely, the signifier that designates "the phallic function."[76] Woman symbolizes man through the Φ that establishes her, $\cancel{L}a$, as a singular woman [*une femme*] only within a nonuniversal series of women. For this reason, Φ as the signifier of the phallic function is at the same time "the signifier which does not have a signified."[77]

But—and this is crucial—eventually woman alone stands for the Other sex: for woman, man is *man* through the symbolic Phallus, whereas, for man, woman is nothing but a—masturbatory, as we shall soon see—imaginary objectification, leaving aside which, in her radical otherness, she "does not say anything to him." In other words, while, in not relating to $\cancel{L}a$, $\cancel{S}$ cannot even relate to $S(\cancel{A})$—to which woman relates in her nonphallic feminine *jouissance* as a radical Other—in relating to one of the two elements that define the masculine sex for *man himself*, i.e., Φ, woman more precisely relates to the contradiction between $\cancel{S}$, the castrated masculine subject, and his being such only in relation to the exceptional uncastrated Phallus (or Father). This contradiction ("All men are castrated only insofar as there exists one Man who is not castrated"), which we will dissect logically in a later chapter, is again intuitively rendered well by Don Juan as a "feminine myth": women are invariably attracted to Don Juan, and end up in bed with him; in this sense he is the Man; but, at the same time, he cannot have them all. In any new relation he has with yet another woman, "it is from the perspective of the One-missing [l'*Une-en-moins*] that she must be taken up."[78] Accordingly, the One embodied by Don Juan's supreme im-potence "is only there [...] to represent solitude—the fact that the One doesn't truly knot itself with anything that resembles the sexual Other [...] that the Other cannot be added to the One [but] only be differentiated from it."[79]

It is thanks to this asymmetry between the contradiction that founds man and the opening of woman onto radical otherness that the $\cancel{L}a \rightarrow \Phi$ vector—i.e., "for woman, something other than object *a* is at stake in what comes to make up for the sexual relationship that does not exist"—does not in the end clash with Lacan's other claim that "woman serves a function in the sexual relationship only qua mother." The two statements are compatible precisely because human sexuality is based on a sexual relationship that is not One, that is, on the noncoincidence between Φ and *a* as crutches of the sexual object. While, for *woman*, Φ is that which makes up for the sexual relationship (that does not exist), at the same time, within the same relationship as not One, for *man*, "woman serves a function in the sexual relationship only qua mother" (as, in the end, the reification of the lost object). For all we know, Don Juan might well have been after his mother; his seducing women one by one, outside of any universal category of Woman, that is to say, as singularities, was in all likelihood sustained by the phantasmatic vector $\cancel{S} \rightarrow a$, the thwarted desire for the One of universal fusion.

This being said, if woman does not relate sexually—i.e., phallically—to the masculine Other as $\mathcal{S}$ —but to its structural contradiction, outside of which there is no man—she nevertheless enjoys a privileged nonsexual relation with the "most radical" Other, the Other as barred, as not-One, or, better, with the barred Other insofar as it can only be half-said in its nontotalizability through the mark of the signifier. Lacan formalizes this relation as $\mathit{La} \rightarrow S(\cancel{A})$, and argues that it is the vector of an unknowable *jouissance*—yet expressible as such (as witnessed by the writings of the mystics)—that is specifically feminine. He also argues that due to its openness toward the radical otherness of the barred Other, this *jouissance* makes woman have "more of a relationship to God than anything that has been said in speculation" about him.[80] More specifically, in experiencing God qua the nontotalizability of the symbolic order, feminine *jouissance* approaches him in a way that is contrary to any philosophy or theology that, following Aristotle's notion of the unmoved mover, or ultimate sphere, has identified the divine with a "supreme Being," a One who fully enjoys himself.

It should be clear by now that Lacan's main assumption here is that God is but a name for the paradoxical status of the symbolic order—"It is indubitable that the symbolic is the basis of what was made into God"[81]—suspended as it is between its making One and its being not-One, its producing the semblance of unity and this very production's reliance on the maintenance of a nontotality. In brief, God, his existence as a hypothesis, is no more than *saying*: "The Other [...] is the only place [...] that we can give to the term 'divine being,' God, to call him by his name. God [*Dieu*] is the locus where, if you will allow me this wordplay, the *dieu*—the sayer [*dieur*]—the saying [*dire*], is produced. With a trifling change [*pour un rien*], the saying constitutes God. And as long as somebody says something, the God hypothesis will persist."[82]

We should not lose sight of the fact that the impasse involved in this seesaw of the symbolic order *tout court*—which is, at the same time, responsible for making it work—is precisely what human sexuality as the absence of the sexual relationship amounts to. If woman existed as *La*, as The Other, if she were ultimately not not-all but not-at-all in the phallic function, and as such universalizable (differently from man, who is universalizable only through the contradiction of the phallic function), then her asexual *jouissance* would correspond to that of the supreme Being theorized by Aristotelian philosophy and theology.[83] But there is no such thing as Woman, no *être-ange*. A woman ex-sists as La, as a *jouissance* that is ecstatically mystical, not mythical, while it is man's desire to be One that attributes angelical features to her—and in parallel "defames" singular women as not-all ("*on la dit-femme, on la diffâme*").[84] Although it is tempting to connect feminine nonsexual *jouissance* as a privileged relation to God qua the nontotalizability of the symbolic order with the asexual angelical being that the phallic fantasy (and hysteria) projects onto it—onto its saying that one feels without knowing—, psychoanalysis should by all means keep them separate. Lacan spells this out very clearly when, in the same context, he claims that "the aim of my teaching [...] is to dissociate a and A by reducing the first to what is related to the imaginary," that is, to the phallic fantasy as $ $ \rightarrow a$, "and the other to what is related to the symbolic,"[85] that is, ultimately, to the Other as irreducibly barred. Again, Lacan insists, the latter should be rendered as S(A̶), as A̶ qua marked by the signifier, rather than just as A̶, in order not to embrace another form of mythical discourse, that of the totalization of non-totalizability, of the idealistic hypostatization of the incompleteness of language into One real not-One.[86]

In other words, God as the symbolic order is, so to speak, more on the side of the barred Other, but, Lacan adds, he is also inevitably "confused" with object a,[87] that is, with that which makes One out of the barred Other. Here we obtain a straightforward understanding of why sexual difference "doesn't make two God," yet "it doesn't make just one either": there is a split between God as the object a, as the support of the masculine phallic fantasy's making One—of its aiming at universal fusion with the angel, i.e., with what is, for man alone, the angelical mother—and God as S(A̶), the nonphallic feminine *jouissance* of the mystic as the concrete instantiation of the not-One. God can be seen as both the making One of man—in both the subjective and objective sense—and the not-One of woman, or better, as their continuous oscillation. This duplicity does not make two, but neither is it reducible to just one. Note, moreover, that Lacan significantly speaks of "two God" [*deux Dieu*], steering clear of the plural; this further stresses the fact that his theo-logical speculation is not to be associated with any attempt to resume a polytheist notion of the divine based on the cosmological complementarity of the opposition between a masculine God and a feminine Goddess. What is at stake for him, rather, is the way in which sexual difference obliges us to rethink, in terms of structure or "God hypothesis," the one and only God of monotheism as continuously moving from one God to two God, and back. God as not-One is not another God. More precisely, the oscillation between God as making One and God as not-One depends on the more general movement from God as *one* symbolic structure (what in earlier years Lacan called "the big Other," i.e., the locus of signifierness where intersubjectivity takes place)[88] to God as one symbolic structure that, as such, inexorably oscillates between the imaginary making One and the real not-One, namely, between the two God.

This oscillation of the one God—i.e., of the symbolic order as such—between the making One and the not-One is also echoed within the making One itself, the totalizing side of God, that of masculine phallic *jouissance*, which Lacan strictly associates with love. As we have already discussed, love is the frustrated, and hence self-sustaining, *desire* to be One, which repeatedly issues into the not-One, and, at the same time and through the same movement, the desire to *be* One.⁸⁹ The latter is as such impossible insofar as human sexuality corresponds to the absence of the sexual relationship, that is, of the relationship between two Ones, whereby the two-as-One would be established: "Love is impotent, even if it is mutual, because it is unaware that it is but the desire to be One, which leads us to the impossibility of establishing the relationship between 'them two' [*la relation d'eux*]. The relationship between them-two what?—Them-two sexes [*deux sexes*]."⁹⁰ We are then left with what Lacan calls the "duet" [*duo*] of genital/organic intercourse and its related phallic *jouissance*.⁹¹ As I have explained, at least on the masculine pole of sexuation, this *jouissance* enjoys nothing else than the object *a*, that is to say, the object that, in the fantasy $ \$ \rightarrow a $, puts itself in the place of what cannot be glimpsed of the Other. For this reason, insofar as *a* takes the place of the real missing partner, or rather, accompanies her absence, phallic sexuality—along with the possibility of reproduction it entails—is always necessarily a perverse *ménage à trois* with God, Lacan adds.⁹²

While in his early discussions of fantasy in the 1950s he had associated phallic *jouissance* with perversion as a non-normative, deviant form of sexuation,⁹³ in Seminar XX Lacan goes as far as arguing that "the act of love" *tout court*, the brutally physical act of lovemaking dictated by the *desire* to be One, "is the male's polymorphous perversion."⁹⁴ In other words, not only is God imaginarily embodied in love in the object *a* so that we ourselves can make One as isolated subjects—in this sense Lacan can claim that "love never makes anyone go beyond oneself," and the very myth of the fusional One with the angelical mother in the end depends on "the mirage of the One you believe yourself to be"⁹⁵—but, following closely his clinical notion of perversion (for which the desire of the pervert is fully aligned with the desire of the Other), this reduction of S(Ⱥ) to object *a* ultimately also amounts to a direct enjoying for the Other/God, for the unity and consistency of its meaning.⁹⁶

As Lacan concludes, man's phallic *jouissance*—including sexual intercourse—is therefore eminently masturbatory and idiotic.⁹⁷ Although this is not spelled out, we need to bear in mind the etymology of the latter term, which derives from the Greek *idios*, that is, "private," "one's own." Seminar XX abounds with reference to idiocy and stupidity (*bêtise* is also associated with *bête*, beast: this perfectly encapsulates the masculine attempt to return to the supposed solipsistic closure of the animal environment). Not surprisingly, in addition to phallic *jouissance*, God—one of his faces—and love are themselves presented as idiotic.

In a passage from the fourth lesson, which we have already scrutinized from a different angle, right after admitting that "it is impossible to say anything without immediately making Him subsist in the form of the Other," Lacan proceeds to diametrically oppose the discourse of history to psychoanalytic practice. If the former is entirely aimed at "making us believe that it has some sort of meaning," the latter, on the contrary, is focused on the stupidities voiced by the patient, which should be regarded as "effects of saying," inseparable from language as such; these effects that "agitate, stir things up, and bother speaking beings" are eventually useful, in that they lead people to "accommodating themselves [...] managing all the same," and to reproduce, by "giving a shadow of life to the feeling called love."[98] In other words, God (as a nonbarred Other) is automatically evoked whenever we say something; for this very reason, saying as such necessarily involves saying something—more or less—stupid (since the Other is actually barred). Yet it is only stupidity, rather than the attempt to formulate a meaningful discourse, which upholds our love stories—as a stand-in for the absence of the sexual relationship—and thus the species.

The connection between God and stupidity is also the theme of a particularly intriguing and complicated part of the second lesson. In this context, Lacan finds in the "collectivization of the signifier"—or, better, in confounding the semblance of linguistic totality, which speech inevitably presupposes, with the alleged completeness of language—the fundamental stupidity of traditional formal logic, and links it with the figure of God as the "supreme signifier," the One, the utmost Being of Aristotelian origins who fully enjoys himself. He then adds that this stupidity is openly witnessed by the smiling angels often portrayed in ecclesiastical paintings and frescos: "If an angel has such a stupid smile, that is because it is up to its ears in the supreme signifier."[99]

This remark gives us an excellent opportunity to stress once again the distance that separates *l'être-ange* from *l'être étrange*. For Lacan, woman is certainly not an idiot. Given the textual evidence, those critics who support the equation between femininity and the angelical being would also need to account for the equation between femininity and stupidity. Far from being reducible to the angel fantasized by man, woman's strangeness precisely amounts to her being *not-all* within the phallic function. What is "strange" here is the inextricability of her active role in the phallic function, through the vector $\cancel{La} \rightarrow \Phi$, from her having a relation with the fact that there is no Other of the Other, that is, $\cancel{La} \rightarrow S(\cancel{A})$. In other words, her opening toward the God of nontotalizability, the not-One pole of structure, is possible only because of the co-dependence of $\cancel{La} \rightarrow S(\cancel{A})$ with $\cancel{La} \rightarrow \Phi$. Woman's *specifically* feminine *jouissance* is possible only because of her feminine *phallic jouissance*, and vice versa. The short passage from the sixth lesson of Seminar XX which seems to associate the feminine *jouissance* of the mystic with woman's strangeness—and which commentators quote out of context[100]—should itself be read along these lines. Mystics are by no means angels.[101] Mystical women who are *not-all* in the phallic function are nevertheless still fully in it; to put it bluntly, although mystics put into practice their not-all *more* than other phallic women, they are not for this reason *less* phallic, since, as I have repeatedly pointed out, feminine nonphallic *jouissance* is additional (by means of negation). Saint Teresa's nonsexual jaculation does not in the least prevent her from experiencing sexual enjoyment when she makes herself be counted as a singular, nonuniversalizable woman by a womanizer like Don Juan.[102]

What I think Lacan fails to unravel when he confronts the inseparability of the feminine "*not-all* in the phallic function" from the "not-all in the *phallic function*" (and vice versa) is the *different* degrees to which each woman (each subject who is not symbolically a man) can "activate," so to speak, the *en plus* / extra component of the *pas-toute*. Not only can a promiscuous libertine and a mystic coexist in the same woman, but a mundane courtesan wholeheartedly complicit in the perverse intrigues of her prince could well become as ecstatic as a frigid saint without ever leaving his palace or renouncing her sexual practices. Conversely, woman's remaining nonetheless "fully" in the phallic function entails very dissimilar ways of concretely relating to the phallus and the organ it symbolizes: if, on the one hand, the hysteric is so phallic that she "plays the part of man" and vainly tries to embody his basic fantasy, i.e., being *The* woman "outside sex," on the other, it is highly unlikely that she will ever sleep with Don Juan after actively seducing him ...

Another contiguous issue that remains overall unexplored by Lacan concerns the exact status of *feminine phallic jouissance*. Besides the numerical consideration according to which the latter gives rise to a notion of the one as singular that differs from the masculine One of fusion, how does woman enjoy *phallically*? Is she also involved in a love triangle with God? My tentative answer is affirmative, but only on condition of adding that her *ménage à trois* cannot take the shape of the fantasy $\$ \rightarrow a$ (as we have seen, it is only woman qua mother who might attempt to realize the masculine phallic fantasy, to pass from the desire to be One to being One by using her child as a phagocyted appendix). By way of approximation, I would suggest that woman's love relation to the other sex—and to God as an Other that shows, in this case, his masculine side—must still be conceived through the vector $\mathcal{L}a \rightarrow \Phi$ or, better, through a desire to be *one* only within a one-by-one series. Having said this, we also need to specify that, from the stance of love and the different light it sheds on the paradigm of feminine singularity, this vector now evinces a wanting to be recognized by man as his "one and only" [*la seule*]—as Lacan suggests in a text written the same year he delivered Seminar XX.[103] Such a request for exclusivity nonetheless still presupposes, as its reverse side, the acknowledgment that even as the one and only, woman remains a singularity in a nonuniversal series.[104]

This matter—which Lacan does not really tackle, and which I can only introduce here—would perhaps eventually oblige us to further complicate the number of God. While God is neither "two God"—since the Other and the barred Other are distinct only as interrelated in structure—nor "just one"—since structure is the Other and the barred Other—he is also making One/one in two co-dependent but utterly dissimilar ways, namely, as a masculine One and a feminine one which cannot be added together. God is the result of the noncomplementarity between not-One, not-two, and two ones (One and one). His faces display $S(\bar{A})$ (neither one nor two), object a (One), but also Φ (one). That is to say, God is the *hole* of feminine nonphallic *jouissance*, the *object* of masculine phallic *jouissance* (fantasized through the angel, potentially annexed by the mother, and negatively embodied by the hysteric), as well as the *symbol* of feminine phallic *jouissance*. Most importantly, thanks to this third face of God, woman has a relation with the *differentiality* of the symbolic order as such, with the "There's such a thing as One" (Y a d'l'Un) that is not-One and making One/one. God, the God of the God hypothesis that is structure, is the happening of the Y a d'l'Un that is not-One but makes One/one, and of the not-two that is not two-as-One.

CHAPTER 2

LOGIC AND BIOLOGY: AGAINST BIO-LOGY

2.1 THERE ARE TWO SEXES, BUT THERE ISN'T A SECOND SEX

In order to advance a structural account of sexuation/subjectivation that culminates in the oscillation of the God hypothesis between the one/One and the not-One, Lacan cannot avoid tackling biological sex. Jean-Claude Milner has recently claimed that Lacan's confrontation with science is mostly focused on the gap that separates the ancient Greek notion of *episteme* from modern physics, and that the French psychoanalyst, "simply for a question of dates," only knew of the beginning of the revolution that has been happening in genetics over the last fifty years.[1] While I cannot but agree with Milner's point, I would nevertheless not underestimate Lacan's biological ideas and pronouncements on the life sciences, especially his late critique of the representation of sex offered by what he deems to be the animistic, pre-Galilean basis of evolutionism as well as of cellular and molecular biology.

In Seminars XVIII, XIX, XIXB, and XX, the discussion of the phallic function as our transcendental logic of sexuation/subjectivation is paralleled by a resumption and complication of the theory of animal and human reproduction introduced in Seminars I and II. Throughout the 1950s and early 1960s, Lacan stressed the way in which the openness of the human world can turn into an animal pseudo-environment only thanks to symbolic mediation, and, together with this, the fact that love, the uncompromising character of its demand, is opposed to such a recuperation of instincts through desire and the drives.[2] On the other hand, his teaching of the early 1970s insists on the margin of compatibility between love's search for the One and reproduction, but, at the same time, accentuates the tenuousness of the ensuing biocultural suture that compensates for the absence of the sexual relationship. The latter is now more plainly considered as an impossible real, an impasse of the symbolic-imaginary that should always be given logical priority, and only consequently, on this basis, ontological value.

I think this shift in perspective is due primarily to Lacan's attempt at dispelling the impression that his taking for granted the dysfunctional nature of Homo sapiens concealed, in the end, a form of negative anthropocentrism. Positing man as the lacking animal grants him an unwarranted, albeit paradoxical, privilege. Although they do, now and then, fall back into the rhetoric of the intrinsically noumenal *malaise* of our speaking species, the Seminars of the early 1970s tend to replace the abstract privative notion of the onto-biological (primarily sexual) disadaptation of mankind with that of an empirical nonadapted adapt-ability—or, to use a more contemporary phrase, of a plastic in-determination—that is more directly rooted in the evidence of psychoanalytic practice, and then theoretically elaborated starting from *Il n'y a pas de rapport sexuel*. Lacan believes he can thus both continue his denunciation of the teleology of selection and linear progression toward higher forms of the living endorsed by mainstream Darwinism, as well as distance himself from the implicit substantialization of lack (and hence of language) that in a way accompanied his idea that, if the speaking animal regularly misses its sexual object, this occurs because it is in itself, as a human *animal*, an inadequate "little upturned turtle."[3]

The apparently minor but crucial novelty of such a change in orientation with regard to a theory that remains, however, firmly based on the tortuous sexuality of our species (an assumption echoed nowadays by scientists, who do not hesitate to define us as "the animal with the weirdest sex life")[4] can be measured more clearly through Lacan's contrasting stance on animal sexuality. Seminar I did not hesitate to define it as the efficiently fitting correspondence of a key with a keyhole.[5] On the other hand, Seminar XIX warns us that the "supposed animal model" of perfectly bi-univocal reproductive complementarity—"the animal image of copulation [that] seems to us to be a sufficient model of what is at stake in the sexual relationship"—from which we would depart, in absolute terms, as a biological exception is itself nothing other than a side-effect of the "fantasy of the soul" through which *we* imaginarily "observe" the animal.[6]

Leaving aside the (para-ontological) issue of the in-itself of animal sexuality—which, in the early 1970s, reemerges with a question mark on several decisive occasions, and eventually leads to the query "Is there something of the One for the animal?"[7]—we need to notice how, precisely when he challenges the objectivity of the discourse of ethology and goes as far as severing the link between psychoanalysis and any "idea of nature,"[8] Lacan also feels obliged to specify that the "There is no sexual relationship" summarizing the condition of human sexuality as evinced by clinical practice should most definitely *not* be regarded as a "nominalist" maxim. On the contrary, it rather indicates that sex is *real*: "That sex is real, that isn't in the least put into doubt."[9] The real of sex, Lacan argues, can be grasped by enunciating the primary impossibility of its relational character. More accurately, "the real [of sex] is there before we think of it"[10]—phallically—through the terms "man" and "woman," yet we can access it only diagonally after realizing—in everyday life and, above all, in the setting of psychoanalytic treatment—that, with regard to the speaking animal at least, copulation is in the first place "not assured."[11] The motto of Seminar XI according to which the originality of psychoanalysis lies in its promotion of a kind of "naturalism" that "give[s] body to psychic reality without substantializing it"[12] in the body finds in this perspective its full expression; it does so, coherently, in the guise of a stance that refuses any naive dichotomy between culture and nature, or reduction of one to the other.[13]

We can shed further light on the multifaceted issue at stake by dwelling on what, in Seminar XIX, Lacan refers to as the "little difference," i.e., the anatomical difference between the sexes. As he explains, very clearly, "when I say that *there is no sexual relationship*, I precisely put forward [...] that, in the case of the speaking being, sex does not define any relationship" between two discrete sexes.[14] This is not at all to imply, he adds, that "I deny the difference that there is, since the earliest of age, between what one calls a little girl and a little boy"[15]—just as much as he does not doubt that the absence of the *rapport sexuel*, as the absence of a "sexual measure," paves the way for a remarkably wide range of polymorphous liaisons sustained by the phallic function.[16] It is indeed from this little difference that Lacan's—and Freud's—entire discourse emerges, yet "as soon as I start from *there*, you don't know what I'm talking about."[17] That is to say: while, on the one hand, we are dealing with a "difference that imposes itself as innate [*native*] and is by all means natural," on the other, "it is not part of a logic."[18] The little girl and the little boy "recognize themselves as speaking beings," and, in parallel, acquire a sexual positioning, only by initially "*rejecting* this [innate] distinction via all sorts of identifications"[19]—suffice it to think of the paradigmatic case of Little Hans and his attribution of the "widdler" to both sexes. Psychoanalysis has taught us to recognize these identifications with the "major source of the phases of each childhood."[20]

The phallic function, our sexuation, thus springs from what appears to us as the illogical nature of sex. To put it another way: for the human progeny, sexual difference as a natural difference can become such only as long as it is symbolized by the surrounding adults: "*We* distinguish them, it is not them who distinguish themselves."[21] However, what is more, in distinguishing girls from boys, adults make the mistake of "recognizing them without doubt on the basis of that from which they [adults] distinguish themselves"—i.e., natural sexual difference—but exclusively "according to criteria formed under the dependence of language"—i.e., the Oedipus and castration complexes.[22] In brief, phallic sexuality is reified, seen as directly natural to the detriment of the real of the absence of the sexual relationship. With the same move, the "little difference" ceases to be taken for what it is, a logical impossibility, and turns into the possession or lack of an organ. Lacan calls this the "common error."[23]

Expanding on Seminar XIX, we could suggest that little boys and girls start off their ontogenetic—linguistic and sexual—process of subjectivation from a traumatic encounter with the *indifference* of the anatomical "little difference" (as "not part of a logic") with respect to the symbolic difference of sexuation, which instead always-already surrounds them through adults.[24] This indifference is overcome (via repression) first, during the Oedipus complex, through the rudimentary difference of infantile sexual theories (Freud's "phallic phase"), for which there are those who have the phallus and those who must also have it—even if contextual evidence points to the opposite—and then through the more accomplished difference of the post-Oedipal repartition between those who are all phallic (man) and those who are not-all phallic (woman). The little difference is at this point retroactively equated with sex organs, i.e., genitalia.

Let us also note in passing that the initial indifference of anatomical difference, as such rejected by the Oedipal child, should certainly also be read together with the fact that, for Lacan, it is by all means possible for anatomical males to be symbolically sexed as women, and vice versa.[25] Yet conversely, even in the case in which there is no overlapping between anatomy and symbolic sexuation, subjects retroactively self-designate themselves biologically as male or female on the basis of the possession or lack of what earlier Seminars appropriately called "the real phallus," namely, the penis—which is real as an organ only through the phallic function. This is not explicitly addressed by Lacan, but follows from what appears to be for him the universality of the "common error" discussed above.[26]

Returning to Seminar XIX, we should now pay particular attention to the way in which Lacan openly associates the real as an impasse of *logic* with the real he is himself resigned to call, for lack of a better term, *natural*. The anatomical "little difference," i.e., sexual indifference that will have been differentiated, stands right at their intersection. That is to say: the initial indifference of the little difference with respect to symbolic sexual difference nonetheless entails that, for us, "There are two sexes,"[27] two different natural sexes. Once more, here we need to acknowledge that we grasp the two different natural sexes only as organic, that is, as retroactively mediated by the phallic function; and that, moreover, it is not necessarily the case that one organic sex is symbolically subjectivized as "man" and the other as "woman." But, more importantly, we also need to concede that the two of the natural sexes thus obtained is itself a logical impasse; that is to say, it goes together with the impossibility of counting woman, the *Other* sex, as *an*-other sex. Woman can only be *differentiated* from man, not added to him. To sum up: (1) indifferent nature gives itself sexually to the child as a logical impasse; (2) this causes the phallic emergence of the two, and thus nature is retroactively the two of the sex organs; (3) nature as two sexes is again a logical impasse, i.e., the missing of the second sex.

Let us unpack this by examining Lacan's text more closely. The "little difference" is, as mentioned, real in that it is "not part of a logic"; this applies not only to the child, but also to his adult audience: "As soon as I start from there, you don't know what I'm talking about." At the same time, the "little difference" is real "for the fact that in the species that names itself *Homo sapiens* [...] sexes seem to be split up into two roughly equal numbers of individuals."[28] When considering this second passage, let us not forget that, for Lacan, the anatomical real is also there before we can think of it (as not part of a logic), since, as he tells us, he is not a nominalist: he is here talking about a *natural* species, the human *animal* (although this is the same human animal that also "names itself"). Yet, on the other hand, following his antisubstantialist naturalism, the emphasis in the same quote should most definitely be put on the number *two* of the species, not on the individual *Homines sapientes* that compose it, or on the species as a whole. The natural species is real as species only retroactively thanks to the two sexes, which are, however, already there anatomically before we can think of them (initially as indifferent to the two).

Above all, merging these definitions of the real of the anatomical "little difference," if we assume with Lacan, at least provisionally, that life does not as such "flourish in significations,"[29] that there is no transcendent bio-logy of the living, then the resulting meaningless pseudo-movement of life—which is not even an acephalic thrust itself ultimately provided with a voluntaristic sense—will indeed amount, for us (adult *Homines sapientes*), to sexual *difference*, or better, *sex as natural indifference in the guise of il-logical difference*. In other words, all that we can access of the real of our species' sex as natural is *numerical*: two roughly equal numbers of individuals. The so-called biological real of human nature is filtered (logically as difference) through the logical real qua the *impasse* of logic: the split into two roughly equal numbers of individuals. We therefore obtain an equivalence of the statement "For logic, there is no sexual relationship, or measure, between the different sexes" with the statement "There are two natural sexes." Or also, *the natural real is perceived as number on the illogical hole of the logical wall that both separates us from nature and connects us with it.*[30] As Lacan himself has it, against biological discourse, psychoanalysis reminds us that the access to the real is the symbolic: "We do not access the so-called real except in and through this impossible that alone defines the symbolic," and, subsequently, "it is within this perspective that we can take what we call reality, *natural reality*, at the level of a certain discourse."[31]

Another way to put this important point, and elaborate on it, is as follows. The formula "There is no sexual relationship" tells us that it is real that there are two sexes, and that the real is thus "dual."[32] But this duality of the real as natural structure[33] is primarily logical, not biological ("it's not because it's biological that it is more real").[34] The bio-logical as a supposed logic of life rather obfuscates the dual logic of the real conveyed by the Il n'y a pas de rapport sexuel, precisely under the pretext of dealing with what is in itself, outside of any symbolic (human) intervention, the—by definition—meaningfully principled/grounded, and thus after all unitary, force of the living. That is to say: biology does not acknowledge that, for us, there are two real natural sexes only to the extent that, logically, "There isn't a second sex"—as Lacan puts it, mocking Simone de Beauvoir.[35] The Other sex—woman's sex— "empties itself" through the phallic function.[36] This means that since the two natural sexes are always apprehended by our species retroactively and, what is more, in an asymmetrical way (i.e., woman's sex can only be represented phallically as not-all), the two of sexual difference is actually equivalent to the "not-two,"[37] the missing of the second sex. Such a deadlock, what we could call the "There is no two-as-One coming from the relation of the one to the Other," corresponds nonetheless to symbolic sexuation to the extent that woman, the "one less," "work[s] for the One."[38]

More generally, Lacan believes that biology cannot be considered as a scientific discourse, or better, that the notion of science on which it rests is pre-Galilean. Instead of separating nature from so-called sensible substance by means of number (and the letters of mathematical formulas), it projects onto nature number as derived from the image of the human body as one form, and the phallic fantasy of totalization that depends on it. Abiding by a "delirium which is without doubt common," and could also be named "common sense," unlike modern science, which interrupts this delirium, biology then proceeds to a "contemplation of the world" and identifies it with "what is."[39] How does biology's understanding of sex, in particular, therefore contrast with that of psychoanalysis? Lacan derives from the axiom Il n'y a pas de rapport sexuel the following corollaries concerning human (biological) sex: (1) "There are two sexes"; (2) "Insofar as there is no relationship between the two sexes, each sex remains one";[40] and, we should add, (3) precisely because there is no relationship, the second sex can be defined as a "one less" only as soon as it is thought from the compensatory perspective of the first— which is itself one only vis-à-vis the not-One of the Other. What Seminar XIX calls the "mythology" of biology, its common sense, moves instead from the opposite presupposition that the two sexes (or the two gametes, or the two sets of sexual chromosomes) as discrete entities invariably merge into One. Lacan has no reason to doubt that, as biologists teach us, "sex is located in two little cells."[41] But such a licit numbering of nature—itself inferred from the irreconcilable real two of human sexual difference, which thus does not necessarily have anything to do with sensible (observable) substance—is far from entailing that when the spermatozoon penetrates the ovum, a fusion follows. This kind of allegedly empirical and objective conclusion stands for nothing but a "vulgar metaphor" for copulation seen as an effortless amalgamation of the sexes: "Sex imagined as the image of what, in the reproduction of life, would be love."[42]

Starting from the axiomatization of the clinical evidence of the *Il n'y a pas de rapport sexuel* and the antithetical fact that the reproduction of life also takes place in the *Homo sapiens* species, psychoanalysis refuses this facile synthesis in order to question whether "discourse is or is not able to articulate the sexual relationship."[43] Ultimately, discourse is not able to articulate it, but can articulate this very impossibility by showing—through a "knowledge of truth," as we will see—how the phallic function allows for the emergence of sexed liaisons against the background of an enduring absence of the sexual relationship.

2.2 BIOLOGY SOUL-LOVES

In the Seminars of the early 1970s, Lacan continues and deepens in multiple directions his dismantling of the fusional bias of biology's take on sex, and of the underlying presupposition that man "serves an end," that "he is founded on the basis of his final cause, which [...] is to live or, more precisely, to survive, in other words, to postpone death and dominate his rival."[44] On the one hand, I believe that this staunch attack on the blatant theo-teleology of mainstream Darwinism still remains extremely topical, up to the point of suggesting that it is precisely through the *bios* of biology that, as Lacan has it, "today, only the *theo* is left, always there, really solid in its idiocy, and logic has [...] evaporated."[45] On the other hand, I am equally of the opinion that, for a question of dates, Lacan has missed not only the full extent of the ongoing revolution in the life sciences, as indicated by Milner, but also their *potential* for theoretical self-critique.

For instance, the psychoanalytic questioning of the imaginary, anthropomorphic basis of our reduction of the real duality of sex to the bipolar complementarity between male and female as a key and a keyhole, a preconception which is operative especially when we consider animals, surfaces distinctively in current cutting-edge debates in fields such as psychobiology and behavioral neuroscience. As Mark Blumberg put it in a book devoted to the co-implication of development and evolution significantly entitled *Freaks of Nature*, "anything goes; when it comes to sex, expect ambiguity."[46] Here he describes, among others, organisms that lack sex chromosomes although their sexes are as identifiable as male and female as those of most mammalian species (crocodiles);[47] possess an erectile penis-like clitoris, a scrotum, and no vagina (the female spotted hyena);⁴⁸ switch sex depending on circumstances (the tobacco fish); are technically asexual, i.e., clones, yet the female mates with males of closely related species, transfer of sperm takes place, but there is no genetic exchange (the Amazon molly).

Without entering into a detailed discussion of these fascinating examples, or intending to use them as an objectively "factual" scientific proof of what psychoanalysis would have merely intuited, we can nonetheless state that, first, they reinforce Freud's broad and, in his time, revolutionary idea that (human) sexuality is not predetermined, that is to say, not bound to an unequivocal standard of what is masculine and what is feminine (behaviorally for Freud; behaviorally, morphologically, and genetically for contemporary psychobiology).⁴⁹ As the author of *Freaks of Nature* has it, in a presumably deliberate wink at psychoanalysis, "sex is a 'syndrome,' a collection of 'symptoms'" that, however, "as a collective, allow for a 'diagnosis' of *male or female*"⁵⁰—note here also his clear and crucial reference to how sex yet amounts, for us, to two natural sexes.

Secondly, these scientific discoveries support Lacan's contention that the il-logical real of sexual difference, understood also as natural, goes hand in hand, for us, with the impossibility of establishing sex straightforwardly on the simple basis of observable physical disparities in genitalia—which are instead phallically constructed as sex organs only in a retroactive way. Seeing a female hyena in Vienna's zoo rather than a lion, or a horse in the street, would no doubt have made Hans even more perplexed as to his sex and that of his mother.⁵¹ Similarly, it is because of the initial indifference of the anatomical "little difference" (even smaller in some other species) with respect to symbolic sexual difference that, as adults, we can continue to confuse the hyena's clitoris with a gigantic penis.

Thirdly, in line with Lacan's resistance in his late work to singling out man's openness as opposed to the closed environment of the animal, such empirical investigations also put in doubt the exceptionality of the convolutedness of human sexuality, as irreducible to instincts, in favor of a more comprehensive approach to human *and* nonhuman sex as a "meandering, unfolding path."⁵² Genes (when they are present) do indeed have an influence on such a path, but this does not in any way allow us to invoke the existence of closed genetic programs in either humans or nonhumans, whereby the biology of sex would ultimately come down to the identity of sex chromosomes.

In this context, it is however also the case that some *technical* aspects of Lacan's denunciation of the life sciences, and in particular genetics, appear to be obsolete. For example, his remark that "things are far from being such that we have, on the one hand, the network of the gonad, what Weismann"—and Freud after him—"called the *germen*, and, on the other hand, the *soma*, the branch of the body"⁵³ has by now lost most of its polemical undertones, and sounds rather *conservative* from the standpoint of contemporary "evolutionary-developmental" theory. Lacan stresses, contra Weismann, the interdependency of the genotype (the germen) and the phenotype (the soma), yet without renouncing the primacy of the former over the latter: "The genotype of the body conveys something that determines sex, but this is not sufficient" insofar as "from its production of the body [...] [the genotype] detaches hormones that can interfere with this determination."⁵⁴ For their part, leading contemporary biologists such as Eva Jablonka and Mary-Jane West-Eberhard not only acknowledge that the view according to which differences in (sexual) phenotype are the result of both genes and the developmental environment is nowadays shared by most researchers in the life sciences, but go as far as suggesting—against mainstream biology—that "genes are *followers* in evolution."⁵⁵ As Jablonka writes, "developmental responses to the environment are *primary*, and can be fine-tuned, stabilized, or ameliorated by *subsequent* genetic changes in populations."⁵⁶

These new and particularly inspiring directions in the life sciences do indeed have the potential to shake the very foundations of the Mendelian appropriation of Darwin, if not of Darwinism *tout court*. They should, however, themselves be approached with caution from a psychoanalytically informed philosophical perspective intending to demystify the theo-teleological kernel still prevalent in evolutionary theory. The datedness of some of Lacan's tirades is not an excuse not to test so-called Evo-Devo through his own even now persuasive anti-bio-logical discourse. While the deconstructive impetus of evolutionary-developmental biology stands out as undoubtedly strong, the "new synthesis" it advocates remains at best vague, if not confusing. Theoretically, Evo-Devo leads in fact to quasi-paradoxical conclusions, such as the following: "Selection is still seen as crucial, but the nature, origins, construction, and inheritance of developmental variations are deemed to be just as important."⁵⁷ To put it bluntly: what, then, is "selection" in this framework, and above all, what is "evolution" for Evo-Devo? What is it that is being selected once genes are no longer "leaders" in evolution? Does this refer to the increasingly fitter, as increasingly plastic, phenotypic responses to the environment? If so, independently of overthrowing *genetic* determinism, there is clearly here a risk of propounding a notion of environment, and of plastic phenotypic responses to it, that continues to partake of the old Darwinian finalism of adaptation aimed at an incrementalist evolution of Life, and ultimately at justifying the fact that "consciousness has to appear, the world, history converge on this marvel, contemporary man, you and me, us men in the street."⁵⁸

At this stage, one should invoke the dialectical Darwinism of Stephen Jay Gould, and the way he lists the alleged increase in "flexibility of behavioral repertoire," and hence in phenotypic plasticity, as one among other possible criteria concocted to defend—more or less explicitly—the tale of "progress," that is, "the fallacy that evolution embodies a fundamental trend or thrust leading to a primary and defining result."[59] Against this stance, he famously proposes that "life has always been, and will probably always remain until the sun explodes, in the Age of Bacteria."[60] More philosophically, he puts forward a "claim about the nature of reality" according to which "*variation itself* [is] irreducible, [...] '*real*' in the sense of 'what the world is made of'"[61]— whereby we seem to be left to infer that selection is just the way in which variation varies. He then proceeds to understand the unpredictable, contingent, and unrepeatable "excellence" of *Homo sapiens* in terms of sheer "trends properly viewed as results of expanding or contracting variation, rather than concrete entities moving in a definite direction," and, more specifically, of the fact that, while not showing any general thrust toward improvement, "life [...] just adds an occasional exemplar of complexity in the only region of available anatomical space."[62]

Leaving aside Gould—not without noting that his idea that life as a presupposed *agency*, albeit occasionally and contingently, adds some *complexity* remains itself problematic for its lingering vitalism and anthropocentrism— we can suggest that, in all likelihood, Lacan would not have supported Evo-Devo's view that "genes are followers in evolution," for the simple reason that he problematizes the very notion of evolution (to which Gould instead clings; we would have to ask him outright: How can there be evolution without progress?).[63] Fundamentally, Lacan sees evolutionary theory as unsubstantiated by the very facts it claims to observe objectively and derive its knowledge from, while nonetheless it resists its self-demise by fashioning a tautological discourse. As he writes, "it is in the most improper fashion that we put there [in matter] a meaning, an idea of evolution, of perfectioning, while in the animal chain that is presupposed we see absolutely nothing which bears witness to this so-called continual adaptation." This is so misleading that "it was necessary all the same to renounce it and to say that after all those who get through are those who have been able to get through. We call this natural selection. It strictly means nothing."[64]

In other words, natural selection does not strictly mean anything, since eventually evolutionary theory rests on the tautology according to which those who survive are those who have survived. Developing Lacan's cursory remark, and taking on board more recent speculation in the life sciences, we could suggest that evolutionary theory leads to the redundant idea that those who have survived would prove through the very fact of having survived that they are those who evolve/adapt, where instead, stressing the role of contingency in "evolution," some respected evolutionary biologists do themselves have to conclude, examining fossils, that surviving organisms did not seem better adapted than their now extinct contemporaneous neighbors.[65]

This specific attack on the tautological character of evolutionary theory (whether based on an explicit teleology or on a professedly nonfinalistic "thrust" of life; whether genetically or environmentally deterministic) should be read together with Lacan's more comprehensive onto-logical debunking of what he deems to be the Aristotelian "animism" of biology, which for the time being we should tentatively define as the imaginary presupposition of a correspondence between thought and what is being thought. Molecular biology is not exempt from such a presupposition, given that it operates on the supposed correspondence between the linguistic notion of information and "the level of the gene's molecular information."[66] This idea is supported by Nobel-Prize-winning life scientists: evolution "entails the generation of information," and man's development of language as a species-specific faculty involves a "plane of information transfer, similar to the primary plane of genetic information."[67]

Here we should also, however, stress that, for Lacan, animism does not apply exclusively to bio-logy but must be referred to what he considers the unfinished character of Galilean science *in toto*. Modern science is only in principle nonanimistic. In his view, modern science proceeds in a contradictory manner: thanks to the use of numbers and letters, it has undone—and this is its great achievement—the ancient association between nature and sensible substance, i.e., between nature qua what is being thought, and the perceived unity of the human body and its senses qua presupposition for thinking. It thus has undone the a priori assumption of a consistent uni-verse. Yet modern science nevertheless equally promotes a new kind of animism, that is, a form of naturalist reductionism for which the presumed totalizability of man's body, including his brain, could eventually be mathematized—e.g., by means of a synergy of statistics, genetics, and cognitive science—as a numerical segment of the whole of nature. The alleged correspondence between thought and what is being thought is thus not eliminated, only displaced. Modern science tries to recompose, in a novel way, the cosmos as harmonic.

We therefore need to conclude that even if biology were to become finally a full-blown algebraic Galilean science, it would still be susceptible to the same kind of criticism Lacan addresses to Galilean science. Miller thus moves too quickly when he argues that, even though "Freudian biology is not biology," for it is primarily an energetics, from the moment that biology no longer has life as its object, but what François Jacob calls "the algorithms of the living world," Lacan could unreservedly support it.[68] I would be inclined to reverse his claim: there can be a psychoanalytic biology that is not a bio-logy as soon as Freudian energetics is challenged,[69] and this can be achieved only if one does not take for granted that "the algorithms of the living world" have necessarily done once and for all with animism.

Moreover, at a much simpler level than that of Galilean sciences such as physics, contemporary biology could be said to remain firmly imaginary, since fundamentally it still treats the letters of its algebra in an analogical way. Everything proceeds from the idea that genes are discrete and divisible particles. For instance, in population genetics, basic mathematical models have until recently considered only one gene locus at a time. Despite the advanced statistics of, say, the gene-finding algorithms elaborated by bio-informatics, can we say, following Lacan's definition of formalization, that in genetics "whatever number of ones you place under each [...] letter"—e.g., in the formula $mv^2/2$—"you are subject to a certain number of laws"?[70] To put it very bluntly: does this modern understanding of the letter also apply to the G, T, A, C of guanine, adenine, thymine, and cytosine that compose the nucleobases of DNA and their forming pairs? Or is our scientific approach to genetic material still intimately tied to "the idea of evolution" ending up "at the top of the animal scale, with this consciousness that characterizes us," an idea which thus simply proposes "a new figure of progress" in the guise of *programing*?[71] If so, is this regressive neo-theo-teleological paradigm not already heavily influencing *all* science?

Our stance toward recent developments in the life sciences should consequently be twofold. On the one hand, we need to listen attentively to Milner's exhortation to Lacanian discourse to take seriously the current consolidation of a "Galileanism of the living."[72] This is decisive to the extent that the latter manages to threaten doxastic Darwinism and its long shadow. The work of Johnston has already demonstrated how fruitful such an opening can be theoretically in terms of a psychoanalytic-philosophical rethinking of the broad notions of realism and materialism, which, more than half a century ago—and availing himself of the findings of zoology, ethology, embryology, and *Gestalt* theory—Lacan rescued from what he deemed the antirealism and antimaterialism of phenomenology. Rather than hastily giving up all that is Darwin-related—if not biological *tout court*—as Lacan sometimes does,[73] taking seriously the "Galileanism of the living" must here go together with the awareness that establishing whether evolutionary theory can be reformulated in a novel manner in line with the principles of Galilean formalization is by no means an easy task. An "evolution" without progress like the one implicitly proposed by Gould stands as a thought-provoking oxymoron, but Lacan-informed philosophy should theoretically push it further.

On the other hand—and this is even more important—we should not lose sight of the complex positioning of psychoanalysis vis-à-vis Galilean science: Lacan condemns the fact that modern science's relentless expansion, or better, intensification of the real goes together with an increasing attempt at totalizing knowledge which forecloses this very intensification. More specifically, in confronting contemporary biological perspectives such as evolutionary-developmental theory, it is crucial to stress that its proponents are at present in search of what they themselves label a New Synthesis—one which would be able to replace the hegemonic link between Darwinism and Mendelianism with a Darwinian epigenetic genetics that recovers the credible elements of the Lamarckian legacy. Although this move *could* strike a definitive blow to the most untenable theo-teleological aspects of evolutionism (that is, the aprioristic presupposition that life as an inexhaustible, continuous, and incrementalist force binds One and One into two-as-One), as has been noted in debates internal to the same scientific circles, such a change of biological paradigm would hardly diminish overall the intolerance of ambiguity.

Sex, for instance, could well be regarded as an agglomeration of "symptoms" more and more recalcitrant to being understood as the bi-univocal fusion of complementary (organic, cellular, or molecular) partners, and this in line with the advancements of physics, which has long ceased to consider matter as reducible to binding particles that are easily identifiable. Yet such an ever more apparent, and empirically testable, real "decomposition" of the world[74] would still most probably aim at the delineation of a unitary worldview, which is what psychoanalysis refuses to begin with as fundamentally onto-theological.[75] This future *Weltanschauung* could eventually even rest on the algebraic formula of an acausal, chaotic universe, and on an evolutionary algorithm accounting for sexual reproduction—if not life *tout court*—compatible with it, without for this reason reducing in the least science's attempted totalization of knowledge.[76] In this sense, the retarded "animism" of traditional biology, together with the life and cognitive sciences' current effort to overcome its embarrassing delay, could, by contrast, unexpectedly teach us a lot about the unsurpassable character of the entirety of modern science's contradictory stance on the real. Lacan's claim that the theory of natural selection strictly speaking "means nothing" also shows that as such it amounts at present to a point of emergence of the real qua symbolic impasse, to the structural impasse of formalization that runs parallel to modern science—which psychoanalysis then inscribes as nonformalizable through its thinking of sexual difference as the indicated limits of what is formalizable.

To dwell on this complex juncture, I propose now to focus on Seminar XX's fierce attack on behaviorism. I take it to be exemplary of the way in which Lacan understands modern science's relation to the real. His arguments are in my view still very much topical, especially if we bear in mind that, forty years later, after the cognitive revolution has swept away behaviorism, evolutionary-developmental biology nonetheless goes hand in hand with a neuroscientific reassessment of behavior. As we have seen, according to Lacan, the problem with classical, Aristotelian science is that it is animistic, since "it implies that what is thought of," the natural object in the world, "is in the image of thought," the human subject. That is to say, it takes for granted that ultimately, "being thinks."[77] This imaginary science, its knowledge, thus does not want to know anything about the real as that which does not work in the symbolic. The novelty of modern science amounts to the fact that it both seizes the real, namely, what is unknowable (albeit formalizable) as lying outside of the phantasmatic correspondence of thought with what is thought of, and at the same time intends to reduce it to the level of imaginary knowledge. Hence, we could add, modern science does not want to know what it already knows about the real: the historical surfacing of psychoanalysis as a direct descendant of Galilean discourse confirms and reverses this in that it endeavors to establish itself as a *savoir sur la vérité*, as the knowledge of the limits of knowledge. Lacan contends that, in the name of founding the human sciences on incontestable criteria, behaviorism epitomizes such an oscillation of modern science in an extreme and self-reflexive way, for it applies it to man himself qua the purportedly empirical object of his own knowledge.

Behaviorism correctly assumes that accessing the real scientifically presupposes the unbinding of the ancient imaginary correspondence between the subject of knowledge and the natural object, between *physis* (the order of the world as such) and man's (self-)perception as a constitutive component of the in-itself. It also apparently suspends the very correlation between the modern subject of science and its empirical object, so as to focus exclusively on the latter in the guise of man's own behavior. However—and this is crucial—instead of removing any subjective cognition from the field of behavior, it only reintroduces noetic intentionality (or, the desire not to know) exactly in behavior, in what it passes for the empirical object of its science. As Lacan writes, "on the basis of a finality posited as the object of that behavior, nothing is easier [...] than to *imagine* it [finality] in the nervous system."[78] In other words, man is himself supposedly reduced to an empirical object (behavior) in order to get rid of any nonscientific intentionality/subjectivity, but actually the harmonious correlation between the subject qua thinking and the object qua what is being thought of reemerges through the intentional matching between the nervous system and its final cause. Animism is thus preserved as the correspondence between the nervous system as the empirical object of science turned into a *natural subject* and its *telos*, which, as Lacan spells out, is eventually to live, or better, to survive. In this way, behaviorism "does nothing more than inject therein"—in the nervous system's serving the "evolution" of life as propounded by the Darwinian *Weltanschauung*—"everything that has been elaborated philosophically, 'Aristotlely,' concerning the soul."[79] Although a close exegetical engagement with this issue is beyond the remit of my present argument, Lacan's apparently far-fetched juxtaposition of Darwin and Aristotle can be supported textually if we pay attention to the fact that the latter not only defines the soul precisely as an original life force—"That which has soul is distinguished from that which has not by living"; "The soul is the cause and first principle of the living body"—but also evidences its teleological course in strict conjunction with the activity of the mind—"Clearly the soul is also the cause in the final sense. For just as mind acts with some purpose in view, so too does nature, and this purpose is its end."[80]

More to the point, I believe that the ensuing closet animism of behaviorism, which is thus both idealist and vitalist, could easily be extended to most of the contemporary cognitive and neurosciences. This becomes especially clear if we invert the terms of the basic correspondence on which the animism at stake depends—Lacan's own assessment lends itself to this—that is, if we understand Life as the definitive thinking and intentional subject, the *selfish* gene, and the nervous system (or, better, the human brain and consciousness) as the object that is being thought by its evolution. In this specific sense, it is especially traditional Darwinian biology, and the way in which its finalism still informs apparently more refined sciences, that are revealing from the viewpoint of psychoanalytic discourse for their adamant inability to confront the real. Darwinian biology and its appendices stand for the science whose critique proves to be most helpful to Lacan's putting forward of a new real logic of sexuation, and a related notion of love and reproduction.

Not surprisingly, with the same move Lacan equally aims at overcoming the "idea of nature." As he writes—and the naturalist reductionism of the cognitive revolution has only confirmed this—the latter "is not close to disappearing from the front stage."[81] Invoking its disappearance does not, however, amount to replacing it with an "idea of culture."[82] For while, on the one hand, psychoanalysis's epistemological orientation does indeed amount to thinking nature as "precisely a fruit of culture,"[83] and thus as a mere idea, on the other, it dialectically counterbalances this claim with that according to which culture is itself founded on the absence of the sexual relationship, which in the end provides us with an innovative, truly nonsubstantialist approach to nature. The traditional idea of nature retrospectively "dresses up" the absence of the sexual relationship, but, at the same time, this absence as a real impasse of logic that founds logic should in turn be regarded as the immanent passage from nature to culture, as the fact that, at least from the standpoint of culture, all we can say about nature is: "There *really* are two natural sexes" (initially indifferent to sexual difference and only retroactively assignable to the imaginary male/female polarities through the phallic function).

As we have seen, Seminars XIX, XIXB, and XX return to this point in many passages. What remains to be highlighted is how Lacan spells it out most clearly when engaging in an often simultaneous confrontation with

Aristotelian metaphysics and bio-logical discourse as its perpetuation. The *Il n'y a pas de rapport sexuel* needs to be taken as an (onto-biological) "principle,"[84] he says plainly, which we can also phrase as follows: the real is dual, or better, the real is dual as not-two, as the irreducibility of the Other sex to an-other sex. This should be, first of all, diametrically opposed to Aristotle's identification of the principle with either the One or Being, which soon "makes it necessary at any price that the One is, and that being is One," whereby onto-logy is turned into an onto-totology.[85] It should also be contrasted with biology's derived tenet that the fusion of "the two unities of the germen, the ovum and the spermatozoon," engenders "a new being."[86] Such a tenet itself depends on a variation of Aristotelian onto-totology.

Again, Lacan is here far from contesting the empirical observation of two different kinds of sexual cells.[87] What he denies is the fact that this real—which is bio-logical only to the extent that it transposes into "life" the il-logical principle of the two as not-two—may be liable to being articulated symbolically in terms of a sexual (organic, cellular, or even molecular) *relationship*.[88] We could therefore suggest that insofar as Darwinian biology takes such a relationship for granted, it should be seen as a discourse that does not in fact focus on sex but on Eros: building on Lacan, Darwinian biology is accordingly a *psycho-erotology*. That is to say, the biological notion of life ultimately issues from nothing other than an animistic metaphor for the allegedly unifying force of love, for that which "makes one from two, as what is supposed to gradually tend in the direction of making but one from an immense multitude."[89] Although Freud himself was not exempt from committing this very mistake in his meta-psychology—"Freud promotes the One"[90]—psychoanalysis "brings about [...] a revamping [...] in the realm of Eros."[91] It does so precisely by, on the one hand, unmasking the connection between love, its metaphorical transposition into the domain of life, and its metaphysical translation into the notion of the soul, while, on the other, promoting a different understanding of the amorous phenomenon starting from the axiom of the absence of the sexual relationship and the associated claim that, conversely, "it is at the level of language that we must investigate the One."[92]

Lacan can in this way state that his own clinical and theoretical work is to be located in between a talking about love and what "would be science."[93] Such a zone is treacherous and borders on contradiction, since all discourses on Eros (religious, philosophical, or pseudo-scientific) have so far always contrasted with science's opening onto the real, to the extent that even the Galilean revolution and its de-facing of *physis* has ended up betraying itself through Darwinian psycho-erotology. Lacanian psychoanalysis thus needs to continue the "subversion of knowledge" initiated by modern science, prior to which knowledge was always fundamentally ascribable to a presumed *sexual* knowledge. Before the Galilean revolution, no knowledge was conceived that did not participate in the fantasy of an inscription of the sexual link. One cannot even say that the subjects of antiquity's theory of knowledge did not realize that. Let us simply consider the terms "active" and "passive," for example, that dominate everything that was cogitated regarding the relationship between form and matter, a relationship that was so fundamental, and to which each of Plato's steps refers, and then Aristotle's, concerning the nature of things. It is visible and palpable that their statements are based only on a fantasy by which they tried to make up for what can in no way be said, namely, the sexual relationship.[94]

Focusing in particular on Aristotle, Lacan also makes a direct link between animism as an alleged correspondence between thought and what is being thought of, love as a phantasmatic stand-in for the absence of the sexual relationship, and the Greek philosopher's notion of the soul. He argues that the fantasy of the presence of the sexual relationship that is presupposed by all knowledge that does not separate the real from what we perceive to be "nature" as sensible substance inevitably relies on "mistak[ing] the other [sex] as [one's] soul."[95] Lacan's multilayered genealogical argument scattered across Seminars XIX, XIXB, and XX, which is, at the same time, a critique of traditional onto-theology, epistemology, and cosmology, as well as of Darwinian biology, can be reconstructed through the following steps:

1. Classical science and philosophy think, first and foremost, the body, the human body in particular. They assume that the body can function only if it "suffices unto itself,"[96] which also means that it must be self-contained: "What is important is that all that hang together well enough for the body to subsist [...]. This means that *the body is taken for what it [imaginarily] presents itself to be, an enclosed body.*"[97] In other words, the body is taken for One body.
2. From this standpoint, "the soul is nothing other than the supposed identity of this body." Or, better: the soul is the supposed identity of the body "with everything people think in order to explain" it. "The soul is what one thinks regarding the body" as enclosed and self-sufficient.[98]
3. The reciprocal necessity that the One is and that Being is One, onto-totology, arises directly from the inextricability between the body and the soul as what one thinks the enclosed and self-sufficient body *is*. In other words, "if there is something that grounds being, it is assuredly the body":[99] the One-Being, God, follows from the One-body as identified by the soul.
4. The foundation of the parallelism between onto-totology and the One-body qua soul allows the alleged bipolarity of the male and female sexual values to be taken epistemologically "as sufficient to support, suture that which concerns sex"[100] (i.e., the absence of the sexual relationship as

absence of meaning), and consequently to set up a theory of knowledge. As long as the Other sex is taken as one's soul qua the supposed identity of one's body, knowledge always revolves around the assumption that the power of knowing relates to the world just as man relates to woman. "The world was that which was perceived [...] as being at the place of the other sexual value. What concerned the *nous*, the power of knowing, was placed on the positive side, on the active side," on the side of man as "in relation with the One."[101]

5. To love amounts exactly to mis-taking the Other (woman's) sex for one's soul. Hence love (*amour*) should more appropriately be rendered as soul-love (*âmour*), a merging of the empirical phenomenon of love with the idea of the soul (*âme*). Strictly speaking, soul-loving does not involve sex as the absence of the sexual relationship, and is thus rather a "hommosexual," or "man-sexual" elaboration.[102]

6. Classical theories of knowledge "think that everything in the world knows what it has to do"[103]—i.e., think that being thinks—because they do always soul-love. Ultimately, Darwinian biology is itself a classical theory of knowledge that soul-loves, or a "psycho-erotology." It assumes that the body thinks in the same way we do precisely when we think the soul as the supposed identity of the body with all we think in order to explain it. That is, as I have already said with regard to behaviorism, biological animism surreptitiously transforms the empirical object of science into a natural subject energetically oriented toward "a meaning, an idea of evolution, of improvement."[104] Darwinism is therefore a narcissistic theory—"there is no doctrine that puts human production higher than evolutionism"[105]— that has not in the least "humiliated" man, not even with regard to its developments in molecular genetics. Rather, it allows man to think, in an onto-totological way, that when the body "thinks secretly, there are secretions. When it is assumed to think concretely, there are concretions. When it is assumed to think information, there are hormones. And still further, it devotes itself [*s'adonne*] to DNA [*ADN*], to Adonis."[106]

2.3 FROM LIBIDO TO DRIVE

If Seminars XVIII, XIX, and XIXB start to develop a new logic of sexual incompleteness—based on the absence of the *rapport sexuel* and how our very subjectivization entwines with it—which Seminar XX then articulates in terms of a rethinking of Eros and *jouissance*, all these works nonetheless tacitly but extensively rely on Seminar XI's earlier treatment of human libido from an anticosmological angle, that is, as an irremediably *partial* drive. In line with earlier works, Seminar XI (1964) carries out an extensive investigation of the specific differences between instinct, desire, drive, and love. Yet at the same time, anticipating the Seminars of the early 1970s, it exposes the way in which their interaction allows for an understanding of sexual reproduction in the species *Homo sapiens* that does not resort to the theo-teleology and onto-totology of biological animism.

It is by no means coincidental that Lacan inaugurates Seminar XI with a discussion of the position of psychoanalysis vis-à-vis those of religion and science. Like both science and religion, psychoanalysis is certainly to be regarded as a kind of praxis, i.e., "a concerted human action, whatever it may be, which places man in a position to treat the real through the symbolic."[107] Lacan also—importantly—adds that the fact that praxis in such a broad sense ends up falling back into the imaginary is on this initial level of secondary value: a certain relapse into the domain of totalizing images appears to be inevitable—also for psychoanalysis—since imaginary knowledge alone guarantees that human (sexual) relationships are livable.

What should instead be deemed crucial when asking programmatic questions such as "What kind of praxis is psychoanalysis?" and "Is psychoanalysis a science?" is the acknowledgment of the extent to which *modern* science has become subjected to the imaginary. At least since the Enlightenment, we have tended to assume that religion is more imaginary than science, in that, as Lacan explains shortly after Seminar XI in "Science and Truth" (1965), in it everything eventually rests on a final cause: *all* will be decided on Judgment Day. In revolving around a meaningful Revelation, religion disavows the truth as the real void of structure that causes the subject.[108] But we must not forget that, as shown by our previous discussion of biology, the Galilean revolution itself ossifies into a cosmology: modern science "refers to a unitary system, called system of the World"; this reference "is always more or less idealist, since it is a reference to the *need* for identification," namely, to what Seminar XX will later define as soul-loving.[109] In other words, modern science excludes the subject as a divided subject from its symbolizations which are ideally considered to be totalizable; or also, it considers truth only as a formal cause, it reduces truth to the knowledge of the laws that are supposed to account for it in an exhaustive manner.[110]

Here modern science's foreclosure of the incommensurability of truth with knowledge could be said to be even more radical than religion's disavowal of it: to put it bluntly, the religious man at least concedes that he does *not* know what the truthful God knows. From this perspective, psychoanalysis should pay close attention to religious discourse and its treatment of the divine and the soul. A sound critique of established science aimed at promoting Freudianism as a praxis that extends Galileanism against its animistic drift can neither ridicule religion as irrational[111] nor invoke a categorical separation of religion from a novel kind of science that would admit psychoanalysis.[112] As Lacan contends following his "excommunication" from the International Psychoanalytical Association, while the psychoanalytic community should obviously not be a Church, "the question indubitably does arise as to what in [that community] can well echo a religious practice," that is, "not a desiccated, methodologized religion [...] but religion as we see it practiced, still alive, very alive."[113] Returning to this passing allusion in Seminar XX, he specifies that a religion is still living when it "bring[s] back what we call the world to its filthy truth,"[114] that is, our dereliction or fall in this world. More importantly, in line with the para-onto-theo-logical opening I have sketched in the preface to this volume, he also suggests that the rationalist qua anti-animistic thought of psychoanalysis, and of a science which would found itself on incompleteness, should not be paralyzed by the prospect that the soul as an essential identity may in the end exist in the afterlife, but tackle it logically. Were it the case that the soul existed, this would only confirm that this world is irrevocably not-all, and the soul is what our world is not.[115]

Seminar XI therefore begins by enjoining psychoanalysis to take seriously the disquieting oscillation, if not reversal, between science and religion with regard to the real-symbolic and imaginary poles of their praxes. In other words, in order to challenge as much as possible any "transcendent complement [...] which always refers to some ultimate unity of all fields"—and which is still as present in scientific positivism as in the confessional systematizations of religion—psychoanalysis should enact a preliminary tactical retreat that contests basic ideas of modern science such as "research" and "experience."[116] Real research, one which searches for a signification that is always new and never exhausted, succeeds only to the extent that it does not invariably meet in its experience the object it had already found (i.e., presupposed) a priori.[117] Science must indeed have an object, but it should equally assume that this object also alters in proportion to the evolution of science itself, or that empirical data emerge only within a given discursive-historical structure, and there never are raw data.[118] If science abandons such awareness, it soon ends up embracing the obscurantist imperative "You would not seek me if you had not already found me."[119] That is, relying on an epistemological vicious circle, it unfailingly *works*, recovers too much empirical confirmation, while, by contrast, being unable to impose any tangible change on everyday reality and common opinion.

Lacan's methodological directives, which are rarely as explicit as in this initial lesson of Seminar XI, thus warn us that modern science's alleged empiricism may well ultimately become nothing but the tautology of a mystical experience. If submitting an experience to a scientific examination always lends itself to ambiguously suggesting that this experience has of itself a scientific subsistence, independently of any discursive contextualization, then we are still covertly taking for granted that the symbolizations of science limit themselves to partaking of the chant of Nature, and that being thinks.[120] In parallel, these critical considerations encourage us to adopt a completely different scientific approach, which, posing the question of the object of psychoanalysis, will retroactively also shed light on the as yet not appropriately elucidated object of modern science. To this end, it is misleading to compromisingly search for the object of psychoanalysis in the various fields of existing scientific praxes that seem to be offering an experimental updating of Freudianism.[121] Having unmasked science's regressive use of empiricism, it does not even suffice to single out *theoretically* the divided and incomplete subject as the empirical fact of psychoanalysis, or the way in which this observable subject remains an "antinomic correlate" of science to the extent that "science turns out to be defined by the deadlocked endeavor to suture the subject."[122] Rather, on a much more straightforward level, in order to circumscribe the object of psychoanalysis, "we shall take our psychoanalysis with us, and it will direct us at once toward fairly well located, specifiable points of praxis."[123] Freud operated precisely in such a way when he initiated the "talking cure": he let hysterics speak, and listened to them. Theoretical elaborations followed from this. As stated in the "Acte de fondation" contemporaneous with Seminar XI, psychoanalysis as an "original praxis" requires not only a theory of praxis, but first and foremost a "praxis of theory," that is, a preemptive casting doubt on the imaginary status of theory as such precisely by means of praxis as the treatment of the real through the symbolic; this move, he adds, is ethical.[124]

Lacan repeatedly emphasizes that the novel scientific experience psychoanalysis advances in opposition to the theo-cosmological empiricism of science is always concerned with one major point of praxis: the traumatic dimension of human sexuality as "the meaningless event, the accident, bad luck."[125] What is at stake here is exactly the same point we have previously discussed, with reference to the Seminars of the early 1970s, in terms of the two as not-two of the il-logical and natural real that underlies the sexuation of our species. In both cases we are dealing with the "truth as cause"[126] or void of structure. This becomes far more evident if we refer to "Science and Truth."

Lacan's basic argument there is that the subject of psychoanalysis as concretely troubled by his sexuality is the subject of science insofar as he is not sutured by science. The subject of psychoanalysis and the subject of science are two sides of the same coin: modern science forecloses truth as resistant to knowledge, yet truth then reappears in the consulting room through the signifying constructions that psychoanalysis as praxis detects in symptoms and the other formations of the unconscious. That is to say: psychoanalysis is the historical product of the subject of science's own renewed quest for truth; to put it bluntly, it is the analysand who demands to know the truth about his symptom, a formation that does not make any sense for scientific knowledge. Here we grasp the twofold paradox of psychoanalysis's relation to science in its purest form: the "*science of psychoanalysis*"[127] cannot be equated with scientific *knowledge*. Moreover, it can nonetheless operate on its subject only as the subject of science.[128]

Moving from such a point of praxis, Lacan can then infer that if science at last does not manage to suture the subject, it is because there is no metalanguage, no totalizing truth of language: language and the symbolizations it creates are structurally incomplete. In other words, the emergence of the differential logic of the signifier is concomitant with the introduction of a void. This is the only truth as evinced in the psychoanalytic setting, from which the (theory of the) subject's *Spaltung* between consciousness and the unconscious ensues. Lacan hence understands the truth of incompleteness in causal terms: the "truth as cause" is nothing else than structure *tout court*. He in fact specifies that this cause is not a mere "logical category" but that which "caus[es] the whole effect":[129] in short, it is real, the real of structure, or better, structure as the real. And this is valid both in the ordinary sense that the would-be cause belongs in an immanent way to nature as the material dimension of the signifying structure—i.e., of the transcendental logic of sexuation—independently from the latter's significations, which it will have caused,[130] as well as in the more technical Lacanian sense for which the real marks the—sexually—illogical limit of the logic of the signifier. As I have explained, these two acceptations of the real are inseparable.

In "Science and Truth," Lacan can thus also conceive of psychoanalysis as a praxis that treats truth as a *material* cause, and in so doing keeps it separate from knowledge. More specifically, psychoanalysis recognizes that the emergence of the signifying structure in concomitance with a real void which is inherent yet irreducible to it should be considered as a material process, one according to which "th[e] material cause is properly speaking the form of impact of the signifier."[131] In other words, as Lacan rephrases it a few months later, "the signifier is nothing other than matter that transcends itself into language"[132]—where, again, the establishment of this transcendental level goes together with the introduction of a void.

We can conclude that already in the mid-1960s Lacan tends to isolate one major leitmotiv in his psychoanalysis: the real of structure (or structure as the real) qua the meaningless event of sex as truth that materially causes the whole effect of sexuation/subjectivation. I think that his claim that this highly abstract argument remains firmly rooted in a praxis—aimed at redefining the role of praxis—is convincing. However, I also believe that, due to his opposition to putting forward any *Weltanschauung* precisely in the name of praxis, all these works remain problematically elusive when it comes to addressing the *phylogenetic* rationale of what they submit. In a few words, why—or, better, with respect to what—does *Homo sapiens*' sexuality as parallel to language stand as "bad luck" in the first place? As we will see, this is in my view a fundamental strategic error on Lacan's part, given his professedly dialectical materialist agenda.

For the time being, we should simply track down the way in which Seminar XI initially dwells in a polemical manner on the ontogenetic development of human libido. What the praxis of psychoanalysis teaches us is that the libido "must not be referred to a natural pseudo-maturation," divided into supposed linear stages, since it always remains opaque, even for the very parameters adopted by biological discourse to study development in general.[133] Psychoanalysis, rather, shows us that libidinal development is entirely dominated by "the stumbling block of the tuché," and that it is only thanks to this "central bad encounter" that the speaking animal manages to "account for the world."[134] More precisely, we are dealing with a dialectic that revolves around a missed encounter at the sexual level.[135] Libidinal "maturation" (which must involve the symbolic assumption of an asymmetrical positioning as man or woman through a phallic logic) as well as, eventually, reproduction always follow the absence of any predetermined sexual communion. Here, Lacan clearly prefigures the axiom Il n'y a pas de rapport sexuel years before its explicit formulation.[136]

If the object of psychoanalytic science is the libidinal unconscious (and, as we shall soon see, the object a is the more refined Lacanian way of conceiving of the very object of libido),[137] we must then first and foremost refuse to understand it in the guise of something "dynamic," of an incremental "force" hard-wired for genital satisfaction.[138] The very term "force" is normally "used to designate a locus of opacity," a "particular mystery,"[139] whose ultimate purpose amounts to reassuring us against a more general, everyday, and tangible order of mystery, that of our linguistically and sexually alienated subjectivity. Similarly, the libidinal unconscious does not by any means consist of an "obscure will" considered as primordial and antecedent to consciousness.[140] The unconscious should instead be thought as a gap or interval located between the evanescent real cause—the traumatic absence of the sexual relationship—and the concrete effects it entails in reality—the many symptomatic misadventures of our sex and love lives.

Consistently with this view, Lacan cannot but show a profound contempt for Jung and his notion of "psychic energy." Approaching libido in energetic terms is already bound to generate confusion. Jung exacerbates this: he goes as far as staging an ultra-animistic repudiation of the very idea of sexual libido for the sake of a "much more generalized notion of [an energetically archetypal] interest."[141] The latter would be based on the alleged persistence in man's cogitative world of a harmonizing "archaic relationship." Yet for Lacan, such an "ancient world" ultimately reflects nothing but "a natural metaphor" of human desire as a desire to be One, whereby "the supposed identity of our perception is decided."[142] It thus deceptively epitomizes within psychoanalysis the same cosmological outlook he will openly fight in Seminar XX.

Although this is perhaps less evident, I would argue that in Seminar XI Lacan also institutes his psychoanalysis's antidynamic stance on libido as similarly irreducible to the dichotomous logic of both the Darwinian theory of adaptation-disadaptation (or selection-extinction) and the Heideggerian reaction to it, namely, the neat opposition between animal closure and human openness he had himself seemed to embrace earlier. For instance, contra Darwinism, it is absurd, Lacan writes—defending Roger Caillois—to explain phenomena of animal mimicry (such as the eyespots of some insects) in terms of the aim of adaptation. This equates to attributing them "to some kind of formative *power* of the organism." Yet "for this to be legitimate, we would have to be able to conceive by what circuits this *force* might find itself in a position to master, not only the very form of the mimicked body, but its relation with the environment."[143] Mimicry is not adaptation to the environment but a contingent, retroactive, and often ineffective camouflage "in the strictly technical sense."[144] Instead of invoking opaque forces preprogrammed for "harmonizing with the background," through which stronger species would prevail in the struggle to the death, reproduce, and evolve, we should rather think here of human warfare: the background is itself nonharmonious, and it is then a question of "becoming variegated [...] against a variegated background," while nonetheless remaining distinct from it.[145]

Along the same lines, Lacan claims that it is untenable to posit that biological "function [...] creates the organ," since "everything that is an organ in an organism always presents itself with a large multiplicity of functions."[146] The life sciences have increasingly confirmed this in an experimental manner over the last thirty years.[147] Thus the normative—Darwinian—view on organs, that is, "the supposed function of instinct in the relation between organism and organ," is to be abandoned.[148] To sum up: against naturalist reductionism, when considering libido we should stop wondering about the so-called preadaptation of the instinct. Yet at the same time, against Heidegger's antidialectical stance on *Technik* as incompatible with the animal's "captivation" [*Benomennheit*] within the environment, we should direct our attention to the palpable fact that "an organism can do something with its organ."[149] This certainly happens in our species: not only is the natural organ, the penis, what immanently gives rise to the logical *organon*, the phallus as a signifying instrument or tool, but the penis itself stands retroactively as a real organ precisely thanks to the transcendental phallic function. *Man* is open precisely qua human *animal*.

Hence, in principle, we have no reason to exclude the possibility that other species *might* also be "doing something" with their organs: mimicry could itself amount to a differential technique in its own right, beyond mere anthropocentric analogies, one which would, however, be fundamentally indifferent to our species-specific phallic difference. To put it bluntly, for all our phallic interest in catching and collecting butterflies to the extent that they seem to be staring at us as a gaze does, should their eyespots express a localized and materially contingent logic, the latter nonetheless remains completely unresponsive to ours. After all, what, for us, is the function of eyespots if not that of a blind spot, which consolidates our difference through its (difference's) indifference to it? In other words, the possibility that other living beings are also open, i.e., not confinable to an essential undifferentiated absorption [*Eingenommenheit*], does not by any means entail that nature is as such fundamentally univocal difference.[150]

At this stage, we should not be surprised that the whole discussion of libido is framed by Lacan within what he calls both, as previously examined, the antisubstantialist *naturalism of psychoanalysis*—which, I would add, should also avoid a reification of difference—and more concretely—a concreteness that comes from the "point of praxis" of psychoanalytic treatment—"the *realism of the unconscious*," namely, the fact that the unconscious is a lacuna, cut, or rupture that "inscribes itself in a certain lack,"[151] that of the sexual relationship. This is why, right after denouncing the organic functionalism of Darwinian theory, Lacan can nonetheless also speak of psychoanalysis as distinctively devoted to *bodily libidinal organs*: "For us, in our referring to the unconscious, what is at stake is the relation to the organ."[152] Yet—and the specification is crucial—the organ on which all other bodily libidinal organs depend (including the mouth, the anus, the eye, the ear, and, only secondarily, the genitalia) is a missing organ: the phallus. The relation to the organ does not stand for "the relation to sexuality, or even to sex [...] but [for] the relation to the phallus, insofar as it is missing [*fait défaut*] in what could be attained of the real in the aiming [*visée*] of sex."[153]

This dense quote will become clearer as we proceed in our unpacking of Seminar XI. It anticipates the main tenets of Lacan's theory of the drive, and has to be read together with his other claim that the phallus is the "false organ" of the drive, while the libido—which Freud considered as an energetic substratum of the drive—stands for the "true" yet "non-existing" organ.[154] What should be evident by now is rather that, in agreement with its professed materialism, Lacanian psychoanalysis as an antisubstantialist naturalism and realism could eventually find—or found—a compatible biology, if and only if the latter abandons its animism, namely, the unifying logic of *bios* as a primordial energy.[155] Accordingly, the sole notion of energy through which Lacan's psychoanalytic "biology" attempts to rethink Freud's libido as a force that accompanies but no longer underlies the functioning and transformations of the drive is that of *potential energy*, a constant force, he says, that needs to be diametrically opposed to kinetic energy and anything that regulates itself through movement.[156] "Drive is not thrust [*poussée*],"[157] something that is irrepressibly pressing in and overflowing despite repression, Lacan maintains programmatically. Consequently, it should not be considered to belong to what traditional biology normally refers to as the "organic register," which applies to the living "organism in its totality" in the guise of a "rhythm" marked by energetic discharges.[158]

Lacan's main antivitalist critical point against conceiving the libido as an archaic and fundamentally free-floating noumenal energy that qua substance predates, sustains, and ultimately unifies the symbolic order—"libido is not something flowing, fluid, it does not divide or accumulate, as a kind of magnetism";[159] "libido is not a field of forces"[160]—can easily be grasped in terms of his overall materialist orientation (although it becomes exegetically problematic when it is presented as a close reading of Freud's texts).[161] Yet there persists a difficulty with regard to the overall status of the drive in Lacan's theory: how can we accept its irreducibility to the register of the kinetic/cyclical organic—to a "shock force"[162]—and, at the same time, assume that its potential/constant energy—which, to complicate things further, originates from an evental trauma—is still directed toward an object/organ, albeit one that is "missing" or "false"? I believe that we can try to account for this second and merely hinted conception of the organic[163] only to the extent that we assume that the drive, for Lacan, amounts always to the *drive of the absence of the sexual relationship*, namely, the *drive that fails to achieve its goal*, and that this very failure (as a paradoxical libidinal satisfaction stemming from unsatisfaction)[164] is what allows a partial stabilization of human sexuality as well as eventually—also thanks to the sublimatory intervention of love in this circuit—reproduction. Lacan's investigation of the *Trieb* in Seminar XI, and in particular of its biological and energetic dimensions, remains antinomical—he acknowledges this in a brief but intense dialogue with André Green[165]—especially if it is not filtered retrospectively through the a priori of the *Il n'y a pas de rapport sexuel* (which already silently informs Seminar XI).

Moving precisely from the axiom of the two as not-two of (logical-natural) sex, and the way in which it allows us to uncover the derived semblance of the One in the sphere of human sexuality, I propose now to dwell at length on the basic arguments of Lacan's "disassembling [*démontage*] of the drive," as well as its interaction with desire and love in a new nontotalizing figure of the organic.

1. The drive, lying at the crossroads of soma and psyche, has "neither head nor tail."[166] It can be conceived as an assemblage [*montage*] without any predetermined finality.[167] Freud is thus right in distinguishing its components, which do not constitute, Lacan adds, an organic instinctual whole, supposedly present in other animals, but a *partial representational*

circuit partaking as such of the symbolic order.¹⁶⁸ In other words, the fragmentation between the source [*Quelle*], thrust/pressure [*Drang*], object [*Objekt*], and aim [*Ziel*] of the drive cannot convey any presumed "totality of the sexual drive."¹⁶⁹ This psychosomatic understanding of the *Trieb* anticipates the very idea from the Seminars of the early 1970s that, at the phenomeno-logical level (of everyday life and of the psychoanalytic clinic), human sexuality, insofar as it is phallic, does not relate to the Other (sex).

2. The partial circuit, as irreducible to a teleological self-accomplishing *cycle* that is exclusively somatic, nonetheless somehow closes onto itself. More specifically, there is an "insertion on one's own *body* of the beginning and end of the drive" precisely *because* "the drive [...] merely represents, and partially the curve of fulfillment of sexuality."¹⁷⁰ To put it differently, in the case of *Homo sapiens*, organic sexuality takes place only retrospectively through its incomplete representation in the psyche. The sexed body gets sealed off phallically and, as Seminar XX will argue, thus stands as a masturbatory monad before its real partner. At the same time, the replacement of the latter with a phantasmatic object sustains copulation/reproduction as a by-product.

3. What takes place in between the absence of finality of the drive and its closing onto itself, which eventually might carry out a reproductive function, is, fundamentally, connected with a "paradoxical satisfaction."¹⁷¹ In Seminar XX, Lacan will refer to it as the "other satisfaction" of phallic *jouissance*. The drive circles around the object, yet does not reach it,¹⁷² and this "movement outward and back" is what structures the drive, whereby its libidinal satisfaction is attained without attaining its goal—which "would be defined by a biological function, by the [direct] realization of reproductive coupling."¹⁷³ We must therefore distinguish the goal of the drive from its aim, which ultimately amounts to its circular (albeit not cyclical) trajectory, the itinerary it has taken. But during this process the very unattainable goal (the object insofar as it would, according to Freud, eliminate the state of tension)¹⁷⁴ is itself subsumed as unattainable under such a "return into circuit."¹⁷⁵ Satisfaction can thus be said to be paradoxical in the sense that it equates with the repetition of non-satisfaction.¹⁷⁶ As Žižek aptly puts it, "the real purpose of the drive is not its goal (full satisfaction) but its aim: the drive's ultimate aim is simply to reproduce itself as drive, to return to its circular path, to continue its path to and from the goal. The real source of enjoyment is the repetitive movement of this closed circuit."¹⁷⁷

4. For Lacan, following Freud, the paradoxical satisfaction of the drive relies on the fact that it is captivated by the Thing, the mythical object of original satisfaction which would precede the constitution of the

subject, and as such should be considered as always-already lost, never there in the first place. This important connection does not feature explicitly in Seminar XI, where Lacan seems to be taking for granted his previous discussion of *das Ding* in Seminar VII. Bringing together arguments from both works, his main argument here is that the drive tries to recover the lost Thing, but finds only "the presence of a hollow, a void."[178] This void qua *presence* is the object *a*, the object around which the drive circles, and from which, in doing so, it obtains *jouissance*. The object *a* is in turn materialized as different evanescent part-objects—the breast, the feces, the gaze, and the voice—relating to bodily organs as erogenous zones—the mouth, the anus, the eye, and the ear. In that they are all phallicized, these part-objects also involve, successively, the genitalia. Lacan here advances a three-layered framework of human sexuality that accounts for the passage from the absence of finality at the level of the innately biological (that of the supposedly predetermined sexual instinct) to the precarious achievement of reproduction through the mediation of the circuit of the partial drive.

5. While there is, strictly speaking, no genital drive[179]—otherwise there would be a sexual relationship—the non-genital yet phallicized drives concur with the possibility of copulation and reproduction. This is an issue that Lacan never discusses openly in Seminar XI. It remains at the level of an antinomy: genitality, he claims, is "nowhere," yet "it is nevertheless diffused."[180] Or also, we could add, the drive, given its partial character, is always to be seen as plural drives, that is to say, the drive(s) can never reach a complete genital organization. Yet conversely, the drives are partial only insofar as they are all phallic: the circuit between their libidinal bodily organs (the mouth, the anus, the eye, and the ear) and their part-objects (the breast, the feces, the gaze, and the voice) is retroactively structured through the phallus, which is, fundamentally, an image of the penis.

6. In his treatment of the drives, Lacan presents the phallus as a "missing" or "false" organ, but it is also—at least since the mid-1950s and his reformulation of the Oedipus complex—a signifier, the one signifier for which "there is no signified."[181] In brief, the phallus is what stabilizes the structural lack characterizing speaking animals, yet without overcoming it. As a signifier, the phallus organizes the absence of the sexual relationship by embodying the differential character of language that goes with it in the image of the male sexual organ—or, better, in the visual alternation of the penis between tumescence and detumescence. Yet this comes only at the cost of rendering this very alternating image as such "elusive" or "ungraspable," cut out from the image of the body:[182] the phallus (or $-\varphi$) amounts to the missing or false organ in the sense that its presence

qua image of the erect penis already implies its absence, and vice versa. What vanishes with the phallus is the mutual implication of presence and absence as the synthesis of presence and absence.

7. The phallus as a missing organ is ultimately what, in the partial drives, takes the place of the always-already lost object, the Thing. This imposes a clarification of the respective positions of the phallus and the object *a* with regard to the Thing. In short, the object *a* is made *present* in the drive as the missing phallus. Or also, more precisely, the object *a* occupies the place of the Thing as the missing *organ*: as we have seen, all libidinal bodily part-objects inhabit object *a* as the *presence* of a void.[183] On the other hand, the phallus occupies the same place as the *missing* organ: no part-object can ever *replace* the Thing. In other words, the stabilization of the absence of the sexual relationship through the vanishing of the phallus requires that its lack be itself symbolized through the object *a*. As Lacan has it, the object *a* "serves as a symbol of lack, that is, of the phallus [...] insofar as it is lacking."[184] This is achieved thanks to the subject's separating himself, in his very constitution, from a "limited number" of part-objects (the breast, the feces, the gaze, and the voice) that are imagined as detachable from the rest of the body, and circled around by the drive.[185]

8. Lacan posits a basic overlapping, or even a homomorphism,[186] between the circuit of the drive through which sexuality participates in the psyche and the gaping structure of the latter as constituted by the incompleteness of language.[187] In his words, "with regard to the agency of sexuality, all subjects [...] deal only with *that part of sexuality that passes* into the networks of the constitution of the subject, *into the networks of the signifier*"; this happens "through the bringing into play of what, in the body, deserves to be designated by the term apparatus [*appareil*]," namely, the phallus, "that with which the body, with regard to sexuality, *may fit itself up* [*s'appareiller*] as opposed to that with which bodies may be paired off [*s'apparier*]."[188] Once again, according to Lacan, the human body functions as a sexed organism only to the extent that as an instrumental *organon* it retrospectively recuperates sexuality via language in spite of a deficit in instinctual mating. More to the point, if sexuality manages to be inscribed on the body as a partial representation, this is the case because the nonteleological drive has, circularly, a *psychic* beginning and an end in the *physical* erogenous zones. The latter are the orifices qua "source" of the drive that allow *Homo sapiens* to establish libidinal investments with the part-objects, i.e., with the blank object *a* as the symbol of the phallus as lacking, as the "cordoned" missing organ.[189] To sum up, the circuit of the drive does not just trace a fruitless repetitive loop that revolves around a missing noumenal center (the Thing turned into the

object *a* via the phallus), since this very repetition is itself phenomenologically organized around corporeal openings that obtain some form of enjoyment,[190] on "something [which] in the apparatus of the body is structured in the same way as [...] the gaps that the distribution of the signifying investments sets up in the subject."[191]

9. In the lessons of Seminar XI under consideration, Lacan initially gives the impression of completely opposing the circuit of the drive to love: "On one side, Freud puts the partial drives and on the other love."[192] However, this is soon revisited and mitigated: at the level of love "there is no trace of drive functions, *except* those that are not true drives," i.e., what Freud calls the *Ichtriebe*, the autoerotic passion aimed at "wishing oneself one's own well-being."[193] I think Lacan struggles here to maintain the early Freudian distinction between preservation (the reality principle) and sex (the pleasure principle), which he will fully merge in Seminar XX through the idea of love as a "desire to be One" that obtains phallic *jouissance*, while already sensing the inadequacy of the late Freudian unification of the two principles into a vitalist notion of Eros. On the one hand, as I have often pointed out, love has, for Lacan, a fundamentally narcissistic, that is, imaginary, structure.[194] On the other hand, love's masturbatory-idiotic search for the *gesamt Ich*, the whole ego, remains inextricable from taking the *other* as one's soul.[195] This certainly does not mean succeeding in entirely containing the drive within the "loving oneself through the other"—since, to say the least, an object and a person are clearly not the same, Lacan specifies, namely, the other subject cannot fully be reduced to an imaginary object.[196] It indicates, rather, that the *champ pulsionnel* and the *champ narcissique* can be linked at the point where a bodily opening in the circuit of the drive overlaps with that which in the other escapes the narcissistic capture of love, that is, the point where "the drive [...] invaginating through the erogenous zone, is given the task of seeking something that, each time, responds in the Other."[197] Although Lacan does not make this connection explicit, we should read object *a* qua aim of the drive together with object *a* qua the "agalma," the hidden precious object, or "spring of love," that, as explained in Seminar VIII, is in the beloved more than the beloved himself, i.e., the irreducibility of his desire to the subject's masturbatory imaginary identifications.[198] As Lacan frankly concedes in a fleeting yet essential answer to Miller, the "whole question"—now contextualized within an attempt at promoting a new anti-animistic stance on the organic—"is to discover how this love object may come to fulfill a role analogous with the object of desire."[199]

10. We have to bear in mind that the object *a* ultimately corresponds to the object of *desire*, or, better, the object-*cause* of desire only qua *object of drive*.

As early as Seminar V, Lacan observes that "drive" stands for a "technical term given to desire insofar as speech isolates it [desire], fragments it, and puts it in a disarticulated and problematic relation with its aim."[200] Clearly, against what many commentators have attempted to do, the two notions should not be accounted for separately.[201] It is the drive that entertains a relation to object *a* as an aim, Seminar XI insists, albeit one that is as such different from a goal—object *a* is *present* in the trajectory of the drive as a *missing* object—whereas "object *a* [...] is never found in the position of being the *aim* of desire."[202] In other words, the Thing qua nothing other than its own disappearance (i.e., its phenomeno-logical symbolization in the guise of the loss of the object, or phallus) originates desire,[203] which repeatedly circles around the missing *object* only qua drive. As Johnston remarks, "although the drives find satisfaction in encircling a never-quite-achieved goal, desire is what remains unsatisfied with the object causing it."[204] The further complication that emerges in Seminar XI is that the circuit of the drive as a lacunary apparatus started by the dis-appearance of the Thing, an apparatus which is as such "a subjectivation without subject," cannot but be paralleled by a subjectivized (although "holed" and primarily unconscious) phantasmatic structure ($ ◊ *a*) that sustains desire vis-à-vis a love object.[205] Desire in phantasy thus mediates between the object *a* as the real object of the asubjective drive and object *a* as an agalmic "lure": in founding imaginary love identifications with the other, the latter sets up the (split) subject *tout court*.[206] To put it differently, the drive can enjoy something of the object while not attaining it qua Thing only inasmuch as the missing object is concomitantly sublimated as an object of desire through love. This is how we should interpret Lacan's otherwise enigmatic claim in Seminar X that "only love-sublimation makes it possible for *jouissance* to condescend to desire."[207]

11. The genitalia are themselves regulated retroactively by the same psychosomatic dialectic. For Lacan, they are, contrary to object *a*, on the one hand, "perfectly graspable"[208] (where object *a* is evanescent), and, on the other, "dissolved," "not reassembled" (where object *a* instead cordons the phallus).[209] This means that their image is apprehended only as a symbolic presence (the penis) that evokes an absence, and as a symbolic absence (the vagina) that evokes a presence; the alternations presence/absence and absence/presence are, however, here in a disparate juxtaposition to each other: presence lacks absence and absence lacks presence, beyond any possible synthesis.[210] Genitality thus partakes of love and the vain search for the *gesamt Ich* as autoeroticism; it simply continues masturbation by other means. As such it could be said to lie on the other side of the drives—which instead enjoy as partial—and is for the same

reason also inextricable from them. In other words, the genitalia appear as discrete objects and are invested libidinally thanks to the gaze and the voice as the two post-Oedipal part-objects that, symbolizing the phallus as lacking, link the drive with desire in fantasy.[211] In this sense, both genitality and all the drives—which are never supplanted by any genital drive—are reliant on the Other. To put it bluntly, copulation, even when it is seemingly devoid of any amorous passion, cannot be disjointed from falling in love with the way in which the Other stares at us or speaks to us, that is, from desiring to be One with object *a*.

2.4 POTENTIAL ENERGY VERSUS THE LAMELLA

According to Lacan, the always-already lost Thing can partially be found in the circular trajectory of the drive, where it appears as the missing object *a*. Such a repetitive loop is from time to time punctuated by the replacement of a libidinal investment in one part-object for another: the part-objects in question correspond to the many gazes and voices we fall in love with. Accordingly, Lacan can also understand this process as a *dérive*, a drift.[212] The important point to bear in mind here is that he believes he can accommodate what would thus seem to amount to multiple series of kinetic "discharges" of libido within a more comprehensive—antivitalist—notion of libido as potential energy.

In brief, this does not simply mean that "a drive is constant because the consumption of an object cannot lower the force or impetus of the drive,"[213] but, more daringly, that the impetus itself (or, better, thrust: *Drang*) needs to be regarded as a sort of nonforce, as a "*tendency to discharge*,"[214] Lacan specifies, which as such remains always potential. In simple terms, we are, as linguistic animals, in a state of "stationary tension."[215] Moreover, if we look at this from the stance of the paradoxical satisfaction—qua not satisfying—that is attained through the *montage* of the drive, we could speak of a discharge without movement, a false movement that does not contemplate any "rise and fall."[216] To sum up—and this is crucial—"drive is not thrust,"[217] but, again, a psychic circuit that is embodied, and in this way partly represents sexuality. It also stands as such as a fundamental theoretical convention whereby psychoanalysis can investigate human sexuality by adopting some notions of energetics while, with the same move, rejecting bio-logical animism.

In this light, the thrust of the drive acquires a meaning exclusively through the *source* of the drive—and the circuit's returning to it—which is to be located in the orifices of the body, the erogenous zones that are homomorphous with the gaping structure of language. These zones are surfaces—or, better, rims—that integrate the thrust into the potential energy of a constant flux (the trajectory of the drive as a "maintained constancy"),[218] in spite of physiological variations, "deep variations [...] subjected to all the rhythms, even to the very discharges that may occur as a result of the drive" (e.g., ejaculation).[219] The *Trieb* can thus admit "discontinuous elements" (the thrust and the source) into a combinatory loop without energetic contradiction, precisely by submitting what are normally conceived as variations of force to a constant force.[220]

Lacan does not, strictly speaking, deny the appropriateness of regarding physiological variations which appear to involve the organism in its totality as cyclic, and of studying them by means of a nonanimistic use of kinetic energy (variations such as those concerning respiration, or digestion). What he rejects is the pertinence of kinetic energy to the partial field of human sexuality. However, a tension remains in his overall argument. Given the central role sexuality inevitably plays in reproduction and the perpetuation of the species, it eventually conditions the very possibility of our representing the human animal as a whole organism. Physiology must therefore pass through psychoanalysis's novel approach to the organic. In his early Seminars, Lacan contended that all we know at the physiological level amounts to metabolism, "that is, the balance sheet—what goes in and what comes out."[221] Seminar XI adds to this picture the idea that man's symbolized life qua these quantifiable cyclic inputs and outputs ultimately rests on the absence of the sexual relationship as a constant force which, as such, cannot really be quantified.[222]

In other words, psychoanalysis, whose object is the sexual unconscious, reduces kinetic energy to potential energy in order to disassociate what we usually conceive as physiological kinetic energy from any idea of a free-floating primordial life instinct, or Eros, that would precede symbolic quantifications. This operation conforms to modern physics's understanding of energy, which is never seen as a substance existing in itself, but as a "calculable function discerned through a series of relations between nonenergetic elements."[223] Lacan's recurrent recourse in different places in his teaching to the metaphor of the dam is helpful: the flowing water that precedes the construction of a dam does not amount to any energy, unless we decide to believe a priori in the "sprite of the current."[224] Water becomes energy only in relation to the machines that will measure it, accumulate it, and transform it into other kinds of energy (e.g., electricity). In order to avoid falling back onto animism, it does not even suffice to suggest that "without this man-made construction the energy of the water remains merely an abstract and potential energy."[225] Lacan contests this very point when he states: "to say that energy was already there, in a virtual state, in the current of the river [...] does not mean anything at all."[226] Rather, his argument implies that *potential* energy itself enters retrospectively on stage only through the dam. We can speak of potential energy as soon as the construction of the dam has been completed but its turbines have not yet been activated; most importantly, we can speak of the integration of variations of force into the constant force of potential energy because the dam's turbines do malfunction when they are activated.

My general point here is that the moment at which the wall of the dam already partly interrupts and channels the flow of "natural" water, while still not bringing about a cycle that leads to the quantification of energy, should be taken as an illustration of the onto-genetic not-two of *Il n'y a pas de rapport sexuel* discussed earlier: namely, the cut of the signifier, the in-difference of the anatomical "little difference" that will have been inscribed on the body as sexual difference once the malfunctioning turbines of the drive/desire/love compound are activated. What is at stake in both instances is, to simplify, the passage from the indifference of the "natural" to the differential character of the logical, which indissolubly knots them as in-difference.

In replying to Green's concerns about a deconstruction of the Freudian *Trieb* that nevertheless needs to merge the discontinuity of its four elements with their energetic combination into a constant system, Lacan concedes that his conceiving of the drive as, basically, a potential energy located in the source of the drive as erogenous zones is just "the beginning of a rational solution to [an] antinomy."[227] The tentative character of this ambitious theoretical elaboration can be perceived most clearly if we dwell on another analogy, the well-known image Lacan provides in Seminar XI to exemplify the *montage* status of the drive: "If we bring together the paradoxes that we just defined at the level of the *Drang*, at that of the object, at that of the aim of the drive, I think that the resulting image would show the working of a dynamo connected up to a gas-tap, a peacock's feather emerges, and tickles the belly of a pretty woman, who is just lying there looking beautiful."[228] While such a "surrealist collage" captures well the anti-finalism of the drive—i.e., its radical divergence from any notion of preestablished instinct or innate "releasing mechanism" à la Konrad Lorenz—as well as the far from irrelevant fact that, however contingently, a certain modest sexual effect is being achieved (a peacock's feather tickling the belly of a woman), it fails to explain how the circuit of the drive—contradictorily originating here in the thrust (*Drang*) of the dynamo—should always be thought in terms of potential energy: nothing is being said in this context about the source of the drive, the *Quelle* associated with the erogenous zones, which, as discussed, are what integrate the thrust into a "stationary tension."

To further unravel Lacan's energetic account of *Trieb* beyond its omissions and discrepancies, we could perhaps venture to juxtapose this surrealist collage with the metaphor of the dam used to explain potential energy in a non-animistic fashion (which does not feature in Seminar XI). Let us picture the physiological cyclic variations, the rises and falls in energy of the human organism—which are themselves dependent on the drive, and ultimately on the absence of the sexual relationship qua our sexuality—as the reversible transformation of potential into kinetic (and other kinds of) energy enabled by a working dam: previously impounded water, in falling, drives a turbine, which in turn activates a generator, which produces electricity, which can either be stored through an accumulator or distributed to our houses, and so on. We should then try to imagine how, in a variation of the same scheme whereby the presumed sexual turbine-generator of smooth instinctual reproduction is not working properly, what the potential energy of the water impounded and channeled by the dam manages to activate in the first place is the dynamo of the above-mentioned collage. According to Lacan, this does not create any cycle of stasis/movement, rise and fall, or even cause and effect; the absurdity of the collage is precisely meant to show that the elements of the drive are discrete, *unrelated* to each other, and, consequently, that their energetic field is unquantifiable. In this particular sense, not only does the drive amount to a circuit rather than a cycle that involves a discharge of kinetic energy, but the physiological cyclic variations rely as by-product on this circuit: they do take place *through* the malfunctioning of the sexual turbine-generator.

In other words, given the dysfunctional dynamo of the drive, energy remains a constant potential energy positioned at the level of the source / erogenous zone (comparable to the head of the dam's pipe where the water is channeled). Or better, we could also talk of potential energy generating a series of fake movements—obviously, a gas-tap cannot trigger the emergence of a peacock's feather—which, however, in the last instance do produce a semblance of cause–effect relationship with a concrete, albeit marginal, result: the peacock's feather that tickles the belly of a beautiful woman—a clear allusion to the fragile imaginary/phantasmatic basis of human copulation, and of its nonsatisfactory enjoyment as obtained through the phallic logic of the signifier.

Undoubtedly this discussion would need further clarification at a nonanalogical level, which Lacan does not provide in Seminar XI or elsewhere. The images we have considered are both fascinating, in that they oblige us to envision a novel approach to the organic that complies with the psychoanalytic axiom of the absence of the sexual relationship, and problematic: for instance, can we really conceive of a potential energy that subdues, if not annuls, its kinetic counterpart?[229] On the other hand, what unmistakably transpires in this context is Lacan's determination to develop, in the wake of Freud, the *Trieb* as a limit notion that links the soma to the psyche, and to investigate the way in which the body of *Homo sapiens* as inextricably connected with language lends its orifices to the drive inasmuch as their physical configuration is homomorphous with the signifying gap in the Other. The apparent cyclic closure of human life itself (i.e., its attainment of the perpetuation of reproduction) depends, after all, on the energetic constant of a series of corporeal openings—which are not genital, and involve genitalia only epiphenomenally—just as the conscious and unconscious identifications (the ego and the phantasy) that suture the subject into a provisional unity rely on the logical precedence of the not-all of language (of the fact that the symbolic order oscillates between its producing the semblance of the One and this very production's reliance on the maintenance of a not-One). Lacan's notion of the drive does not only articulate this psycho-somatic parallelism but also attempts to overcome its very dualism in a materialist manner: it is both a theoretical construction of psychoanalysis that dismantles the idea of a substance qua organic living energy and, conversely, an embodied fiction—operating in the phantasy in conjunction with desire and love—by means of which the subject represents sexuality partially, gains enjoyment out of non-satisfaction, establishes sexual liaisons with other human beings and, in some cases, eventually reproduces. It is therefore misleading to affirm that the drive "has nothing to do with biological sexual difference."[230]

Toward the end of the lessons from Seminar XI under consideration, Lacan expands this account in that he approaches the drive as a meta-psychological "convention" of post-Freudian psychoanalysis and as a transcendental "fiction" of the soma–psyche compound[231] also in terms of what he calls a "myth" concerning the "pure life instinct," "immortal life."[232] This is the so-called myth of the libido as lamella, "something extra-flat, which moves like the amoeba" and "inserts itself into the erogenous zones" (the lamella qua myth thus seems to correspond, on this level, to a critical reading of the "sprite of the current"—i.e., pre-symbolic kinetic energy).[233] Consistently with his antivitalist premises, Lacan initially presents the lamella as the organ of the drive "whose characteristic is not to exist,"[234] namely, as an organ that was never there in the first instance, which nonetheless stands as a structural retrospective illusion of both psychoanalytic theory and the human subject's ontogenesis.

The problem with this highly speculative scenario, the point at which Lacan contradicts his own antivitalist premises—once again, the entire theory of the drive as potential energy clearly aims at instituting psychoanalysis as a materialist doctrine of the linguistic body of *Homo sapiens*—is when he repeatedly labels the lamella as "what the sexed being"—which obviously cannot be restricted to the human *parlêtre*—"loses in sexuality," "what is subtracted from the living being by virtue of the fact that it is subject to the cycle of sexed reproduction."[235] What Lacan evokes in this way is a Thing qua living One of *nonsexed* reproduction that precedes the advent of the two of sexed reproduction qua loss. This necessarily poses the question of what *noumenal* process of disaggregation (Freud's understanding of the death instinct as a force inscribed in nature looms in the background) transforms the "immortal" and "indestructible"[236] One of asexual life into the deficient two of sexed reproduction. In other words, *the two no longer emerges in concomitance with the not-two of the absence of the human sexual relationship as inextricable from language*; it ceases to be conceived as a split—that is also a continuity—between noumena and phenomena as experienced from the perspective of phenomena, but is made to derive from a dispersive decomposition of the One inherent to the in-itself of nature (or at least of asexual life).

The key issue to grasp here is that the image of the lamella would amount to a mere myth—about that which is left out of the psycho-somatic circuit of the partial drive yet lies at its core—and, as such, be consistent with Lacan's materialist attempt to account for a structural retroactive illusion created by language, if he did not apply it to nonhuman sexual reproduction. Since, on the contrary, it focuses on an alleged fundamental rupture between, on the one hand, nonsexed life and, on the other, human *and* nonhuman sexed life, it ends up presupposing that the human impossibility of representing the totality of sexuality—which gives rise to the drive and the unconscious—automatically entails that sexed life as such is a differential nontotality, which, moreover, would in turn be preceded by a living totality. To put it even more explicitly, Lacan oversteps his own materialist directives when he assumes that sexed life as such is difference, a difference that lacks something. This argument emerges in other passages of Seminar XI, for instance when he speaks of a "real lack" existing in sexed nature independently of language: "The real lack is what the living being loses [...] in reproducing himself through the way of sex"; the linguistic lack, that "around which the dialectic of the advent of the subject [...] turns," "takes up the other lack, which is the real, *earlier* lack, to be situated [...] at sexed reproduction."[237]

Given its importance, I wish to repeat this last argument. The story of the lamella cannot be regarded just as a myth of retrospective origins, and treated accordingly as part and parcel of the incomplete (meta-psychological and ontogenetic) libidinal structure that inevitably fabricates it, but stands as a direct *ontological* assertion ultimately based on an illicit anthropocentric projection of the *Il n'y a pas de rapport sexuel* onto sexed nature. Lacan himself vehemently criticizes this kind of pronouncement every time he warns us against positing any facile—animistic—equivalence between thought and being, or, better, between thinking (phallically the oscillation between the not-One and the One) and what is being thought of as outside of thought (while, agnostically, he does not exclude a priori that there might be an illogical correspondence between the planes of thought and being, whereby the not-One *as* One is the definitive divine One). In a sense, Lacan accomplishes with the myth of the lamella a radical reversal of his earlier assumption that opposed the perfect unity, the One of the animal, to the disharmony, the two of man, since the two now issues from sexed life as such. Yet both claims share the same ambition of establishing a final positioning of, respectively, the difference between man and animal and that between sexed and nonsexed life in the cosmos. Here we are facing some deep and possibly irresolvable tensions in his oeuvre. For the time being, our methodological imperative will be to abide by the axiom of the absence of the human sexual relationship and, following some aspects of Lacan's thought, to conceive the difference (or potential energy) this axiom postulates as the in-difference of nature.

2.5 LESS THAN LESS THAN NOTHING: IN-DIFFERENCE

It should by now be evident that there are two conflicting ways in which Lacan understands the status of (sexual) difference in nature. According to the first, which I deem incompatible with his overall materialist-realist agenda opposing vitalism and animism, being is ultimately difference. This inevitably ends up presupposing the One as that which is different from difference, as that without which there could be no difference. Lacan senses the problem, but fails to solve it: for instance, in Seminar XI, where, as we have seen, he finally advances the idea of a "real lack" in nature, introduced by sexual reproduction and thus "earlier" than the differential character of language, he also states that the One does not precede discontinuity[238]—be it that of the gap of the human unconscious, or that of sexual reproduction in general on which such a gap would rely. The issue is not discussed any further; this statement limits itself to marking a vague grasp of the difficulty in reconciling the primacy of difference with the not-all.

I believe that the ontology of difference in question could be subdivided into four increasingly broader variants, all leading to the same logical deadlock, namely, a return to the One:

1. The One of the animal. Man is open; the animal is closed. Man is open in that there is no human sexual relationship, whereas the sexuality of the animal functions smoothly, like a key and a keyhole. However contingent the material reasons of *Homo sapiens*' predicament may be—the sequence prematurity of birth / prematurity of sexual maturation / sexual neoteny in adulthood, as inseparable from the phylogenetic and ontogenetic emergence of language—they oblige us to think of what is not human, and of life in particular, as a whole about which we cannot know anything.

2. The One of nonsexed life as implied by the myth of the lamella. This would be "immortal," "irrepressible," and "indestructible" life that "survives any division, any scissiparous intervention."[239] It is "unreal" in the sense that it can be thought of only mythically, that is, in a retroactive way, from the standpoint of difference as what confines differential sexed life to "the zone of death."[240] At the same time, it cannot be regarded as a substantial "field of forces." Yet, Lacan says, although the lamella is unreal it is not simply imaginary: it articulates itself through the real—the

difference of sexed life—i.e., it embodies itself in it.[241] In other words, the One *will have been* through the difference that divides it. But—highlighting an unwanted implication Lacan does not contemplate—if we do not specify that what will have been the One *remains nonetheless not-One*, or, better, *indifference* to the phenomeno-logical dialectic between the One and difference, even after becoming the One through difference, then it is presumed that *that* which will have been the One *is* and could only be the One through differential sexed life.

3. The One as that which does not live. Lacan draws the dividing line of difference a step further when, in a passage from Seminar XXI, he suggests that bacteria, which reproduce asexually, do already partake of something similar to the absence of the sexual relationship. Endorsing Jacob and Wollman's *La sexualité des bactéries* (1959), he speaks of bacteria's capacity for being infected by viruses, and of the mutations that then arise as a form of enjoyment of the host. More precisely, *jouissance* would stem from the fact that "between two mutations of bacteria of the same lineage there is no possibility of relationship."[242] What we should recognize in this first—asexual—"sexuality of limited scope" is the idea that not only sexual specification but life *tout court* go together with difference, with the "nonrelationship between two branches of the same tree."[243]

4. The One as that which is different from cosmic (living and nonliving) nature as difference, yet also contains it. This is the logical consequence of Lacan's assumption in Seminar XI that, as we saw in our discussion of mimetism, the (organic and inorganic) environment would be as such not harmonious, and the defining characteristic of a living being (especially, but not exclusively, of one that speaks) consists of "becoming mottled against a mottled background," of establishing, as its second nature, we may add, a difference—even just in the guise of a minimal genetic mutation—from cosmic difference. We could in the end agree that the ontological argument implicit in the myth of the lamella amounts simply to the side-effect of a misleading image, and that Lacan never espoused the view that nonsexed life—or the inorganic, if we also bring in his sporadic remarks on bacteria—corresponds to the One. But there is good reason to believe that he is attracted to the perspective according to which the cosmos as not-all could be seized as pure difference. However, he does not fully appreciate that this very stance automatically positions the cosmos in contrast to what would differ from difference, from the One/God who would seal it as a differential whole, as *a* (not-One)—something he seems to be profoundly aware of elsewhere.

The other, more promising, take on nature and difference Lacan adopts on various occasions throughout his oeuvre is that for which, first and foremost, "nature is there"[244] as indifferent to difference. "Everything emerges from [...] the signifier,"[245] but nothing really changes with it; the signifier is indifferent matter that transcends itself into the differentiality of language, while in so doing it also persists, or insists, as the indifference of the nonsignifying letter. The signifier can thus appropriately be thought of not as the becoming difference out of a differential background but as the immanent splitting of indifferent nature into in-difference—whereby difference not only was and will be indifference before the appearance of language and after its disappearance, but is *currently* indifference as we speak.

According to Lacan's argument here, it is a fact that "nature is always there, independently of whether we are there or not"[246]—or, at the very least, this presumed fact cannot be dismissed easily. *Es ist so*, as Hegel is reported to have said when confronted with the natural beauty of the Alps.[247] Yet once we have acknowledged this, in order to avoid falling back into a philosophy of nature that has nothing to do with materialism and inevitably always hides an idealist agenda (a presupposition of the One) even when it postulates—as Lacan himself sometimes does—a real lack, or difference, in nature as such, our ontological and epistemological point of departure should be that "discourse does not have consequences in nature."[248] It does have consequences in discourse *as* nature—most blatantly, through modern science—only to the extent that discourse *forgets* language as just another—indifferent—"natural reality," whereby there is a "reduction of its material" dimension, i.e., the "commencement of logic" and its necessary imposition of the semblance of a meta-language.[249] Again, against any "sprite of the current"—independently of whether it is considered as always-already "alive" or merely as a differential potential preceding discourse—"energetics is not even conceivable if not as a consequence of [the] discourse"[250] of physics, which has consequences for the real inasmuch as it is a consequence of discourse. What needs to be stressed here, as implicitly present in the argument I have just made, to refrain from giving the impression of embracing another form of idealism, that of "idealinguistery," is that, for Lacan, structure as differential linguistic structure is nonetheless that which is "the most real," the "real in itself" as he calls it in a nonmetaphorical way, i.e., in my own terms, in-difference.[251]

Such an ontology of in-difference, as opposed to one of difference as a real lack of nature independent of language, makes several appearances in Lacan's work, although it is never developed systematically. For instance, we can detect it in his early contention that "asymmetry in nature is neither symmetrical nor asymmetrical—it is what it is."[252] In other words, language as natural difference should not be resolved into an ultimate principled order of nature (the One), just as it should not be led back to a more primordial difference of nature (which in turn evokes the One via a detour), for nature is indifference, in spite of language as *natural* in-difference. Even if we can admit the *retroactive* presence of "pseudo-significant asymmetry" in nature—from which man immanently "produce[s] his fundamental symbols"—it is man (language) "who introduces the notion of asymmetry."[253] In-difference equally transpires in Seminar XIXB, where, in stark contrast to his observations about bacteria and the lamella, Lacan denies that *jouissance* could ever be ascribed to anything but man's absence of the sexual relationship, and that the animal's apathetic copulation involves the differential "dissociation" of enjoyment.[254]

Significantly, Lacan argues most convincingly for this truly dialectical materialist[255] view in the very same lessons of Seminar XVI in which he returns to a noteworthy discussion of the drive as nonkinetic energy. He vehemently rebuts those who criticize him for allegedly neglecting the energetic dimension that had been so prominent in Freud. As I argued above, his claim that nature is simply "always there" as indifferent to discursive difference entails rather than denies that discourse has *real* consequences on *nature as discursive nature*: this is in line with the promotion of a "true energetics" that takes as its guiding principle a *constant* to be referred to a "closed system"[256]—to the *making* One of linguistic structure as thus tentatively sutured. Any energetics that does not start off from such a principle should be regarded as "delirious," since it inevitably supposes a primeval "life drive" [*pulsion de vie*], named libido in the context of psychoanalysis.[257] So, on the one hand, "all that we are as 'sentient' falls under the aegis of the consequences of discourse."[258] Yet, on the other, such confinement of the in-itself of the drive to the domain of a discursively produced myth aims, against mistaken impressions, at emphasizing that the partial satisfaction the subject derives through the drive is that which *is* tout court: in our jargon, it is indifference as in-difference. Here, in the "nativism" of the drive as an apparatus of partial enjoyment molded by the signifier, lies the "*naturalism*" of psychoanalysis, Lacan importantly specifies.[259] More to the point, the "rim structure" (the erogenous zones) of the drive that integrates its thrust into a "stationary tension" or potential energy stands as a "conjunction of logic and corporeity" (in short, language as in-difference), whereby *jouissance* can psychosomatically be experienced as a "hole."[260]

What remains problematic in my view is, given this scenario, Lacan's admonition that "it is not worth talking of anything except the real within which discourse as such has consequences."[261] I believe the opposite is the case: it is worth talking about the real within which discourse has no consequences, since such talking does not necessarily imply advancing a mythical discourse—as Lacan seems to suggest. This is valid for one simple but crucial reason, which, as we have seen, constitutes the core of Lacan's own argument: the real within which discourse as such has consequences (difference) is also *at the same time* a real within which discourse has no consequences (indifference), and it is only in this sense that it can be defined as "the most real" (in-difference). It is only in this sense that Lacan's materialism of the signifier cannot be labeled "idealinguistery," and that it does not rely again tacitly on the One necessarily summoned as that which differs from difference (a difference which is here—rightly—equated with the real-of-language, the absence of the sexual relationship, within which discourse has consequences). What is more, he himself provides us with several good hints to defend him against this—otherwise justified—accusation. Even just positing the drive as the "place-holder" of sexuality as what is "unthinkable" for *Homo sapiens* qua being of language, yet conversely as what originates "the idea of sexuality,"[262] paves the way for an investigation of the very absence of the sexual relationship—the axiom of Lacanian phenomeno-logy—in terms of the *Es ist so*, an investigation which cannot be content with considering absence (or differential lack) as the ultimate horizon of thought. After all, Lacan moves in this direction precisely when he declares that asymmetry in nature is neither symmetrical nor asymmetrical.

Before discussing how the ontology of in-difference (concretely centered on the absence of the sexual relationship) I have so far outlined can be articulated as a broader agnostic para-ontology that overcomes the level of phenomeno-logical critique, and only thus effectively exorcizes the One, I would now like to turn to the way Žižek—arguably the author who has insisted most on the dialectical materialist dimension of Lacanian psychoanalysis—tackles the notion of the drive and the possibility of elaborating a strictly connected philosophy of nature.[263] Žižek's treatment of the naturalism, materialism, and realism of the drive is illuminating on several accounts, yet he also conceives it as an "immortal insistence-to-repeat," a "moving" that "striv[es] to reach the void," a "less than nothing"—to be understood as *less than the void of signifierness*—which would as such be an "original excess, an excess 'in itself.'"[264] In doing so, he adopts and elaborates the Lacan who ontologizes the myth of the lamella, or at least the Lacan of cosmic (living and nonliving) nature as difference—of a fundamentally Schellingian "radical gap, instability, discord into [the] pre-subjective/pre-reflexive Ground."[265] In contrast to this stance, we have been trying to follow and develop the Lacan of linguistic potential energy as "stationary tension" and real in-difference. Let me make this point clear: the question here is not that of identifying the "true" Lacan (there are many, as we have contended) but of selecting and adopting those of his arguments which can most profitably be put to work for the delineation of a new dialectical materialist agenda.

Having a profound awareness of the fact that, as already maintained in Seminar VII, the *Trieb* "is an absolutely fundamental ontological notion,"[266] Žižek advances a series of observations on Lacan's drive that allows us to accurately contextualize it within the framework of post-Kantian philosophy:

1. The drive qua the signifier's material intervention in the real should be read in the wake of both Kant's transcendental turn and his acknowledgment that trying to conceive reality as One exposes irreparable antinomies, a "crack," as well as Hegel's radicalization and solving of this problem, whereby "it is our very division from absolute Being which unites us with it, since this division is immanent to Being."[267]
2. Given the immanence of this division, the drive is satisfied through the repeated failure to reach the object; as opposed to the lost object of desire, in the case of the drive, "the loss itself [is] an object."[268]
3. This object—or, more precisely, the enjoyment the drive obtains from it—has a properly ontological value. Not only is the drive a conceptual threshold situated between biology and psychology, but "the drive is natural [...] it is culture in its natural state."[269]
4. As culture in its natural state—or, which is the same, as a division that is immanent to Being—the drive is "pure difference." As such, it is logically prior to both the (imaginary) difference between "positive entities" and the "symbolic differentiality" that sustains it (the fact that "there is no positivity in a signifier, it 'is' only a series of what it is *not*").[270]

Žižek also rightly acknowledges that if, for the pure difference of the drive, the loss itself is an object, this object cannot be regarded as a lack: the latter appears only retroactively from the perspective of symbolic differentiality. He nonetheless thinks the pure difference of the drive as immanent to Being in terms of a "hole": a lack would designate a "void within a space," whereas "a hole is more radical, it designates the point at which the spatial order itself breaks down (as in the 'black hole' of physics)."[271] Most importantly—and this is where my Lacan-inspired ontology parts ways with his—such a hole qua drive would indicate that, fundamentally, "things move":[272] they move in that they would strive to reach the void/lack, i.e., the drive *as articulated with desire through symbolic differentiality. There is something rather than nothing because there is something less than nothing* (a "black hole") *that moves toward nothing* (the void/lack of symbolic differentiality). True, Žižek assumes that this moving *toward* can be formulated as such only retroactively from the stance of symbolic differentiality, and that symbolic differentiality—and thus the "toward"—is contingent: it could have not happened. Yet at the same time—against Lacan's dissociation of the drive from any sort of natural thrust—he also unequivocally posits that something less than nothing, a "negative energy,"[273] has always been there as a "push to directly enact the 'loss'—the gap, cut, distance—itself,"[274] thus determining the real as a "curvature"[275] independently of symbolic differentiality.

In dealing with these vast ontological claims, we need to be particularly cautious not to throw the baby out with the bathwater. I agree with Žižek that the transcendental horizon of symbolic differentiality—what I called in earlier chapters the phenomeno-logical oscillation between the One and the not-One (qua void/lack)—allows us to grasp substance (which Žižek capitalizes) as not lacking anything, and in so doing access the "real outdoors," against accusations of "correlationalism." I also agree that this nonlacking substance should be thought as in itself differential (or "curved" into-itself, or folded, using Deleuzian jargon), and that such a pure difference appears retroactively through symbolic differentiality while it cannot be reduced to it. Yet this is valid only to the extent that we specify that pure difference *is and is not* difference, for it is in-difference, indifference that contingently becomes difference yet also remains indifferent to difference. To reiterate this point: my problem with Žižek is not his putting forward a notion of the real as "less than nothing" qua less than the void/lack of symbolic differentiality, but his inability to conceptualize this pure difference as in-difference; this then leads him to understand the "less than nothing" in terms of the differential movement of a barred real, which at times seems to bring with it a *presubjective* ("acephalic") notion of *nature/substance as quasi-subject* with clear vitalistic undertones ("humans are not simply alive, they are *possessed* by the strange drive to enjoy life in excess, passionately attached to a surplus"—the *"eppur si muove"*—"which sticks out and derails the ordinary run of things").[276] In spite of all my sympathy for Žižek's project, I cannot but observe that Lacan would have condemned this as animism, maybe with the addendum that we are facing here a peculiar animism of the not-all.

Let me expand on these issues by taking a closer look at how Žižek reads Hegel and Deleuze vis-à-vis his central ontological axiom of the "less than nothing." He follows Hegel to the extent that the dialectical process is primarily concerned with the fact that "what first appears as a mere sign [...] of the Thing turns out to be the Thing itself," and that "the Real is *simultaneously* the Thing to which direct access is impossible *and* the obstacle which prevents this direct access."[277] This is perfectly compatible with the dialectical materialist stance I am trying to extract from Lacan's naturalism and realism of the signifier (which Žižek also discerns in him). He can thus claim that "the 'primordial difference' is not between things themselves"—which would automatically entail an identity of things as different from each other—"also not between things and their signs"—following the early Lacan's naive Kojèvian view that the symbolic order kills the Thing—"but between the thing and the void"—of symbolic differentiality—which "distorts our perception of the thing so that we do not take the thing for itself."[278] Consistently, the sign does not replace the Thing; pure difference, rather, amounts to "the movement from things to their signs," "the thing itself becoming the sign of [...] itself, the void at its very core."[279]

I would argue that the last part of this reasoning is both correct and incorrect, depending on how we read it. In my own terms, we are here concerned with the becoming difference of indifference, indifference's becoming itself as difference, yet—and this is the key distinction—indifference itself becomes difference as also indifference to difference: the "primordial difference" is in-difference. Everything hinges on how we conceive "the void at the very core of the Thing." If by this Žižek means simply—in a properly Hegelian fashion—"the void/lack of symbolic differentiality at the very core of the Thing as nonetheless non-lacking," i.e., indifferent, I would have nothing to reproach him for. But as we have seen, he distinguishes such a void from a "more radical" hole (a "black hole"), which is what he is ultimately referring to in this passage, in spite of some terminological confusion. Pure difference, for Žižek, is the Thing itself becoming the sign of itself. On closer inspection, what he seems to be suggesting is that pure difference is *the pure difference of the Thing itself*—qua hole or curve—that becomes contingently the *sign* of pure difference—as void/lack of symbolic differentiality; nonpure difference, which nonetheless gives us pure difference. If this is the case—and I would very much welcome a reply—Žižek grants *too much* to his less than nothing, reverting to a pre-Hegelian (Schellingian) ontology. As he puts it, "we [...] get two emptinesses": not only "emptiness marked as such within the symbolic space," but also "direct presymbolic emptiness."[280] My basic objection here is not that—correlationally—we would not have access to the presymbolic (Hegel, Lacan, and Žižek are far beyond Meillassoux's critique of critique), but rather that we can and should postulate the "presymbolic"— *and the symbolic to the extent that the materiality of the signifier is immanent to it*—as indifferent to "emptiness" / the void, not as "direct emptiness" / the hole.

To sum up: why, then, cannot Žižek think pure difference as in-difference (qua "the most real," for Lacan) and the less than nothing as a *merely* retroactive movement from indifference to difference which holds true—as an immanent truth that can in fact only be half-said—exclusively from the perspective of difference? Because he presupposes *movement* to begin with: "things move"; "'moving' is the [immortal] striving to reach the void."[281] Although this striving is not teleologically aimed at the void of the signifier, it is nonetheless always-already present in the "curvature" or "out-of-jointedness" of nature. As primordial difference, nature / the Thing is as such an "unnatural excess"[282] driven to repeatedly "enact the loss"—an enactment that should be seen as an exuberance, the exuberance of repeating a deadlock, where the latter is perceived as a loss only through linguistic distortion.

Žižek claims on several occasions that such "radical openness" as acephalic and immortal repetition—what I deem to be the mistaken assumption of his ontology—is precisely what Hegel does not grasp.[283] Perhaps not so unexpectedly—but dangerously, if one still gives prominence to his dialectical materialist agenda—he also juxtaposes this understanding of the drive as difference and repetition with Deleuze's and Guattari's "desiring machines": "Whenever Deleuze and Guattari talk about 'desiring machines,' we should replace this term with *drive*."[284] I agree with Žižek that correctly approaching the Lacanian drive in terms of an apparatus of enjoyment, as we have done, somehow imposes on us a comparison with desiring machines. I even agree with Žižek that Deleuze's ontology (yet is this ontology the same as that of desiring machines?) is rich in materialist suggestions; for instance, when he singles out "a perception as it was before men (or after)"[285]—but also in concomitance with men?—"released from their human coordinates," or when, according to Žižek, he would claim that "'things-in-themselves' are in a way *even more phenomenal* than our shared phenomenal reality: they are the impossible phenomena, the phenomena excluded from our symbolically constituted reality"[286]—that is, in Lacanese, language as real linguistic nature, its material dimension, as what needs to be "forgotten" qua point of impossibility (or in-difference) is both "more real" than our symbolically-imaginarily constituted reality and the immanent bedrock of the latter's phenomenologic. But the inevitable question here is: why not stick to Hegel (and certain aspects of Lacan's thought) to uphold this crucial dialectical position, and develop it further?

Here we should not be afraid to be more Hegelian and less Deleuzian than Žižek. It is not sufficient to state that, while Lacan and Deleuze converge on the idea of what we could bluntly call a phenomenalization of the noumenal, which *is* the noumenal as such, Lacan diverges from Deleuze in that he would replace Deleuze's notion of desire as the "free flow of the libido" with the notion of the drive "as constitutively marked by a basic insoluble deadlock."[287] What Žižek still assumes here is that *both* Deleuze and Lacan would first posit "an anonymous/acephalous immortal insistence-to-repeat": while for Deleuze this repetition is "free," for Lacan it is instead "the repetition of the impasse," nature as a basic derailment of nature, which as a holed exuberance will have been perceived linguistically as lack.[288] In stark contrast to Lacan's drive as a potential energy or "stationary tension" which does *not* really move, this understanding of *Trieb* is what then makes Žižek speak of its "excessive intensity" as something that is "too strong," and hence transcendentally repressed/forgotten.[289]

Žižek thus determines a priori the less than nothing as an alleged (negative) exuberance, or energy, of nature, which equates with a "getting stuck."[290] In order to highlight the proper dialectical materialist dimension of the Lacanian drive, I believe we need to un-determine this unwarranted ontological determination—unless, of course, we are content to accept such a botched "sprite of the current" as a metaphysical first principle. In short, we should aim at dialectically conceptualizing the "less than nothing" (the less than the void of the signifier, which Žižek rightly senses as seminal)[291] as *less than* "less than nothing" (as less than Žižek's deadlocked, yet excessive, intensity), that is, as in-difference.[292]

The recent debate between Johnston and Žižek on the "weakness" of nature is helpful here in clarifying my own position. Johnston's main claim is that the alternative between naturalism and antinaturalism should be rejected if one intends to revive the dialectical materialist tradition in the wake of German idealism and Lacanian psychoanalysis. Both are "worse." As we have also shown, Žižek appears to be profoundly aware of this: the drive is culture in its natural state; at the same time, it is only with humans/language that a transcendental emergence of desire (and lack) qua symbolic differentiality takes place. That being said, Johnston correctly discerns another trend in Žižek's thought—which I would claim has become more than "occasional" in *Less Than Nothing*—whereby not only is the false alternative between naturalism and antinaturalism replaced by a Hegelian dialectic of nature and culture, but such dialectic is itself supplemented, and even superseded, by an "enigmatic neither-natural-nor-cultural third stratum."[293] In answering the brusque but more than legitimate question "what sort of material is posited by Žižek as the groundless ground of not-whole being?," Johnston cannot but acknowledge that Žižek ultimately "talk[s] of there being, in addition to the two dimensions of nature and culture, some sort of un-derived third vector," whose name is "drive."[294] Johnston does not force Žižek in characterizing it "as the *root-source* of what comes to be subjectivity proper in and for itself"[295]— what I have earlier referred to as presubjective nature/substance as quasi-subject.

The "untamed excess" of this third vector corresponds exactly to the curvature, or exuberant hole, we have been trying to criticize so far, of which Johnston is, with good reason, suspicious. As he asks, where does what Žižek calls the "moment of thoroughly 'perverted,' 'denaturalized,' 'derailed' nature which is not yet culture" come from?[296] Should we not rather conceive it as a "by-product" of the dialectic between nature and culture?[297] Žižek's concise reply to Johnston, where he anticipates arguments later developed in *Less Than Nothing*, only reinforces our doubts: there is something rather than nothing because of the drive as the "'undead' obscene immortality of a repetition which insists beyond life and death"; there is something rather than nothing "because, energetically, something is cheaper than nothing"; basically, there is therefore something rather than nothing because there is *something less than nothing* (less than the void, here associated not only with the lack of human desire—culture—but also with the "vacuum" of the universe—nature) that sustains or "maintain[s] the nothing."[298]

Does Johnston successfully counter Žižek's stance on what the Slovenian philosopher calls "the minimal ontological coordinates of the universe"?[299] While I endorse his critique of the "third vector" proposed by Žižek, I think the "transcendental materialism" he puts forward in its stead falls short on two strictly related points, revolving around the notions of "denaturalization" and "the barred Real," where he himself ends up granting too much to the "less than nothing" qua less than the void of signifierness / symbolic differentiality. Johnston persuasively calls for an account that "would identify what the material possibility conditions are within the physical being of 'nature' for the internal production out of itself of structures and phenomena (with which subjects are inextricably intertwined) that eventually achieve [...] a type of transcendence-in-immanence,"[300] or better, I would specify, a transcendental-in-immanence. He also convincingly observes that without such a genetic/material explanation of the being of language we inevitably "open the door to the irrationalities of obscurantist idealisms, spiritualisms, and theisms"[301]—Žižek's third vector, Johnston would concur with me, is in this light the wrong solution to the right problem, which, thanks to Hegel and Lacan, he has been in fact one of the first to have intuited after the untenable dismissal of naturalism operated by mainstream poststructuralism and deconstruction.

However, Johnston then frames this genetic/material explanation in terms of a process of "denaturalization": the emergence of the being of language would mark a "break with nature."[302] My objection to Johnston here is simple: from a properly dialectical materialist standpoint focusing on the materiality of the signifier, the emergence in question, i.e., symbolic differentiality, *is and is not* a break with nature. This follows from both, as we have seen, Lacan's tenet that discourse has *no* consequences in nature while, at the same time, it *does* have consequences in nature qua *discursive* nature; and Johnston's own adherence to a transcendental-in-immanence that, if one assumes its full implications, remains *immanent*. Again, indifference contingently becomes difference (i.e., symbolic differentiality, or the phallic logic of sexuation/subjectivation) yet also remains indifferent to difference. What is "most real" as pure difference is the point of in-difference (i.e., there is no sexual relationship); this is the correct way to conceptualize Žižek's "less than nothing" without resorting to his third vector.

Johnston's insistence on a denaturalization that is "not too-radical" with regard to the physical being of nature that would precede it is in this respect misleading.[303] The issue at stake is not the *degree* of the being of language's "break with nature," but the fact that we can dialectically think this rupture as equally "radical" and as such, in Johnston's terms, "uneven, partial, incomplete, failed";[304] or also, that it is all the more radical the more it is not *really* able to sublate indifference.

To do full justice to Johnston's transcendental materialism, and with the same move distance ourselves from it more neatly, we need to tackle one further issue: the so-called "barred Real." What is the rationale behind Johnston's pledge for a denaturalization / break with nature that is not too radical? Let us first summarize what he—and I with him—cannot accept in Žižek's ontology. The latter's three vectors are the following: (1) the drive or "night of the world"; (2) the world; (3) the subject of the drive. To cut a long story short, beneath the *meta-stasis*[305] of Žižek's Hegelian-Lacanian and dialectical materialist retroactive ontology of substance-subject-substance lies a Schellingian-Lacanian irremediably idealist *hypo-stasis*. The not-one that appears as One only retroactively through its splitting into two, and as such remains not-one—but also in-differentiates itself as not-One—hides a pre-subjective One-as-not-one that becomes the two only to give rise (not so coincidentally after all) to the *subjective* One-as-not-one. According to this second view, presubjective nature/substance as quasi-subject sustains/moves toward the void of the universe only to fully actualize itself in the subject of the drive—where the void/lack of desire, the subjective *oscillation* between identity and difference (i.e., symbolic differentiality), is sublated into difference *as* identity.[306]

In other words, what is (circularly through the subject) primary for Žižek is the One-as-radical-break: "The drive is quite literally the very 'drive' to *break* the All," yet simultaneously, "the Whole is never truly Whole."[307] The being of language—qua subject of the drive beyond desire—would *radicalize* the primordial radical break—the out-of-jointedness of nature as a deadlocked excessive intensity that sustains nature itself—*and* supersede it by wholly assuming the break (that is, by assuming the Whole as break). Contra this problematic stance, Johnston wisely sticks to the two dimensions of substance and subject, eliminating the third (but ontologically first for Žižek) vector—"noumenal monstrosity."[308] For the sake of an anti-idealist genetic approach to subjectivity "conducive to a solidly materialist theory of the subject,"[309] the break of the being of language should be regarded as not too radical, because the real (or, for Johnston, "weak nature")[310] is *already inconsistent*, barred. As he conclusively puts it in an article entitled "The Weakness of Nature": "the Real of nature already is holey [...] prior to having holes bored in it by the impacts of signifiers (in terms of language introducing nothingness, non-existence, and so on into being)."[311] This does not point back at Žižek's One *as* break; clearly, according to Johnston, the real of nature is differential not as a (deadlocked) excessive intensity that is, for Žižek, "too strong," but indeed as weakness and powerlessness.[312] Johnston replaces Žižek's "strong" groundless *Ground* for which the One *as* not-One *is* with a "weak" groundless ground for which the *not-one* is.

So why should we not be satisfied with Johnston's solution when invoking a dialectical materialist ontology of in-difference derived from (a certain) Lacan and (a certain) Hegel? First, Johnston does not draw a distinction—one that, in terms of what I have said, is *and* is not really such—between difference (the barred symbolic, or not-two; the—linguistically sexual, for Lacan—oscillation between the One and that which is other than One) and indifference (the barred real, or not-One, that in-differentiates itself into the barred symbolic). Putting forward this distinction is in my opinion the only way in which we can account for the preservation, justifiably defended by Johnston, of the distinction between the barred real and the barred symbolic. However, Johnston argues, contradictorily, that the barred real is different from the barred symbolic, yet the barred real is just as differential as the barred symbolic, even *prior* to having holes bored in it by the impacts of signifiers: "Nature *too* (i.e., the not-All material universe of physical beings) could be described as 'at war with itself.'"[313] Or, similarly, forgetting that nature first and foremost gives itself to us as Hegel's *Es ist so* (or as Pascal's "eternal silence" of infinite space), that it can be thought as meta-statically persisting as indifferent irrespectively of discursive/differential nature (and the imaginary cycles of movement/rest, rise/fall it induces), Johnston states that "naturalizing human beings"—i.e., stressing the continuity between the real and the symbolic—"entails a reciprocal denaturalization of natural being"—i.e., a barring of the real as prior to the symbolic.[314]

As I said above, this view, supported at times also by Lacan, seems to me to be derived from an illicit anthropocentric projection of the absence of the sexual relationship—as phenomeno-logically axiomatic evidence highlighted by psychoanalysis—onto the (organic and inorganic) cosmos. In contrast to the other Lacan, for whom we cannot even take for granted that linguistic asymmetry is in nature *just* asymmetrical/differential, Johnston's stance, if not mediated further dialectically, promotes what I would again call an "animism of the not-all," different in kind from Žižek's only to the extent that the latter openly posits an equation of the not-all with the All/One, and infuses it with a pre-subjectively subjective "movement." (Moreover, as we will soon see, this departure from Žižek by no means inoculates Johnston against the shadow of another, even more insidious, form of the One.)

Johnston has the great merit of having stubbornly insisted on how a dialectical materialism inspired by Lacan should, despite some of his claims, investigate the genesis of the transcendental / symbolic differentiality, opposing any veto against enquiring into the origins of language. For instance, commenting on my previous work, he correctly observes that it is not enough to suggest that humans are disordered and out-of-joint (differential) with regard to nature. One must indeed interrogate this phenomeno-logical out-of-jointedness as itself real. Yet calling into question the apparent exceptionality of the human condition—as I am no doubt doing more thoroughly in the present book than in the past—should not necessarily lead us to hurriedly conclude that "nature itself is disordered and out-of-joint," "a disharmonious, self-sundering Real."[315] This conclusion—whereby the human "dis-adapted" condition is universalized, and thus paradoxically exalted—only displaces our basic ontological problem, that of the immanent genesis of the transcendental: the barred symbolic is differential because the barred real always-already was so, but, if this is the case, (1) how does symbolic difference differ from real difference?; (2) where does the difference of the barred real qua "prior" to the difference of the barred symbolic come from?

Having said this, I grant that a variant of Johnston's transcendental materialism—not acknowledged by Johnston himself—could accommodate in-difference, that is, the contingent becoming not-two of the not-one, which nonetheless as not-two remains not-one. The advantage of introducing this variation is that it neutralizes, or at least renders more rigorously thinkable, the issue of anthropogenesis, releasing it from any dependence on "more than material" elements. From the standpoint of in-difference, the question concerning the historical location of the "moment" of emergence of symbolic differentiality—still a key concern for Johnston[316]—loses its significance. Not only, following the Freud of *Civilization and Its Discontents*, should anthropogenesis be seen as always tentative, partial, and, to put it simply, renewed each time a baby of the *Homo sapiens* species starts to speak, whereby it is precisely such tentativeness that accounts for the *anthropogenetic* factor; but this apparently "dis-adaptive" character of anthropogenesis is more fundamentally indifferent for nature, for our own nature as human animals—and for that of the trillions of bacteria prospering as parasites in our body, or of the chemical bonds constituting the fingers I am using right now to type these very words. Conversely, given that indifference can equally be thought as in-*difference*, the empirical experience of the absence of the sexual relationship as inextricable from language, the fundamental tenet of Lacanian theory, is sufficient to factually *prove* anthropogenesis. This does not in any way mean relinquishing a genetic approach to the transcendental but adopting one that subsumes onto-logical difference under *empirical difference as onto-logical in-difference*.[317]

In other words, as Livingston aptly puts it in his critique of Johnston, "if the constitutive inconsistency of the world"—i.e., indifference in my own terms—"can indeed be traced to the specific formal structure of the reflection of the totality of the world from a position within it"—i.e., onto-logical in-*difference*; Lacan's structure-as-the-most-real, empirically given as such to the differential being of language—"then this formal structure can indeed be seen as conditioning the specific existence of what is called a 'subject'"—i.e., onto-logical *difference*—"and the various phenomena of consciousness, freedom, and autonomy typically associated with it. But this does not exclude, as well, that the underlying structure"—i.e., onto-logical in-*difference*—"is both more general and more deeply rooted in the very formal dynamics that link totality, reflexivity, and inconsistency as such"—i.e., in the *onto-logical becoming* in-difference of indifference that also remains onto-logically indifferent to difference. "With this, the familiar dilemma of the 'natural' or 'cultural' origin of the subject is apparently overcome."[318]

To sum up, I would claim that the basic theorem of such an ontology would be "the in-different not-one is." Yet this rectified version of Johnston's transcendental materialism still presents in my view a major, and more profound, problematic aspect: in short, it assumes too much precisely in that it relies on the barred, "weak," and now in-differential real as the indisputably ultimate horizon of being.[319] In other words, it fails to ask the following *para-ontological* question: might the out-of-joint barred real, the not-one, be as such the One? This question is crucial for dialectical materialism, since it prevents us from *directly* implying the One as that which is *different* from the (differential, or even at this stage in-differential) inconsistency of the barred real. In brief, Johnston falls back into Meillassoux's God of atheists, or what I call a deceiving God who deceives us but not himself: the not-one here limits itself to paving the way for *a* (not-One), for the One (not-One).

Note that, crucially, in asking the question "might the not-one equate as such with the One?" I am recuperating on another level *some* aspects of Žižek's "minimal ontological coordinates of the universe." While his One as not-One, or Whole-as-not-Whole, is posited as an ultimate first principle (that is not-One)—which in addition amounts as such to a "break"[320]—and could thus be described as *theological*, my One as not-One points in the direction of *materialist agnosticism* (developed from and compatible with Lacan's "God hypothesis" as discussed above). In other words, the ontological dialectic between dialectic and nondialectic—that is, the in-difference between difference and indifference I have been delineating so far—leads to a para-ontological either/or: *either* the not-one is—in line with the modified version of Johnston's "transcendental materialism"—or the not-One is One—in line with Žižek's appropriately self-professed "materialist theology." Either Johnston is right, or Žižek is right, but they are both worse insofar as they do not put forward this either/or as onto-logically undecidable.

Most importantly, as I hinted in the preface, it is precisely this very ontological undecidability that then allows us to *decide* for "the not-one, i.e., in-difference, is" without falling back into the "God of atheists" (difference as contained by the One) to which a direct endorsement of the very same position inevitably leads us. In brief—and this is the point where the para-ontology sketched here opens up onto an ethical and political dimension I intend to develop in the near future—the undecidability in question awards us the *freedom to act* as though the One/God did not exist (qua divine essence), for if he existed, he could only be fooling us by also fooling himself (he would in fact be One *as* not-One). In this most radical configuration of the "evil genius," which already undermines transcendence, God as One would not simply be willingly "indifferent" or uncaring toward our differential (fallen) condition, while, as forever different from the difference that *He* wills, maliciously enjoying this predicament—the God of those who have no God always entails such an (in the end) comforting implication—[321] but his very oneness as incomplete not-One would itself amount to nothing else than inconsistent indifference.[322]

To conclude, there can truly be difference and change (the not-two is) as different from and immanent to indifference (the not-one is—and the not-two ultimately is as such not-one) if and only if we dare to think and preserve the thought of the eventuality of an *equation* between indifference and the One (the not-One is One), yet at the same time *practically* discard it. Or, to put it bluntly, we need Žižek's mistake, his *materialist* theology, to save Johnston's excavation of Lacan's dialectical materialism—as centered on the absence of the sexual relationship—from Meillassoux's insurmountable impasse, i.e., his *idealist* theology.

CHAPTER 3

LOGIC, SCIENCE, WRITING

3.1 SEXUATING THE EXPLOSION OF SEXUALITY

Starting with Seminar XVIII, where the psychoanalytic discourse is investigated in detail as a knowledge of truth (the truth of incompleteness) that counters any pronouncement on the totalizing truth about truth, and culminating in Seminars XIX, XIXB, and XX, in which the so-called formulas of sexuation are constructed within this context, Lacan's main preoccupation lies in the development of a new logic based on "There is no sexual relationship." More precisely, as programmatically stated at the beginning of Seminar XIX, he aims at "writing the other relationship,"[1] namely, the phallic function. In the same way as, in the early Seminars, the symbolic was considered as both a remedy for the faultiness of human sexuality and a sealing of it, the phallic function stands for a relationship "that functions as a cork" for the absence of the sexual relationship, but also as a "barrier" to the sexual relationship.[2] As we saw in chapter 1, it in fact revolves around man's masturbatory *jouissance* and the erotic desire to be One, whereby the Other (woman as sexual partner) is as such inevitably missed qua "radical otherness."

The main objective of the second half of this book is a close examination of Lacan's psychoanalytic logic of sexuation, that is, his *formalization* of the phallic functioning of the transcendental logic of sexuation/subjectivation that compensates for the absence of the sexual relationship by phenomenally establishing a semblance of the One, while also presenting incompleteness as a phenomenal impasse. Our first step at this stage should be a more direct interrogation of the axiomatic principle of such a psychoanalytic logic: what does Lacan precisely mean by "There is no sexual relationship"? A blunt yet persuasive way to answer this is simply to say that most men and women do indeed make love, but with all kinds of difficulties (while for the same reason some men and women, such as certain hysterics, refuse to engage in the sexual act altogether).[3] These difficulties are not only experienced in our everyday life but can be observed, studied, and treated as symptoms in the consulting room. They are, more widely, what generated the request for psychoanalytic treatment in the first place at a specific historical moment. Psychoanalysis emerged out of an interest in this predicament—which was quite possibly also a major concern for previous discourses (such as early Christianity or courtly love)[4] that are, however, by now opaque to us—and discovered an "element of indetermination," something "nonmeasurable" pertaining to sexual need that renders vain any attempt at founding and understanding the sexual liaisons we undoubtedly establish with the other sex—which at times lead to copulation and reproduction—as a *relationship*.[5]

In other words, the investigation of the unconscious initiated by psychoanalysis shows that "all that which is of language has to do with sex."[6] But, this very relation is one in which the sexual relationship between man and woman cannot be written as $a \to b$ (or $b \to a$), as an "application" of a to b (or of b onto a),[7] or, better, as a *ratio* between them. Again, the speaking being cannot symbolically represent sex as such; hence this remains a logical impossibility: the absence of the sexual relationship amounts to the fundamental absence of sexual meaning. In a similar sense, stressing the biological/ethological dimension of his argument, Lacan can claim that the absence of the sexual relationship is the "habitat" of the speaking being, and, conversely, that the sexual nonrelational "relations" that we nonetheless achieve are made possible exclusively by speech.[8]

Language thus goes together with a positioning of sexual nature in the "disjunction" between man and woman,[9] yet this disjunction *can* as such be formulated: what does not stop not being written, the impossibility of the relationship, can itself be written as a nonrelational "relation." This is precisely what Lacan intends to elaborate through the discourse of the analyst and the subsequent formulas of sexuation. How, then, should we understand more accurately the fact that language cannot "account" for the sexual relationship?[10]

In Seminar XVIII, Lacan is careful in detailing three different levels of language's confrontation with the sexual relationship: "enunciation," "inscription," and "effective inscription."[11] We do certainly spend a lot of time talking about sex and contiguous matters, especially—if not exclusively—when something does not work in what we call inappropriately our *rapports*,[12] and very much enjoy indulging in this activity.[13] We are also able to comment on the way in which language inscribes sexed nature in the disjunction between man and woman, up to the point of formalizing this disjunction as a logical function $F(x)$—which is precisely Lacan's project throughout these Seminars. It remains, however, impossible to obtain an "effective inscription" from this formalization: language cannot render the inscription of sex, which it itself carries out, as a sexual relationship between the two allegedly complementary poles of the masculine and the feminine. Man and woman are, rather, inscribed as the real of a disjunction, and are such (man and woman) only thanks to the phallic function outside of any "sexual bipolarity."[14] Thus the specific import of psychoanalysis is precisely its having shown that "it is untenable to stick in any way to this duality as sufficient."[15] To sum up: psychoanalysis amounts to the discourse that constitutes itself as the enunciation of the fact that the sexual relationship cannot be written, or, more precisely, formulated as a measurable ratio between two discrete and substantial elements, a and b, man and woman. The disjunction between man and woman is fundamentally illogical. Yet psychoanalysis can write as a logical function $F(x)$—the phallic function—such a disjunction, that is, the impossibility of writing the relationship.

As I argued in chapter 2, this stance diametrically opposes psychoanalysis to all traditional notions of sexual knowledge qua the animistic basis of *any* theory of knowledge, which invariably took for granted sexual bipolarity, for instance, in the guise of the *yin* and *yang* of ancient Chinese culture, but also of basic ideas in Western philosophy such as action and passion, form and matter. Lacan insists on this point: "The general model of [the] relationship between male and female is what has always been haunting [...] the speaking being's mapping of the forces of the world."[16] Possibly beyond Freud's own explicit intentions (Freud did not formulate the impossibility of the sexual relationship as such, yet "it is written in what Freud writes"),[17] psychoanalysis thus produces an "explosion of the notion of sexuality,"[18] which allows us historically to consider the history of the sexual relationship, and of the theories of knowledge that go hand in hand with it, as revolving around the illusory belief that the sexual relationship is logical / can be written.[19] The organization of language into social discourses, i.e., into intersubjective effects of language's incompleteness, therefore relies on a primary structure of fiction, which Lacan names "semblance," aimed at veiling the impossibility of the sexual relationship, whereby man and woman themselves emerge as "beings of fiction."[20]

With specific regard to the process of sexuation—that is, the fact that adult speaking beings are, after all, divided into men and women, that they acquire what Lacan himself refers to as an "identity of gender"[21]—semblance entails quite simply the fact that a boy becomes a man as long as he *feigns* to be a man, and, vice versa, a girl becomes a woman as long as she feigns to be a woman: a boy must "make-man"[22] [*faire-homme*] and a girl must "make-woman" [*faire-femme*]. "Man" and "woman" are nothing but such feigning. More importantly, this can be achieved only if the boy acts as a man *for women*, and the girl acts as a woman *for men*: "sexual identification does not consist in believing oneself to be a man or a woman, but in taking into account, for the boy, that there are women, and for the girl, that there are men."[23] At this stage we can clearly see how sexuation founds itself as a nonrelational "relation": the disjunction between the sexes, the structural absence of the sexual relationship where beings of language are concerned, paradoxically promotes gender identity only to the extent that "what defines man is his *relation* to woman, and inversely."[24] For the same reason, this "relation" cannot be written as a relation $a \to b$ or $b \to a$ since "man" and "woman" are not as such predetermined (there is no essence of masculinity or femininity), and become "man" and "woman" only in "relation [*relation*] to the other party," which is to say that "nothing allows us to abstract these definitions of man and woman from the entirety of the speaking experience, up to and including the institutions in which they are expressed, namely marriage."[25]

When thought of as outside of symbolic institutions and the phallic function that sustains them, man and woman can only designate sex as a *real* "unknown."[26] We saw in chapter 2 that this can at best be articulated through the oxymoronic maxim "There are two sexes, but there isn't a second sex"; we have also seen how the XY and XX of biology do not supersede this logical impossibility, but rather have again recourse to a traditionally animistic understanding of sexuality, for which XY $\to$ XX still tacitly relies on the supposed bipolar complementarity $a \to b$. At this stage, expanding on the incompatibility between the notion of relationship as $a \to b$ and human sexuality, we could suggest that a boy becomes a man (a) only as an x that relates to preexisting women (b), and, conversely, a girl becomes a woman (b) only as an x that relates to preexisting men (a), yet the "relations" ($x \to b$) = a and ($x \to a$) = b are as such *unrelated*, do not give rise to a relationship $a \to b$. Man as a is not in relation to woman as b, and vice versa, although man emerges as a from x only in relation to b, and vice versa.

What we have just sketched out here, developing some passing remarks made in Seminar XVIII, is the basis of the phallic function as Lacan's reelaboration of Freud's Oedipus and castration complexes, which he then moves on to formalize in detail by means of an innovative logical writing, especially in Seminars XIX, XIXB, and XX, whose construction we will from now on follow step by step. For the time being, drawing some provisional conclusions from this simpler algebraic notation, we need to emphasize that *castration* amounts for Lacan to the fact that the other sex qua *unrelated*—woman for man, and man for woman—stands precisely for the *phallus*, that is, the signifier of an impossible absolute *jouissance* ("the real of sexual *jouissance*, insofar as it is as such detached"), the One *jouissance* that *would be* if there were a sexual relationship, yet also concomitantly of the *sexual jouissance* that replaces it ("sexual *jouissance* insofar as it is coordinated with a semblance").[27]

But then, we should ask, how does the phallus *sexuate* the absence of the sexual relationship? In Seminar XVIII, Lacan presents it very clearly as a "third term"—which as such contests any alleged bipolarity—that allows for the formation of a nonrelational "relation" while not being a "middle term" [*médium*] between the other two terms: "If we link it [phallus] to one of the two terms, for instance that of man, we can be certain that it will not communicate with the other, and inversely."[28] In other words, we obtain a semblance of the sexual relationship $a \rightarrow b$ (the phallic nonrelational "relation") only to the extent that $a \rightarrow \Phi$ is given and $\Phi \rightarrow b$ is not given, while, at the same time, $b \rightarrow \Phi$ is given and $\Phi \rightarrow a$ is not given. In terms of the creation of gender identity as necessarily related to the other sex that we have just discussed, this will mean that being a man as nothing other than feigning to be a man for women, $(x \rightarrow b) = a$, is precisely what women relate to as the phallus in $b \rightarrow \Phi$, just as feigning to be a woman for men, $(x \rightarrow a) = b$, is precisely what men relate to as the phallus in $a \rightarrow \Phi$.

To this point one should importantly add that, as we saw in chapter 1, both a and b relate sexually to the signifier Φ: the nonrelational "relation" remains *asymmetrical*, woman having to borrow from man a signifier that was derived from the image of the penis—which is quite possibly the ultimate explanation for the fact that language fails to convey sex as a sexual relationship. Consequently, woman will have a privileged approach to phallic incompleteness, i.e., to the fact that human sexuality manages to *feign* the relation $a \rightarrow b$ only at the cost of severing $a \rightarrow \Phi$ from $b \rightarrow \Phi$. To put it differently, woman emerges as the support of the truth about "what there is of *semblance* in the relation between man and woman," in the sense that by remaining in the end the Other sex, resisting full identification as Other-than-One—as Other than the phallic signifier that nonetheless anchors her, not having a second signifier at her disposal—she interrupts, "punctuates the equivalence between *jouissance* and semblance."[29] That is, woman bears witness to the fact that this very equivalence remains "disjunctive," i.e., that the phallic *jouissance* of semblance amounts to nothing other than a semblance of *jouissance*.[30] Lacan's overall argument therefore also entails that if, on the contrary, woman had a signifier for her sex, if a second sexual signifier existed, the phallus would not signify castration (i.e., sexual *jouissance* as marked by it), and language would thus be whole, that is, it would cancel itself out: there would be a sexual relationship.

3.2 SEMBLANCE AND TRUTH

The major argument Lacan intends to put forward is that "There is no sexual relationship" stands for the limit of logic, and that logic is structurally coextensive with this limit, sustains itself through it. The truth of phallic incompleteness lying at the core of *Homo sapiens'* transcendental structure equates with the incompleteness of our logical thought as a species-specific linguistic trait capable of founding knowledge. Reciprocally, logic's ability to fully justify itself formally by, in the end, also accounting for sex as a *rapport* would totalize language and lead to its demise. Lacan's complex point about psychoanalysis as a "junction between knowledge and truth"[31]—which coincides with the very possibility of writing the *absence* of the sexual relationship as "There is no sexual relationship"—is here fourfold:

1. The absence of the sexual relationship imposes a limit on discourse, which emerges most evidently in the discourse of neurotics (above all, of hysterics), whose *knowledge* is precisely that *il n'y a pas de rapport sexuel* and, in parallel, that *jouissance* is hence caused by phallic semblance.[32]
2. This limit of discourse that coincides with discourse itself can properly be appreciated as a truth through psychoanalytic discourse. That is, thanks to psychoanalysis, discourse does not hysterically divide itself into the reduction of discourse to a nondiscursive limit and its opposing sublation into a meta-discourse on the limit (i.e., into a limit qua knowledge), precisely by demarcating logical failure, which as such needs to be inscribed, supported by writing.[33]
3. The knowledge of truth that must be written in order to be grasped qua incompleteness also positively institutes itself as the *knowledge* of truth, as a "new logic."[34] The logical exploration commenced by psychoanalysis "is not only the questioning of what imposes a limit on language in its apprehension of the real" but also, in this very attempt to approach it, a demonstration of "that which of the real may have determined language."[35]
4. Psychoanalytic discourse should closely follow the development of *formal* logic throughout history, that is, find an orientation in confronting the productivity of its deadlocks, which have already delineated the co-implication of language and the real. In this sense, formal "logic bears the mark of the sexual impasse."[36] Yet psychoanalytic discourse should shun *logicism*, the mirage of containing the real of discourse within logic, of promoting a meta-linguistic knowledge that tells the truth *about* truth.

To sum up: any discourse, without exception, gives itself as a semblance.[37] The discourses of the hysteric, of logicism (which has by now engulfed modern science, Lacan contends), and of psychoanalysis all emerge in history approximately at the same moment by measuring themselves against this state of affairs, which before had been effectively veiled by traditional— especially religious—knowledge. But we should nonetheless carefully distinguish between the ways in which they confront this structure of fiction. In Seminar XVIII, Lacan struggles to express such a subtle yet decisive distinction; he eventually manages to convey it in two brief—and distant—passages through a manipulation of the Seminar's title, *On a discourse that would not be of semblance*, which refers to psychoanalysis.

In opposition to the hysteric's denunciation of discourse for its semblance, her unmasking of a "discourse that would not be the *discourse* of semblance,"[38] but mere semblance—i.e., of the fact that, faced with the absence of the sexual relationship, discourse would not as such hold up, "would not be"[39]—psychoanalysis does not believe semblance to be an "artifact" beyond which "the idea of something that would be other, a nature" would arise, since "truth is not the contrary of semblance" but, rather, supports it.[40] On the other hand, in opposition to positivist logic's search for a "discourse that would not be a *semblance* of discourse,"[41] namely, a *true* discourse as aprioristically opposed to a false discourse, psychoanalysis proposes to develop a logical writing of the limit of logic (as surfaced in the hysteric). In other words, psychoanalytic discourse rejects logicism's "putting a signified to the test of something that decides by yes or no," and "what does not lend itself to this test [...] is defined by meaning nothing."[42] Psychoanalytic discourse, rather, formalizes the "dialectic between truth and semblance."[43]

However, it must be stressed that Lacan does *not* identify truth with semblance: for speaking beings, semblance is nothing but the signifier,[44] while truth amounts to the fact that for signifierness [*signifiance*] to be able to signify, "signifiers cannot be there all together."[45] In other words, discourse is both a semblance *and* an effect of truth, the truth of incompleteness that is not pregiven in opposition to what is false, but becomes true through discourse's repression of it ("truth progresses only through a structure of fiction").[46] The moment at which psychoanalytic logic attempts to give body to this truth then amounts to the moment when discourse as a "representative of representation"[47] is suspended. Yet it can be suspended only because it has always been structurally suspendible, Lacan adds. While not refuting semblance, the effect of truth kept in a state of repression cannot be reduced to semblance either; this is the very reason why the question about a discourse that would not be of semblance can be posed precisely at the level of the structure of discourse.

If psychoanalytic logic explicitly formalizes this conundrum, renovating discourse by displacing itself into a "dis-universe" of incompleteness, then discourse no longer simply represents representation but also turns into an open "continuation of discourse that is characterized as an effect of truth."[48] However, such a displacement of discourse remains itself *intrinsic* to semblance: the *désunivers* in which psychoanalysis operates is indeed not *divers* from discourse qua semblance, Lacan spells out. Rather, it promotes a discursive "diversion" that gives a different tinge to semblance.[49] More to the point, a discourse that *would* not be of semblance—psychoanalysis—*is* a discourse of semblance, for discourse gives itself only as semblance: "Of *a discourse that would not be of semblance* posits that discourse [...] *is* of semblance." But the great advantage of putting it in this way is that "we do not say a semblance of *what*," i.e., that we do not posit semblance as the opposite of a supposed true discourse, which is what logical positivism does.[50]

A discourse that would not be of semblance is thus a discourse about that which, *from within semblance*, is *not* of semblance: the real as impossible, which can be written/formalized as such. At the same time, as witnessed by Lacan's insistence on *logically* revisiting and revising the *myth* of the Father of the horde, a discourse that would not be of semblance is also a discourse about that which, for semblance, would necessarily *be tout court* if semblance were not there—namely, the sexual relationship that would write itself, hence ultimately a nondiscourse. The key issue at stake in this context is therefore not an interrogative "Is it or is it not of discourse?"—i.e., "Is it or is it not of semblance?"—but the acknowledgment of an alternative available within discourse: "It is or it is not said."[51] For discourse, facts are such only by virtue of the fact of saying them, yet there is something, the real, that is a fact by virtue of being unsayable. Psychoanalysis as a discourse that would not be of semblance attempts to approach and articulate it discursively from two inseparable perspectives: that of the real as impossible, and that of what this very impossibility allows us to posit as mythical necessity.

Before dealing more closely with Lacan's scrutiny of formal logic—including his assessment of Aristotelian logic, which is inextricably bound up in Seminars XVIII, XIX, and XIXB with the putting forward of the formulas of sexuation (the propositions of the phallic function Φx, i.e., the logic of incompleteness or not-all)—we first need to further articulate his understanding of the co-dependence of language, logical writing, and truth from the perspective of psychoanalysis as a discourse on the real as impossible (the absent sexual relationship that would not be of semblance). Although, in Seminar XVIII, Lacan does not mention Derrida once, his point of departure in unraveling this articulation is precisely a critique of the notion of archewriting, which he refers to on different occasions, and which in his opinion gives rise to "regrettable confusions."[52] In stark contrast with any idea of writing as something "which has always been there in the world, prefiguring speech," language no doubt precedes writing. Yet no less importantly, it is writing that can question the place of truth as indissolubly bound up with the structure of fiction produced by language; it achieves this to the extent that formal logic constitutes itself only in the guise of writing—"There is no logical question unless it starts from writing."[53] In other words, while on a first level writing clearly stands for a "representation of speech," it also indicates "something that is found not to be simply a representation," in the sense that it is at the same time a "repercussion" on speech, an "event of discourse" through which the subject as an instrument of discourse interrogates the very way in which discourse manages to master itself.[54] Note that in this regard, from the stance that openly tackles the dialectic between semblance and truth evidencing the place of truth qua incompleteness, strictly speaking, "writing is precisely not language," Lacan specifies, for there is no language of language, no meta-language: writing, in logically interrogating the incompleteness of language, is not language—since it could be language here only as meta-language—even though writing presupposes language.⁵⁵ But, conversely, given that there is no meta-language, writing, the logical demonstration it supports (which is ultimately a demonstration of incompleteness), requires speech: "It would be enough for me to give you a mathematical demonstration, you would see that I am forced to talk about it because it is something written, otherwise nothing would get across. If I *speak* about it, it is not at all *meta-language*."⁵⁶

To expand on this subtle series of arguments, why, given the co-implication of writing and speech, should the former retain any privilege in approaching truth (the real of the absence of the sexual relationship)? Lacan suggests that speech cannot convey the incompleteness of language without immediately giving it a meaning, and thus transforming it into an *apparent* completeness. Saying "There is no meta-language" inevitably institutes this very statement as a meta-linguistic semblance, or—which amounts to the same thing—indirectly claims to *mean* that "There is no meta-language" is a meta-language.⁵⁷ On the other hand, writing insofar as it is different from speech, i.e., does not limit itself to representing speech in a written form, highlights a *literal* element that resists signification, and puts into play the real not as an after-all *meaningful* deficit of meaning (the meta-linguistic implication of "There is no meta-language") but as the *meaninglessness* from which meaning qua deficit of meaning originates. This is the case, for instance, when we replace the sentence "There is no meta-language" with the algebraic notation $S(\cancel{A})$.⁵⁸

For Lacan, this advantage of writing becomes all the more evident as logic qua a form of "developed language" increases its ability of "making holes in what is written," moving from Aristotle's term logic to modern predicate logic.⁵⁹ Aristotelian logic already contains the letter in principle; as Lacan has it, "'All animals are mortal': you strike out 'animals' and 'mortal' and put in their place the high point of writing, namely, a quite simple letter," i.e., "all x are y."⁶⁰ But modern predicate logic goes much further in this direction. Its basic presupposition is, after Frege, an "empty place," that of the so-called argument or variable of the function, such that, in the holed sentence "all _ are mortal," "the x marks an empty place in what is at stake."⁶¹ More precisely, the holed sentence can thereby be formalized as $\forall x . Mx$ only insofar as "x, to the extent that it is unknown, can legitimately be posited [...] as being able to find *its place* in what happens to be the function that corresponds to it; namely, where the same x is taken as a variable."⁶² In other words, the x functions in a function as nothing more than the marking of an empty place, ultimately that of incompleteness, by means of writing. In parallel, the x does not presuppose any essence; rather, as unknown, it acquires meaning only as a variable of a function, which is itself dependent on the empty place.[63]

At this stage, we should not lose sight of the fact that writing's ability to pin down the place of incompleteness does in the end confirm the inextricability of language qua semblance and truth qua incompleteness, which would otherwise pass unnoticed, since speech amounts to this very inextricability—as Lacan famously puts it, we always speak the truth and, for the same reason, all the "supposed paradoxes that classical logic stops at [...] hold exclusively from the moment when they are written."[64] In other words, from a more explicitly psychoanalytic perspective, the truth about the absence of the sexual relationship cannot be separated from the truth about phallic *jouissance*: the inextricability of language qua semblance and truth qua incompleteness positively entails that language is a "little phallus that tickles us gently,"[65] while truth also involves "enjoying being a semblance."[66] Consequently, Lacan's putting forward the insubstantial character of the sexual relationship—and of the *jouissance* obtained from it—by adopting the writing of logic will coincide with a writing of *sexuation*. Lacan writes the sexual no-thing [*l'achose*] that, like the empty place of a function, "is absent there where it holds its place," but with the same gesture, he inscribes sexuality as castration, as the phallic function Φx.[67]

The favoring of writing over speech in trying to circumscribe the sexual no-thing and the phallic corking that both compensates for it and seals it as unattainable has thus basically to do with the fact that *l'achose* cannot be said, yet can be demonstrated.[68] For Lacan, this turns psychoanalysis into a continuation, but also a problematization, of the discourse of modern science and its use of the algebraic letter of logic and mathematics. When Galileo and Newton abandoned the closed universe of totalizing knowledge, science acquired the ability to establish itself as a network that makes "the right holes appear at the right place,"[69] that is, to verify empirically a written hypothesis, precisely because it began taking as an ultimate referent the real as impossible—i.e., in the first instance, the collapse of the Ptolemaic cosmos's monolithic structure of fiction. Scientific deductions have ever since returned to the real as impossible: "The apparatus of discourse insofar as it is what, in its rigor, encounters the limits of its consistency—it is with this that we aim, in physics, at something that is real."[70] To put it differently, the appearance of the right holes at the right place starts from and leads to the real as that which "makes a hole in semblance,"[71] makes a hole appear at the *wrong* place, namely, in appearance itself. Lacan claims that if the "essence of language" is nothing other than its "structure of fiction," modern science's adoption of the algebraic letter has been able to produce for the first time a "sort of questioning, of pressure [...] which puts the truth" as real "up against the wall of verification."[72] Verification, insofar as it is logically inscribable, leads in the end to a point where "the fiction comes up short," whereby what brings it to a halt, the real, cannot only be vaguely grasped, but written "within the very system of fiction [as] a contradiction."[73]

Seminar XVIII stresses at several points that this way of proceeding, which emerged out of dissatisfaction with all "allegedly intuitive"[74] premises of knowledge (first of all, the geocentric model), makes modern science share with psychoanalysis the same de-universalized stance. Unlike philosophy, both discourses move from a refusal of what Lacan calls a meta-linguistic "mapping" of "where we have got to" in our accumulation of wisdom. They start off, rather, from hypotheses that do not claim to be dealing with the "foundation of things" but with the "conditional of a truth," namely, an if that can be articulated and verified in its empirical consequences only at a logical level, without this predicating anything about the truth of the hypothesis.[75] The scientific, inscribable verification of a hypothesis—for instance, the heliocentric hypothesis—does not amount to the latter's truth, which would be an absolute truth about a conditional truth. To put it bluntly, it is true that the Earth revolves around the Sun on condition that, as part of a galaxy among billions of galaxies, the solar system is not deemed to be at the center of the universe. For Lacan, logical implication allows us to derive a true conclusion from a premise that is as such not true: taken in isolation, at word value, heliocentrism as a hypothesis has indeed, for the time being at least, been proved false (i.e., there are other cosmic "centers," not only the Sun, and the Sun itself orbits around the center of our galaxy).

This being said, we have already discussed how Lacan then sees modern science's confrontation with the truth of incompleteness as profoundly ambiguous, if not openly contradictory. In its historical progress since the seventeenth century, scientific discourse has continued to "bite the real" and expand the breach in the uni-verse, yet, in parallel, it has ceased to concern itself with its status as a semblance, replacing the conditional truths derived from its hypotheses with the supposedly true hypotheses to which the members of the scientific community consent.[76] Science therefore paved the way not only for psychoanalysis but also for a different discourse, the university discourse, that reinforces its quasi-psychotic adherence to the certainty of existing knowledge all the more as this certainty is increasingly discredited in a *scientific* way (if yet another tinier particle has been discovered, disproving previous hypotheses while confirming new ones, it must be because we are finally dealing with the ultimate particle that holds the fabric of the universe together, the "God particle" ...).

In the next section we will return to this issue by showing how, in Lacan's opinion, logical positivism intensifies modern science's structural oscillation with regard to truth and the real. For the time being, it is important to dwell on two contiguous questions that remain unsolved in Lacan's positioning of his attempt to logically write the impossibility of writing the sexual relationship, i.e., to write the limit of logic, vis-à-vis the discourse of science: the status of intuition and the role of history. With regard to the first, on the one hand, Lacan claims that what psychoanalysis has fundamentally in common with modern science is, following the collapse of the traditional structure of fiction, "precisely the abandoning of any recourse to intuition in order to keep to a certain inscribable."[77] That is to say: both discourses dispose of any allegedly intuitive knowledge of the cosmos, which eventually relies on the association between nature and the perceived unity of the human body as, in turn, always amenable to a presumed sexual knowledge (the bipolarity between man and woman). On the other hand, in apparent contrast with this argument, Lacan understands the real qua the limit of algebraic logic precisely in terms of intuition. A passage from Seminar XVIII leaves little room for doubt: "Can everything be reduced to pure logic, that is, to a discourse that sustains itself from a well-determined structure? Is there not an absolutely essential element that remains, whatever we do to insert it into this structure, to reduce it, that all the same remains as a final kernel and is called intuition?"[78] Lacan goes on to say that scientific writing should therefore be appreciated according to its two sides, deductive reasoning and "intuiting," where the latter is responsible for the effectiveness of the former—a fact, he says, that has been especially valued by mathematics, from Descartes to Brouwer, against endeavors to reduce number to pure logic. Even more surprisingly, he states that "the writing of the little letters [of modern science] has no less of an intuitive function than the one outlined by our friend Euclid."[79]

How are we to resolve this tension? Developing Lacan's argument, it could be suggested that intuition acquires a completely different facet with the detachment of truth from knowledge brought about by the advent of modern science and the end of the closed universe. Intuition moves from being the perceptual knowledge man can take for granted as part and parcel of an absolute and immutable Truth that transcends him (of the God who has created the world in seven days, and placed the Earth at the center of it, as "proved" by our senses), to standing for the kernel through which truth presents itself as an impasse of verification that can logically be inscribed as a contradiction. In brief, intuition no longer preserves fiction but undermines it, in order eventually to give rise to new fictions.[80] But, even if we are convinced by this embryonic explanation—which faces the difficult task of accounting for what seems to be the historical shifting of our (at least partly hardwired) intuitive skills from the domain of imaginary wholeness to that of real incompleteness—is it possible to reconcile it with the above-mentioned reference to Euclid, whose isosceles triangle theorem, Lacan insists, "is nothing other than a writing [*écrit*]"[81] that forces the "norms of writing" [*les normes de l'écriture*], and as such already announces (modern) logic's ability "to make holes in what is written"?[82] I believe that it is not, and that an unsurmountable problem emerges here in Lacan's own discourse. Although these two passing remarks on ancient geometry remain extremely vague, if one reads them together it would be no exaggeration to suggest that Lacan recovers in Euclid the seeds of an intuition of the real, of a real intuition, which contrasts with his determination in singling out the Galilean-Newtonian scientific revolution and its use of the letter as the precondition for any de-universalized universe. To put it straightforwardly: does Lacan deem that the truth of incompleteness was somehow already sensed and written, if not formally proved, by—possibly among others—the ancient Greeks? This would seem to be the case when he treats Aristotle's term logic as already implicitly containing the "empty place" of Frege's predicate logic, not to mention his assertion that "Plato was Lacanian" since, in the *Parmenides*, he "shows that once you begin to say it in an articulated fashion, what is outlined in terms of structure creates a difficulty [...] and that it is along this path that one must search for the real."[83]

Here we come to the second, more extensive and delicate matter concerning Lacan's logic of sexuation as the logic of the not-all, and the extent of its dependence on the writing of modern science. Is the absence of the sexual relationship *the* basic transcendental invariant of the speaking animal? Or should it be understood as a historical product, not only in the sense that discursive changes epiphenomenally condition the *il n'y a pas de rapport sexuel* but in the deeper sense that there were—or will be—historical periods for which this axiom, and the ensuing dialectic of semblance and truth, does not hold? Also, from a slightly different angle, assuming that language is as such structurally incomplete, and therefore that *Homo sapiens* cannot avoid the dialectic of semblance and truth that now goes with the phallic function, does this necessarily entail that the absence of meta-language always corresponds to the absence of the sexual relationship?

I believe that in the early 1970s, when he repeatedly hints at these issues, Lacan develops two incompatible narratives, one for which the *il n'y a pas de rapport sexuel* is legitimate only from within the epistemological horizon set by modern science and complicated by psychoanalysis, and another that posits its trans-historical validity with regard to *Homo sapiens* as such, thereby pointing to wider ontological interrogations (which, against the implications underlying his own arguments, Lacan is too quick in dismissing as irrelevant to psychoanalytic discourse). Preliminarily, we should note that this alternative is connected with, yet does not directly touch on, the vexed question of the origins of language and the role of sex in it—which is vetoed by Lacan— since this question not to be asked already *presupposes* that the absence of the sexual relationship is the fundamental transcendental of the speaking animal, as is made explicit in the following passage: "Speech, the way it functions, depends, is conditioned as speech by the fact that it is for it, as speech, precisely forbidden to function with regard to the sexual relationship in any way that allows it to account for it. *I am not in the process of according primacy to anything in this correlation*: I am not saying that speech exists because there is no sexual relationship. [...] I am not saying either that there is no sexual relationship because speech is there. But there is *certainly* not a sexual relationship because speech functions at a level of which psychoanalytic discourse has discovered the preeminence, specifying the speaking being in everything that is of the order of sex, namely semblance."[84]

I would argue that the first narrative acquires all its significance if we give the right emphasis to the fact that "There is no sexual relationship" does not involve an impossibility to represent sex *in general*, but more specifically to write it in the guise of a *ratio* $a \to b$ that adopts the algebraic reasoning of modern science and, most importantly, follows its logic as a *deductive* logic that nonetheless stems from and leads to the limit of logic qua *real* intuition. The real of the absence of the sexual relationship thus amounts here to the persistence of this real intuition that resists *science*'s written manipulations of it—a real on which the latter paradoxically rely, as well as periodically return to—and subsequent attempt at foreclosing truth into a progressive accumulation of—continuously contested—knowledge. As openly conceded by Lacan, we can, for instance, still write the sexual relationship as $\male \to \female$,[85] as well as believe that a better grasp of the universality of these allegedly complementary principles would solve our sentimental problems.[86] What we cannot write, I would add, to unpack Lacan's cursory observations, is the $E = mc^2$ of sex. Or better, we can write the way in which the E and m of the two sexes are not related by any predetermined constant c^2 but in so doing are nonetheless involved in a contingent phallic nonrelational relationship that *may* give rise with difficulty to copulation and reproduction.

In other words, from this stance, psychoanalysis itself is nothing but the product of the historical impasse of subjecting sex (initially, the hysterical symptom that did not make sense for medicine) to modern scientific discourse, by which psychoanalysis is nonetheless contained. Not surprisingly, despite his discovery of the unconscious's transgression of the law of non-contradiction, Freud's project always follows a scientistic motivation, even when he identifies the final word of psychoanalysis with the deadlocks arising with the "rock of castration" and the "negation of femininity": fundamentally, it is because, for the time being, these cannot be explained by the discourse of science, now enriched by provisional psychoanalytic findings, that men and women do have problems with sex, not vice versa. Lacan's step forward in this context would be to develop a logic of the not-all—the phallic function as our logic of sexuation/subjectivation—that writes precisely the logical irreducibility of sex to the logic of modern science, and thus challenges the latter from within by reminding it of its co-dependence with a de-universalized universe, which imposed itself historically at a given point in time.

According to this account, it seems that the truth of the absence of the sexual relationship marks, as Lacan admits on some occasions, just a "historical phase": it signals a certain "frontier between the symbolic and the real," namely, an articulation between castration, copulation, and phallic *jouissance*, that is due to "the historically recent emergence of psychoanalytic discourse" in the wake of the discourse of modern science.[87] Even more explicitly, he writes: "the interest of what I am highlighting does not lie in saying that from all time things have been the same as the point to which we have got to"; although we hear tell of it only from the outside, hypothetically at least ("perhaps," Lacan says twice in a single sentence), there were and there will be "places where there occurs between men and women this harmonious conjunction which makes them believe themselves to be in seventh heaven."[88] In one instance, in an unexpected anticipation of Deleuze and Guattari's fascination with Taoist sex and *coitus reservatus* as a means of accessing the body-without-organs, Lacan goes so far as to suggest that the relational "sexual life of ancient China will perhaps flower again."[89]

It seems to me that, however cautious and fragmentary these statements may be, they nonetheless blatantly clash with Lacan's much more frequent view that, as we saw in the passage quoted above, language and the absence of the sexual relationship are structurally reciprocal independently of any cultural variation. Even if we limit ourselves to a scrutiny of Seminar XVIII, we find ample evidence that Lacan supports the idea of the trans-historical (if not extra-historical) validity of the *il n'y a pas de rapport sexuel*: "Language does not account for the sexual relationship";[90] "Language [...] has its field reserved within the gap of the sexual relationship";[91] "Language [...] only connotes [...] the impossibility of symbolizing the sexual relationship among the beings that inhabit language."[92] Conversely—again, Lacan does not intend to privilege one of the two terms of this correlation—"it is from this habitat," i.e., from the impossibility of symbolizing the sexual relationship, "that they are able to speak."[93]

Leaving aside his most extreme pronouncements—such as those about Taoist sex, which might be deliberately provocative—we could argue that Lacan in the end compromises between the two alternative narratives we have just exposed. That is to say: *for us moderns*, the speaking being is inextricable from the absence of the sexual relationship because the anti-totalizing orientation of (the origins of) scientific discourse has for the first time in history let the speaking being grasp the *constitutive* incompatibility between language and sex, which was efficaciously veiled by all traditional theories of knowledge as structures of fiction about the existence of the sexual relationship.

But opting for such a reading actually raises more questions than it answers. Regardless of whether this is achieved through a rigid matrimonial codification of copulation and an oppressive stigmatization of nonreproductive sexual practices (as in the Christian West) or, on the other hand, by means of a no less regimented set of sexual techniques able to promote the joyous *belief*—Lacan himself specifies—that one "is in seventh heaven" by retaining one's semen as long as possible (as in ancient China), does a structure of fiction that is capable of perfectly corking/veiling the *il n'y a pas de rapport sexuel* not amount, *precisely as semblance*, to a prehuman *rapport*? Note that in the early 1970s, Lacan continues to uphold the idea, already present in his writings of the 1930s and 1940s, that semblance also regulates at an imaginary level the reproduction of *nonspeaking* animals, as shown by the link between sexual display [*parade*] and copulation.[94]

So it seems that, after all, the two accounts of the impact of history on the absence of the sexual relationship remain diametrically opposed, and our attempt at mediating between them only gives rise to a trickier pair of options, which underlie Lacan's arguments, but between which, this time, he himself would most probably find it, for good reason, difficult to choose. Either Galileo was responsible for the loss of our—Edenic-animalic, albeit as such fictional—innocence about sex, and thus, by the same token, for rendering us strictly speaking human. Or, on the contrary, "man and woman, insofar as we might define them by a *simple biological* pinpointing, [are] these beings who are in difficulty with sexual *jouissance*";[95] hence there is no way of *structurally* distinguishing the dialectic of truth and semblance at work in traditional knowledge from that which allows for the de-universalization of the universe supposedly introduced by modern science and continued by psychoanalysis.

This further tension is rendered all the more palpable, but also as such short-circuited, when Lacan brings biology into play. While he keeps on repeating that sex can only be represented phallically, and that castration is thus "biologically essential for the reproduction of [speaking] beings as living beings, for their race to remain fruitful,"[96] he also does not exclude the possibility that the science of biology (the life sciences to come, which, bypassing modernity, would move from their current premodern animistic status to a literally postmodern understanding of the limit—and precondition—of modern science) may well be able to find a way to write the sexual relationship.[97]

Does this mean that biological science has, in the near or not so near future, a chance to change or, better, to rectify our deficient biology, and consequently—considering that castration is "biologically essential for the reproduction of [speaking] beings"—turn us into another species? If so, will this transformation, and the ensuing elimination of the risk of extinction inherent to the very perpetuation of our species as the species for which reproduction is not guaranteed, paradoxically entail a dissociation of reproduction from the sexual act? Lacan seems to suggest precisely this when he claims that "what *jouissance* leads to does not strictly have anything to do with copulation, insofar as it is, let us say, the usual style—*it will change*—through which reproduction is carried out in the species of the speaking being."[98]

Moreover, following his conflicting arguments, it is hard to establish whether he thinks that a science able to write the sexual relationship would indeed involve the emergence of a post-human nonlinguistic meta-language centered on an effortless self-programing of the species,[99] or, instead, the opening up of a new kind of logical impasse, a new real, in a domain different from sex. The further, and even more likely, possibility Lacan appears to envisage is that such a "science-fiction" scenario[100]—as he himself calls it—could just amount to another obscurantist phase of consolidation of phallic semblance, namely, to the imposition of a regressive holistic *belief* in the techno-religious ability to write what actually has never stopped and will never stop *not* writing itself for *Homo sapiens*.[101]

3.3 BEYOND ARISTOTLE AND FREGE

With the exception of his most radical claims on the topic—which I have highlighted on purpose so as to oppose any facile and normative reading—we should assume that with regard to the influence of history on the *il n'y a pas de rapport sexuel* Lacan eventually adopts an intermediate position. This is similar to the one we discussed earlier, but also presents a minor yet considerable difference from it: the absence of the sexual relationship constitutes the transcendental condition of possibility of the speaking animal, which is throughout history more or less *imperfectly* corked by the phallic function. Thus the phallic function is itself an integral element of the transcendental.[102] Plato can in this way literally be a Lacanian *ante scientificam litteram*, and Saint Paul can found Christian theology on an oblique understanding of the irreducibility of sexual difference.[103] Yet, on the other hand, the passage from the closed premodern universe of religion and *episteme* to the open universe of modern science marks a weakening of the phallic suture that could nonetheless be again reinforced in the future—for instance by means of genetic engineering—in concomitance with an ossification of science into a unitary *Weltanschauung* unable to accept the proliferation of incompatible *Weltanschauungen* science has itself given rise to.[104]

However, following closely Lacan's own logical and methodological premises, this complex scenario still remains problematic on another level. The transcendental absence of the sexual relationship as the axiomatic truth of logic *tout court*, as the truth of incompleteness, should *not* be turned into a truth about truth. In other words, the axiom of conditional truth is itself to be taken as *conditional*, that is to say, its truth, as seen, cannot be predicated of the "foundation of things." The if clause that can be articulated and verified in its concrete consequences only at a logical level, without this claiming anything about the truth of the hypothesis, applies also to the *il n'y a pas de rapport sexuel*. If there is no sexual relationship, as emerged *intuitively* in the psychoanalytic clinic at a specific moment in history thanks to the discourse of the hysteric, then Lacan can derive a logic of sexuation that accounts for both our structural difficulty with sex and the palliative value of the talking cure. Yet *this logic does not ontologically corroborate the truth of the hypothesis*.

Maybe Lacan's multiple oscillations in this context—including what we could call his relativistic-historicist temptation (e.g., the statements he makes about the harmonious sexual life of ancient China)—are due precisely to his sensing the risk of ending up installing the truth of sexual incompleteness as a truth about truth. The failure to articulate openly and possibly solve such a tension marks, in my opinion, the most noticeable limit of Lacan's theory of sexuation. This is the point where we need to move beyond his work while availing ourselves of its logical impasses as much as of the unacknowledged, or repudiated, extra-psychoanalytic insights prompted by them. In order to do so, it is necessary to transgress the prohibition to venture into an enquiry on the origins of language, or genesis of structure, which he would consider traditionally philosophical, that is, devoted to the discourse of the One.

On this level, we eventually need to confront the if function of the transcendental *il n'y a pas de rapport sexuel* as an *ultimate* conditional truth—on which all other logical conditions are based—that is in itself *unconditionally* either true or false, but, most importantly, remains for us *truly undecidable* with regard to its truth-value. The truth of incompleteness is the transcendental, which is *as such* either true (the truth about the truth of incompleteness) or false, in which case, incompleteness is in the end complete, and the absence of the sexual relationship eventually resolves itself into a relation/*rapport* from the standpoint of *outside* language, that of a God who willingly deceives us. Furthermore, the absence of the sexual relationship could also *equate* as such with a relation/*rapport* from the very standpoint of language, should the latter be inseparable from a God who deceives us by first and foremost deceiving himself. In this case, the conditional truth of the absence of the sexual relationship would ultimately be both true and false at the same time.

In other words, the truth of incompleteness is, for Lacan, a *function*, which, at the same time, amounts to the phallic function as a suturing of incompleteness. For speaking animals, such truth as a function is neither true nor false: this is the outcome of critique. But stopping here only leads Lacan to the two incompatible narratives I have described above, namely, that which absolutizes incompleteness (by tacitly relying on the One) and that which historically relativizes it. To overcome this impasse we have to fully acknowledge that truth as a thus-defined function can nonetheless be *meta-critically* thought as in itself either true, or false, or both at the same time. Undecidability should then make us *decide* for incompleteness, on a level that is no longer logical, but *ethical and political*. That is, we should do *as if* the deceiving God/One (in its two variants) did not exist: in this way the truth of incompleteness is practically absolutized only by acquiring a new and more viable kind of conditionality.

This brief summary of issues I have tentatively explored in the preface and chapter 2 is particularly important insofar as the entirety of Lacan's convincing critique of logical positivism revolves around his assumption that the latter ultimately intends to assert the truth about truth, the truth of hypotheses. Bracketing for the time being the fact that he himself occasionally seems to be taking for granted the truth about the truth of incompleteness (for example, as discussed, when he identifies a lack in the very texture of nature) without tackling the truth of incompleteness at the meta-critical level of the genesis of structure, we should now focus on what Lacan critically perceives to be modern logic's basic error—and as such a profound betrayal of the de-universalized perspective introduced by Galilean science. The key question we should ask in this context is the following: why does he believe that "the position of logical positivism," which he associates primarily with Frege, "is untenable, at least starting from psychoanalytical experience" and its discovery as well as therapeutic manipulation of the unconscious's linguistic disrespect for the law of non-contradiction?[105] First and foremost, because "truth cannot be settled through a yes or no,"[106] an alternative of the kind "it is either true or false," since discourse stands structurally (i.e., synchronically) as a semblance with which truth is indissolubly aligned. Truth does not rest on a primordial dichotomous opposition between true and false propositions but emerges as a truth-effect, a consequence, only thanks to the unchaining of discourse that necessitates a discursive interpretation (one for which, to begin with, it is true that, diachronically, we "cannot say, at the same time, yes and no about the same point").[107]

In other words, logical positivism's mistake amounts to taking truth as an ultimate extralinguistic referent.[108] This leads to a "fabulous paradox," Lacan says: if referring to truth presupposes a division between propositions that can be marked as in themselves true and propositions that can be marked as in themselves false with regard to states of affairs, this means that truth at last amounts to "positing an *absolute false*, namely, a false to which one could refer oneself as such."[109] That is to say, logical positivism's attempt to institute the fundamentals of a meta-language as the true language of language goes together with the exclusion of the relative non-sense from which it itself emerges. For Lacan, "if we start from the principle that something that has no meaning cannot be essential in the development of discourse, we quite simply lose our bearings."[110] Language is in fact structurally incomplete, not-all—as further confirmed by logic's own incapacity to define itself, and by the very possibility of its search for a meta-language, which derives from such an impasse. Hence designation can, in absolute terms, be neither true nor false, but metaphoric, i.e., "it can only be done through the mediation of something else."[111]

As Lacan nicely puts it, "even if I say 'That' [Ça] in designating it"—in pointing at it—"I already imply, by calling it 'That,' that I chose to make it nothing but 'That'"—that is, a metaphor—"even though *that is not That* [*ça n'est pas Ça*]." "The proof is that," Lacan continues, "when I light it [my cigar], it is something different, even at the [linguistic] level of 'That'"—i.e., "That" does not even coincide with "Cigar"—"this famous 'That' which is supposed to be the redoubt of the particular, of the individual. We cannot omit that it is a fact of language to say: 'That.' What I have just designated as 'That,' that is not my cigar [*Ça, ça n'est pas mon cigare*]. That is so when I smoke it, but when I am smoking it, I do not talk about it."[112] All this does not by any means idealistically imply that the signifier, for instance *Ça*, cannot support or evoke a referent as an objective state of affairs, but that its referent can never be the "right one."[113] In this sense, the final referent of language is always the real (of the absence of the sexual relationship) as that which is "impossible to designate,"[114] or, from a slightly different perspective, the phallus that sutures the real into a semblance of linguistic totality while not appearing in language. Lacan stresses this point: "Nothing of what language allows us to do is ever anything but metaphor [...] The something that every word, whatever it may be, claims to name for an instant"—i.e., to denote as a referent, Frege's *Bedeutung*—"can only refer back to a connotation"—i.e., a sense or meaning, Frege's *Sinn*—issuing from a metaphoric replacement. In the previous example, this is the case with the replacement of "That" with "Cigar": *that* can be "That" only as long as "That" can be replaced with "Cigar," while, on the other hand, "Cigar" is not "That," which in turn is not *that* cigar. In the end, "if there is something that may in the final term be indicated as that which is denoted by any function apparelled in language [...] there is only one *Bedeutung, die Bedeutung des Phallus*. It is only there that we find what is denoted by language, but without ever anything answering to it."[115]

We should, however, bear in mind that, despite such a harsh condemnation of logical positivism,[116] Lacan nonetheless regularly praises Frege for his capacity to supersede Aristotelian logic through a formalization of the "empty place" of the letter, the quantifiable _ of the unknown *x* that satisfies or does not satisfy as argument a given function $F(x)$. As I have shown, it is also thanks to this written invention—or, more precisely, the failure of advancing "a correct usage of this language"[117] which would also be able to account for itself qua meta-language—that psychoanalysis manages to denounce the fact that the sexual relationship cannot be written: "Undoubtedly, without a reference to logic, which of course cannot just be to classical logic, to Aristotelian logic, it is impossible to find the correct point in the subjects that I am putting forward."[118]

Lacan's position vis-à-vis logical positivism thus remains profoundly ambivalent, and this can be felt most strongly when he scrutinizes the challenges it only partly poses, in his opinion, for Aristotle. On the one hand, modern logic de-essentializes traditional logic for, as Morel has observed, "Frege has invented a new way of analyzing the sentence, which is different from the Aristotelian [pregiven] decomposition into subject and attribute or predicate," since "the new couple 'function, argument' [...] is *deduced* from the sentence when we decompose it in a certain manner."[119] In starting with the couple subject–attribute, Aristotle's logic presupposes the copula as the singling out of the signifier/verb "to be"; this actually always-already relates subject and attribute as discrete entities—and, moreover, sees the former as a fundamental entity—even when negation is apparently at stake. Such highlighting of being in language—which is not even employed in all natural languages, and which tacitly relies on the assumption that there is a language of being as a whole[120]—is on a first level effectively undermined by logical positivism's "holing" of the sentence.

Yet, on the other hand, modern logic has not been able to think thoroughly and draw all the consequences from the fact that this emptying of the ontological relation presupposed in the copula linking subject and predicate does, with the same move, also implode the privileged axis of Aristotle's logic. According to Lacan, the latter amounts to the "complete homology between universal and particular [propositions], affirmative and negative respectively."[121] More specifically, he believes that, given his highlighting of the copula—and thus of the alleged being of the subject—the only "logical discrimination" Aristotle would think is that of the contradiction between the universal affirmative and the particular negative propositions (i.e., "Every human is mortal" and "There are some humans that are not mortal"). This is to the detriment of the particular affirmative and the universal negative propositions: "I emphasize that at the level of the Aristotelian articulation, it is between these two poles, UA and PN, that logical discrimination is carried out. The universal affirmative states an essence. [...] Nothing runs contrary to any identifiable logical statement whatsoever, nothing, except the remark that 'There are some that ... do not' [*Il y en a qui ... pas*], a particular negative. [...] This is the only contradiction that can be made against the affirmation that it is a matter of essence. And the two other terms are, in the functioning of Aristotelian logic, quite secondary. Namely, 'There are some that do ...' [*Il y en a qui ...*], a particular affirmative, and afterward how can we know if it is necessary or not? This proves nothing. And to say that 'There are none that ...'

[Il y en a pas qui ...], namely the universal negative [...] well, that does not prove anything either."[122]

In order to elucidate this difficult juncture, which Lacan only hints at in a few passages of Seminar XVIII but which, I argue, gives us the rationale of how he contextualizes his logic of sexuation as a logic of the not-all both within and outside the history of formal logic, we need to approach it in two steps—that of his critique of modern logical writing, and that of his new writing. Critically, first and foremost, Fregean logic would not be able to grasp that, once written, a function (such as, in Lacan's example, "numbers that are real") "is what it is," that is, it is neither true nor false.[123] This apparently trivial remark is crucial. If, given a variable/argument qua unsubstantial and unknown x (such as "root of a second-degree equation"), there are cases in which the latter does not satisfy the function F (since there are roots of the second-degree equation that are imaginary numbers which are not part of the function of real numbers), it makes no sense to say that "the function is not always true," or that it is true only on some occasions.[124] This would in fact amount to contaminating function logic with Aristotelian onto-logic, for which the particular negative limits itself to falsifying the universal affirmative as a presupposed essence. Rather, according to Lacan, we should maintain that "as regards the unknown that constitutes the root of the second-degree equation, I cannot write the function of real numbers *to lodge the unknown in it* [function],"[125] i.e., I cannot write that the unknown that constitutes the root of the second-degree equation *is* a real number.

Above all, we have to acknowledge, Lacan insists, that this very state of affairs should not in any way lead us back to Aristotle's universal negative ("No root of the second-degree equation is a real number"), now reshaped as the nonvalidity of the function as such with regard to the argument/unknown—whereby the fact that the function is not always true ultimately involves its absolute falsity (i.e., True and False gives us False). As we will see shortly, this is what eventually happens in logical positivism. In other words, the function of real numbers is as such far from being negated by the inability of the root of the second-degree equation to satisfy it as "lodging the unknown in it." In parallel, as we have noted, the fact that, at times, it does satisfy it is taken by Lacan to be, after all, irrelevant. Lacan's overall argument could thus be summarized as follows: given $\exists x . Fx$, where $\forall x . Fx$ is not given, this means both that (1) I cannot write the function F to lodge the unknown x in it, i.e., I cannot write that x is F; and, at the same time, that (2) I can still write this as Fx, as *function* of x. The problem with logical positivism is, for Lacan, that it renders (1) above as $\overline{Fx}$, as $\exists x . \overline{Fx}$, in the sense that the function would be *as such* negated, which, as we will see, inevitably leads to what he calls the "nonvalue" of the Aristotelian universal negative.[126]

Lacan's phallic logic of sexuation thus adopts Frege's writing while also modifying it in the wake of his theoretical critique of logical positivism's inability to fully surpass Aristotelianism. He does so by focusing on the demise of Aristotle's privileging of the axis between the universal affirmative and the particular negative, as well as on the eradication of the classical understanding of the universal negative. From a more openly psychoanalytic perspective, this primarily involves thinking a new form of the negative—the not-all, or incompleteness of woman—in concomitance with a universal affirmative—the fact that all men satisfy the phallic function—which emerges only through contradiction—the Father as an exception to the phallic function. At the same time, such an operation brings about, against Aristotle, an *uncoupling of existence from essence*, whereby essence is itself de-substantialized: "Essence is essentially situated in logic; it is a pure statement of discourse";[127] or also, being phallic is a semblance. Lacan believes this uncoupling is already somehow anticipated by Freud's juxtaposition of a primordial symbolic affirmation (*Bejahung*) or "judgment of attribution"— the phallic function as castration—that does not have any import for existence and a logically simultaneous negation (*Verneinung*) that "implies the existence of something which is precisely what is denied"[128]—the Father who exists as the noncastrated phallus. Yet beyond Freud, the separation of existence from essence applies here most evidently not only to the Father's symbolic existence as a founding exception to the phallic logic of sexuation, but also and especially to the fact that, although all men are phallic and there is no woman who is not phallic, woman nonetheless exists or, better, ex-sists extra-logically in the real by *not being* wholly contained by the phallic function.[129]

Let us now dwell on these intricate issues as Lacan introduces them in Seminars XVIII and XIX—in a far from systematic and convoluted manner that initially does not hinge on sexuation. Again, his point of departure is the idea that Aristotle marginalizes the particular affirmative and the universal negative propositions up to the point of depriving them of any logical value. As we have seen, following this, the only possible "logical discrimination," "the only contradiction that one can make against the affirmation [of the universal as] a fact of essence" that exists, lies in the particular negative ("some humans are not mortal").[130] Any interrogation of the *particular affirmative* ("some humans are mortal") turns out to be immediately neutralized by the universal affirmative ("every human is mortal"), which, however, tacitly relies on the particular affirmative. Given that Aristotle assumes that the use of "some" carries with it existence, and that the "every" includes the "some," then the "every" assumes a value (e.g., the essence, or essential attribute of mortality) from that which it is not, i.e., an affirmation of existence (of the human being), while *the latter is taken for granted*.[131]

Lacan believes that Frege's formal writing partly manages to break this vicious circle between universality and particularity, according to which the particular takes its essence from the universal that includes it, only because the universal takes its existence from the particular. In fact Frege manages to destabilize the existence of the particular by detaching in the universal affirmative $\forall x$. Fx the unknown x that is held by the quantifier $\forall$ from its being an argument ("human") of the function F ("mortality"); as we saw above, he isolates in the proposition the preliminary "lack, void, hole, or hollow that is made of what must function as argument."[132] This means that x does not have any meaning before functioning as an argument, which, at the same time, calls into question the very idea of the existence of the "some." As Lacan has it, "What is this x? I said that it is defined as a domain. Does that mean [...] that we know what it is? Do we know what man is by saying that *all men are mortal*? We learn something about him by the fact of saying that he is mortal and precisely by knowing that for all men it is true. But before introducing the *all men* we only know his most approximate features and they can be defined in the most variable way."[133] That is to say, there can well exist some x that satisfies the function $F(x)$ but, unless *all* x satisfy it, we know nothing about such a "problematic" x, apart from the fact that there exists some x that, as unknown, satisfies F while others possibly do not.

Lacan contends that, in spite of this advancement, logical positivism has not been able to undermine classical logic's overlooking of the *universal negative*. Since Seminar IX, he has been convinced that Aristotle neglects its potentialities on purpose in favor of a strengthening of the universal affirmative.[134] This would be corroborated by a passage in *De Interpretatione*, where the Greek philosopher states that "it must not be said, *not all men*, but the negation *not* must be added to *man*; for *all* does not signify that the subject is universal, but that he is taken universally."[135] As Morel comments, Aristotle thus solves the question of the negation of the universal, and a fortiori of the way in which one should think the universal negative proposition, which he senses as insidious, by deciding that "if we encounter 'not-all,' we never exit from what we could call the universal point of view. 'All' is a prosdiorism (quantifier) that does not signify a universal 'thing,' but has the function of universalizing the assertion that follows it. 'All' thus remains external to the assertion; it simply renders it universal."[136] This has vast repercussions for how we understand negation, which is thereby restricted to two options: "Either we negate the verb or the copula, but we do not touch the prosdiorisms"—such as in "*All* men are *not* doing well," which is what eventually underlies the universal negative "No man is doing well." "Or the prosdiorisms are modified in the contradiction"—i.e., in the contradiction between the universal affirmative and the particular negative, where "all" is replaced by "some" followed by a negation—"but we remain within the same category, namely, that of the universal point of view. [...] If we translate 'not all men are doing well' [pas tout homme se porte bien] as 'some man is not doing well' [quelque homme ne se porte pas bien], we obtain a particular [negative], which Aristotle situates always within the logic of the universal."[137]

In other words, the particular negative as a negation of universality is itself something that is ultimately predicated of the *universal affirmative*.[138] As Lacan has it in Seminar IX, if for Aristotle "it is not the qualification of universality that negation must relate to," i.e., the negation of the *all* must never be understood as "not-all," then what is at stake in "not all" as the difference between the universal affirmative and the particular negative is merely "something which simply presupposes the *collection* as realized": that is to say, what is at stake in "not all" is the "qualification of the *omnis*, of the *omnitude*" as the "*aliquis, the some man*."[139] Moving from these considerations, Seminar XVIII's later attack on the "homology" between the universal affirmative and the particular negative, as that which prevents any serious consideration of the universal negative and the particular affirmative, seems thus well directed.

According to Lacan, given its meta-linguistic, i.e., universalistic aspirations, the writing of the Fregean function ends up consolidating the "nonvalue" of the Aristotelian universal negative.[140] He grants that, in logical positivism, a given domain x that as such cannot be inscribed in the function F clearly differs from what he calls a "negativized universal" [*universelle négativée*] or *universal* "nil" [*nul*] of the Aristotelian kind:[141] despite the fact that the domain x does not satisfy F, there can well exist, at the same time, some x from that domain that does satisfy it. This approach to the particular affirmative as unknown x is precisely what undermines Aristotle's short circuit between particular existence and universal essence. Yet, more importantly, the noninscription of the domain x in F is nonetheless still written by logical positivism as $\forall x . \overline{Fx}$. What is annulled is the function.

While for Lacan the function "is what it is" and always remains such, according to this writing it would seem that, at least for the domain x, the function is *as such false*, which takes us back to the Aristotelian "nonvalue" of the universal negative: here, eventually, "whatever x you speak about, one must not write $F(x)$"[142] independently of whether there exists some x that satisfies F while remaining an unknown. Rendering "the domain x does not satisfy F" as $\forall x . \overline{Fx}$ is therefore "inept";[143] it reiterates an a priori exclusion of the possibility of negating the universality of what, in the passage quoted above, Aristotle calls "the subject."

If, on the other hand, we render "the domain x does not satisfy F" as $\overline{\forall x} . Fx$, i.e., negate the domain x, this cannot be read as "not all the x in the domain" / "not every x in the domain," at least if we take seriously logical positivism's tentative departure from Aristotle in considering existence as only a *de-essentialized* unknown. Unlike Aristotelian logic, there is no self-sufficient particular negative here that, as existent, ends up qualifying the universal it actually presupposes to begin with. The negation of the domain can therefore refer only to "not-all the domain," i.e., to the domain as itself not whole.

More specifically, Lacan believes that writing "the domain x does not satisfy F" as $\forall x . \overline{Fx}$ does not allow us to properly understand what happens when, dealing with the articulation of a phallic function that rests on the *absence* of the sexual relationship, we are faced with the question of "what cannot write itself in the function F(x) starting from the moment when *the function F(x) is itself not to be written*";[144] that is, of how to inscribe woman as *not-all* phallic within the phallic function, within a function that writes precisely the sexual relationship as that which cannot be written.

In other words—and here we move to the pivotal point where Lacan joins his critique of formal logic with his own new writing of the logic of sexuation—in order to grasp the phallic function as a nonrelational sexual relation that sutures the *il n'y a pas de rapport sexuel* we need first and foremost to give some value to the universal negative, cease to neglect it. Such value should go beyond the alternative between true and false values. In the first instance, Lacan does this by highlighting what he calls a "discordant" negation[145] that, instead of negating—or better, as he has it, foreclosing—the function ("the function will not be written. I want to know nothing about it"),[146] negates the universal quantifier: "It is not from *all* x that the function Phi of x inscribes itself," i.e., $\overline{\forall x} . \Phi x$.[147] He then applies the same argument to existence, and negates the existential *quantifier*: "It is not from *an existing* x that the function Phi of x inscribes itself," i.e., $\overline{\exists x} . \Phi x$.[148] Evidently, the crucial idea Lacan intends to put forward here—at a moment when, in Seminar XVIII, he is only beginning to construct the formulas of sexuation—is that *the phallic function Φ of x can be written independently of whether x is whole and independently of whether x exists. Incompleteness and inexistence do not refute the function but lie at its core.*

The negation of the quantifier that articulates this independence should therefore be conceived as discordant precisely in that it introduces a disjunction between the quantifier and the possibility of writing the function—or of writing it as negated, but nonetheless not falsified/foreclosed. That is, "it is not insofar as there would be a *for all* x, $\forall x$, that I can write or not write Φx," which is to say that the function Φ of x can also be written when $\forall x$ is negated.[149] Similarly, "it is not insofar as *there exists an* x, $\exists x$, that I can write or not write Φx," which is to say that the function Φ of x can also be written when $\exists x$ is negated.[150] Unlike the foreclosing negation of logical positivism, which ultimately stipulates that a universal essence cannot be written in the case of something that is nonetheless already taken to exist particularly,[151] albeit as unknown, Lacan's discordant negation refers primarily to the symbolic "existence of writing" [*existence de l'écrit*]¹⁵² of a function, the phallic function, that does *not* stop writing (since, once written, "it is what it is") what *cannot* be written (the sexual relationship).

We will now need to look closely at how the not-all (or, negation of universality) and the negation of existence (which in turn paves the way for the positing of *one* exceptional existence that *negates* the function and only *thus* supports universality as a semblance) acquire a preponderant role in the formulas of sexuation and their subversion of the Aristotelian square of opposition. For Lacan, the four propositions (universal affirmative, particular affirmative, particular negative, universal negative) are logically related to each other in a new configuration which, instead of "building a consistent logic of the universal and of the principle of contradiction [...] puts into perspective the rests, impasses, and waste of this formalization," thus giving rise not to "a system but [to] a series of points of impossibility and paradoxes, that need to be collected attentively."¹⁵³

More precisely, the dominant axis that, in Aristotle, united in a "homology" the universal affirmative to the particular negative as its only *apparent* contradiction becomes a "wall" that, in marking the absence of the sexual relationship between man and woman, divides the logic of sexuation into two noncomplementary (nonhomologous) halves.¹⁵⁴ Conversely, the phallic function partly supplements for such *il n'y a pas de rapport sexuel* thanks to the establishment of an indirect relation that links the sexes logically along a ground-breaking reconceptualization of the so far curbed axis between the universal negative and the particular affirmative, which renders obsolete these very phrases, along with those of universal affirmative and particular negative. In the place of the universal negative and the particular affirmative Lacan thinks the not-all of woman, of her domain, as incompletely contained by the phallic function, and the exceptional existence of the Father as not subjected to the phallic function.¹⁵⁵

CHAPTER 4

THE LOGIC OF SEXUATION

4.1 THE TWO FORMULAS OF SEXUATION: ESSENCE AND EXISTENCE

In the early 1970s, Lacan puts forward four formulas of sexuation that write the logical impossibility of writing the sexual relationship, and the way in which the (masculine and feminine) subject is nonetheless tentatively sexed through the phallic function, that is, the function of castration. The first two formulas, located on the left side one above the other, inscribe man as $\exists x . \overline{\Phi x}$ ("There exists a man for whom the phallic function cannot be written") and $\forall x . \Phi x$ ("For all men the phallic function can be written"). The other two formulas, located on the right side one above the other, inscribe woman as $\overline{\exists x} . \overline{\Phi x}$ ("There does not exist a woman for whom the phallic function cannot be written") and $\overline{\forall x} . \Phi x$ ("For not-all of woman the phallic function can be written").

$$\exists x . \overline{\Phi x} \qquad \overline{\exists x} . \overline{\Phi x}$$
$$\forall x . \Phi x \qquad \overline{\forall x} . \Phi x$$

First of all, we should stress once more that, taken in isolation, the x in the formulas of sexuation stands for an unknown that becomes a quantifiable (masculine or feminine) subject only as an argument/variable of the phallic function. Prior to his inscription in the phallic function, the individual speaking animal is merely what Lacan called in earlier Seminars an undetermined *asujet* deprived of any preestablished attribute, passively subjected to language and the symbolic laws that stem from it, which he initially encounters in the guise of already existing kinship relations and family complexes that appear inscrutable to him. In this regard Lacan's formulas advance nothing other than a reelaboration through a formalized writing of his own version of the Oedipus complex and its resolution, as elaborated especially in Seminars IV and V. The logic of sexuation thus amounts to a transcendental logic of subjectivation revolving around a symbolic identification with the phallus, one which works in different ways for man and woman, yet at the same time always presupposes the other sex; as we have seen, man becomes a man only against the background of woman, just as woman becomes a woman only against the background of man.

What is especially important to bear in mind here is that the phallus acts as a common third term for both sexes while not implementing any direct mediation between them: man does not relate to woman *via* the phallus, but only insofar as she refers to it while he also refers to it, and vice versa. More precisely, as Le Gaufey has rightly noted,[1] the phallic function should primarily be understood in terms of the establishing of a relation between the speaking animal (which, lacking any innate essence, cannot originally even be regarded as a speaking *being*) and *jouissance* (which is sexualized only through the phallic function) as elements belonging to disparate series, and *not* between man and woman. In fact both man *and* woman stand as x, or speaking animal, in the formulas. Having said this, and going beyond Le Gaufey, we should add that, with the same move, the phallic function as a *generic* species-specific relation between the speaking animal and *jouissance* (masculine and feminine phallic *jouissance*, feminine nonphallic *jouissance*, and the structural mirage of an absolute *jouissance* liberated from the phallic function are all inscribed in the formulas) also supplies a stand-in for the absence of the sexual relationship that somehow manages to relate *man and woman*, but only in a nontransitive and asymmetrical fashion *as x*. This is the case since: (1) it is impossible for Φ to fully represent woman—which would allow us to write her as y and obtain a binary function with two variables, $\Phi(x,y)$, whereby x and y could phallically be determined as the domains "man" and "woman";[2] (2) there is no independent feminine function—such as *yin*, ♀, or XX—that would be alternative to the phallic one yet bi-univocally connected with it.

For the most part, commentators tend not to address these important preliminary issues, since they focus exclusively on the final version of the formulas ($\exists x.\overline{\Phi x}$; $\forall x.\Phi x$; $\overline{\exists x}.\overline{\Phi x}$; $\overline{\forall x}.\Phi x$), introduced by Lacan in the third lesson of Seminar XIX, and further developed with respect to how one should read them together throughout this Seminar, Seminar XIXB, and Seminar XX.[3] Such an approach overlooks the long and convoluted gestation of the logic of sexuation,[4] which we have already partly explored by examining Lacan's challenge to the Aristotelian notions of existence and universality through his critical appropriation of Frege, and which we will continue to analyze in this chapter. What I find most striking is that very little, if any, attention has been paid so far to the fact that, toward the end of Seminar XVIII, Lacan already proposes two formulas of sexuation for man and woman, which he explicitly defines as such:[5] $\overline{\exists x}.\Phi x$ and $\overline{\forall x}.\Phi x$. The first will no longer openly appear in later Seminars, and the negation of existence will be attributed to woman in the guise of a double negation that also concerns the function, i.e., "there does not exist a woman for whom the phallic function cannot be written." In spite of this, I am of the opinion that this early account is crucial for a correct understanding of the four formulas as the final writing of the phallic function.

Following Lacan's own description of the negation of the existential and universal quantifiers as a discordant negation, which he considers to be his innovative contribution to logic, I propose to read in the first instance the formulas from Seminar XVIII as follows: "It is not insofar as *there exists some man* that I can write or not write Φx"; on the masculine side of the four formulas, the function will be in fact both written and written as negated irrespective of $\overline{\exists x}$. Similarly, "it is not insofar as there would be a *for all women* that I can write or not write Φx"; on the feminine side of the four formulas, the function will be again both written and written as negated irrespective of $\overline{\forall x}$. Here, two specifications should immediately be made. First, note how the formula for woman involves in this case a discordant negation that questions the traditional Aristotelian universal affirmative "all women are ...," while in Seminars XIX, XIXB, and XX, the same formal writing will refer primarily to the "all of woman." The way in which Lacan moves logically from one understanding of the negation of the feminine universal to the other, which actually surpasses any clear-cut distinction between the universal and the particular, will be clarified in due course. For the time being, let us limit ourselves to pointing out that statements such as "we cannot say *all women* [*on ne peut pas dire toutes les femmes*],"[6] or "there is no *every woman* [*il n'y a pas de toute femme*]"[7] do not mean exactly the same as statements such as "woman is not whole [*la femme n'est pas toute*]."[8]

Secondly, and most importantly at this stage, $\overline{\exists x} . \Phi x$ and $\overline{\forall x} . \Phi x$ are to be taken, in my view, as the axiomatically intuitive starting points of Lacan's logic, the formal notations of the way in which the *il n'y a pas de rapport sexuel* manifests itself blatantly to the speaking animal precisely through its sexually subjectivizing *participation* in the phallic function. To put it bluntly, Lacan considers "There does not exist *some man*" and "There is no *every woman*" as self-evident given the flagrant failures of our everyday sexual lives, and the associated common knowledge we tend to have, in various degrees, about our inadequacy at fulfilling our supposedly reciprocal sexual roles as man and woman.[9] This matter of fact is in turn further supported by the discoveries, as well as the many impasses, of the psychoanalytic clinic and its literature. On the one hand, no *particular* man does embody the Father as the bearer of the phallus: "What is a Father? [...] The Father is only ever a referent. We interpret one or the other relation with the Father. Do we ever analyze anyone qua Father? Let someone bring me a case-study!"[10] On the other hand, in accordance with Freud's *Was will ein Weib?* and the inconclusive debates on feminine sexuality of the 1930s, women cannot grasp "what they want" *as a whole*, that is, beyond their singular involvement with the phallus; the supposed shared essence of their sexuality that would be distinctively feminine remains an "enigma" even to the expert eye of the most consummate female psychoanalyst.

Let us now look more closely at the couple of intricate sentences from Seminar XVIII where Lacan addresses $\overline{\exists x} . \Phi x$ as the formula of man's sexuation. In line with the way in which we have tentatively defined it above, he indeed begins by claiming that what the formula expresses is that "it is not as particular that he is [phallic]."[11] Rather, "man is [the] phallic function insofar as he is *every man*," that is, as universal.[12] Yet, as we saw in chapter 3, Lacan's logic of sexuation started off precisely from the difficulty of assigning any universal essence to man who, like woman, can initially be conceived only as an unknown *x*, and from a critique of the "confusion" between essence and existence in Aristotle's logic.[13] He briefly reminds us of this: "As you know, there are the greatest doubts to be had about the fact that *every man* exists."[14] If man existed straightforwardly as *every man* he would possess a predetermined, innate or instinctual sexual essence logically equivalent to the *yang* or the XY postulated by Taoism and modern biology; consequently the phallus would work not as a third independent term but as an inherent attribute of man as noncastrated (i.e., all men would have *the phallus*). A sexual *relationship* would thus be established in the guise of "every man is phallic; every woman is not phallic."[15]

Lacan at this point ingeniously proposes that it is only by means of what he calls a *touthomme*,[16] a "whole man"—and this neologistic difference in writing turns out to be crucial—that we obtain the universal *tout homme*, that is, the *every man* through which particular men will in turn retroactively be inscribed in the phallic function. How should we understand the *touthomme*? First, "it is a signifier, nothing else,"[17] a pure symbol that supports the otherwise indefinable man of *every man*: "The man of *every man* [...] implies a function of a universal that precisely gives him as a support only his symbolic status, namely that something is enunciated as the *man*."[18] Secondly, the *touthomme* is therefore a mythical, artificial creation of man—or, better, of the generic speaking animal *x*—without which man would not be a man: "Nothing can be grounded of the status of man [...] except by constructing artificially, mythically, this *whole man*."[19] It could as such be identified with the Father of the horde, the one who has all the women (*toutes les femmes*), or, more precisely, "the one who is capable of satisfying the *jouissance* of all the women"[20] (we will return to Lacan's disparaging assessment of the Freudian story, and the specific value he gives to this universal feminine as impossible). Thirdly, and most importantly, the *touthomme* founds the universal *tout homme* without which man could not be inscribed as particular in the phallic function only by *negating* this very function, that is, by *symbolically existing* as the non-castrated phallus, as the exception that does not only confirm the phallic rule for all other men (the "sexual law" of castration that comes in the place of the missing "sexual relationship")[21] but, in terms of what we have just explained, establishes it. Lacan will consequently write the whole man, or Father, as $\exists x . \overline{\Phi x}$.

At this stage, we could also conceive of the *touthomme* as an existence without essence—inasmuch as the phallic function is negated, the whole man is not like all other men—that determines every man as $\forall x . \Phi x$, namely, as an essence without existence—or "being without being,"[22] since the phallic function is nothing but a semblance, sustained only through its negation. The *touthomme* achieves this precisely by *contradicting* $\forall x . \Phi x$, a contradiction that could also succinctly be rendered as "the phallus is not phallic" (i.e., not castrated).

To sum up and return to the formula of man's sexuation as found in Seminar XVIII ($\overline{\exists x} . \Phi x$, or, "It is not insofar as *there exists some man* that I can write or not write Φx"), according to Lacan, not only does there not exist some man who embodies the *phallus*—in the sense that there would exist some man able to *be* the whole man, or Father, for whom Φx *cannot* be written—but there does not even exist some man who is by himself *phallic*, i.e., castrated, as a particular man for whom Φx *can* be written. This being said, on closer inspection it would possibly be more correct to argue that the particular men subsumed under the essence without existence of the universal *every man* do after all acquire a phallic *existence* through the existence without phallic essence of the *whole man*.

Lacan undoubtedly believes that "in order to stand up, the universal ['every man is phallic'] does not have the need for the existence of any man."[23] The same point is reiterated even more strongly when he tackles $\overline{\exists x} . \Phi x$ directly and reads it as: "There does not exist an *x* that satisfies the function [...]. That there does not exist any, it is from this that one formulates what concerns man."[24] However, he then continues this same sentence by stating: "But precisely here the negation [...] is only posited by having first of all put forward that there exists *some man* [quelque homme]."[25] We could still claim that this *some man* concerns in all likelihood the *whole man* that exists as an inherent exception to the phallic function—although the use of "quelque homme" apropos the *whole man* is somehow infelicitous, given that he is also repeatedly defined as the "not-more-than-one" [*pas-plus-d'un*].[26] Yet in the very same passage with which we started our analysis, Lacan unequivocally also maintains that "*some man* is [phallic]," which obviously cannot refer to the nonphallic *whole man* and seems to oppose $\overline{\exists x} . \Phi x$, only to specify promptly that "it is not as particular" that the *particular*—*quelque homme*—is phallic, but as universal.[27] While acknowledging Lacan's oscillations on this issue,[28] it is reasonable to interpret *"some man is phallic"* as $\exists x . \Phi x$, a *particular existence* which is not readymade as in Aristotle (who assumes that the use of "some" carries automatically with it existence) but follows logically from the contradiction between the essence without existence of $\forall x . \overline{\Phi x}$ and the existence without essence of $\exists x . \overline{\Phi x}$.

In other words, on the one hand, particular men are phallic only insofar as every man is phallic and not because they would phallically exist as particular. On the other, as David-Ménard claims, "man exists through his way of posing an exception with regard to what encloses him in the universal of the masculine," that is to say, by "always taking himself a little for the father of the horde, even if he knows that every man is castrated."[29] But to this remark we should add at once that such a particular existence emerges only because a particular man is and remains at all times nothing but an element of the universal *phallic* set, as itself determined by an exceptional nonphallic element that does not belong to it. Otherwise, we run the risk of mistakenly understanding man's existence as a masculine variant of the feminine being not-all phallic, which clearly goes against the grain of Lacan's teaching. The "all phallic" includes the "nonphallic" that does not belong to it without for this reason turning into a "not-all phallic."[30]

In the end, man thus exists as a particular, he manages to escape his condition of *asujet*, but just as a phallically sexed subject originating from the contradiction between universal and existential judgments, between "every man is phallic" and "there exists one and only one man who is not phallic"; moreover, this phallically sexed subject bears the mark of his indetermination by existing solely as a *barred subject $. $\exists x . \Phi x$ will indeed disappear from the final version of the formulas, which nevertheless presuppose such a discordant negation of man's existence. One could even venture the suggestion that this disappearance is already anticipated by Lacan's own choice of the *indicative* verbal mode ("there *exists* some man") in Seminar XVIII's formula of man's sexuation, which we are now in a position to rephrase in a more comprehensive manner. While, in the case of woman, it is not insofar as there *"would be"* in the *conditional* a "for all women"—which there is *not*—that I can write or not write Φx, in the case of man, it is not insofar as particular men *nonetheless exist*—in a sense different from that of Aristotle, for whom particularity automatically brings with it existence—that the phallic function can be written or not. Rather, it is insofar as there is *every man* that it *can* be written, and insofar as there exists *one whole man* that it *cannot* be written, *as a result of which* (as a result of the writing of the function as entwined with the writing of its negation—whereby, contra logical positivism, the function cannot be said to be absolutely true or false) particular men do ultimately exist.[31]

As we will now see in detail, if man exists (as a contradiction), it is woman who famously "does not exist" for Lacan. While commentators usually associate this statement with Seminar XX, he already puts it forward in Seminar XVIII.[32] Let us begin by pointing out what is obvious: her formula from Seminar XVIII ($\overline{\forall x}.\Phi x$, i.e., "it is not insofar as there would be a *for all women* that I can write or not write Φx") will be incorporated in the four formulas from Seminars XIX, XIXB, and XX. How should we interpret this continuity—which, as noted, also entails a displacement, since $\overline{\forall x}.\Phi x$ will prevalently be read as "for not-all of woman the phallic function can be written"? And how does it lead to the promulgation of *la femme n'existe pas*? Lacan's axiomatic starting point—again, supported in his opinion by common knowledge and the clinic—is that "there is not *every woman* [*il n'y a pas de toute femme*],"[33] there is not a feminine universal that can be inscribed in the phallic function (such as that $\forall y.\Phi y$), or not inscribed in it as an indicator of an alternative sexual function that could be written otherwise (such as that $\forall x.\overline{\Phi x} \rightarrow \forall y.\Omega y$). This latter point remains for the most part implicit in Lacan's argument, aside from when he ridicules in passing the alleged yin or XX functions,[34] but I regard it as crucial.

More specifically, he begins his investigation by returning to Freud's myth of the Father of the horde, in order to develop it in a critical way. In *Totem and Taboo*, Freud would already indicate the impossibility of the sexual relationship precisely via the negation of the feminine universal: the "all women" [*toutes les femmes*] is indeed what is at the start precluded to the horde by the presence of the Father, and, after his killing, what each particular member of the universal band of brothers must as such renounce.[35] But, according to Lacan, Freud would not acknowledge this as the impossibility of the sexual relationship. That is, he would rather give the opposite impression that the Father, whom the father of psychoanalysis regards as a really existing prehistorical being,[36] embodies or lives the sexual *relationship*, instead of merely founding its phallic *semblance* as an exceptional logical existence deprived of essence.[37]

While Lacan's deconstruction of *Totem and Taboo* is limited to short hints spread across a number of different lessons of Seminar XVIII, we can nonetheless reconstruct it precisely through three consecutive stages, which increasingly challenge Freud.[38] First, "what the myth of enjoying all women designates, is that the there is no *all women* [*toutes les femmes, il n'y en a pas*]. There is no universal of woman."[39] If we read between the lines of Lacan's own interpretation, the myth therefore basically shows that "every man" stands as that which does not have access to "all women." Moreover, we should also infer from it that "all women" is graspable and negated as such only retrospectively following the killing of the Father; before this, "every man" and the concept of universality *tout court* are in fact not yet constituted.[40]

Yet, second, all the above is "written in what Freud writes [...] and one just has to read it" provided one realizes that the negation of *all women* is given in *Totem and Taboo* without putting forward the structural impossibility of the sexual relationship, on the basis of which only such a negation can be conceived correctly.[41] From a slightly different perspective, and expanding on Lacan, Freud's speculation would remain confined to the level of the deadlock of defining feminine sexuality as a *positive* whole. Or, better, he would chauvinistically decide to solve it by answering the hysteric's *Was will ein Weib?* with the infamous *Ablehnung der Weiblichkeit* from "Analysis Terminable and Interminable," the "*repudiation* of femininity" shared by men *and* women, as his last pronouncement on the topic.[42] To put it bluntly, what women would ultimately *all* want is *not* being women; this would be their essence. Clearly, such a predicament does not preclude the possibility of postulating an all-enjoying Father, and of deriving from it a functioning masculine sexuality whereby every ("healthy," non-neurotic) brother would moderately partake of his potency through the resolution of the Oedipus complex and the acquisition of genital sexuality. Against Lacan, man would relate here to woman through the Father/phallus as a *direct* mediator through which *all* women would be taken, and take themselves, as that which, by definition, negates itself (first and foremost by means of so-called "penis envy").[43] Freud would thus confuse the negation of universality with a universal nil; for him, women form a *negative* whole.

Thirdly, and most importantly, if we understand Freud's misogynous bias, and thus supersede his reductive reading of the myth of the Father of the horde, which, for Lacan, speaks for itself beyond the author's intentions, we come to the conclusion that what is at stake in it is not only the negation of the feminine universal, but, concomitantly, the fact that the Father does not have a partner. To express it better: the Father has "all women" (as such negated for "every man") since "the whole woman" epitomizing womanhood has always-already disappeared. As in all myths, Freud would hence mitigate a real impossibility of which he seems unaware—namely, the absence of the primordial Father's companion—with a fabricated impossibility, that is, "own[ing] all women," which "is manifestly the *sign* of an impossibility."[44] In this way "the whole woman" is materialized as "all the women of the Father" (all the women the Father had once upon a time), and in turn both prohibited—as "*all* women"; no brother can have all women, not even after the killing of the Father—and distributively awarded to every man—as "all *women*"; more precisely, "for each [man] there is his each [woman]," who bi-univocally answers to him as "*his* woman."[45]

Although Lacan will articulate this complex point about the solitude of the Father in a logical form only in Seminar XIX apropos the "there does not exist a woman for whom the phallic function cannot be written," in Seminar XVIII he already emphasizes that the negation of the feminine universal extrapolated from the hesitations of *Totem and Taboo* ultimately involves the fact that "it is unthinkable to say *The* woman [*La* femme]."[46] What is unthinkable is a universal essence of womanhood, which, one should add preemptively, as in the case of the founding of "every man is phallic" (of *The* man) on "something enunciated as the *man*," as the *whole man*, would be obtained only via the existence of a woman, the *whole woman*, who negated the phallic function.[47] On the other hand, what Lacan deems thinkable is "*a* woman [*une* femme]."[48] As *a* woman, woman evades both the vicious circularity between the existence of the *some* and the essence of the *all* of Aristotle's logic, *and* man's logic of exception qua its hidden support—which, as we have seen, preserves in the end both the universal and the particular affirmatives thanks to a detour through the Father. While later Seminars mainly develop *une femme* in terms of *singularity*, at one point in Seminar XVIII such a singularity is, interestingly, also presented as a "multi-unity";[49] this is a definition we will have to bear in mind especially when considering how, despite the absence of the sexual relationship, the phallic function nonetheless manages to let woman somehow be counted by man.

Lacan's sarcastic evaluation of the "buffoonery" of the "hyper-myth" of the Father of the horde[50] identifies, thus, through the negation of the universal feminine, a basic transcendental kernel regarding the real as the impossible of the sexual relationship, which would be in Freud more than Freud himself, and now puts us in a position to read correctly the otherwise enigmatic explanation of the formula of woman advanced in Seminar XVIII. What "it is not insofar as there would be a *for all women* that I can write or not write Φx" ultimately means is, not surprisingly at this point, that "*The* woman [*La* femme] cannot occupy her position in the sexual relationship"—or, better, in the sexed liaisons supported by the phallic function. "She cannot be it," Lacan adds—i.e., be *woman* qua the impossibility of the universal "*The* woman"—"except under the heading of *a* woman [*une* femme]."[51]

Moving from such a definition of woman's sexuation as *une femme*, we can also attempt to elucidate provisionally the logical passage from $\overline{\forall} x$ as "not for *all women*" (i.e., as the negation of *toutes les femmes*) to $\overline{\forall} x$ as "for *not-all* of woman" (i.e., as the negation of *la femme toute*) in the following way: woman is *not-all* (*pas-toute*) insofar as there is not a universal set (*toutes les femmes*) to which she could belong that would provide each particular *x* with an essence of womanhood Ω, and, concomitantly, insofar as there is no possibility of turning such an unknown *x* into a discrete element *y* of the phallic universal either. This second impossibility emerges clearly through Freud's impasse, where *toutes les femmes* is given only through a negative essence. That is, all women are phallic by being nonphallophores, and, most importantly, all women are such by rejecting this state of affairs. Thus, all women are *essentially* not women; all *y* are as such elements *y* of the phallic set only by *not* being *y*, by refusing themselves as *y*, i.e., by envying those who have the phallus.[52] Like

Freud, Lacan believes that woman is inscribed in the phallic function—outside of which there is neither man nor woman, and within which only man is, albeit as $.[53] But unlike him, he also deems that woman is caught in it merely as *a* woman, where, as we have just seen, her singularity cannot be thought as a whole particular element belonging to a universal, but as a being *not-all* phallic.

To sum up, it is as not-*"all women"* that woman is singularly not-all phallic. David-Ménard is therefore right in suggesting that there are two meanings of "not-all": "'Not-all' [pas tout] refers to the logical fact that women do not form a whole. But when Lacan comments on what he writes, the 'not-all' acquires a different meaning: it is not all of a woman that is bound to the phallic."[54] I would further argue that, as I have shown, not only are these two meanings related—the second being derived from the first—but, for the same reason, they also prevent us from understanding the "not-all" in terms of the Aristotelian distinction between universality and particularity. In this regard, I consider the rationale of Le Gaufey's admittedly meticulous reading of the *pas-tout*, which is aimed at conceiving it as a new kind of particular negative, to be highly problematic.[55] For his part, Lacan increasingly tends to avoid using Aristotle's terminology, and whenever he feels obliged to resort to it for the sake of illustration, he invariably identifies the "not-all" as a universal.[56] This is not to say that this barred universal could not be read as a singular replacing a particular, given that, as we have seen, the impossibility of "*The* woman" equally applies to not-"all women" and to "*a* woman."

As for the explicit textual articulation between the two meanings of the "not-all," although he never explains it thoroughly, Lacan nonetheless highlights what is at stake in Seminar XIX—tellingly, as he returns for a moment to his critical discussion of *Totem and Taboo*. Here he claims that "the story of the original man who would precisely enjoy what does not exist, namely, all women," is a myth about a man who enjoys what is "not possible, not simply because it is clear that we have our limits, but because there is no *all* of women [il n'y a pas de tout des femmes]. Nothing can appropriate the *all* to this not-all [rien ne peut approprier le tous à ce pas-toutes]."[57] It is easy to see how this ambiguous "there is no *all* of women" [il n'y a pas de tout des femmes]—as different from the far more straightforward "there is no *every* woman [il n'y a pas de toute femme]" from Seminar XVIII—and, what is more, its translation into a hyphenated plural *pas-toutes*, could equally be read as "there is no 'all women'" *and* as "women are singularly not-all." This short passage hints precisely at what we have tried to uncover, namely, the logical passage from the "it is not insofar as there would be a *for all women* that I can write or not write Φx" to the "for not-all of woman the phallic function can be written."

In this context, Lacan also importantly specifies that the *pas-toutes* should in no way be read as a particular negative, since "contrary to the function of the particular negative, that is to say, that there are *some* of them which are not so, it is impossible to extract such an affirmation from the *pas-toutes*. It is reserved to the *pas-toutes* to indicate that *somewhere she* [woman] *has a relation to the phallic function.*"[58] Before moving on, in the rest of this book, to explaining how precisely this link is established as an amorous sexed liaison that is not a sexual relationship, first, between the two formulas of sexuation, and then, in a more comprehensive way, between the four formulas of sexuation—a link which, as phallic function, nonetheless opens up the not-all of woman to another *jouissance* beyond the phallus—one final point needs to be made concerning the statement "woman does not exist" drawing on these provisional conclusions.

Commentators tend to identify *la femme n'existe pas* directly with the negation of feminine universality. Evans offers us a good example of this approach: "As is clear in the original French, what Lacan puts into question is not the noun 'woman,' but the definite article that precedes it. In French the definite article indicates universality, and this is precisely the characteristic that women lack. [...] Hence Lacan strikes through the definite article whenever it precedes the term *femme*."[59] This statement is only partly correct, and raises more questions than it solves. For instance: Why does Lacan claim at times that "woman does not exist" (*la femme n'existe pas*), where the negation clearly focuses on existence, while at others he rather maintains that "There is no such thing as The woman" (*Il n'y a pas La femme*)[60]—or also, similarly, that "it is unthinkable to say The woman"—where what is negated is primarily universal essence?[61] Is there any difference between the two? Unlike Evans, who takes one assertion to be simply the "rephrasing" of the other, I think what is at stake in such an apparently trivial rewording is a significant intersection of distinct logical and ontological considerations on femininity, although undoubtedly these pronouncements hold only if they are read together.

I would argue that we can uncover four different—albeit contiguous—meanings of *la femme n'existe pas*, which are not necessarily emphasizing the striking through of *La* as a universal. To begin with, we should pay attention to the fact that, in Seminar XIX, precisely when he is trying for the first time to inscribe the two formulas of feminine sexuation in the phallic function, Lacan—surprisingly—seems to privilege a *third* formal notation for woman, which he then abandons: $\overline{\exists x} . \Phi x$.[62] Note that, importantly, this is exactly the same formula with which he started his analysis of man's sexuation in Seminar XVIII ("It is not insofar as *there exists some man* that I can write or not write Φx"). While, as we have seen, particular men do eventually exist as phallic—although only *after* the writing of the function ("for all men Φx can be written") which goes together with its being not written ("there exists one man for whom Φx cannot be written")—in the case of woman, $\overline{\exists x} . \Phi x$ means that there does not *at all* exist some *particular* woman who is castrated, or phallic. Or, better, it is not insofar as there *would exist* some particular woman that I can write or not write Φx. Rather, it is insofar as *singular* women are not-all (*pas-toutes*) castrated, or phallic, that the function can be written or not. But, conversely, this also entails—and here the dismantling of Aristotle's logic as sustained by the logic of exception is brought to completion—that there does not even exist *one* particular woman who is *not* castrated (which is precisely what the second formula of feminine sexuation expresses). It is thus possible to infer that all singular women are not-all castrated, provided that the first "all" in this sentence is itself conceived outside any notion of universality. More precisely, then, all singular women are not-all phallic, but as such they never add up to a *whole*; or also, *each* singular woman is not-all phallic, in a manner—so-called "multi-unity"—that does not allow us to deduce "*all* women are (as not-all) phallic" from "there does not exist a woman, *not even one*, who is not phallic."[63] We are facing a subtle and resourceful series of arguments, which we now limit ourselves to introducing by taking a step back and looking at its specific implications for the negation of the existence of woman.

What Lacan explicitly puts forward in defining *woman's* $\overline{\exists x} . \Phi x$ is that "there does not exist an x that is such that can satisfy the function Φx."[64] Shortly thereafter he explains that this is the case since "leaving aside an insignificant little nothing [*un petit rien insignifiant*]"—we shall revisit in due course this crucial onto-logical expression as Lacan's most accurate characterization of the *void*—"they are not castratable."[65] In other words, in complete contrast to the *Ablehnung der Weiblichkeit*, "the essence of woman [...] is not castration,"[66] for, as we have explained at length, there is not a universal "for all women" that is subjected to the phallic function. Yet—and this should also be evident by now—Lacan also regards such a negation of universality as the other side of the fact that women "*have to do with castration*" as *pas-toutes*.[67] Hence, to sum up, we could suggest that woman is *not* essentially, i.e., universally castratable only to the extent that she is nonetheless not-all *castrated*[68] as a singular that, at the same time, evades any notion of the particular. Emphasizing *both* consequences of the mutual elimination of universality and particularity on the feminine side, not only does woman not exist as a particular castrated subject, but, by the same token, there does not even exist *one* particular noncastrated woman who would negate the universality of the phallic function. This is the case since, for her, there is no such universality in the first place, nor an alternative feminine universal (again, there does not exist a feminine exception to the phallic function, whether, as in Freud's myth, as the harem of partners qua nonphallus—pure "minus"—of the Father/phallus—pure "plus"—or, as in Taoism or modern biology, as his "vaginal"[69] companion supporting an independent—cosmological or chromosomic—function of womanhood).

Returning to *la femme n'existe pas* and its overlapping meanings, which critics fail to acknowledge, we are now able to advance that on a first level, that of $\overline{\exists x} . \Phi x$, the statement means that—as for man—contra Aristotle, the existence of the *some* cannot be taken for granted, namely, it is not insofar as there exists x that the phallic function can be written or not: here "'some woman' does not exist," but remains x. Yet on a second level, that of $\overline{\forall x} . \Phi x$, unlike man, for woman there is not an "all women" through which the existence of the particular affirmative would nonetheless be recuperated retroactively through a universal essence: here "*The* woman (or *W*oman) does not exist"; there does not exist an essence of woman (or, "it is unthinkable to say *The* woman"; "There is no such thing as *The* woman"). But, on a third level, that of $\overline{\exists x} . \overline{\Phi x}$ —and this is possibly the most important meaning of the statement, the one that most directly involves the specificity of woman (differently from the first level, which also regards man) and the negation of her existence (differently from the second level, which also concerns essence)—there is no "all women" precisely insofar as there is not an exceptional existence that negates the phallic function and would as such found universality (and consequently the existence of the *some*, as well as in turn that of the *all*) as in the case of man. Here "*woman* does not exist." Contra Evans, Lacan does indeed call into question the noun "woman," or, more precisely, adopting the terminology he uses when defining the masculine exception, he strikes through "something that is enunciated as the *woman*," the *toutefemme*, or whole woman, who would couple with the mythical, albeit symbolically existing, Father as the *touthomme*, or whole man.[70]

Finally, however, *la femme n'existe pas* in various guises because, as anticipated in chapter 1, she, rather, *ex-sists*. In her singular being not-all *phallic*, unlike man, whose existence is sustained in a tortuous manner only through a symbolic subterfuge, a contradictory semblance, woman nonetheless ex-sists *as real* "beyond the phallus"—her not-all standing for the not-all, that is the real, of the phallic function or symbolic order as such. Thus feminine ex-sistence—or Other *jouissance*—and in-existence—the, evocatively, "insignificant little *nothing*" through which she is caught by the phallus—"divide" woman, Lacan will argue, into an *undecidable* being in a way that is very different from the manner in which castration splits up man into a *contradictory* being. This being said, as we will see, it is precisely *in-existence* that lays the foundation of an ersatz sexed liaison as amorous bond between the logical necessity of the Father and the ontological impossibility that he may ever find his feminine matching pair.

4.2 THE HYSTERIC AND THE FATHER

As I have repeatedly pointed out, for Lacan there is no sexual relationship, in the sense that it stands for a logical *impossibility*, but there are sexed liaisons sustained by the phallic function. The phallic function is, however, universally *possible* for man through the *necessity* of the exception (the Father) only inasmuch as woman is *contingently* inscribed within the phallic function. Here we should always bear in mind that "sexual identification does not consist in believing oneself to be a man or a woman, but in taking into account, for the boy, that there are women, and for the girl, that there are men":[71] if the boy cannot take into account women he remains an undetermined *asujet*; the not-all of woman is a precondition of man's universality (and vice versa). Readers of Lacan who lose track of this run the risk of falling back onto Freud's *Ablehnung der Weiblikeit*, and the ontologically essentialist and chauvinistic view of sexuality it entails.

While the specific modality in which woman is contingently taken within the phallic function is investigated in detail starting from Seminar XIX—a topic to which we shall turn in the next section—in Seminar XVIII, Lacan already discusses woman's relation to the phallus in innovative logical terms precisely when he advances his two formulas of sexuation. He does so by focusing on the hysteric and the Father. It is the hysteric's love for the Father, and concomitant confrontation with him, that allows for the establishment of sexed liaisons that compensate for the absence of the sexual relationship. Yet—and this is crucial—such a love/confrontation leads itself into a sexual deadlock that founds sexual liaisons only to the extent that it preserves the *il n'y a pas de rapport sexuel* at another level. In fact, on the one hand, the Father qua bearer of the phallus is just a disembodied symbol: as we have seen, no man is a Father, and the Father ultimately amounts to a *name*,[72] "the *man*," "the *whole* man," which can hence also be understood as a *number*, the One exception founding the rule. On the other hand—and the importance of this definition has been underestimated so far—"the hysteric is not *a* woman."[73] Thus woman as undetermined *x* becomes a woman inscribed in the phallic function against the background of man—who is himself inscribed in it through woman—thanks to the hysteric who "introduces" her therein, Lacan says,[74] but who is not herself a woman.

To put it bluntly, the hysteric chooses to say "yes" to the phallic function, and therefore paves the way for sexed liaisons. Yet at the same time, the hysteric remains outside of sexuation, since woman is such in the phallic function only inasmuch as she says "yes" *and* "no" to it (where the "and" is additional, not disjunctive). How should we understand this paradox? In brief, *woman as a woman is introduced in the phallic function by the hysteric's failure to be* "every woman," that is, to answer the question "What is *The* woman?" by recovering an essence of womanhood. The hysteric wrongly believes that such presumed essence would institute her as the partner of the Father, i.e., as the existence of the whole woman. From a slightly different perspective, we could suggest that the hysteric does not realize that men as essentially phallic/castrated can only take themselves "a little" for the Father, and, what is more, that this happens through contradiction, or also, the (initial) severance of existence from essence.

Lacan explicitly articulates the hysterical position vis-à-vis woman in four different passages scattered across Seminar XVIII, which must be read together. First, "it is in relation to *every woman* that *a* woman locates herself."[75] Secondly, "*every woman* is the enunciation whereby the hysteric is decided as a subject."[76] But thirdly, as discussed, "there is no *every woman*."[77] Consequently, hysteria is "the point where is articulated the truth of [the] failure [of] the sexual relationship"[78]—since there is no essence/universality of woman matching that of man. Before addressing further these complex arguments, which Lacan only delineates and I am attempting here to systematize, we need to take a step back and consider how he accounted for sexuation prior to developing the logic of the not-all. This will in turn enable us to show that if the hysteric is not a woman, conversely, woman is not a hysteric, although the impasse of hysteria is needed for the emergence of *a* woman as woman's only way to be (not-all) sexed.

Already in Seminar VI, Lacan proposes that while man is not without having the phallus, woman is the phallus without having it.[79] In brief, man has the phallus via an identification with the Father only insofar as his essence is contradictorily determined as a negation (hence he "is not") by castration.[80] On the other hand, by herself identifying with the Father (since "there is no symbolization of woman's sex as such")[81] woman lacks the phallus, yet this very lack, equally caused by castration, is also a form of possession with regard to man. Lacan advances this in straightforward terms as early as Seminar IV: "Not having the phallus symbolically also means participating in it out of absence and therefore, in a way, having it"; or also, "given that she is taken up into the intersubjective relation, there is for man, beyond her, the phallus that she does not have, the symbolic phallus, which exists here as an absence."[82] I have attempted to explain this issue in detail in *Subjectivity and Otherness*: in a few words, insofar as man is such only as castrated, he does not have woman's not-having as a form of symbolic having, thus his desire depends on such a lack; even possessing the phallus (+) always means lacking the oppositional − on which the + depends.[83]

Hence, as Lacan does not fail to remind us fifteen years later in Seminar XVIII, castration ultimately amounts to the fact that the other sex indicates the phallus, that is, the signifier of an impossible absolute *jouissance*, the *jouissance* that *would be* if there were a sexual relationship, yet *also* concomitantly of the phallic *jouissance* that replaces it. In other words, in spite of their co-dependence, here we should carefully distinguish between the Phallus with a capital P, that is, the Father qua exceptional existence that does *not* abide by the phallic function, and *thereby* founds it, and the phallus as that which man is for woman and woman is for man as defined by the phallic function, or function of castration.[84] While I thus agree with David-Ménard in saying that "in Lacan the phrase 'phallic function' has a contradictory sense depending on the context, as if it referred at the same time to the two propositions of the 'man' position"[85]—i.e., to both "There exists a man for whom the phallic function cannot be written" and "For all men the phallic function can be written"—it will also be apparent by now that we are not in the least dealing with a conceptual confusion, but, as we have seen, with the fact that the phallic function is itself sustained by a logical *contradiction*, which is accurately reflected in the terminology.

Moving from these premises, the basic distinction between the hysteric and woman, or, better, between their respective, albeit entwined, identifications with the Phallus/phallus—which are as such both required for the establishment of an indirect, asymmetrical, and unmediated relation with the male sex[86]—could as an initial approximation be expressed as follows: if woman identifies with "being the phallus without having it," the hysteric identifies with "not having the phallus." Or also, as Colette Soler puts it, while the former embraces a "phallicism of being" which leads her to "turn[ing] herself into the objectal guarantor of man's phallic lack," the latter rather sides with a "phallicism of having" that associates her with "what is subjected to castration."[87] Elaborating on this, we could suggest that the phallus that woman *is* without having is the *phallus of man as castrated*, i.e., the "minus" that the phallic "plus" will never have. Yet the phallus that the hysteric, like woman, does *not* have is in her case, unlike woman's, primarily associated not with man's castrated "plus," but with the *Phallus of the Father as noncastrated*.

We need now to specify in what precise sense woman is the phallus without having it, while the hysteric does not have the Phallus, as well as how it is the latter that paves the way for the emergence of *a* woman.

1. Lacan's rendering of woman as "being without having" in his early work is still partly dependent on Aristotle's totalizing onto-logic, since this phrase does not account for her being phallic only through *incompleteness*. We must therefore rectify it and state that not-all of woman identifies with "being the phallus of man without having the phallus." Our decision to merge Seminar VI's formula of feminine sexuation with the much later negation of woman's universality is textually supported by Lacan's continuing to speak, in Seminar XVIII, of "the phallus [...] not introducing [...] in the gap of the sexual relationship [...] two [natural] terms definable as male and female, but a choice between terms [...] of a very different *function* that are called *being and having*."[88] This passage appears in the very same lesson in which he discusses for the first time the idea that there is no "*every woman*" and that *La femme* does not exist. The phallic

function $\Phi(x)$ formalizes the not-all of feminine sexuation also in the guise of being and having.

2. The hysteric does not partake of woman's not-all, since, for her, not having the Phallus entails not being *tout court*; she is simply *not*. Or better, in not accepting being subjectivized as "not-all phallic" (which goes together with a "beyond the phallus") in the name of the universal "every woman," she *is not-at-all*, she embodies an "empty parenthesis."[89] We could hence advance that if on the one hand, eventually, not-all of woman "is without having," and man "is *not without* having" (where incompleteness and double negation signal well the intricate fragility of their reciprocal sexual *determination*), on the other, the hysteric "*is not without having*," again, in the sense that she could be only by having the Phallus. On this level, she remains closer than man and woman to the truth for which, given the absence of the sexual relationship, the speaking animal remains as such an *undetermined x*.

3. The hysteric's identification with not having the Phallus of the Father and not being finally amounts to a desire to *be* the Phallus/Father (the Father qua bearer of the Phallus), or rather, to be One as his fusional partner—as shown by psychoanalysis since its first clinical case histories, the hysteric in fact identifies with the Father. On this level, the hysteric remains closer than woman to *semblance*, insofar as woman is, rather, identified as not-all. The hysteric stands here as a "man-sexual," in that she ultimately shares with man a desire for totality, for the existence of a uni-versal essence, where the One exception would not found the $+/-$ of the phallic function (the minus of the plus and the plus of the minus) but obliterate it. Man's and the hysteric's similar amorous striving for the Phallus (love is indeed understood as "the desire to be One") provides the most basic, although insufficient alone (since the hysteric is not a woman) palliative for the establishment of a phallic liaison between the sexes as unrelated.

Lacan thus, somewhat confusingly, applies "being the phallus" to both woman (her sexuation) and the hysteric (her failed sexuation which is, however, necessary for woman's sexuation). The distinction I propose between the phallic phallus and the nonphallic Phallus proves useful for clarifying this point. As Soler has highlighted, woman's identification with being the phallus of man does not, strictly speaking, "indicate an identification but a place, that of the complement of masculine desire. The formula of fantasy, $\$ \lozenge a$, visualizes this asymmetry between the desiring subject and the partner as the complementary object of his desire"[90]—which has imaginary, symbolic, and real (qua object of *jouissance*) values. I would name woman's occupation of this objectal place "identification with the phallus." Here we should stress that woman's "*being* the phallus of man" does not go against the fact that, as we have seen, she possesses, as *a* woman, neither essence nor existence, but rather confirms it: being the phallus of man merely means being the phallic/castrated minus that the phallic/castrated man as plus does not have.[91] Moreover, once again, woman is *not-all* "being (the phallus of man) without having it." To put it better: as discussed in the previous section, woman is without having it only with regard to "an insignificant little nothing." Consequently, we should also note that insofar as "*being* the phallus of man" reduces the phallic function to such an insignificant little nothing seen from the exclusive viewpoint of *man*, that is, to the fact that man desires and woman consents to being desired (ultimately as the object *a* of man's *jouissance*), the identification at stake leaves open the question of a "properly feminine desire."[92] Beyond Soler's observations, this concerns both woman's nonsexual *jouissance* beyond the phallus ($\cancel{La} \to S(\cancel{A})$), whereby she ex-sists, *and* her *active* sexual involvement with phallic *jouissance* ($\cancel{La} \to \Phi$), whereby she in-exists.

On the other hand, the hysteric's identification with being the Phallus/Father entails a pure desire *to be*, as opposed to woman's identification with being the phallus as an insignificant desire to enjoy by making man enjoy—which is far from exhausting her phallic and nonphallic enjoyment. As Soler puts it, this also means that the hysteric's identification with the Phallus "excludes identifying oneself with the object of [man's] *jouissance*."[93] In other words, woman is (not-all) the phallus *for man*, while the hysteric wants to *be* the Phallus *without or even against man*, that is, by means of a direct identification with the Father. This accounts for the reason why she approaches (or rather, fails to approach) man by means of a peculiar twofold strategy; while she seduces man insofar as she confounds him (his +) with the Phallus (the obliteration of the +/−), at the same time, she inevitably ends up refusing him to the extent that she is perfectly aware that man does not have the Phallus, and that there is no man who is a *whole* man. Woman acknowledges that there is *no more than one* [pas-plus-d'un][94] whole man, as well as that her man can thus not be Him—or also that there cannot be a man who is what Lacan calls "the *man*" as "a signifier, nothing else." In so doing she replaces her not having the phallus with her being not-all taken as the phallus of man qua castrated man. On the contrary, the hysteric's reluctance to be the object of man's castrated *jouissance* stems from her assumption that there must be *at least one* [au-moins-un][95] *man* who is a whole man, and that her man must be Him, yet inevitably does not succeed in this task, and should constantly be reminded of it.[96]

The hysteric's desire for totality therefore goes even beyond that of man, with whom she ultimately cannot connect qua castrated "every man." As a "man-sexual" oriented toward the uncastrated Father she is in fact, unlike man, also "outside sex."[97] As long as man undergoes castration he manages to situate himself within sex; or better, as we have seen, the *possibility* of his universal sexuation amounts to nothing other than the contradictory split between castration and a belief in the Father/Phallus. For the hysteric, the very same split gives rise instead to an unsurpassable *impossibility*, which leaves her without sex. More accurately, the impossibility of being the noncastrated partner of the Father, of *unifying* with Him, anchors her tightly to the impossibility of "there is no sexual relationship," which is in part sublated by man and woman through the phallic function. It is as if the hysteric remained nondialectically fractured between her identification with not having the Phallus—which makes her take the "insignificant little nothing" of woman's castration far too seriously—and her concomitant identification with being— or wanting to be—the Phallus. Man himself identifies with not having the Phallus and with wanting to be it (both his universal essence and his particular existence are indeed convolutedly derived from the Father). Yet unlike the hysteric, on the one hand, he is able to mitigate castration by also identifying with having the phallus (+). On the other hand, most importantly, his identification with the Father is an identification with the logical necessity of an *exceptional "one more"* [un-en-plus][98] contradictorily added to the universal law of castration, which as such *sustains* the +/−, rather than subverting it once and for all like the hysteric's supposedly embodied "*at least one*."

By identifying first and foremost with the speaking animal's irremediable subjection to castration, or absence of the sexual relationship—and in this regard all feminine and masculine *subjects* are as such to different extents hysterical—the hysteric's strictly speaking asexual role in sexuation is thus limited to soliciting man's desire to be One, that is, his love, while subtracting herself from the position of his object of *jouissance*. Yet, as I have stressed, Lacan sees the hysteric's extreme not-having—and her consequent renunciation of participating in sexed, i.e., phallic enjoyment—as a fundamental precondition of woman's not-all "being without having," and consequently of the emergence of the phallic function *tout court*, which alone allows a compensatory relation between the two sexes. Why is this more precisely the case? In a seminal passage of Seminar XVIII, Lacan spells out that the hysteric has the merit of establishing an (as yet asexual) connection with the Phallus, with the *whole* man, *independently of man* (of his contradictory logic of exception/castration whereby every man is phallic only insofar as there exists one whole man who is not phallic). In his own terms, "what the hysteric articulates is clearly that as regards constructing the *whole* man [touthomme], she is just as capable as the *every man* [tout homme] himself. [...]. So then, because of that, she does not need him."[99] In other words, the hysteric does not need man as "every man" qua castrated, and as such nonexchangeable with the *whole* man, to establish her desire *to be* the Father/Phallus's partner as the *whole* woman (but also at the same time as *The* woman, or *W*oman), whereby the essence of "every woman" would exist through the hysteric.

However, given that "there is no 'every woman,'" no universal essence of womanhood—not even via the route of an exceptional logical existence that would contradict the law of castration, as for man—Lacan adds the important point that, on the other hand, "if *by chance*" the sexual relationship—qua sexed liaisons that partly compensate for the absence of the sexual relationship—"interests [the hysteric], she has to be interested in this third element, the phallus"[100]—i.e., the phallic "plus" that man has as opposed to the Phallus that obliterates the differentiality of the $+/-$. Moreover, "since she can only be interested in it through the relationship to *man* insofar as it is not even sure that there is even one"—i.e., insofar as no man is a whole man although he issues from the latter's purely symbolic existence—the hysteric's "whole politics will be turned toward what I call *having at least one* [au moins un] *of them*"[101]—i.e., toward finding a man who embodies the whole man. Finally, it is precisely this hysterical search for the "at least one" (which Lacan now writes *hommoinzin*, a merging of *homme* and *au moins un*) or better, its inevitable deadlock, that stands out as an "inaugural" moment that "situates *woman* with respect to the key third term of the phallic function."[102]

Due to the complexity of the arguments at stake, which is increased by some dubious editorial decisions in the published version of Seminar XVIII,[103] let us unpack this further. Here Lacan delineates three logical—and retroactive—stages by means of which the hysteric as the failure of "every woman" paves the way for woman as "*a* woman." We should distinguish:

1. The purely hysterical autonomous relating to the Phallus, or *whole* man, as a castrated desire-to-be that mistakenly takes itself as an essence and is uninterested in really existing men;

2. Following the impossibility of "every woman" and "the whole woman," the contingency of the hysteric's interest in the phallus as owned by "every man," and her parallel overlapping of "every man" with the transformation of her desire-to-be into the desire to have at least one man who is a whole man;

3. Woman's own constitution as a singular *not-all* "being without having the phallus" on the very basis of the *at least one* (qua the repressed persistence of hysteria in woman as *a* woman, we could say). The latter is, however, in woman's case sublated into *a no more than one*, and as such both associated with really existing men *and* dissociated from them—in a way that echoes the contradictory relation of "every man" to the exceptional Father as a *one more*.

More specifically, singular women emerge vis-à-vis a symbolic *no more than one* by letting it take them only "one by one"—as opposed to as a hysterical alleged One. At the same time, they found sexed liaisons with really existing, castrated men as "every man," in the hope of finding the man who will love a woman as his "one and only."[104] On the other hand, what is again crucial to highlight when focusing on the hysteric is her irremediable asexual fracture, and the importance this has in the end for sexuation, and hence subjectivation *tout court*. Tackling from a slightly different angle the hysteric's flawed dialectics of not-having the Phallus while concomitantly wanting to be the Phallus, we could suggest that she implodes as a subject precisely through a correspondence, or rather, a short circuit between her making the *at least one* subsist *irrespective of man*—that is, irrespective of his contradictory logic that masks castration through an exception, which she constantly works to expose and ridicule—and her searching for the *at least one* inevitably *in man*. Man is in this respect unacknowledged as castrated, confused with the Father, and ultimately reduced to an *impotent* Father. Confusing the *at least one* with the *no more than one*, that is, her man with the Father—by both degrading the Father to "every man" and potentially dignifying "every man" as a Father[105]—leads the hysteric, after all, to embrace the cause of the *no one*, even in the guise of giving up copulation *tout court*. We could also call it the cause of the *no-body can truly be One (with me)*, which thus reminds the phallicized sexes of the truth of the not-two, of the persistence of the absence of the sexual relationship in spite of the phallic function.

And yet the impasse of the search for this *at least one* never to be found among really existing men, with whom the hysteric would like to couple as the whole woman giving existence to "every woman" (to "every woman wants to be the Phallus"), is nonetheless the "inaugural" moment of the phallic function, Lacan concludes. This is the case in the sense that not only does the hysteric's unsatisfied desire play the role of the "functional schema" of woman,[106] but because of this, more generally, "without the hysteric there would have never come to light what is involved in what I am writing as Φ of x"; man himself can be inscribed in $\overline{\Phi x}$ as $\forall x . \Phi x$ only insofar as woman is inscribed in it as $\overline{\forall x} . \Phi x$ through hysterical nonsatisfaction.[107]

In other words, psychoanalysis claims that it is the hysterical "outside sex" that in the first instance sustains logical quantification.[108] The *at least one* of the hysteric establishes sexed subjectivation as a counting that revolves around a suturing of the absence of the sexual relationship through different figures of the One—namely, the *no more than one* of woman's incompleteness, and the *one more* of man's contradiction. Lacan explicitly maintains that the hysteric's belief in "every woman," in *The* woman, which imposes "the passage to being" (i.e., her desire to be the Phallus as the fusional partner of the Father), allows "*a* woman [*une femme*] [to be] connected with a *no more than one* that locates her in [the] logic of the successor."[109] This is the logic whereby woman can make herself be singularly counted "one by one" [*une par une*] as not-all "being the phallus of man without having it." As we will see in the conclusion, woman as phallic thus stands for the one, *and* again one, *and* again one, etc.—for the repetition of the zero counted as one which is, however, irreducible to the one—that allows man to move from one to two, three, four, etc.

More precisely, and this seems to me the tortuous but fascinating and convincing point of arrival of Seminar XVIII's logic of sexuation—which will be clarified numerically and onto-logically in the following Seminars—"the hysteric locates herself by introducing the *no more than one* from which each woman [*chacune des femmes*] is instituted through the route of the *it is not from 'every woman'* [which should also be read as *it is not from 'all of woman'*] *that we can say that she is function of the phallus*."[110] Yet precisely insofar as the hysteric identifies with "every woman" and refuses to understand the *at least one* as a disembodied *no more than one*, the very process through which she institutes woman defines her as a failed nonwoman: "The hysteric is not *a* woman."[111] Or also, more comprehensively, "that it is from *every woman / all of woman* [that we would say that she is function of the phallus], it is there that [the hysteric's] desire is made, and this is why this desire is sustained by being unsatisfied, it is that *a* woman results from it, whom the hysteric could not be in person."[112]

To sum up, with *a* woman the *at least one* the hysteric relates to as *every woman* (the "at least one really existing man must be a Father!")—which alone can initiate logical quantification, and hence sexuation/subjectivation for the two sexes—is brought down to the level of the *no more than one*. The latter can then overlap with man's *one more*, since both amount to the symbolic exception of the Father/Phallus; from now on Lacan numerically conceives it in terms of "There's such a thing as One" [Y a d'l'Un]. It is through Y a d'l'Un that really existing men are universalized as not being the *whole* man, as "all men are phallic," and singular women make themselves be counted one by one as "not-all of woman is phallic." Leaving aside for the time being the question of how precisely this overlapping unfolds along the noncomplementary vectors $\Phi \leftarrow \$ \rightarrow a$, for man, and $\cancel{La} \rightarrow \Phi$, for woman, we now need to tackle three final issues concerning the hysteric. These are the ontogenetic value of her unsuccessful quest for universality as applicable to each singular woman; Lacan's radical departure from Freud in considering her difference from woman; her ontological status as pure in-existence.

The first point has remained implicit throughout our exposition, and now requires additional explanation. When discussing his two formulas of sexuation in Seminar XVIII ($\overline{\exists x} . \Phi x$ and $\overline{\forall x} . \Phi x$; "It is not insofar as *there exists some man* that I can write or not write Φx" and "It is not insofar as there would be a *for all women* that I can write or not write Φx") Lacan makes it clear that "the negation [of the quantifier] has here the function of *Verneinung*, that is, it is not posited before having advanced that there exists *some* man, whereas it is in relation to *a every woman* that *a* woman is situated."[113] In other words, following the initial meaningless encounter with sexual difference as already symbolically present in the adults surrounding them, and prior to their own subjectivation as, respectively, "all men are phallic" and "not-all of woman is phallic" (both entailing a repressive negation that founds the gap between consciousness and the unconscious as either a masculine *Spaltung* or a feminine "division"),[114] boys and girls go through an *affirmation*. This is a primordial act of symbolization whereby the former directly identify with the *some man* who has the Phallus, as yet to be properly referred to as an exceptional *one more* (and thereby perceived as an encumbering and menacing pure "plus" with whom they compete), while the latter identify with the *every woman* who does not have it, which thus makes them embrace (what will be) the *hysterical* position.

Here Lacan's logical considerations should also be interpreted from the angle of a concrete *ontogenetic* experience with which will-be women and will-be men are faced. The still unsexed, presubjective speaking animal as *x* is initially introduced to sexuation either as a failed woman hysterically searching for the essence of *The* woman or as an impotent man overshadowed by the existence of the *whole* man. This first time of sexuation already implies a certain circulation between the sexes: the question of hysteria (which is itself a question about the Father in the guise of "Does man exist?") arises for girls as long as the question of the Father (which is itself a question about hysteria in the guise of "What does *Woman* want?") arises for boys, and vice versa.

Focusing on the feminine side of this process, what should interest us the most is that, in Seminar XVIII, Lacan seems to concede that the original (proto-)symbolic moment of woman's sexuation is the affirmation of the *every*, of "every woman is castrated." Most importantly, the girl's inevitable affirmation of "every woman is castrated" amounts in the end to an affirmation of *absolute negation*, since, unlike the case of adult men—who are also all castrated—she cannot partake of the nonphallic exception that contradictorily sustains the law of castration as its inherent transgression (which is as such yet to be established even for boys). Woman's first access to sexuation/subjectivation is given through a *pure minus*.

From a slightly different perspective, we could say that *all* women are hysterical before becoming not-all, namely, not-all castrated—and thus, strictly speaking, women. Conversely, each *a* woman has once been—and to a certain extent continues to be—a hysteric, which is not, however, to say that *a* woman is merely a hysteric. As Soler points out (without engaging with Seminar XVIII): if, on the one hand, "hysteria encourages a confusion with the feminine position," on the other, Lacan's primary concern is to address the question of "femininity in its difference from hysteria."[115]

This leads us straight to our second point. For Lacan, the hysteric wants to be *every woman*, *The* woman as universal—and hence she is not a woman, since woman is such only as *a* woman, although *a* woman emerges exclusively through the ontogenetic impasse of hysteria (of *every woman's* clearing the way to woman as ⧸a). In opposition to this, as discussed, Lacan believes that for Freud every woman in the last instance does not want to be a woman, that is, every woman is hysterical. Or also, we could advance that the hysteric as conceived by Lacan equates with the abortive woman who identifies with what is, for Lacan, Freud's idea of woman. Here we should keep in mind Freud's *Ablehnung der Weiblickeit*, the alleged refusal of femininity for which *all* women would be taken, and take themselves, as that which, by definition, negates itself (especially through "penis envy").[116]

As discussed, for Lacan, the hysteric's identification with not-having the Phallus, as diverging from woman's identification with not-all "being the phallus of man without having it," is concomitant with her desire to be the Phallus. "Every woman is castrated" goes together with "every woman should not be castrated"; the hysteric aspires to exist as *every woman* embodying the alleged essence of femininity Ω, as the fusional partner of the Father/Phallus. But given that there is no Ω, the hysteric can at most only fake being *every woman* precisely as the *harem* (the pure "minus") *wholly subjected* to the mythical Father/Phallus (the pure "plus"), that is, in line with Freud's rejection of femininity, as a negative *universality*.

Therefore, the hysteric eventually returns to the girl's ontogenetic point of departure ("every woman is *castrated*")—which woman shares during the Oedipus complex but successively overcomes through the not-all. The hysteric, however, modifies the girl's position precisely by masking the negation of feminine universality—which woman, on the contrary, assumes as singular ⧸a —in the guise of what we could call the *antinomic affirmation* of absolute negation: the "not-at-all" is affirmed as "every woman *is* castrated."

We could thus add—and this is our third conclusive remark on the crucial role the hysteric plays in the logic of masculine and feminine sexuation while remaining herself "outside sex"—that she embodies the "There does not exist a woman for whom the phallic function cannot be written" ($\overline{\exists x} . \overline{\Phi x}$) *without* also concomitantly embodying the not-all, the "For not all of woman the phallic function can be written" ($\overline{\forall x} . \Phi x$), and thus without being a woman. In brief, either woman is not-all or she is hysterically not-at-all, in which case she mistakes the absence of a feminine exception to the phallic law of castration for a form of negative universality. As not-all phallic, woman both in-exists as ⧸a $\rightarrow \Phi$ (in relation to *man* thanks to the indirect mediation provided by the Father) and *ex-sists* as ⧸a $\rightarrow S(\bcancel{A})$ (in relation to *her* Otherness "beyond the phallus"). These are the two sides of *a* woman. The hysteric is needed for the emergence of a woman, but she *merely in-exists* at the level of "There does not exist a woman for whom the phallic function cannot be written" vis-à-vis the Father as "There exists a man for whom the phallic function cannot be written." In other words, she does not partake of ex-sistence, which is itself a precondition for relating as in-existence to *really existing* men as castrated.

Ultimately, the hysteric thus fully identifies with the o as bi-univocally *coupled* with the 1. She proposes herself as the One's vanished *partner*, whereby the "not-at-all" could nonetheless itself be counted as a negative whole. Although, as Lacan warns us, it is tempting to "love the truth that the hysteric incarnates,"[117] namely, the translation of the logical absence of the sexual relationship into the physical/affective materialization of woman as an empty set, such truth is not really truthful. This is the case since it eventually proposes yet another way to avoid the irremediable incompleteness of the two as not-two, that is, the irreducibility of the feminine Other to "another one," in any of its forms, including the zero. The zero of in-existence—which, it is important to stress, *supports* sexuation—should, on the contrary, rather be considered as "the truth of lack, which consists in the fact that 2 *lacks* 1."[118] What is lacking is Woman as the "One-missing" [l'Une-en-moins], or also, the "one-less" [l'une-en-moins] woman that forever separates counting woman one by one, as *a* singular woman, from her alleged universality. Woman thus does not allow us at any point to add the Other to the One.[119]

4.3 THE FOUR FORMULAS OF SEXUATION: MODALITY AND NUMBER

Seminars XIX and XIXB offer the most in-depth discussion of the four formulas of sexuation, i.e., Lacan's formalization of the phallic function as *Homo sapiens'* fundamental logic of subjectivation. This discussion is then by and large taken for granted in Seminar XX's schema of sexuation, where what is at stake is primarily an exploration of man's phallic love for woman and woman's concomitant Other *jouissance* "beyond the phallus."[120] In ... *ou pire* and *Le savoir du psychanalyste* Lacan not only significantly expands on man's phallic universality ("For all men the phallic function can be written") and woman's not-all ("For not-all of woman the phallic function can be written") but also, going beyond Seminar XVIII, fully unravels the status of the exception to the phallic law ("There exists a man for whom the phallic function cannot be written"), which nonetheless founds it through contradiction, and of the feminine *negation of the exception* to the phallic law ("There does not exist a woman for whom the phallic function cannot be written").

This unpacking aimed at explaining how the four formulas—and hence the "sexual values"[121] of man and woman who do not preexist the phallic function—fit *together*, and cannot be obtained in isolation from each other, is carried out especially by means of an investigation into the logical and extra-logical status of *number* as well as a subversion of Aristotle's *logical modalities*. The former revolves around the *theorem* "Il y a de l'Un," "There is something like/of the One," or better, "The One *happens*" (whereas the One is *not*), which is derived from the *axiom* of the absence of the sexual relationship. What is involved here is both a definitive de-mythicization of the Freudian Father as the embodied One, and a further complication of the tripartite understanding of the One as "at least one," "no more than one," and "one more" which Lacan advanced in Seminar XVIII in terms of the precondition for subjectivation/sexuation. In short, "the One is not Being, it *makes* Being."[122]

As for the subversion of logical modalities, this focuses precisely on how the *Il y a de l'Un* should be grasped by juxtaposing its necessity with a structural impossibility—without which the One would not happen in language. With this move Lacan unveils the fact that "the alternation of necessity, contingency, possibility and impossibility is not in the order given by Aristotle"—who opposes what is necessary to what is contingent and what is possible to what is impossible—since what has logical priority "is the impossible, that is, in the end, the real" (i.e., the real impossibility marked by "There is no sexual relationship").[123]

In this light, it is also crucial to bear in mind that, in corking the impossibility of the sexual relationship while also reproposing it at another—sexed—level, the phallic function does not allow man to relate to woman via the Phallus—that is, via the necessity that, as happening of the One, arises within the phallic function. The Phallus is not a pacifying *mediator*, whereby the phallic function would give rise to a sexual *relationship*. The phallic function allows man to approach woman only insofar as she relates to the Phallus in a way—contingent singularity—that is logically different to the one in which he relates to it—possible universality, which stands as such in contradiction to the necessity of the exception to the universal.[124] In other words, both sexes are sexed and thus emerge as masculine and feminine subjects exclusively to the extent that they symbolically identify with the Phallus—which from now on, in line with Lacan, we will mostly refer to in terms of the necessity of the One. That is, $\forall x . \Phi x \to \exists x . \overline{\Phi x}$; $\overline{\forall x . \Phi x} \to \exists x . \overline{\Phi x}$. But this does not entail $\forall x . \Phi x \to \exists x . \overline{\Phi x} \to \overline{\forall x . \Phi x}$ nor $\overline{\forall x . \Phi x} \to \exists x . \overline{\Phi x} \to \forall x . \Phi x$ as phallic mediation. With regard to the other sex, the phallic function and the necessity of the One as one of its structural components rather locates *Homo sapiens* as a being of language in $\exists x . \overline{\Phi x} \leftarrow \forall x . \Phi x \to \overline{\forall x . \Phi x}$, in the case of man, and in $\exists x . \overline{\Phi x} \leftarrow \overline{\forall x . \Phi x} \to \forall x . \Phi x$, in the case of woman, where the two sets of relations cannot be given independently of each other, and, furthermore, should also take into consideration $\overline{\exists x} . \overline{\Phi x}$. We should tentatively associate this fourth formula with the impossible (one of the chief purposes of Seminars XIX and XIXB we will then have to explain is Lacan's articulation of the link *and* the gap between impossibility and inexistence as both designated by the negation of exception). Last but not least, let us also not forget that, due to the fact that sexuation amounts to an asymmetrical *phallic* function in which the symbol/signifier of the Phallus ultimately issues from the *Gestalt* of man's sexual organ, the feminine sequence emerges only thanks to the hysteric, her not being *a* singular woman but a "*man*-sexual" who in vain attempts to collapse the distance between the Father and every man—i.e., in searching for the "at least one," she does not accept the phallic logic as contradictory.

More generally, we could suggest that Seminars XIX and XIXB put forward three increasingly detailed logical explanations (in lessons III, VII, and XIV) of how the "bandaging" provided by the phallic function, which can be written as the precarious sticking together of the four formulas, allows a "circulation" between the sexes, yet does not establish a "relation with the [other] sex."[125] In what follows, I will reconstruct the first two explanations in a step-by-step fashion; the third and more complex explanation will be dealt with in the conclusion. This will also oblige me to make some significant detours to further clarify the import of Lacan's original take on number and modalities, which are his privileged tools for constructing the four formulas. Although we have already approached these matters from different angles, in order to cover them one final time in a more exhaustive manner it is important, first, to briefly recap the main directions of Lacan's overall project in the early 1970s.

As he programmatically states at the very opening of Seminar XIX, the main—theoretical and clinical—task of psychoanalysis is "to go without any ceremony to the hole in the system" of knowledge (and of language *tout court*), that is, to the real.[126] This, he claims, can be accomplished through logic, which thus means that we should not embrace any form of mystical "non-knowledge" [*non-savoir*].[127] Rather, we should endorse a certain "function of knowledge" as a "knowledge of truth" that ultimately amounts to nothing other than *saying* the absence of the sexual relationship as a real hole/void.[128] However, such knowledge of truth [*savoir sur la vérité*] that says there is a real hole/void in knowledge cannot be the truth of knowledge [*vérité sur le savoir*].[129] In other words, truth can only be half-said, since as soon as the knowledge of truth utters "It is true that there is a real hole/void in knowledge" it inevitably presents itself as a truth of knowledge, which as such is no longer truthful. Yet—and this specification is crucial—half-saying the truth of the absence of the sexual relationship as a real hole/void in knowledge is the best we can say. All other sayings are *worse*.[130] Not only do they confuse the knowledge of truth with the truth of knowledge (a confusion which half-saying the truth cannot itself fully avoid; one is tempted to suggest that it can half-avoid it …), but also tend in varying degrees to replace truth with the mirage of absolute knowledge as the supposed whole truth about truth, granted by one ultimate signifier.

In line with this, Lacan can argue that the four formulas as a symbolic articulation of the real hole/void are to be considered as a way to *escape fantasy*.[131] The link between the barred subject S and the object *a* in fantasy is in fact the (always insufficient) containment, already operative at the level of the unconscious, of the truth of the absence of the sexual relationship, which is carried out by means of an objectification of woman as the Other sex missing in the order of language. This porous barrier then sustains masculine universality at the level of consciousness, where men believe they can, by fraternally "holding hands," and by each of them thus owning his woman (*à chacun sa chacune*), "encircle the whole world" as a uni-verse of knowledge.[132] In brief, the four formulas openly *expose* the functioning of the phallic logic of semblance without which "each man would have to confront a girl all alone, which is something they do not love to do," since "it is too risky"[133]—the fantasy whereby each and every particular man takes himself a little for the Father of the horde in fact manages to assuage the real hole/void only to the extent that it ultimately *presents* it as *castration*, and is thus repressed. With the same move, such an exposition as saying the absence of the sexual relationship does for its part take risks—for instance, as we shall see, by investigating the extreme consequences of thinking one sex as all alone, and hence unable to add up to the two-as-One of love—so as to "found something other than semblance as regards sexual relationships."[134]

This delicate point deserves particular attention: "Founding something other than semblance" does not eliminate semblance (just as escaping fantasy entails the repetition of its "traversal"). Rather, it turns it upside down in order to seize logically, from within semblance, what is not of semblance (the absence of the sexual relationship), or contiguously, what for us, beings of language, *would* not be of semblance (the mythical sexual *relationship*), if only it were not given to us as *semblance*'s real void, as its structural impossibility. What *would* not be of semblance here is imaginary absolute *jouissance* that would *be*, i.e., the *jouissance* of the Phallus, which, however, is *not*.[135] As a symbol, the Phallus only exists "all alone,"[136] Lacan says, missing its Other; in this sense, it exists as *real*.

Lacan never tires of repeating that all discourses sustaining our sayings are as such fundamentally of semblance; he is unequivocal on this. More specifically, semblance is that unvarying position of discourse the matrices of Seminar XVII referred to as the "*dominant*" position, the position of the "*agent*." But psychoanalysis, which as a discourse is no exception to semblance, destabilizes such agency precisely by putting in its place the *object a*,[137] that is, the very element through which the absence of the sexual relationship is tamed and tentatively fixed, but which, when given dominance, causes a continuous "displacement of meaning"—a subversion of knowledge as uni-versal—and eventually allows *discourse* to "grasp [...] something that would be beyond meaning," something real.[138]

In the Seminars of the early 1970s, Lacan approaches these broad questions in terms of number and logical modality. Something which is not of semblance can be said of man and woman through a logical investigation of how semblance works, as long as we realize that essence should not be confused with existence; "There exists" (the *man* that exists) cannot initially be predicated of any Aristotelian (gendered) *some* but only of number, which "partakes of the real" and thus conveys truth (by half-saying it).[139] More to the point, moving from the axiom *Il n'y a pas de rapport sexuel*, "There exists. There exists what? A signifier [*Un signifiant*]."[140] Or, better, "There exists *one*" [*Il existe un*], a real one as symbol, and it is only insofar as it precariously exists as necessity vis-à-vis the inexistence of woman that the phallic function and a circulation between the sexes (*les relations sexuelles* that are not a *rapport*) is obtained.[141]

In parallel, the emergence of the existence of the real one from the absence of the sexual relationship, and the ensuing *relations sexuelles*, should be considered on a second logical level, that of modalities (possibility, impossibility, necessity, contingency). These are traditionally tackled, following Aristotle, by privileging what is possible, what "one can" [*ce qui se peut*].[142] Not surprisingly, Lacan dismisses this primacy. In a first attempt at delineating the logical sequence of modalities, and the fact that they cannot be read separately, in lesson I of Seminar XIX,[143] he limits himself to highlighting how what is necessary—the "not to be able not to" [*ne pas pouvoir ne pas*]—surfaces in the passage from what is impossible—the "not to be able to" [*ne pas pouvoir*]—to what is contingent—the "to be able not to" [*pouvoir ne pas*].[144] Il-logical priority thus rests with the impossible. However, instead of dwelling on the way in which necessity (the necessity of the real one) amounts to a "going" from impossibility to contingency—as is evident if we take necessity's *pouvoir* as the last term of the definition of the impossible and as the first of that of the contingent—and on the role of possibility in this—as the "to be able to"—he brings in a fifth concept, that of *impotence*. Impotence, as "to be able not to be able" [*pouvoir ne pas pouvoir*], is what transpires "if you take this route the other way,"[145] that is, if one tries to return to impossibility (*ne pas pouvoir*) from contingency (*pouvoir ne pas*).

Lacan is not trying here to introduce an additional modality in the guise of impotence, but to grasp impossibility—which is strictly speaking just illogical, logically impossible—from the logical field that it itself opens up as, as such, inaccessible from this field. Psychoanalysis should thus be seen as a discourse, and hence as a semblance, that founds something other than semblance in the precise sense that, passing through necessity, contingency (and possibility), it discloses logic's loop the loop from impossibility as its precondition (the absence of the sexual relationship, about which we cannot know anything)[146] to impossibility qua impotence as its inevitable conclusion; i.e., as the delimitation of this absence, which can be posited only retroactively in what does not work, what we are able not to be able to do in our *relations sex-uelles* orchestrated by the phallic function.

Such a return to impossibility as impotence should broadly be regarded as the subject's *active* assumption of *castration*;[147] as such it is of fundamental importance for any assessment of the peculiarity of psychoanalytic discourse with regard to other discourses. As David-Ménard has suggested, "to speak of a 'psychoanalytic discourse' involves admitting a theoretical contribution of psychoanalysis that makes appear in kinds of knowledge different from it what they do not take into account in their statements," that is, in brief, the fact that "there is never such thing as completeness."[148] In other words, psychoanalysis achieves a "phenomenon"—i.e., an appearance—"of disillusionment," or, as I would put it, an appearance of *dis*-appearance, which is yet another way of conceiving of a semblance that founds something other than semblance.[149] In particular, according to David-Ménard, this applies to the "failure of the search for an alterity that would fulfill what is expected in love"—but we have also explored how, beyond the specificity of psychoanalysis, for Lacan, a certain form of animistic "soul-loving" underlies knowledge *tout court*.[150]

If we now turn to the explanations of the *circulation* among the four formulas in Seminars XIX and XIXB, we can in fact see that logical modalities, and the concomitant happening of the One, are meant to be understood in terms of a transcendental logic of sexuation/subjectivation sustaining the logic of any other discourse (including that of formal logic). In his initial attempt at unraveling them (in lesson III), Lacan begins by associating necessity and possibility with the masculine sexual value, impossibility and contingency with the feminine sexual value. He first takes each value in isolation, showing how they should both be read in terms of an intrinsic "opposition."[151] Then, he briefly sketches the way in which these very oppositions allow one sexual value to be approached by the other in a noncomplementary manner—which is precisely what renders them inextricably linked as *different* sexual values of the same phallic function. "Man" is the result of the opposition between necessity, the necessity that the One happens in discourse ("There exists one man for whom the phallic function cannot be written")[152] and possibility, the possibility of the universal ("For all men the phallic function can be written"),[153] whereby the masculine opposition should be read, as we have seen, in terms of a contradiction. On the other hand, "woman" is the result of the opposition between impossibility ("There does not exist a woman for whom the phallic function cannot be written," i.e., there does not exist an exception on the feminine side) and contingency, the contingency of the fact that woman is taken in the phallic function as the nonuniversal not-all ("For not-all of woman the phallic function can be written").[154]

Here Lacan does not yet openly investigate this feminine opposition in terms of *undecidability*, as he will at the end of Seminar XIXB. He seems to stick to a rather traditional definition of contingency as the "not impossible": "It is not impossible for woman to know the phallic function."[155] This is at first sight confusing, for it would appear to make contingency superfluous, since he has just identified impossibility with "There does not exist a woman for whom the phallic function cannot be written" (i.e., who does not know the phallic function)—where impossibility is thus formulated as a double negation, a negation of the nonphallic/noncastrated relation between the sexes that would be, if the masculine One as an exception had a partner. But we should follow him closely in this difficult but crucial passage. Contingency as the "not impossible" is by no means redundant if we read it bearing in mind that what is primarily under investigation is the disclosure of a logic of incompleteness, or, the incompleteness of logic. The impossible as "There does not exist a woman for whom the phallic function cannot be written" is *not* impossible precisely to the extent that, contingently, it is *not-all* impossible for woman to know the phallic function. Or also, contingency stops the sheer impossibility of the sexual relationship by inscribing woman in the phallic function as not-all; but, for the same reason, impossibility is nonetheless preserved at a logical level as a double negation (the negation of the exception). The negation introduced by contingency—the "not" of the "not impossible" as, in turn, a contingent not-all—thus complicates impossibility, defined as a double negation, in a manner that renders it unrecognizable from the standpoint of the *not to be able to* of conventional logic. As I have repeatedly pointed out, woman as singular is indeed *able* to ex-sist "beyond" the phallic function, that is, *as an opening onto her own impossibility*, as long as she in-exists as nonuniversal contingency *within* the phallic function.

In order to avoid a fundamental mistake, we should, however, stress that the contingent not-all stands as a negation of the double negation of impossibility not in the sense that it affirms that there may exist a noncastrated woman for whom the phallic function could not be written (as the Other One, the partner of the Phallus as One). This would reduce the negation of impossibility to a mere contradiction. Rather, as we saw in the sections above, the contingent not-all negates the double negation as impossibility ("There does not exist a woman for whom the phallic function cannot be written") in the sense that each woman as a nonuniversalizable singular woman is *not castrated* apart from "an insignificant little nothing."[156] By the same token, the contingent not-all also prevents the double negation of impossibility from itself becoming an affirmation of the feminine universal (as negated), whereby "There does not exist a woman for whom the phallic function cannot be written" would surreptitiously be transformed into "For all women the phallic function can be written"—which would give rise to another version of the partner of the Phallus as One, in the guise of *every woman* as the zero of the One.[157] Contingency is therefore a negation not only of impossibility—which it reinstates on a different level—but, more originally and against classical logic, of possibility, the possibility of universality to which men desperately cling and women threaten; or, better, contingency is an affirmation of the mutual implication of nonuniversality and the semblance of universality.

On this basis, Lacan concludes that the *relations sexuelles* established by the phallic function are noncomplementary, since woman's "approach [*abord*] of man" is via castration, whereas man's "access [*accès*] to woman" is ultimately dependent on the fact that "they are not castratable."[158] Lacan's overall argument is clear, but I think that his use of terminology is to a certain degree misleading with regard to the sexual asymmetry he intends to describe (an asymmetry which is given *within* the phallic function). In line with his reasoning, I would rather propose that while woman has *access* to men as contradictorily castrated in relation to the *man* who is not castrated, and, most importantly, as *wholly* contained by such contradiction—which explains why Lacan underlines how it is woman who reminds man of castration[159]—man, on the other hand, only *approaches* woman in her "indetermination" (as Lacan says), or better, I would specify, as determined qua undetermined.[160] To sum up, woman can be inscribed in the phallic function only inasmuch as she is for the most part—i.e., with the exception of an "insignificant little nothing"—noninscribable in it. That is, her inscription—and hence the inscription of the phallic function *tout court*—depends on encircling an impossible real. Lacan fully supports my argument in what might initially seem one of the most obscure sentences of Seminar XIX: "It is starting from the moment when it is from the impossible as cause that woman is not essentially linked to castration that access to woman is possible in its indetermination."[161] This encircling or "*saying of the impossible*," through which the affirmation of the in-existence of woman as not phallic eventually conceals the real of her not being castratable, amounts to a "saying of *man*."[162] It should as such not be confused with woman's opening onto this same real as ex-sistence—which, however, itself depends on the phallic function.

Lacan's account of the circulation between the four formulas of the phallic function is then deepened in lesson VII. What this analysis adds to the introduction of the anti-Aristotelian sequence of logical modalities of lesson I and the exploration of the *relations sexuelles* seen as a noncomplementary connection between the oppositions inherent to each sexual value of lesson III is basically: (1) a much more explicit critique of modern propositional logic that further substantiates that of logical positivism in Seminar XVIII, in particular, of their use of the notions of negation and truth; (2) together with this, a post-Fregean numerical understanding of the masculine and feminine sexual values, where the happening of the necessity of the One can be thought only against the background of the impossibility of the Other, whereby the

One exists "all alone"; (3) an initial explanation of how the contingent not-all by means of which woman is caught up in the phallic function stands structurally—to the best of our knowledge as a knowledge of truth that is not a truth of knowledge—for the contingency of discourse *tout court*, although discourse appears to us as the necessity of the One (which in turn makes the universal whole possible).

We could thus suggest that Lacan's overall aim here is to understand the transcendental logic of sexuation/subjectivation as a logic of incompleteness where the circulation of logical modalities should itself be conceived of as a circulation between different versions of the one/One: the impossibility of the Other as One (i.e., the Other as the missing One that is nonetheless counted as an in-existent zero, and eventually phantasized as another One); the necessity of the *One* that happens (and *exists* all alone); the possibility of the One as a universal *all* (the One that *is* of classical ontology); the contingency of the other one (i.e., *une femme*) as a *singular not-One qua not-all*.[163] Overall, the oscillation between the One/all and the not-One/not-all, that is, the not-two which itself cannot make One—and can thus only be half-said—would seem to provide us with the definitive true kernel of discourse. Yet it also opens up the para-ontological question concerning whether, as such, the not-One is and hence the One is not, or the not-One is eventually the One (as a deceiving God that contains the not-One—i.e., the not-One is the *One*—or as a *self*-deceiving God—i.e., the not-One is the One, which is the not-One, which is the One, etc.).

Let us now take a step back. For Lacan, the phallic function of which he details the four formulas as the logic of sexuation/subjectivation underlying the logic of any discourse fundamentally concerns, as he openly states, the foundation of *les relations sexuelles* on universals. Yet, given that woman is not-all, and hence not a universal, "how does the universal *man* relate to the universal *woman*"?[164] On the one hand, woman remains an "absolutely foreign Other."[165] On the other, the above question is—theoretically and ontogenetically—"imposed on us by the fact that language requires that it is through that [universals] that they [*relation sexuelles*] are founded."[166] In very general terms, as previously discussed, language cannot represent the Other sex—and consequently sexual difference *tout court*. This impossibility is inextricable from language. But, at the same time, language represents this impossibility, which it contains while reproposing it at a different level, by means of universalization. In other words, woman participates in the phallic universal; however, this very participation "does not universalize her":[167] the universals amount to man's phallic universal and woman's *not-all*, the phallic nonuniversal. This also means that woman participates in the phallic universal, rendering it possible, precisely to the extent that she continuously challenges it as not-all (and also by reminding man of the contiguous contradiction on which the phallic universal is based on the masculine side). Hence, in the end, not only the universals but the universal cannot be separated from the non-universal.

The phallic function, Lacan claims, is "unique."[168] This is what distinguishes it, as a writing of the impossibility of writing the sexual relationship, from the traditional writings of sexual difference as a supposed relationship between two bi-univocal female and male essences (*yin* and *yang*; matter and form; etc.). Psychoanalysis teaches us that sexual difference is, rather, internal to the phallic function—i.e., "man" and "woman" as nonsubstantial values follow their quadruple positioning as argument *x* of the function[169]—and it does so by borrowing the formal notation of modern propositional logic. However, the fact that sexual difference is obtained only within the phallic function is far from entailing that such difference is itself, strictly speaking, phallic.[170] That is, it cannot be exhausted by an either/or choice between what is phallically true and what is phallically false (Freud's error, which makes him relapse into sexual essentialism): "man" is in fact written universally as an argument of the function only in contradiction with the nonphallic exception, and "woman" is written as not-all phallic only because of the absence of such an exception. If we understand this, we then also realize that modern propositional logic has a limited—or even "abusive"[171]—notion of negation, whereby the negation of the function is reduced to what is false. Seminar XIX has no hesitation in defiantly proclaiming its distance from the logical tradition inaugurated by Frege: "I am putting forward that the way in which our positions of function and argument are written is such that the relation described as negation by which what is posited as truth can only be denied by the word 'false' [...] is unsustainable here."[172]

Going against modern propositional logic, Lacan thus postulates that, when negated, the phallic function is not false: "It is phallic both as a truth," i.e., as $\forall x . \Phi x$; $\overline{\forall} x . \Phi x$, and as something to be "discarded," i.e., as $\exists x . \overline{\Phi x}$; $\overline{\exists x} . \overline{\Phi x}$.[173] More specifically, the two upper formulas—where no *rapport* or even *relation sexuelle* is given, since the nonphallic exception misses its counterpart—should as such, i.e., as negating the function, be read as functional to the two lower formulas, in terms of an "obstacle" (or "opposition," as we saw earlier) to them, yet not as their negation. Hence saying that the function is phallic "both as a truth" and as what propositional logic would consider false, ultimately entails that all four formulas are true. However, their truth is not the "true truth" [*vraie vérité*], Lacan specifies. The latter would be what does not stop not writing itself—that is, the sexual relationship as a sheer impossibility—and can be rendered only as what "contests the phallic function"—the phallic function qua the contingent stopping of what does not write itself—that is, as *It is not true that the phallic function is what founds the sexual relationship*."[174] Unlike what happens in modern propositional logic, in the phallic function, the function is, in the end, *not* true, precisely insofar as *all* its four propositions have truth-value, pointing in the direction of the "true truth" of the absence of the sexual relationship.[175]

If we then focus on the negation of the quantifier, itself alien to propositional logic, we similarly find that, according to Lacan, the "*subsistence as negated*"—and as such *not* falsified—of the feminine "there does not exist a woman" and "not-all of woman" should not be taken as a negation of, respectively, the masculine "there exists a man" and "all men," but as "legitimate"—phallic—"oppositions" that as such "*enclose*" the four formulas as a function.[176] Lesson VII therefore generally contends that a circulation between the four formulas is achieved by means of four oppositions: to the *intrasexual* oppositions of lesson III (contradiction and indetermination) we should add two further (as yet unnamed) *inter*-sexual "gaps"—as Lacan will call them in his third and final exploration of the formulas in lesson XIV.

Expanding on the intersexual gaps, Lacan shows how, along with the equation of negation with falsity, the four formulas also contravene logical *conjunction* and logical *disjunction* as understood by modern propositional logic. The value of a conjunction between two propositions is true, for propositional logic, when both propositions are true. If we take the two formulas for which, even according to the standards of propositional logic, the phallic function is true—the other two being simply meaningless as false—we notice, however, that "universals cannot be conjoined," for the masculine universal can relate to the feminine universal only as not articulated universally, i.e., as not-all.[177] Although "all men are phallic" and "not-all of woman is phallic" are both true according to the standards of propositional logic and Lacan's own, for him, we nonetheless do not obtain a conjunction from them so that "it is true that all men *and* not-all of woman are phallic." This would indeed stand as a non-oppositional relation between universals tacitly presupposing "*all* women (as not-all phallic) are phallic"—which is precisely what all men phantasize about. ... In other words, a logical conjunction between the masculine universal and the not-all as, in turn, a feminine *universal* would involve a new kind of hystericization of woman, whereby "every woman *is* (not-all) castrated."[178]

As for a disjunction between two propositions, its value is true, for propositional logic, if at least one of the propositions is true: either one proposition is true, or the other, or both. Lacan here focuses on the two formulas that negate the phallic function—"discarding" it without falsifying it—i.e., "There exists a man for whom the phallic function cannot be written" and "There does not exist a woman for whom the phallic function cannot be written." He stresses how, because of their not complying with disjunction, they establish what he calls a "veritable disjunction."[179] That is, within the four formulas as a *writing* of the impossibility of writing the sexual relationship, the two upper formulas write this very *impossibility* as an opposition between existence and inexistence. Or also, they contest the phallic function by writing "*It is not true that the phallic function founds the sexual relationship*," not even when the phallic function negates itself. More precisely, what comes in the place of conventional disjunction as "the strongest logical relation"[180] (for which it would be true that "there exists a man who is phallic or there exists a woman who is phallic" if there existed a man who is phallic, or if there existed a woman who is phallic, or if there existed both a man and a woman who are phallic)[181] is, on the one side, the existence of the nonphallic One, and, on the other, nonphallic inexistence as the *zero*.[182] Note that here the zero stands simply for the *missing* One, which is counted as zero-as-one (the *in-existence* of woman as a singularity) and phantasized as the other One (woman as object *a*) only thanks to the circulation between the four formulas. In other words, the phallic function's not abiding even by logical disjunction brings to our attention that "at the level that the sexual relationship might [...] be hoped for beyond the abolition [...] of the phallic function [through its negation], we only find as a presence [...] one of the two sexes."[183]

Leaving aside for the time being a more in-depth analysis of the One and the zero—or better, of the One and the zero as in turn "*the relation of one to zero*"[184]—what is important to stress here is, once again, that phallic sexuation as the "differentiation of man and woman" emerges only at the level of the universals, of the "discord" between the phallic universal and the not-all phallic.[185] On the other hand, at the level of the particulars, the phallic function inscribes the Other sex as absent or inexistent, something which Lacan already formulated fifteen years earlier in his algebra as $S(\cancel{A})$—the identification of $S(\cancel{A})$ with $\overline{\exists x}.\overline{\Phi x}$ is made explicit and should always be borne in mind in what follows.[186]

Here we encounter a further complication. If "what will be *founded* as male and female" in terms of a "repartition" of sexes depends on the opposition between the all and the not-all, why does Lacan then, a few pages later, conceive of the level of existence/inexistence as "*the foundation of sex*"?[187] Although his use of a synonym is somehow infelicitous, I think he is far from refuting himself. While the former foundation concerns the twofoldness or two-sided status of the phallic function as unique, that is, as he puts it, the "*duality*"[188] between the sexes, the latter refers to the fact that there are *two* sexes, but the *second* is missing, or rather, is given in the phallic function as missing: "For there to be a foundation of sex [...] they must be two. Zero and one, undoubtedly that gives two on the symbolic plane."[189] Yet this two is more properly a "gap"; the gap between 0 and 1, or not-two. More to the point, "the gap as such is always that of the two" as "the essence of the first couple," 0 and 1.[190]

Lacan stresses the importance of such a "voiding" of the Other sex as the basis of the transcendental logic of sexuation/subjectivation *tout court*, and goes as far as claiming that it "conceals the very possibility of the articulation of language."[191] I would add here that it is, by the same token, hidden/repressed by language's own actuality in discourse. Precisely because of this structural occultation, Lacan warns us against thinking of the first couple, o and 1, as logically *implying*—in a traditional sense—the repartition of the feminine and masculine sexes as the opposition between the all and the not-all, whereby the foundation of sex at the level of existence/inexistence would found sexuation at the level of the all/not-all (or vice versa). Implication as understood by propositional logic—i.e., as the relationship between propositions (paired up in our case) that holds true when one logically follows from the other—is as alien to the phallic function as conjunction and disjunction are: "Nothing of what [is] at the lower level, at the level of the insufficiency of the universal specification, implies that it should be *if and only if* the syncope of existence at the upper level is effectively produced, that the discord at the lower level is required, and reciprocally."[192]

In other words, the circulation between the two levels—where one would expect implication to be at work—rather involves a logical "abuse of authority,"[193] which we will have to investigate numerically later on. Let us preliminarily point out that what in the phallic function in the end *functions*—the *discord* at the universal level of sexuation *stricto sensu*, which is imposed by the not-all as "the only point where duality has a chance to be represented"[194]—does not imply the "syncope" of the o *and* 1 (or is implied by it),[195] but, abusively, just the One. This One (or Phallus; or Father) stands for the *"ideal* point" that, as we have seen, allows sexual *identification*, respectively, for man, as the "one-more" that sustains phallic universality as an exception to it, and, for the hysteric, as the "at least one" that paves the way for the singularity of woman as not-all phallic.

The phallic function thus functions discordantly at the level of the all and not-all, and a circulation is achieved with the level of existence, precisely insofar as both *"all men are phallic"* and *"not-all of woman is phallic"* are independently co-implied with the One in an abusive manner,[196] i.e., they attempt to eliminate the zero as irreducible to the one/One. Yet at the same time, woman as *not-all*—and hence nonhysterical—also maintains and *reinvigorates* the gap between the zero and the one/One by relating to her own inexistence (i.e., by actualizing this very gap through her feminine Other *jouissance* "beyond the phallus"), as well as, with the same move, by reminding man that the compound One-as-ideal point / phallic universality rests on a contradiction.[197]

In this context Lacan finally makes a series of fascinating but quite obscure remarks about necessity and contingency, which we—like him—are unable to fully unfold by means of the theoretical tools provided in Seminars XIX and XIXB. They would in fact seem to open up his speculation onto a meta-critical/para-ontological level—concerning, in brief, the origins of language—which he always consciously discourages us from venturing into. First, he affirms that the discord that makes the phallic function work is due to the fact that, on man's side, "we have the universal founded on a *necessary* relationship with the phallic function," whereas on woman's side this relationship is "*contingent*, since she is not-all."[198] While understanding woman's being contingently caught in the phallic function does not present any evident problem—i.e., it is not impossible for woman's nonrepresentable sex to eventually be represented as nonuniversal via the symbol of the male sex—claiming that the universal "all men are phallic" is based on a necessary relationship with the phallic function does raise many questions. Here Lacan would seem to presuppose that the contradictory relationship between the *possibility* of the universal and the necessity of the exception—which defines man in the phallic function—is itself ultimately ruled by *necessity*. Although we are dealing with a fleeting remark, it is difficult to dispel the impression that he is adopting in this case an (impossible) extralinguistic perspective, thereby tacitly concluding that man's transcendental logic of sexuation/subjectivation relies in the end on the *necessity of contradiction* (where woman's logic would be contingently entwined with this necessity of contradiction).

This view—which in my opinion he does not intend to promote but should nonetheless be carefully considered, as it can justifiably be derived from his words—is, however, opposed when, later in the same lesson, he tackles woman's contingency more closely. What is primarily at stake here is woman's (or, more correctly, the hysterical woman-to-come's) search for the "at least one"/Phallus. Lacan appears to be suggesting that such a search is a "gratuitous" i.e.,—contingent—"requisite" of woman's phallic sexuation (note in passing that this oxymoron already locates contingency, more precisely, in the field of the contingency of necessity), which, as a requisite, is "imposed" (gratuitously) by *man's* own *contingent* identification with the One/Phallus as the ideal point (the "one more"). He then speaks of such an ideal point, or of such identification with the ideal point—the text can be read both ways—as a "logical *necessity*," which, in terms of what we have just said, *logically follows its contingency*. Given its complexity, it is worth quoting the passage in full:

> The requirement [*exigence*] that there exists *at least one man*, which is the requirement that appears to be expressed at the level of this feminine that is specified by being a *not-all* [*pas-toute*], is the only point where the duality has a chance of being represented. There is here nothing but a gratuitous requisite [*réquisit gratuit*], if I can say so. This *at least one* is imposed by nothing else than the unique chance—and again it needs to be played out—of the fact that something functions on the other side, but as an ideal point, as a

possibility for all men to achieve it. By what? By identification. There is there nothing else than a logical necessity that is imposed only at the level of a wager [pari].[199]

Here, the emergence of the phallic function as such is eventually due to the unique chance of a wager that needs to be played out (in the Oedipus complex). In referring to *both* man's identification with the One as an ideal point, in the first instance, *and* its imposing a *"gratuitous* requisite" on woman, this contingently consensual *pari* denies that logical necessity (itself referable to the One as an ideal point, the possibility for all men to achieve it contradictorily by identification, but also the triad One/man/woman)[200] is derived from necessity. The necessity of the One, that of its contradiction with universal possibility, and that of this contradiction's contingent encounter with woman, all rely on contingency (as the "not-impossible," the stopping of the not writing itself of the sexual relationship—which is contingently written as the impossibility of writing the sexual relationship). As Lacan will succinctly put it in Seminar XX, "the *apparent necessity* of the phallic function turns out to be mere contingency."[201] More precisely, this is the contingency of the *bodily* inscription, for both man and woman, of the Phallus as the signifier of absolute sexual *jouissance as removed* in the image of the tumescence/detumescence of the male sexual organ, and in that of the female sexual organ's being deprived of the male sexual organ (as we have seen, man himself "is *not* without having the phallus," i.e., to put it simply, he has an "alienated," symbolically mediated relation to his penis).[202]

This being said, the acknowledgment of the prevalence *within discourse*—for both sexes—of the contingency of necessity over necessity itself runs the risk of being posited as an *extralinguistic* truth: discourse—and its production of the One as a necessity of discourse that is concomitant with the delimitation of the absence of the sexual relationship as an impossibility—would be *in itself* contingent. Lacan is well aware of this dimension, which he is not prepared to accept, except as a foundational hypothesis that remains logically undecidable, for otherwise such a *contingency* of necessity inevitably brings with it its reification into the *necessity* of contingency.[203] In other words, the phallic function (i.e., discourse *tout court*) is as such *for us*, beings of language, ultimately contingent in terms of the Oedipal *onto-genesis* of its (necessary) structure, but we simply do not know if the same applies to its phylogenesis as a *natural* language, i.e., whether the bodily inscription of the Phallus is extralinguistically contingent.

On the other hand, neither is Lacan himself totally immune from committing this error (i.e., turning the *contingency* of necessity into the *necessity* of contingency). This is shown by the fact that the contingent inscription of the phallic signifier in the phallic *Gestalt* of the penis seems at times to be defining our species in *absolute* terms, as an objective truth of nature, rather than as a factual knowledge of truth concerning the speaking animal in nature. In parallel, Lacan does not fully grasp how a tactful pondering of the contingency of necessity as an extralinguistic hypothesis *along with* a development of the other extralinguistic hypothesis implicit in his arguments on modality, i.e., that of the necessity of contradiction, may after all enable us to think contingency in absolute terms. In brief, para-ontologically, *either* contingency is ultimately a modal name for the *point of in-difference* we discussed in chapter 2 (the point of the contingent emergence of difference, the not-two, from indifference, the not-one, where the not-two also remains not-one), and is in *this* sense absolute, *or* contingency cannot be separated from the absolute necessity of a *deceiving God* (as contained by or equated with him). This undecidability prevents us from logically choosing the contingency of necessity as an absolute—and thus inadvertently reifying contingency into a divine necessity of contingency—yet at the same time it allows us to decide practically for it—by acting as if the deceiving God did not exist, since if he existed he would only be fooling us.[204]

Returning to lesson VII and summing up its conclusions, what, for Lacan, is certain intra*linguistically, given the contingency of phallic necessity, is that for sexuation to take place—on the basis of a discord at the level of the universals—man and woman must comply with two requirements. First, for woman, that of the *at least one / no more than one man*, which in spite of its gratuitousness is nevertheless "desperate" given her being voided as Other sex; second, for man, that of *castrating all women* without exception (or, better, of "the assurance that there does not exist any woman that is yet to be castrated").[205] The latter requirement—without which man's own universal could not be sustained—is accomplished to the extent that "There does not exist a woman who is not phallic/castrated." Yet, as we have seen, this is far from corresponding to "All women are phallic/castrated." What man, in the end, obtains is only a "gratuitous assurance," Lacan says, inasmuch as the "fragile conjecture" by means of which he attempts to universalize woman (i.e., $\overline{\exists x} . \overline{\Phi x}$) is itself, by referring at the same time to an impossible/real, the indicator of "the opposite of a limit."[206] Thus the more man tries to impose a universalization anchored to the One, and the zero as one/One, the less he manages to control the not-all and its precipitation into the *zero as limitless*. Accordingly, the conclusion of the logico-sexual-numerical tour de force of lesson VII is that "far from giving consistency to any *all* [feminine or masculine], the *without exception* gives still less consistency to what is defined as *not-all*."[207]

In view of future discussions, let us finally highlight that there is in lesson VII one isolated instance in which Lacan speaks of the all and the not-all—of their discord which allows sexuation—as a *disjunction* (having shown that they do not form a conjunction and that, at the level of existence, there is no disjunction).[208] We will take this remark at face value, i.e., we will assume that Lacan is using "disjunction" in the technical sense of the term as conceived by propositional logic, but also that this is, after all, what he understands—against propositional logic—as a "veritable disjunction." More specifically, then, "all or not-all" is true because "all" is true and "not-all" is true[209] (although, as we have seen, against propositional logic, the conjunction "all and not-all" is not true even if both terms are true). For us, beings of language, structure—as a semblance from which we can found something other than semblance—ultimately amounts to *"all" is true and "not-all" is true in the form of the lingering disjunction "all or not-all" is true.*[210] Contravening Lacan's prohibition placed on investigating the origins of language, the question will then be: given that establishing logically whether all is true or not-all is true remains undecidable, what kind of practical philosophy can we para-ontologically construct out of such an alternative (which could also involve the alternative between all-*as*-not-all is true or not-all is true), while abiding by the above definition of structure?

4.4 LOGIC: PRODUCING A NECESSITY OF DISCOURSE

Before dealing with Lacan's third and most comprehensive treatment of the circulation between the four formulas as the transcendental logic of sexuation/subjectivation, we first need to take a closer look at his concurrent claim that logic as such—the logic of every discourse, or at least of all the discourses that are accessible from the historical perspective of psychoanalysis as invariably sustained by the phallic function—consists in the *production of a necessity of discourse*. In the conclusion, we will then also have to further detail how such a discursive production of necessity amounts to a production of the One: first and foremost, of the One of "the One happens" as "all alone," i.e., of the fact that, despite its imaginary idealization on the *phenomeno*-logical level, structurally (that is, logically), the One *does not access the two*, since it can be obtained only along with the inexistence of the zero.

In chapter 3, I characterized discourse as the intersubjective (i.e., intersexual *in primis*) effect of language's incompleteness, that is, of the latter's co-dependence on a logically impossible real. Such an effect of the real establishes itself as a fundamental "semblance," aimed at veiling precisely the absence of the sexual relationship. This specific definition should always be borne in mind. At this stage, however, it is useful to spell out some of the main tenets of the notion of discourse—which Lacan infers in Seminar XVII, and which are implicit in the following Seminars.[211]

1. Discourse further articulates Lacan's longstanding conception of the inessential being of our species in the guise of a dialectical interaction between the structurally synchronic field of language and the subjectively

psychological, or diachronic, function of speech. To put it differently: discourse provides us with a third and more thorough viewpoint on the symbolic order (or Other) as *Homo sapiens'* pseudo-environment, a world of desire for intersubjective recognition, and thus of love. Discourse preserves the primacy of language over the psychological subject, whereby the former is not simply a faculty that can be actively acquired by individual members of the species, but also something that speaks the human animal, unbeknownst to his self-conscious ego. Yet at the same time, discourse highlights how this relation between language and speech is in turn dialectically associated with a nonlinguistic, or rather, nonlogical element, the object *a*, that concerns the real of *jouissance* (i.e., more precisely, the phallic *jouissance* stemming from the absence of the sexual relationship and accompanying our love as a desire to be One).

2. Discourse, for Lacan, is fundamentally the unconscious discourse of the Other. Discourse situates the unconscious outside of the psychological subject, in the sense that it is not constituted as the abyssal/archetypal container of what he represses, but rather constitutes his sociohistorical reality. Or, the discourse of the Other as a structure logically counts the subject before the subject is able to existentially count the Other (and the other subject) as One. In eliminating any clear-cut division between the socially external and the psychically internal, this theory also overcomes the rigid dichotomy between subject and object, as well as the confinement of the symbolic order to the intersubjective relation between two or more subjects. The subject and the object (object *a*) become combinatory elements of discourse as the discourse of the Other, while the other subject is understood as one of its invariant places.

3. Discourse develops Freud's meta-psychology, and corrects it. On the one hand, it dispels the idea of the unconscious as the sealed repository of potentially unbridled sexual instincts lying in the depths of the individual's psyche—an imaginary misconception that is in part still present in Freud. It also has done with the concomitant assumption that the erotic vicissitudes of the linguistic animal, however convoluted they may be, are ultimately motivated by a primordial living energy as a naturally binding force of the One. On the other hand, it preserves a tripartite—topical, dynamical, and economical—perspective with regard to the way in which the culturally determined being of language comes to terms with sexuality. *Topically*, the notion of discourse entails a distribution of places within structure, which is constant and fourfold:

$$\frac{\text{agent}}{\text{truth}} \qquad \frac{\text{other}}{\text{production}}$$

The place of the agent is the dominant position of discourse; the place of truth indicates what is repressed by discourse and as such returns in discourse; the place of the other limits intersubjectivity to a specific location within discourse; the place of production marks what is extracted from discourse—and the intersubjective relation it regulates—as its inassimilable remainder, that is, as a discursive loss. In addition to the four constant places, discourse has four constant elements occupying them in a clockwise order: $\bar{S}$, the split, inessential subject; S_1, the master-signifier; S_2, the battery of all other signifiers; a, the object. While this order is itself fixed (i.e., there cannot be a direct conjunction between $\bar{S}$ and S_2, and between S_1 and a), the elements need also to be considered *dynamically* in two ways. *Intra*discursively, as a sequence, their being topically fixed within discourse nonetheless promotes a movement such that the element occupying the place of truth relates to the element occupying that of the agent, which in turn relates to the element occupying that of the other, which in the end relates to the element occupying the place of production.[212] *Inter*discursively, while preserving the same clockwise order, the elements do also vary their structural position, thus giving rise to four different discourses: the discourses of the master, of the university, of the hysteric, and of the analyst, where the place of the agent is occupied, respectively, by S_1, S_2, $\bar{S}$, and a.[213] Finally, the *economic* dimension of discourse depends on the place the object a—as the element of phallic *jouissance* linked with discourse yet fundamentally extraneous to it—occupies in these four possible permutations.

4. The four discourses, including that of the analyst, ultimately rest on the discourse of the master. The latter is the discourse that has the master-signifier—the *one* signifier that is not included in the set of signifiers, the S_2 of knowledge it nonetheless sustains discursively—in the place of the agent, and the object a, the extraneous element of phallic *jouissance*, in the place of production, or discursive loss. As Recalcati claims, "the discourse of the Maître is the *prime discourse* for it has a foundational characteristic with regard to the other discourses"; in this sense, it is "the very discourse of civilization."[214] In other words, the disposition of $\bar{S}$, S_1, and S_2 in the discourse of the master (respectively, in the places of truth, the agent, and the other) provides us with a schematization of the basic alienation of the linguistic animal—what Freud called the "discontent" of civilization—as caused precisely by language, or, as Lacan puts it in Seminar XX, by "signifierness." A signifier in the battery of signifiers represents a subject for another signifier in this battery—ultimately, under the aegis of the master-signifier—and thus "prevents the subject from consisting in himself as an *ens causa sui*. There is never a single signifier in which the subject could reflect himself and consist but rather a signifying chain that operates on the subject in the sense of a 'constitutive division.'"[215]

Furthermore, the discourse of the master openly shows how this universal of alienation, whereby the subject is constituted as divided, offers itself only together with a remainder, the object *a* of phallic *jouissance*, which is *produced as a loss* (of mythical absolute *jouissance*), i.e., as discursively inassimilable.

Recalcati's remarks are not isolated. Feltham, for instance, similarly suggests that "the master's discourse also schematizes the *primordial* structure of the speaking being," as concomitant with the production/loss of the object *a*.[216] While I do agree overall with this interpretation, I also believe that these authors, among others, underestimate one crucial intersection—which Lacan himself addresses only in an oblique manner, and which we should instead unravel. It seems to me unproblematic to assume that his investigation, in rapid succession, of the four discourses (Seminar XVII), a discourse, psychoanalysis, that is of semblance but "founds something other than semblance" (Seminar XVIII), and the phallic function—along with its nonphallic feminine supplement—as the transcendental logic of discourse for which discourse is as such a semblance (Seminars XIX, XIXB, XX), develops a common theme. This is, in simple terms, the interaction between symbolic and real, signifier and *jouissance*, structure and subject. The key question will then be: How can we map the logic of the discourse of the master (and the reliance of the three other discourses on it) onto the transcendental logic of sexuation? Or, more simply, why does Lacan's teaching focus, in the span of a couple of years, first on the four discourses, and then on the four formulas of sexuation?

My contention is that this is no mere coincidence. First of all, I would argue that the discourse of the master presents us with the basic social bond deriving from the *masculine side* of the transcendental logic of sexuation. Although it is quite obvious, such a link has not yet been made sufficiently explicit. In a few words, the discourse of the master—as well as its university and hysterical variations (for the former keeps the master-signifier in the position of truth, and the latter, as discussed, ultimately amounts to a "man-sexual" logic)—tries to reduce the not-all of woman, that is, her phallic in-existence and ex-sistence beyond the phallus, to the object *a*, which is produced by this "prime discourse" but nonetheless irreducible to it. Here one should immediately oppose the discourse of the analyst to that of the master. This discourse does originate from the discourse of the master—which stands as its "other side," as Lacan famously claims, and to which, at the same time, it also returns with a significant twist, as we shall shortly see.[217] Yet in spite of this, by putting the object *a* in the position of the agent, the discourse of the analyst uncovers the way in which the object *a* eventually stands only for *man's* phallic construction of woman: it does so precisely by articulating the two formulas of feminine sexuation—as both distinct and inseparable from the two formulas of masculine sexuation—where in fact woman emerges as objectified exclusively through "an insignificant little nothing."[218]

More specifically, it is thanks to the notion of the *knowledge of the analyst*—as a knowledge of truth, an S_2 which indeed occupies the position of truth in the matrix of the analyst's discourse in Seminar XVII, as well as tellingly featuring as the title of Seminar XIXB—that Lacan ties his theory of the four discourses as social bonds to that of the four formulas of sexuation as their transcendental logic. We could go as far as suggesting that the four formulas are the analyst's knowledge. But what the analyst's discourse thus confronts head on by means of formalization (in short, the absence of the sexual relationship) is already openly displayed by the master's discourse. That is, the latter's attempt at objectifying woman always results in failure. As I have just observed, in this "prime discourse," the nonlogical element, the object a as the real of phallic *jouissance*, takes the place of production as the place of a discursive *loss*. Critics commenting on the theory of the four discourses fail to spell out that this coincidence is then occulted, or, better, *dis-placed* in the discourses of the university and the hysteric. On the one hand, these two discourses are mere variations on the discourse of the master, for they all share a common avoidance of the positioning of the object a in the place of the agent. On the other, they try unsuccessfully to assimilate, or make sense of, the object a produced by the discourse of the master as an inassimilable discursive loss, and as such dangerously exhibited in it. What they actually achieve is merely a redistribution of the object a into different discursive loci (that of the other and of truth) and, in parallel, a dislocation of discursive elements (in turn, $\$$ and S_2) onto this loss, whereby these very elements are nonetheless affected by object a, precisely to the extent that they themselves become discursively incomprehensible. While a thorough examination of Lacan's understanding of these combinations (a in the place of the other and of truth; the occupation of the place of production by $\$$ and S_2) is beyond our remit here, with regard to what interests us most directly—i.e., the logic of sexuation—we should simply point out that when it comes to the hysterical discourse, its locating S_2 in the place of production is nothing other than "the impotence of knowledge to say the truth about *jouissance*"[219] (i.e., to say the object a in the place of truth). In other words, the hysteric knows a lot about the master's impotence, but, in turn, this very knowledge renders her impotent, that is, prevents her from accepting herself as the object of his (loss of) *jouissance*.

For our purposes, the overall point to bear in mind at this juncture is that all four discourses, *the very possibility that discourse is as such produced, relies on the agency of the S_1 and its production of the object a as a loss*. This, not surprisingly, means that the law or logic of structure, i.e., the phallic function underlying the permutations of the four discourses—and hinging on a master-signifier exempted from such a function only at the price of being himself left "all alone" without a partner—attempts to cork a more fundamental principle of the human animal. That is to say, the absence of the sexual relationship as co-dependent with this animal's linguistic nature; the impossibility of logically conceiving of the second sex, which is then presented in discourse in the guise of the object *a*. To put it differently, the fact that the economy of discourse, which seems in the end to prevail over its topical and dynamical dimensions, can only lead to the production of the loss of *jouissance*, even when the productive place is occupied by elements other than the object *a*, entails that—contra a certain simplistic approach to dialectics—discourse is as such not founded on an exhaustion of what is real into what is logical. Rather, discourse rests on the gap of their noncoincidence,[220] on an irreducible illogicality, which the analyst's discourse—going beyond that of the master—tackles *logically* as the springboard for the dialectics between subject and structure. As Lacan already put it in Seminar XVII, paving the way for his treatment of the phallic function in subsequent years, for psychoanalysis, it will then primarily be a matter of "articulating a logic, which, no matter how feeble it may seem to be [...] is still strong enough to involve what is the sign of this logical strength, that is, incompleteness."[221]

As we have observed, the analyst's discourse is itself derived from the master's discourse. It is thus as such also determined by the agency of the master-signifier—to the extent that, as a discourse, it remains a semblance. Yet the analyst's discourse places the master-signifier, S_1, in the very place of production, that is, it *shows how the agent of discourse is itself discursively produced starting from incompleteness*. Let me restate this decisive passage. All discourses consist of (variations on) the logic of the phallic function as the structural/synchronic agency of the S_1, which in this sense produces them (by ultimately producing the object *a* as a discursive loss); but only the logic of the analyst's discourse diachronically produces this very production as logical necessity by putting the S_1 in the place of production, and thereby highlighting the *contingency* of its emergence.[222] We are then back where we were at the end of the previous section, namely, Lacan's juxtaposition of the axiom of the absence—or impossibility—of the sexual relationship with the contingency—or nonimpossibility—of necessity as the logical necessity of the phallic function. In other words, not only does the object *a* condense the master-signifier's inextricability from the production of phallic *jouissance* as a loss of *jouissance*; it also reveals that it has a concomitant *agency* in the production of this one signifier, or signifier One—as signaled by the matrix of the analyst's discourse—if we adequately expose it as the cipher of the *incomplete* objectification of woman, of the fact that woman is contingently not-all taken by the phallic function, and thereby phallically in-exists (and ex-sists beyond the phallus). This is precisely what Lacan does through the four formulas of sexuation, which do not, strictly speaking, equate with the analyst's discourse,[223] but rather formalize his knowledge, S_2, as a knowledge occupying the place of the truth of incompleteness.

Moving from these premises, we should now find it easier to follow Lacan's convoluted treatment of discourse vis-à-vis logic in Seminars XIX and XIXB. His discussion revolves around a pair of definitions which he fails to signpost properly as parts of the same argument. According to the first definition, "the *object* of logic [is] what is produced from the necessity of a discourse."[224] As for the second, *logic* is the production of a "necessity of discourse."[225] The difference involved is minimal, but should not be overlooked; it emerges clearly if we try to read the quotes together on the basis of what has been acquired from the theory of the four discourses (in particular, of the master's discourse) and the role of the S_1 and the object *a* in them. That is, logic as the production of a necessity of discourse, i.e., of the One, has as its object a real loss—or not-One—that is itself produced from, or by, this One, or necessity of discourse.

This statement, however, is far more insidious than it appears at first sight, for the phrase "production of the One" remains extremely vague: we can, and should, read it as both a genitive subjective and a genitive objective. That is, logic as the production of the One refers to the One's synchronic production, to discourse's producing (and re-producing) itself as a necessity—i.e., as we have seen, to the ultimately invariable discursive *agency* of the S_1, through which discourse is One,[226] but which nonetheless results in the production of a real object as a loss. But it also refers to the diachronic production of the One as a *contingent* necessity of discourse—whose veritable coordinates emerge only through the analyst's discourse by putting the S_1 in the place of production and the real object in that of the agent.[227] As will become apparent, Lacan's interest lies mainly in unraveling the overlapping between these two levels of logic—and of its object as, also, an object-*cause*.

Before explicitly confronting the One's production as distinct from the production of the One, yet also entwined with it, let us first focus on how they already surface in the definition of the object of logic. Again, the bottom line here is that the object of logic is a real illogical loss that is produced synchronically by the One as a necessity of discourse, and that it is up to the—psychoanalytic—art of the logician to diachronically tackle this object as that which in turn produces the One. Lacan thus contends that the object of logic does not amount, as usually claimed by logical treatises, to "the art of conducting one's thought well," in the sense that this would entail "resorting to a [logical] normality from which what is rational would be defined independently from what is real."[228] Such a view merely points to the *ideal* object of logic's "conquering ambition," whereby there would be a one-to-one correspondence between the autonomy of thought and that of what is being thought, between the network of discourse's own articulation as a unitary object—supposedly revealed as such by formal logic—and reality as a closed uni-verse. Formal logic cannot indeed keep to its pretentious plan: its shortfalls, and the ensuing proliferation of different logics, themselves show that the *actual* (and factual) object of logic—whether acknowledged or not—is, rather, the real "as it affirms itself in the impasses of logic."[229] Psychoanalytic logic therefore moves from conceiving the object of logic as an ideal One[230] to conceptualizing this nonetheless structural idealization (which it then understands in terms of a purely symbolic existence without essence) as ultimately effected—and affected—by a real not-One. This is precisely what Lacan proposes when he states, in an apparently paradoxical fashion, that "logic can completely *change* meaning according to the point from which *every* discourse takes its meaning. Now, every discourse takes its meaning starting from another discourse," namely, from the real as the objective impasse of the logic of that other discourse.[231]

The fact that structural change as a—localized—change of discursive logic always takes its meaning from an unchanging—transcendental—logical failure to overcome meaninglessness has a noticeable implication for the psychoanalytic thinking of the One. Expanding on Lacan's arguments, if the object of logic, the not-One of the real object *a* as "what is produced from, or by a necessity of discourse," i.e., from/by the One, in turn causes this very One, then the latter is itself somehow *objectified* by the discourse that exposes this reversibility. In this context it is thus all the more relevant that, like the phrase "production of the One," the definition of the object of logic—"*ce qui se produit de la nécessité d'un discours*"—allows for two interpretations in the French original (as Lacan himself readily acknowledges, "*c'est ambigu sans doute*").[232] In other words, the object of logic stands also for "what is produced of a necessity of discourse," what is produced of the One, to the extent that the product of the analyst's discourse is indeed a master-signifier as *Il y a de l'Un*. Or, better, "the One happens" as a symbolic existence deprived of any essence because discursively "there is *something* like One," or "such a *thing* like One" (all three are legitimate translations of *Il y a de l'Un*, but the last two do at this juncture better emphasize the factually material dimension of the One as a letter, as *Yad'lun*—Lacan's privileged way of expressing it). Even the One, in occupying the place of discursive production, is obtained only as a discursive remainder that does not communicate with the other elements of discourse, or also—juxtaposing the terminology of Seminar XVII with that of Seminar XIX—it is obtained only as a One that is "lost," for it has been left "all alone." Any future discourse that, as a new "style" of the S_1, will follow the analyst's discourse and adopt its transcendental logic of sexuation should therefore take its meaning from this meaningless logical impasse of the *real* One.

Such an unusual and ticklish aspect of the One, according to which the symbolic and real orders are so close that they become almost indistinguishable, is not new to Lacan's investigations. Starting at least from the late 1950s, it is absolutely central to his uncoupling of the One from the traditional way in which philosophy and formal logic have understood it in terms of imaginary completeness. Hoens is thus right in linking the production of the S_1 in the analyst's discourse from Seminar XVII to the much earlier concept of sign, or better, of "a signifier becoming as sign," especially as discussed in Seminar VIII. As he writes, the analytic discourse aims at "mak[ing] the S_1 as sign appear, that is as a signifier *isolated* from the others (cf. the lower part of the discourse: $S_2 \mathbin{//} S_1$)."[233] Leaving aside how Lacan had indeed understood in previous years the notion of the Name-of-the-Father, the precursor of the S_1, in terms of a sign that knots the symbolic and real orders,[234] we should limit ourselves here to stressing the fact that the isolation of the S_1, objectified in the place of production in Seminar XVII's discourse of the analyst, becomes then, in Seminar XIX, the primary object of psychoanalytic logic, an object defined as what is produced as "something like One," and only thereby constituting a necessity of discourse.

Another way to put this would be to claim that the objective or purpose of psychoanalytic logic is to show that not only does discourse speak the subject without him knowing it, but that this is the case because, more fundamentally, "*discourse does not know what it says*" through him (and here lies the "origin of all dialectic");[235] as that which cannot but institute itself synchronically as the logical necessity of the One—and as such is already given to the subject—discourse, however, finally says the One as the production of the not-One (in the $S_1 \rightarrow S_2 / a$ of the master's discourse) *and* the not-One as the production of the One (in the $a \rightarrow \$ / S_1$ of the analyst's discourse). By enacting this second way of saying in its clinical setting, as well as by elucidating it in its theory of the phallic function, psychoanalysis could thus justifiably be considered as a modern form of sophistry, where this term is far from having any derogatory implication. Psychoanalysis is a sophistry directed against discourse *tout court*—which does not know what it says—in that it unmasks the semblance of the One: "It is discourse itself that the [psychoanalytic] sophist takes on,"[236] its confusion of what it always poses as truth, the truth of the One, with what it is actually saying, i.e., the productive oscillation between the One and the not-One. To put it otherwise, psychoanalysis exposes and discursively recognizes the fact that discourse—in spite of itself, of its logical necessity—resists meaning, and that this resistance is ultimately due to the "ab-sense," as Lacan calls it, of the sexual relationship.[237]

Moreover, Lacan believes that, with regard to his sophistry, the analyst is in good company with the contemporary mathematician—this, we will see, then has vast consequences in terms of psychoanalysis's *extralogical* understanding of number. By rebutting the ideal of the exhaustiveness of logic allegedly achieved by logical positivism, "Gödel proceeds to demonstrate that there will always be in the field of arithmetic something that can be enunciated in the proper [or necessary] terms that it involves, which will not be within the grasp of what it posits to itself as a means to be held as acceptable in the demonstration."[238] In Gödel's wake, delving deeper into this, Lacan "privileges" the real as the logically impossible—which "is proved from what the very discourse of the logician grasps"—as "the paradigm of what puts into question that which can emerge from language."[239]

Some types of discourse establishing some specific types of social bond have no doubt emerged from language; but when we "interrogate language about what it founds as discourse,"[240] that is, we should add, when we address if not the origins of language as such, at least those of the master's discourse as a prime—phallic—discourse (Lacan is always hesitant when he ventures in this direction), then we face the impossibility of answering this interrogation otherwise than via the creation of a logical meta-language that paradoxically reduces itself to a particular discourse, and thus begs the question about the foundation of discourse. Yet what we *can* demonstrate is the correspondence between language's foundation of discourse as a social bond and this persistent impossibility—by theorizing the production of the transcendental phallic function. This can be done on condition that we acknowledge, as psychoanalysis does or should do, that even the very statement "There is no meta-language" (for every attempt at creating one turns into a particular discourse) inherently brings with it on some level a self-refuting meta-linguistic claim. In brief, the truth of incompleteness can only be half-said.[241]

This sophistic-Gödelian discussion of—to sum up—how we can demonstrate that demonstration is always a failure of demonstrating is then taken up and fully developed through the idea that logic is "the art of producing a necessity of discourse"—the second crucial definition we are dissecting in this section. The sexual element becomes mostly implicit at this juncture,[242] but we need of course to keep it in mind, for logic ultimately amounts to the transcendental logic of sexuation, or phallic function. More precisely, we must not lose sight, as signposts of the bigger picture Lacan is delineating, of:

1. The axiom regarding the absence of the sexual relationship: logic, logical *possibility*, goes together with logical *impossibility*, the impossibility of logically representing sexual difference, which is as such represented in the phallic function.
2. The two basic theorems of the phallic function derived from this axiom, which provide us with the main coordinates of logic as the representation of the impossibility of logically representing sexual difference. The first concerns the *necessity* of the One, of the no-more-than-one/one-more man,

so that "The One happens," or, "There is something like One"; the second refers to the *inexistence*, or *zero*, of woman, so that "Woman does not exist."

3. An additional theorem—for which Lacan does not seem to have a specific catchphrase—pertaining to the *contingency* of the way in which the inexistence of the zero, and thus also, concomitantly, the oscillation between the necessity of the One and the inexistence of the zero, arises from the impossibility of logically representing sexual difference: in my own words, *it is not impossible that the impossible as indemonstrable can be demonstrated as inexistent*. After all, it is then only contingency that allows us to retroactively put forward the very axiomatization of the real of the absence of the sexual relationship, which as sheer logical impossibility cannot as such be enunciated, in the guise of "There is no such thing as a sexual relationship," and derive the phallic function from it.

Lacan's central point in lesson IV of Seminar XIX is that defining logic as the production of a necessity of discourse entails, as I have already observed, the overlapping of two different levels of logical necessity. In comparison with the explanation I provided above, Lacan also takes a step further and tries to think the One's production and the production of the One *together*. To put it better, logic stands here for the art of producing the One's production—as synchronic logical necessity—through the production of the One—as diachronic logical necessity. This is what surfaces if we focus on the twofold way in which *production* can be understood here. Lacan in fact stipulates that "producing a necessity of discourse" refers both to "demonstrating what was there before" it, and to "realizing" a necessity of discourse "through a work."[243] On the one hand, producing a necessity of discourse as demonstrating what was there before it (i.e., before the One's synchronic production of logical necessity), and must as such be presupposed if we do not assume discourse's logical necessity to be in itself necessary but to have emerged contingently, is *impossible* from within discourse. That is, ironically, what was there before the necessity of discourse appears to us as discourse's "necessity of always."[244] Logic structurally seems to have always been there. Lacan already spelled this out in Seminar II: inasmuch as "discourse closes in on itself [...] ever since the first Neanderthal idiots"—as a semblance of the One, we must add—it "extends itself indefinitely into perpetuity, *prior to itself*."[245]

Yet, on the other hand, we can produce a necessity of discourse (qua diachronic production of the One as a logical necessity) in the sense of *realizing* it through a work: again, think here of the S_1, the necessity of discourse, located in the place of production in the discourse of the analyst, i.e., the place of the real. This is doable precisely if, from within discourse, *we demonstrate how the necessity of discourse (qua the One's synchronic production of logical necessity)*[246] *relies on taking up discursively the very impossibility of demonstrating what was there before and* on positing it as an inexistence (or zero). Schematically: $1 = (0 \rightarrow 1) \rightarrow 1$, where the $0 \rightarrow 1$ stands for the taking up of "what was there before" as now inexistent, and the 1 is finally produced as "all alone," or "in isolation," for the 0 as inexistent entails that the 0 remains nonetheless a missing 1.[247]

Here, we need to insist on how, when referring to the demonstration of what was there before, logic as the production of a necessity of discourse amounts to *logic as logical impossibility*. It is impossible to demonstrate how language produced (or founded, or caused) discourse, because language as such is co-implied with the impossibility of logically representing the sexual relationship, and the production of discourse—as the transcendental phallic function, or One of discourse—follows from it. The fact that what was there before is given to us only as discourse's apparent "necessity of always" is due to nothing other than this state of affairs. To put it otherwise, the "necessity of always" does not insinuate that logical necessity is inherent to a more comprehensive language of being/nature that would underlie human discourse—although we can never be absolutely certain about it, "*it seems that nothing appears that can be properly speaking called ananke* [necessity] *elsewhere than in the speaking being*."[248] It rather suggests the opposite: what was there before the contingent emergence of human discourse is not demonstrable—at least, not by our logic, or one which would be compatible with it—and is thus necessarily mediated in a discursive manner. Or, better: what was there before the necessity of discourse as impossible to demonstrate can be treated as inexistent because discourse—which is, for this reason, a "necessity of always"—can seize it only as what is *not* discursive.

Let us now conclude by taking a closer look at the tortuous line of reasoning adopted by Lacan, which is definitely less systematic, but also more far-reaching, than our exposition above. This is the case especially because it continuously oscillates, without coming to a synthetic solution, between an investigation of the production of the necessity of discourse in general, and an interest in the production of the necessity of *new* particular discourses, as itself evidenced by the historical surfacing of the novel discourse of the analyst.

1. "What constitutes a discourse is constructed from the absence of meaning."[249] This construction of discursive meaning from the absence of meaning, or logical impossibility, remains veiled within a discourse. More precisely, as the production of a necessity of discourse, the logic of each particular discourse institutes meaning from the absence of meaning of a *previous* discourse, that is, it unveils the latter's meaning as meaningless (i.e., its truth). This new meaning will in turn stand for the absence of meaning from which the logic of a subsequent discourse will institute its meaning.

2. "The analytic discourse does not take meaning only from another discourse, but from a set of discourses" (those of the master, the university, and the hysteric) whereby "something original is produced from the closing of this circle."[250] Like the other discourses it brings to an end, psychoanalysis has to unfold its logic, if it is to acquire the status of a discourse. But unlike their logic, psychoanalytic logic constructs meaning precisely by giving *logical* form to the way in which meaning is constructed in these discourses, including psychoanalysis, from a structural absence of meaning. Such absence of meaning amounts to the ab-sense of the sexual relationship. Conversely, the meaning of psychoanalysis is that this very knowledge occupies the position of truth, i.e., of the meaninglessness of meaning. Psychoanalytic logic thus knows that the ab-sense in question can only be half-said. The originality of psychoanalytic discourse finally lies in the fact that the construction of meaning from the absence of meaning is unveiled within one and the same discourse.
3. "The art of producing a necessity of discourse [*nécessité de discours*] is something other than this necessity itself."[251] A necessity of discourse is not itself necessary, but contingent: or, a *nécessité de discours*, discursive necessity, does not equate with the *nécessité du discours*, the necessity as such of discursive necessity. More specifically, the sophistry of psychoanalytic logic (along with that of post-Gödelian mathematics) demonstrates that logic produces a necessity of discourse, yet this necessity of discourse cannot itself be produced, i.e., cannot be demonstrated.
4. "In the absence of a demonstration, what is to be produced must in fact be held as inexistent before."[252] A necessity of discourse cannot be proved, in the sense that it is impossible to demonstrate what preceded it. Or also, a necessity of discourse can only be produced as un-producible, and henceforth merely be reproduced, or repeated as un-producible. The production of a necessity of discourse as its logical realization through the work of the logician, or logical demonstration, therefore goes together with the impossibility of producing what was before this necessity of discourse (as its own cause). But, most importantly, this impossibility surfaces in the logical demonstration, which ultimately rests on it: whether overtly or, most often, covertly, the production of a necessity of discourse takes this very necessity of discourse as inexistent before its production.
5. "What must be supposed to have been already there by the necessity of the demonstration, as a product of the supposition of the necessity of always, bears witness to the no lesser necessity of the work to actualize it [necessity of always]. Yet in this moment of emergence, this necessity [of always] provides at the same time the proof that it cannot be supposed at first except under the title of what is inexistent."[253] Logical demonstration realizes through a work a necessity of discourse as a *logical* necessity, but

this logical necessity is *not* as such logical, precisely insofar as in the absence of a demonstration of what was before a necessity of discourse, the latter "extends itself indefinitely into perpetuity, *prior to itself.*" This apparent "necessity of always" of discourse in general, as filtered through each and every particular discourse,[254] consequently amounts to nothing other than the necessity of discourse as inexistent before its production. The equation in question emerges as such through the work of those logicians who, despite being always-already subjected to the necessity of always, produce a *new* necessity of discourse precisely as un-producible. That is, these are the logicians who do not limit themselves to reproducing/repeating the logical necessity of an existing discourse as a supposed necessity of always.

6. "Inasmuch as the unconscious exists, you realize at every instant the demonstration through which inexistence is founded as a precondition of what is necessary."[255] The fact that a necessity of discourse is given as a repetitive "necessity of always" that must, however, be held as inexistent in the logical demonstration producing a new necessity of discourse—since it is il-logical—is what is witnessed, independently of the logician's work, by the existence of the automatism of the unconscious, and the creative perturbations of the action of psychoanalysis on it. Even if they do not know it, subjects already answer the question "What is necessity?" by logically carrying out their monotonous "everyday *bricolage*" consisting of symptoms.[256] Psychoanalytic treatment then tackles symptoms as originating from the inexistence of truth and *jouissance*, an inexistence which is inextricable from the transcendental necessity of discourse that is the unconscious.

7. "Inexistence is not nothingness."[257] The production of a necessity of discourse is, one could say, a creation ex-inexistence which is not a creation *ex nihilo*. Nothing could come out of nothingness.[258] Inexistence thus "already inexists"[259] as what was before a necessity of discourse and is as such logically impossible. Yet precisely for this reason, *logical impossibility* as "what is inexistent" emerges only retroactively through the "supposition of inexistence," that is, as a *consequence* of the *production* of a necessity of discourse.[260] Inexistence "can inexist"—can strictly speaking *be* inexistent—only by "com[ing] to the symbol that designates it as inexistence, not in the sense of not having existence, but of being existence only because of the symbol that makes it inexistent, and which for its part exists."[261] The symbol in question, through which inexistence, as already irreducible to nothingness, is obtained in parallel with existence, is the number zero. The logical inexistence designated by the zero sustains the epistemo-logical inexistence of truth, which can only be half-said, and the phenomeno-logical inexistence of *jouissance*, which is always structurally in default. Inexistence becomes a question only insofar as it already

finds the double answer of the inexistence of truth and *jouissance*, that is, of the "functional use of inexistence"[262] (i.e., inexistence as given within the phallic function). But what *was* before a necessity of discourse and can be grasped only retroactively as what *is* inexistent through a supposition of inexistence should not, in the first instance, be thought as the *inexistence* of truth and *jouissance*. If we are to understand the "backbone of structure," it should rather be conceived numerically as the "impossibility of numbering"—which is precisely "the real attached to the One."[263] This prevents us from confusing what was before, and as such can inexist only after, with a "certain substance"[264] of truth and *jouissance* that would have been rendered inexistent by discourse.

8. "This necessity [of discourse] is repetition itself, in itself, by itself, for itself, namely, that through which life demonstrates itself to be [for us] only necessity of discourse."[265] The necessity of discourse as the apparent necessity of always that extends itself indefinitely into perpetuity, prior to itself, and as such always-already inexists as logical impossibility, also corresponds to our species-specific "necessity to speak"[266] in terms of natural need and reproduction, as living beings. This has nothing to do with "the power of life"[267] as an alleged intelligent design; on the contrary, it concerns discourse's retroactive creation of the notion of "life" (as the apparent necessity of always) out of a logical impasse. The fact that discourse, whereby logical necessity manifests itself exclusively through repetition, "*seems to rejoin*"[268] the programming of life right down to what happens at the level of the combinatory of DNA, is just an *après-coup* semblance, in the sense that it goes together with an inability to account for what was before the necessity of discourse, however far back in time we locate its—organic and even inorganic—beginnings (it is a semblance at least for our logic, i.e., excluding the eventuality of a meta-language that is for us forever inaccessible, or of a strict equation of meta-language with "there is no meta-language").[269] But on the other hand, this fiction is, to the best of all the knowledge we will ever acquire as a species of speaking animals—i.e., excluding the eventualities mentioned above—nonetheless *immanent* to nature as indifference. The necessity of discourse as necessity of always also means that, although the logician can only suppose it as inexistent, insofar as his own production of a necessity of discourse cannot demonstrate it, this apparent necessity of always has always been there as the (living and pre-living) *matter* from which language emerged, and which as such *persists* in discourse as a "*fact of language.*"[270] What is ultimately at stake here is the *contingency* of logical necessity that must be thought as inherent to nature—and still indifferent for it, assuming it is in itself logically impossible[271]—yet also, at the same time, as the materiality of every given particular discourse, a materiality that, for the logician, precedes as a necessity what he can produce out of it as inexistence.

CONCLUSION

0, 1, UNDECIDABILITY, AND THE VIRGIN

The phallic function as the transcendental logic of sexuation/subjectivation, along with the phenomenal/imaginary reifications it gives rise to, is, according to Lacan, ultimately founded on number. I have already discussed how the core of structure equates with the real (of in-difference). If in turn what is for us fundamentally real is number,[1] it then follows that the core of structure as real must be numerical. More precisely, Lacan posits that structure as real corresponds to two numbers: the zero and the one.[2] To put it better, it corresponds to the oscillation between the zero and the one, which prevents us from considering them in isolation, and to which he thus also refers as the "bifidity of the one."[3] The interdependent couple zero/one is real in the sense that its noncomplementarity structurally marks the impossibility of the sexual relationship as the il-logical: there are two sexes, but there is not a second sex; there is a first sex only to the extent that the Other sex in-exists as irreducible to an-other sex, and can therefore be counted as the difference of the "One-missing." This "gap of the two" is "certain" for Lacanian psychoanalysis as an onto-logical critique:[4] it takes it to be already intuitively evident in the everyday experience of sexual difference, and aims at formalizing such intuition in terms of the "knowledge of truth."

Lacan's understanding of number is no doubt heavily indebted to Frege's. We could go so far as to suggest that Frege's antipsychological definition of natural number is adopted by Lacan in order to account for the onto-genesis of the human *psyche*, where subjectivity emerges exclusively in concomitance with a transcendental treatment of sex as number. In so doing, Lacan also profoundly subverts Frege. To put it bluntly, against the latter, number as real *exceeds* logic. One and zero amounts to one and *not-one*, hence there is "a *logical insufficiency* in any deduction of the one."[5] Following Frege, the one necessitates the zero, which is however not one, but the one missing; zero and one gives us two, yet as one and not-one this couple is really a *not-two*. The series of natural numbers is then made possible only via an error of counting, or "abuse of logic,"[6] whereby the zero as the not-one is turned into another one: "From 0 to 1, that makes 2. Then, that will make three since there will be 0, 1, and 2."[7] In other words, the series rests on the mistaken assumption that the zero as one of inexistence, with which the one of existence is inextricably bound, can then be transferred on from n to n+1. In the end, for Lacan, structure as real is 1 and 0; the numbers that follow are semblance.

Frege's logicism is therefore specifically opposed by Lacan with regard to two basic and related points:

1. The zero should not in any case be equated with nothingness, since nothing can come out of nothingness.[8] The zero, rather, opens onto the "*impossibility of numbering*" *qua extra-logical real*; this is "the real attached to the one."[9]
2. The one is derived from the zero, but one cannot really derive the two from this derivation. The derivation of the one from the zero, rather, installs the one as "all alone." This is schematized as follows: $(0 \to 1) \to 1$; $\overline{(0 \to 1)} \to 2$.[10]

With regard to the first point, for Lacan, Frege has the merit of having thought the one on the basis of the *duality* of the zero, namely, as the successor of a first zero, which then positions the one on the level of a second zero, that of inexistence. Lacan subscribes to the fact that the second zero founds "the number 1 on the concept of inexistence."[11] The problem for him is that instead of conceiving the first zero as the real impossibility of numbering, Frege defines it as the number that belongs to the concept "not identical with itself," and identifies this with nothingness, for such a concept would subsume no object (no object in the world is not identical with itself).[12] Here Lacan has a straightforward reservation: "If it is true [...] that there is no meta-language, from where can we designate in language an object that we can be assured is not different to itself?"[13] Or also, in the absence of a meta-language—which Frege's own differential explanation of number as in excess of itself (n+1) contributes to challenging—structure is as such not identical with itself, yet this is hardly a good reason to conclude that it is not. With the assumption that what is must be—*ex nihilo*—identical with itself, Frege relapses into an onto-theo-logy for which the One is and Being is One.

As for the second point, according to Frege the zero as "that which is not identical to itself,"[14] or "zero-*concept*," nonetheless ultimately subsumes one object, the number zero itself, or "zero-*object*," thus the *number* one is assigned to this concept.[15] Lacan expresses this as $(0 \to 1)$: the zero inexists as one, the "1 of inexistence."[16] According to Frege, from the number one we then automatically also obtain the *concept* of the number one. I think this is what Lacan expresses as $(0 \to 1) \to 1$. Although he does not preserve the distinction between the notions of concept, number, and object with which Frege investigates number, we could say that the concept of the number one is what Lacan calls the One as the "*signifier of inexistence*."[17] In his jargon this amounts to nothing else than the exceptional *existence* of the Phallus ($\exists x . \overline{\Phi x}$): the One as the signifier of inexistence—of the zero that inexists as one—is the *Il y a de l'Un* that exists.

After this logical passage, Lacan parts ways with Frege. As Collett puts it, for Frege, "to the concept of the number one is assigned the *number two*, since the concept of the number one subsumes two objects: the zero-object and the number one (which we have seen is the number zero considered as one object, the zero-object). To the concept of the number two is assigned the number three, and so on."[18] On the other hand, for Lacan, crucially the One as the signifier of inexistence, or Phallus, cannot be said to subsume the zero-object and the number one as two objects. This is the case because the counting-as-one of the zero-concept does not ever really generate the zero-object as *one* object: the zero-object remains exposed to the real of the impossibility of numbering. Accordingly, the Phallus signifies the zero-object as the one *missing*.[19] The concept of the number one as Phallus is that which lacks one to obtain two, and thus remains "all alone." Contiguously, *Il y a de l'Un* will also mean that the One "becomes something that undoes itself":[20] what the One is about, its bifidity, Lacan argues, is the fact that it happens in an instant only to disappear.[21] In other words, the existence of the One and its inexistence—i.e., the inexistence of zero as one—are inseparable.[22] *Il y a de l'Un* in this way indicates that which exists by *not* being-One/All, and eschewing univocity, thereby initiates a nontotalizing dialectic,[23] which is retroactively sustained through the very process of sexuation/subjectivation.

***

Lacan believes that what allows us to reach the two, and any other successor up to actual infinity, is an *error of counting*. In short, the counting-as-one of the zero needs *itself* to be counted as one; or, better, the zero-object that inexists as the number one must be counted as *one* object. Lacan also refers to this twofold process, repeated again and again in the progression of number, as the turning of the counting-as-one into a "monad"[24]—an element which would be in itself *supposedly* complete.

Structure as *real* stops at the oscillation between 0 and 1; it is in this sense that "number simply reduces itself to *Yad'lun*."[25] But structure is also symbolic and imaginary. All the three orders are involved in the phallic function as a transcendental logic of sexuation/subjectivation. Strictly speaking, the Phallus itself could not exist without the error of counting. The very gap between 0 and 1—namely, the real not-two—is in fact *preserved* through this error. That is, *pure difference*[26] is maintained by means of the *repetition* of the counting-as-one of the zero. The latter is repeated, since it both fails to transform 0 into 1 and, at the same time, succeeds in reifying the 0 into the semblance of a monadic object. If turning the counting-as-one of the zero into *one* were really possible, the count would terminate and the not-two would give rise to the *identity* of two-as-One. Conversely, if the counting-as-one of *zero* could not itself somehow be counted as one, the count would not progress, and the not-two, or pure difference, as openness onto the extralogical and thus real "impossibility of numbering," would collapse into this very impossibility as sheer indifference. The series of numbers therefore requires that "the property [that] is transferable from n to n+1 can only be that which is transferred from 0 to 1":[27] what is transferred in 0 → 1 and then from n to n+1 is ultimately the absence of the sexual relationship or, better, "saying" such absence as a sublation of impossibility qua indifference into impossibility qua phallic inexistence. This saying is the subject as *sexual difference*.

The relevance of number to sexuation/subjectivation is especially evident when we focus on woman's inexistence. Not having a symbol for her sex, and given the asymmetry of the phallic function, loosely speaking woman is: 0 as the *impossibility of numbering* at the level of the real; 0 as the *inexistence of the* 1 at the level of the symbolic; 0 counted as *one* at the level of the imaginary. This tripartite division becomes, on closer inspection, much more nuanced, for in spite of the il-logical dominance of the real, each level depends retrospectively on the others. More specifically, then, woman *inexists* as the counting-as-one of *zero* where the 0 and 1 of the real of structure is concerned: this zero is the One *missing*, which is as such opened onto the impossibility of numbering and thus provides her with *ex-sistence*.[28] But, in concomitance woman also symbolically *in-exists* as a singular *one-by-one*, which should now be revisited in terms of the *repetition* of the counting-as-one of zero. This is in turn paralleled by her imaginary *objectification* as object *a*, that is, numerically, the counting as *one* of the counting-as-one of the zero (the one of inexistence).

Let us briefly recall what we concluded earlier with regard to woman's overall positioning in the phallic function vis-à-vis man:

1. Woman is phallic as *a* singular woman;
2. As such, woman is *not-all* phallic;
3. As a singular not-all phallic woman, woman is both "actively" that which makes herself be counted one by one ($\cancel{L}a \to \Phi$) and, in parallel, that which is "passively" implicated in the fantasy as object *a* ($\$ \to a$).

In other words, since *The* woman does not exist, man has access only to *a* woman, or better, to the "insignificant little nothing" through which *a* woman is herself not-all *phallic* (which by no means exhausts her ex-sisting also "beyond the phallus"). Even more limitedly, man has phantasmatic access only to that part of *a* phallic woman that is passively captured as the object *a*. The active dimension of *a* woman's being in the phallic function as the one-by-one itself escapes man, or also is presented to him as the impasse of his attempt at constructing The woman out of the object *a*. Independently of how many women he has, to have The woman—and reach the two-as-One with her—he should have all women, where instead there is always one more he lacks.

The unorthodox Fregean considerations of Seminars XIX and XIXB, which in addition draw freely from set theory, allow us to better specify this numerical scenario. We could suggest that the universal "all men" ($\forall x . \Phi x$), their world, emerges precisely through the repetition of the counting-as-one of the zero of woman, a repetition that is as such sustained by the fact that the zero, the one of inexistence, is at the same time turned into one unachievable object—the monadic object *a* that is "circled around" and thus delimited, but never attained. In other words, the series of man (one man, two men, three men … the actual infinity of *all* men) is obtained by repeatedly adding woman as the "one more"[29] (the phantasmatic partner with whom the duet of love is founded) to each man, so that "for each [man] there is his each [woman]."[30] Woman singularly makes herself be taken one by one by man: while man encircles this singularity as $+1$ in phantasy, establishing thereby a semblance of unity as the two, woman nonetheless also remains related to inexistence as -1 and the impossibility of numbering it marks,[31] for she is not-all.

***

Just as we have tried to define woman through the imaginary, symbolic, and real aspects of the 0, so we can attempt to locate man through the way in which the 1 is articulated according to these three entwined orders. The *imaginary one* is the One/All of "all men are phallic," as such inextricable from phantasy. We have "all men" only because each woman can phantasmatically be added to each man, and, vice versa, each woman could not be added to each man if we did not have "all men." But all men are thus determined as *phallic*, or castrated. The addition to each man of each woman as the "one more" ($+1$) also entails that there is always one more inexisting woman (-1). Or similarly, all that any man can secure in phantasy is that he now needs one less woman to reach The woman. To hold together equinumerosity between men and women (the "sex-ratio")[32] and the very possibility of the masculine universal finally requires contradiction: all men are phallic by each having his woman, because there exists one ideal man who is not phallic by having all women. Man as "all men" cannot but take himself a little for this *man*.

As for the *symbolic one*, this is what Lacan calls the "one of repetition."[33] It is the one of the "sameness of difference"[34] through which man manages to count woman. More specifically, the counting-as-one of the zero (o → 1), that is, pure difference, becomes through repetition[35] the *sameness of difference*. What man extracts from the one-by-one of woman is the counting-as-one of her zero as *one* difference. This is what precipitates the number one into the "one more" as one object, and gives rise to the series of numbers. For woman, however, such sameness of difference is also carried on as *difference*. In other words, on the one hand, the "There does not exist a woman who is not phallic" as different from "There exists a man for whom the phallic function is not valid" stands for the "fragile conjecture" with which man attempts to universalize woman as one difference, as "*each and every woman is phallic*." On the other hand, the lack of a feminine exception indicates the opposite of a limit: through the one-by-one as a nonadditional counting anew of the zero (o → 1; o → 1; o → 1; etc.) woman is in fact installed as a *singular not-all phallic* that remains exposed to her purely differential inexistence and the impossibility of numbering.[36]

This very inexistence is what, on a presubjective level that founds subjectivation and is as such only retroactively thinkable for the subject, is necessarily accompanied by the *real one* as man's symbol: the Phallus, or S_1. Emphasizing its proximity to the Fregean "concept of the number one," we have previously referred to it as the "signifier of inexistence." Not surprisingly, Lacan also understands the signifier of inexistence as the One-without-repetition.[37] Logically preceding the counting-as-one of the zero as *one* difference—and its monadic reification—the S_1 stands thus as "One alone."[38] Or also, the S_1 is alone because it emerges "together" with the One missing (woman as the missing partner) resulting from the counting-as-one of the *zero*.[39] The real one, or *Yad'lun*, can therefore be appropriately described as "bifid": as the absence of relationship between the S_1 and the One missing, the real one is One *and* Other as Other-than-one. It is the S_1, which as symbol can then imaginarily be idealized as an exception to the phallic function, *and* this very S_1 as the signifier S of S($\bar{A}$), which can never really count the barred Other as *one*. This bifidity of the real one, its oscillation between zero and one—or nottwo—as the sameness of *difference*, is then *pure* difference. The rise of *one* difference (or the *sameness* of difference) through an error of counting does not eliminate it. Pure difference in the end means that the One exists as different from the zero because it also inexists as indifferent to the zero.

***

"How to seize then this two, without which it is clear we cannot construct any number?" Lacan asks.[40] As we have seen, the answer is: through the symbolic-imaginary fabrication of "*un autre Un*,"[41] that is, *an-other* One which is not Other, whereby the counting-as-one of the zero is itself counted as *one*, and the "*nade*"[42] of woman as the one of inexistence is turned into a *monad*. To seize the two, and then any successor, we must repeatedly add this other One—which is always the same, the *sameness of difference*—as the "One more" or "extra One" [*Un en plus*] to the predecessor.[43] To put it better: this other One is the "One more" "insofar as it is counted as such in what is enumerated [...] at each passage of a number to its successor."[44] But if any number bigger than one requires an additional One more, the "inaccessibility of the two"[45] as what is structurally given in the real not-two of the dyad one/zero will resurface as the inaccessibility of any successor of two. It will thus be overcome only by concomitantly constructing actual infinity, the *whole* series of numbers—where there can no longer be any successor—as an apparently completed totality.

Looking at this from the standpoint of sexuation/subjectivation, we can hence state that two (as one man plus one woman as the zero counted as *one*) ultimately rests on "all men." Here we should bear in mind that in the progression of number one, two, three, etc., up to actual infinity / all numbers, woman is always zero *as one*, repeated as such to move from one number to the next. Strictly speaking, there never are *two* (or more) women. As One more, woman remains nonetheless singular. On the other hand, man is "two men, three men, etc.," moving from the "One alone" to actual infinity.

Although Lacan does not spell this out, we should therefore distinguish between the two of the couple, or duet of love, i.e., the two of one plus zero counted as one (or one plus object *a*), from the two of "two men," i.e., the two of two particular men as one unit made up of one man plus one man (leading then to "three men," "four men" etc.). Yet above all we should also link them: not only is "two men," or more, achieved by repeatedly counting the zero of woman as One more, but, more importantly, both "two men" and the two of the couple depend on actual infinity. As we have seen, with the exception of one man as all alone, who is nothing but the bifidity of the one, two or more men can be determined as *particular* only because of the universal.[46] Here, Lacan is numerically rewriting the conclusion of the myth of *Totem and Taboo*. Both man's approach to woman and his relation to other men as fellows [*semblables*] revolve around the constitution of a *band* of brothers.

Predictably, however, the further problem is that the actual infinity of all men presents us again with the solitude of the one man as all alone: "Actual infinity is found to realize the same situation as the 1. [...] That which is lacking at the level of 1, this flaw of inaccessibility, is reproduced at the level of [actual infinity]."[47] Two requires actual infinity. Two is equal to one plus zero counted as one: one man plus woman's zero counted as one. At this point we obtain two men, where one man is paired with woman's zero counted as one, but the other is not. "Two men" as a unit becomes subject to the same impasse as one man. We will then count again the zero as one, and obtain three men. This will be repeated up to the actual infinity of all men as One/all, which will nevertheless require One more woman. The actual infinity of all men as one infinity, as the infinity of a set, still goes together with the one of inexistence of woman as zero. All men are phallic.

Although actual infinity reproduces inaccessibility, at this point something else is posited in the process of man's phallic sexuation/subjectivation: "The inaccessibility of something beyond actual infinity,"[48] namely, another kind of infinity, a feminine infinity. On the one hand, this infinity is in a sense always-already there throughout the progression of number—it punctually reemerges as a "return of the numerical repressed"[49] in each passage from a number to its successor[50]—for the counting as one of the zero does not eliminate the zero as the one of inexistence. On the other hand, woman is established as phallic in-existence only precisely by ex-sisting in relation to this Other infinity—which makes her not-all phallic—as soon as the actual infinity of "all men" reproduces what is lacking at the level of the "One alone" by realizing it. As Lacan himself seems to suggest in the quote above, the real of structure as the gap between the zero and the one, or sexual inaccessibility, thus realizes itself through the subject as sexual difference.

∗∗∗

The repetition of the count as one of zero gives rise to "all men" only at the price of constituting in parallel woman as not-all. Woman as not-all is both symbolically a "multi-unity" of singularities, where the one-by-one never reaches, for woman, the two, not to mention the universal, and as such she is in relation to a real infinity beyond actual infinity. While Lacan's attempt to understand this Other infinity mathematically through Cantorian set theory is for the most part confusing, he effectively sketches it out with regard to sexual difference as uncountable crowds of virgins.[51] What "There does not exist a woman who is not phallic" ultimately concerns is the virgin.[52] Clearly, virginity does not refer in this context to not having experienced sexual intercourse, but to woman insofar as she would not be phallic, and as such does not exist, for woman is inevitably phallic, caught up in the phallic function, albeit as a singularity. The virgin, or vanished partner, does not exist, but that which in woman is more specifically feminine, i.e., Other jouissance, ex-sists in relation to it. Or also, woman can never be a virgin:[53] she in-exists in the phallic function starting from the counting-as-one of zero, or $S(\cancel{A})$, which then turns her into a One more. However, she also returns to the zero, enjoying her own inexistence, and in this way, as $\cancel{L}a \rightarrow S(\cancel{A})$, she opens onto the uncountable crowds of virgins, or $\cancel{A}$. Here the zero of inexistence, on which actual infinity is built, subjectively meets through woman infinity as the impossibility of numbering.

Lacan locates this impossibility of numbering "in between the 1 and the 0."[54] We should therefore at this stage reconsider the way in which he adopts and modifies Frege's duality of the zero. Strictly speaking, for Lacan, the zero amounts to the Fregean zero-object, or one of inexistence—which is successively counted as *one* object. On the other hand, the Fregean zero-concept, which he had already dissociated from nothingness and postulated as the impossibility of numbering, is now better defined as lying in between zero and one. The duality of the zero thus gives way to what Lacan calls the duality, or "division" of woman. Woman is dual because the "gap between the zero and the one"[55] is not only the insurmountable *distance* between the masculine One of existence and the feminine zero as one of inexistence, where One is what lacks one to get to two, through which woman then nonetheless in-*exists*. It is also this very in-existence's concomitant *ex*-sistence toward what *lies* in between the zero and the one. To sum up: the two of love is always only too big for man; for woman, it is also too small.

***

As we have seen, the actual infinity of "all men" is self-refuting, for "all men" is obtained as "all men are *phallic*." Or also, "all men" is given as One only together with the inexistence of woman, which thus reproposes the impasse the "One alone" faced to begin with. The universal nonetheless *holds* as One/all. It can hold only because of contradiction. What holds it is in fact one ideal *man* who is *not* phallic, having all women. The actual infinity of "all men" is contradictorily One through an additional man who is not like all other men. In his numerical discussion of sexuation/subjectivation, Lacan analyzes this exception in terms of an "edge" of the set "all men," which thus also works as its "complement."[56] If we want to overcome Freud's mythical understanding of this exception—which in short leads him to foreclose feminine infinity as beyond actual infinity[57]—we need to think of it as an "inclusive function": "What is there to be said about the universal except that the universal is enclosed, enclosed precisely by negative possibility?"[58]

The basic point to grasp here is that with the constitution of the edge/complement of the universal phallic set by means of its negation, the *logical existence* of the One as the One "all alone" of the real of structure is turned into "what we can call *one being*" [un être], *an idealized individual*.[59] In other words, the $\forall$ of "all men are *phallic*," a self-refuting actual infinity emerging only as the inaccessibility of something beyond itself—since basically, the One really is and will always remain all alone—is as such, at the same time, "reversed" into the A,[60] Lacan says, the A of *le grand Autre*, namely, the semblance of completeness that guarantees for us structure as a symbolic *order*. More precisely, the ∀ is reversed into the A, a *whole*, each time that the ∀ is embodied in the *particular phallic men* who contradictorily all identify with the exceptional "one being," taking themselves a little for the Father of the horde.

It is important not to lose sight of the fact that for the universal, or actual infinity of men, to be possible, not only must woman be repeatedly counted as One more, but this very count holds because the masculine One as all alone is, as "one being," itself counted throughout as One more. We discussed earlier how the Father as that which all men contradictorily relate to as a necessity is indeed also defined by Lacan as the *Un en plus*. In other words, the pure difference of the bifid One as the real of structure, which is never overcome, concomitantly gives rise, for man, to the *sameness* of difference even on the *masculine* side: the Father as the idealized individual who is not phallic is difference as *one*; the brothers, or *semblables*, who emerge as such by identifying with him are the different *units* "two men," "three men," "four men," etc.

***

Fundamentally, "there exists only the One" [*Il n'existe que de l'Un*]:[61] the real One of *Yad'lun* all alone, the bifidity of the One as the 0 and 1 of structure. As such, "the One is not found on every street corner,"[62] even if man believes himself to be One, by contradictorily taking himself a little for the "one being" he is not, which strictly speaking does not exist.[63] Man is not One but, rather, "innumerable" [*innombrable*] and "finite."[64] To put it better, Lacan argues in a difficult passage, he is innumerable *because* he is finite.[65] The progression of countless natural numbers nevertheless reaches actual infinity as a semblance of totality. We never really obtain one man in isolation: one man is always contained in "two men," "three men," innumerable men, which can be obtained as long as we have "all men." "All" is inseparable from the innumerable; as such, the innumerable should be regarded as finite.

On the other hand, woman is "countable" [*dénombrable*],[66] yet infinite. Woman is countable because she herself is related to what is, for man, the "ideal point" of the "one being," albeit in her own way, i.e., through the one-by-one; the one-by-one as repetition institutes her, on the masculine side, as the *sameness* of the zero as *one* (the object *a*), but with the same move she is also instituted, on her side, as a *singular one of difference* (*Ⱡa*). In other words, woman is countable as *not-all* countable. More to the point, woman's very exposition to Other infinity as the uncountable [*non-dénombrable*]—i.e., to the crowds of virgins—goes together with her linking to the exceptional One more [*Un en plus*] of man, which is however, for her, no-more-than-one [*pas-plus-d'un*]. Woman identifies with the exception, yet she also takes it for what it is beneath man's idealization: a symbol, which is really all alone and which, in spite of being contradictorily embodied by all men, does not turn them into "one being." As I have argued, woman acknowledges that there is no more than one "the *man*"—as "a signifier, nothing else"—and in so doing she parallels her not having an independent feminine symbol with her being not-all counted as an additional object that phantasmatically sutures the disparity between man qua castrated man and his idealized symbol.

Again, woman's being countable and her simultaneous exposition to the uncountable, or infinity beyond actual infinity, subjectivizes woman as a duality—which is first and foremost the duality of her *jouissance*, as phallic and "beyond the phallus." In the final account of the circulation between the four formulas of sexuation, Lacan discusses this in terms of *undecidability*. The undecidable is the gap between the contingency of woman's being not-all phallic and her inexistence; it is the "gap [...] between the *pas-tout* and the *pas-une*."[67] More precisely, undecidability arises because it is specifically by in-*existing* as not-all *phallic* that woman relates to her very inexistence, that she *ex*-sists toward the impossible, i.e., the infinity as impossibility of numbering *beyond* the phallus. This undecidable—concerning fundamentally whether woman is or is not phallic—will then be more generally the undecidability of the phallic function *tout court*: there is no sexual relationship, *but* there are sexed liaisons, *but* there ultimately are sexed liaisons only because woman opens onto the absence of the sexual relationship.

***

Let us now look at Lacan's final explanation of the circulation between the four formulas of sexuation as the functioning of the phallic function. As in his previous treatments of this matter, he states that the formulas are separated by four gaps, and that to understand how the function works we need to consider the formulas as a circuit of logical modalities (impossibility, necessity, possibility, contingency), sustained as such by the gaps. The gaps are now listed as that of *existence*, between $\exists x . \overline{\Phi x}$ and $\overline{\exists x} . \Phi x$; of *contradiction*, between $\overline{\exists x} . \overline{\Phi x}$ and $\forall x . \Phi x$; of the *object a*, between $\forall x . \Phi x$ and $\overline{\forall x} . \Phi x$; and of the *undecidable*, between $\overline{\exists x} . \overline{\Phi x}$ and $\overline{\forall x} . \Phi x$.[68]

Lacan so far characterized $\exists x . \overline{\Phi x}$, $\overline{\exists x} . \overline{\Phi x}$, $\forall x . \Phi x$, and $\overline{\forall x} . \Phi x$, as respectively, "There exists a man who is not phallic," "There does not exist a woman who is not phallic," "All men are phallic," "Not-all of woman is phallic." These definitions remain valid, but if we follow his text closely, we can see how the introduction of these specific gaps pinpoints aspects of the formulas which had not yet been spelled out so neatly. Moreover, they also show that the formulas work differently, depending on which other formula they relate to via a gap. Thus, the pair $\exists x . \overline{\Phi x}$, $\overline{\exists x} . \overline{\Phi x}$ evidences that, in accordance with our discussion of the bifidity of the One, existence lies *between* "the there exists" and "the there does not exist," where man and woman are not as such yet involved.[69] The pair $\exists x.\overline{\Phi x}$, $\forall x.\Phi x$ highlights that contradiction is, more specifically, the contradiction between the there exists as here to be more properly conceived as "there exists one that is," the "one being," and the universality of castration, which is in this case to be better grasped in negative terms as "there is not one that is not."[70] The pair $\forall x.\Phi x$, $\overline{\forall x}.\Phi x$ underlines the fact that the object a is "the lack, the flaw, desire," that is, the absence of the sexual relationship inscribed as such in the phantasmatic relation $\$ - a$, which manages to create the semblance of what Lacan calls here, surprisingly at first sight but consistently, "the two $\forall x$," masculine and feminine.[71] Finally, the pair $\overline{\exists x}.\overline{\Phi x}$, $\overline{\forall x}.\Phi x$ stresses that, on the feminine side, undecidability arises because the particular there does not exist "is not the negation of universality"[72] (where instead, on the masculine side, there exists one that is negates there is not one that is not); on the contrary, there does not exist as, in this instance, "There does not exist a woman who is not phallic" somehow manages to limit, to universalize a universality which, unlike what is suggested in phantasy, is really not such, for it is not-all.

As for the logical modalities, they are again the same as in Aristotle: $\exists x.\overline{\Phi x}$ denotes necessity; $\overline{\forall x}.\Phi x$ denotes contingency; $\forall x.\Phi x$ denotes possibility; $\overline{\exists x}.\overline{\Phi x}$ denotes impossibility. But, again, the modalities operate in a different order than in Aristotle: roughly speaking, the phallic function starts with impossibility, which leads to necessity, which leads to possibility, which leads to contingency, which leads back to impossibility. More precisely, we should also take into consideration the gaps: "We start from the gap of the undecidable, between the not-all and not-one [pas-une]. And afterward it then goes to existence. Then, after that, it goes to the fact that all men have the potential of castration; it goes to the possible, for the universal is nothing other than that. [...] And after that, where does it go? It goes to the object a. It is with the object a that we are related. And after that, where does it go? It goes where woman distinguishes herself by not being unifying. One only needs to complete it here and go toward contradiction, and come back to the not-all [pas-toutes], which is in short nothing but the expression of contingency."[73]

In other words, Lacan takes the undecidable to be the most important point of the phallic function as the transcendental structure of sexuation/subjectivation. That is, the undecidability between the impossibility of representing woman's sex, for she lacks a symbol, and the contingency of her phallic in-existence as not-all. This necessitates the One of existence, to which woman relates. Such One is, if taken in isolation, "the signifier as One,"[74] the real Phallus as all alone, its bifidity. But the only interest it has for the circulation between the formulas is "the equivocations that can come out of it,"[75] first and foremost, the equivocation according to which it would allow for the melting of the not-two—given by the upper formulas—into One [fondre d'eux en Un]. What is interesting is the fact that the dyad one/zero as "the place of our loss" is forced into the forging of "the One of the idea,"[76] the One more, or Father. The necessity of the One of existence thus gives rise to the possibility of the universality of castration, because all men contradictorily identify with the "one-being," and they do so in phantasy, where man relates to woman, to the absence of her symbol, as *one* object, the object *a*. Yet woman is not entirely contained by phantasy (she is not "unifying") and dwells in it only by relating to the very contradiction between all men and the One more, which is for her no-more-than-One. This, in turn, makes woman "come back" to the not-all, installing her as *not*-all phallic, as an "expression of contingency": the phallic function is not-impossible, but neither is it necessary, as man is led to believe through the subterfuges of the ideal and of the error of counting.[77]

What Lacan at this point fails to add is that woman's *decision* for contingency nonetheless plunges her back into the undecidable. As discussed, woman's contingent not-all ($\cancel{L}a$) is not simply not-all *phallic*, due to her relation with the Phallus, or, better, with its contradictory embodiment in man ($\cancel{L}a \rightarrow \Phi$); she is also not-all phallic precisely insofar as she simultaneously relates to her inexistence ($\cancel{L}a \rightarrow S(\cancel{A})$), which opens onto the *impossibility* of numbering/representing her sex. We therefore return to the undecidability between impossibility and contingency, where the function restarts.

It is worth noting that such a closure of the circuit of sexuation/subjectivation equally shows that it is undecidable whether woman's relation to her inexistence stands for a subjectivation of impossibility (of the fact that there does not exist a symbol for woman) through the *not*-all, or for a containment of the not-all as not-all *phallic* through the "There does not exist a woman who is not *phallic*." Woman *ex*-sists toward the virgin, i.e., the non-phallic woman who does *not* exist, but with the same move such inexistence is tentatively limited as "There does not exist a woman who is not *phallic*," the fragile universality of in-existence. Without the latter, man would not be able to delude himself into believing in the existence of another One, that of "all women are phallic"; phantasy could not be constituted, as we have seen, as the semblance of "the two $\forall x$."

So there is undecidability because "There does not exist a woman who is not phallic," and at the same time, "Not-all of woman is phallic." But on closer inspection this means that there is undecidability *both* because (1) "There does *not* exist a woman who is not phallic"—or, better, "There does *not* exist a woman (who is not phallic)"; there is no symbol of woman's sex, no exception on which to found sexuality on the feminine side—and at the same time "Not-all of woman is *phallic*"; *and* because (2) "There does not exist a woman who is not *phallic*" and at the same time "Not-all of woman is phallic." Undecidability is thus truly undecidable.

***

Lacan's extremely succinct account of the circulation between the formulas, which I have tried to spell out in a systematic fashion, presents itself as *structural*: man and woman are already asymmetrically in place here.[78] But his renewed emphasis on the priority of the real of impossibility over the other logical modalities[79]—sexuation starts from impossibility and returns to "veritable impossibility" as, we should add, a *femininely* subjectivized "demonstration of impossibility"[80]—allows us to unpack the circulation further in *onto-genetic* terms. In order to do so we need to return to some crucial arguments concerning the way in which the hysteric "inaugurates" the phallic function, and the fact that the real of this function is numerical. Lacan's vetoes against any investigation of origins become more and more paradoxical toward the end of Seminars XIX and XIXB; for instance, he admits that "there is no discourse on origins except by treating the origin of a discourse [...] there is no origin that can be grasped other than the origin of a discourse."[81] So in spite of the fact that no formula of sexuation, and no logical modality, holds for an instant without the others, it is nevertheless legitimate to scrutinize how "the hysteric *makes* man," and "the One"—the bifidity of the real One—"*makes* Being," the idealized "one-being."[82]

We can at least provisionally attempt to describe the phallic function in onto-genetic terms as follows:

1. The point of departure is what we discussed previously in terms of hysteria as a pure not-having, which goes together with the creation of the Phallus and the hysteric's identification with it, independently of man. In this sense, the hysteric makes man because she makes his symbol. This pure not-having of the hysteric arises immanently from impossibility as indifference: the absence of a symbol that would represent woman's sex is indifferent in nature. The point of departure is thus what we discussed earlier as the point of in-difference: to be more accurate, it will have been the point of in-*difference* only when phallic sexuation is accomplished through a first circulation of the function. The point of in-difference, however, already coalesces around pure difference—itself strictly speaking graspable only retroactively—because the hysterical pure not-having, the one of inexistence ($0 \to 1$), emerges along with the one of existence ($0 \to 1$) → 1, that is, the Phallus. The point of in-difference that will have been the point of in-*difference* will also have been as such the point of undecidability (between the impossibility of representing woman's sex and her phallic contingency; more generally, between the absence of the sexual relationship and the presence of sexed/phallic liaisons). The undecidable can thus also be seen as the undecidability between in-difference as difference, i.e., sexual difference, and in-difference as indifference, i.e., woman's exposition, through sexual difference, to her own impossibility to be numbered.

2. Language is inextricable from the absence of the sexual relationship, and vice versa; woman's sex cannot be represented in language. This could easily have led to the indifferent extinction of the species. But man's sex can be represented in language; this is because the unfolding of the *fact* of language as the very "absence" of the sexual relationship, which amounts first and foremost to indifference, is paralleled by its differential inscription in the alternation tumescence/detumescence of the male sexual organ. The absence of the sexual relationship can thus tentatively be signifierized bodily in a phallic way. Men (or, better, will-be men) are impotent (given that woman's sex cannot be represented), but there is a symbol of omnipotence (eternal erection), the Phallus, to which will-be men relate.

3. The hysteric creates the phallic symbol autonomously: in this way, as man-sexual, she paves the way for woman, her indirect sexuation through the symbol of man's sex. Yet the hysteric is not a woman, since she confuses the phallic symbol with particular male members of the *Homo sapiens* species; she relates to them as if at least one of them could fully embody the Phallus, which they cannot. When all men are indeed constituted thanks to an idealizing identification with the Phallus as an exceptional One more—whereby the One makes "one-being"—the hysteric cannot accept that particular men emerge through the possibility of universality only by paying the price of *"not being* without having it" (i.e., castration). The symbol of omnipotence is embodied as omni-impotence, for this is what it originally stood for: the Phallus as all alone. In not accepting such a contradiction, which is structurally inseparable from the representation of man's sex, and therefore from sexual difference, the hysteric relapses into the desubjectivized impossibility of representing her sex: she is sexually indifferent.

4. The contradictory identification of all men with the One more as one-being is sustained in phantasy, where man attempts to reduce the Other sex to another one, with which to fuse. This is the hysteric's own objective: her not-having is a desire to be the Phallus, to fully identify with the zero as one, and thus bi-univocally couple with the One. Yet the hysteric refuses to be the object of man's *phantasy*, for this is nothing but an index of castration. Woman, however, arises from this failure of feminine universalization: she is not-all caught in man's phantasy precisely by relating back as a singular one-by-one to the contradiction between man and the Phallus. There is no more than one "the *man*"; no particular man can be "the *man*"; it is a dis-embodied symbol, which should as such be both associated with and dissociated from all men's taking themselves a little for it. Woman maintains the hysteric's structural reference to the One: the speaking animal is in fact, independently of its sex, a desire to *be*, a

manque-à-être or "want-to-be." Yet, as *not-all*, she displaces such desire (to fuse into One with the "one-being") onto wanting to be the "one and only"[83] [*la seule*] of a particular castrated man in her own version of phallic love. Her desire for exclusivity, to be recognized as unique, nonetheless acknowledges the in-existence/ex-sistence of other women as non-universalizable singularities.

5. Woman as contingently not-all phallic is also exposed, as *not-all*, to her impossibility to be numbered that lies beyond the phallus. It is this exposition that retrospectively sutures all the stages of the phallic function and their logical modalities (the impossible/indifferent not-one of the hysteric; the necessary One of the Phallus; the possible universal of men) given that woman's incompleteness can equally be seized as "There does not exist a woman who is not *phallic*." The concomitance of woman's exposition to infinity, whereby she ex-sists, and her being limited as positive in-existence, makes the phallic function as such coalesce around the undecidable questions "Does woman exist? What does a woman want?," which support its circulation.

Contingency has thus a certain logical priority over necessity and possibility: in this sense, "the not-all [*pas-toute*] is the key point" of the phallic function.[84] More precisely, the contingency of *woman*'s not-all as an opening onto impossibility retroactively has a logical priority over the contingency of the hysteric's creation of necessity (the necessity of the One) out of indifferent impossibility, as well as over the contingency of the emergence of possibility (the possibility of the "all") out of the One. Or, better, a feminine *subjectivation of the impossibility of the sexual relationship, which demonstrates it as phallic undecidability*, is needed for sexual *difference* to hold through the circulation of logical modalities.[85] The hysteric's alienating identification with the Phallus, through which existence is obtained only against the background of inexistence, as well as the translation of this very gap, which first symbolizes the "absence" of the sexual relationship, into the +/− of the male sexual organ and thereby activates the contradiction between the universal and its exception, do not alone manage to differentiate themselves from indifference.

***

The phallic function is the transcendental logic of *Homo sapiens*' sexuation/subjectivation. The theoretical aim of Lacan's psychoanalytic discourse—as closely linked to but, strictly speaking, different from the clinical discourse of the analyst—is to formalize it.

To put it bluntly, thanks to the phallic function, *man* is subjectivized as a phantasmatic belief in *saying* the impossible: by turning the fact that there is no symbol to represent woman's sex—that language goes together with the absence of the sexual relationship—into the statement "There does not exist a woman who is not phallic," and by reading this as "All women are phallic," man represses the truth that woman is not castratable, aside from an insignificant little nothing. For her part, *woman* is subjectivized as an ex-sistence that says the impossible as *unsayable*: the example of the mystic, who speaks about what she cannot put into words, stands here as a paradigm of more mundane experiences of miscommunication between the sexes.

Moving from this general conclusion, we could suggest that, in formalizing the masculine and feminine subject as sexed through a circulation of logical modalities, psychoanalytic discourse in turn says the *impossible* as real—as the real of number, the bifidity of the one, or not-two, and of the impossibility of numbering "attached" to it, the not-one. Like woman, psychoanalytic discourse recognizes that sexuation *leads* to impossibility. But, against the risk of drifting into an illusory transcendence, which is a possible outcome of the unsayable as mystical—encouraged by the hysterical acknowledgment of impotence[86]—it stresses that, precisely through woman, this return to the absence of the sexual relationship amounts to a *demonstration* of impossibility as phallic undecidability. Psychoanalytic discourse is in this sense a "knowledge of truth," which thus exorcizes the feminine temptation of "non-knowledge." With the same move, however, it also dispels the masculine delusional claim to *say* the impossible as a "truth of knowledge."

Lacan's final approach to the question of truth becomes, however, increasingly complex, overall inconclusive, though also particularly fruitful in view of further para-ontological enquiries. On the one hand, "truth can be constructed only starting from o and 1."[87] Truth is a *knowledge* of truth "that takes truth as a simple *function*,"[88] as the truth of the phallic function, i.e., the bifidity of the One. Here Lacan states that such knowledge "also entails a real that has *nothing to do* with truth," a real "that is mathematical."[89] This is somewhat surprising, given that, as we have repeatedly seen, the bifidity of the One—truth as a function—is also presented as the numerical real of structure, to which mathematical infinity (an infinity "beyond" actual infinity), or real impossibility of numbering, is immanently "attached."

Our surprise is increased by the fact that, on the other hand, Lacan reiterates this last point; he claims that there is a "dimension of *truth*" that cannot be contained by the "*formal void*" (by the zero, qua one of inexistence, as pivotal to the emergence of natural numbers out of the bifidity of the One).[90] This dimension, which is explicitly described as "positive" for psychoanalytic discourse, springs out of a "love for truth in itself," whereby what we should call "matheme" is opposed to a certain fashion of doing mathematics that revolves around a "requirement for the veridical."[91]

How can we reconcile these two apparently conflicting lines of argument, in spite of Lacan's tangible terminological difficulties? Is truth to be distinguished from the real or not? Let us consider the first argument. I believe that here the context is prevalently polemical. Against logical positivism,[92] to begin with, truth should methodologically be separated from the real. Why? Because the real is what is given as something that resists formalization, and more generally meaning [*sens*], which can nevertheless be formalized as resistant to formalization.[93] It is therefore highly misleading to base formalization on an adherence to the "preconceived idea" that to account for the real, to give it a meaning, we should start with an opposition between what is true and what is false.[94]

Truth does not lie in a veridical correspondence between language and reality, but rather in a signifying articulation that is "secondary" to the real as impossible.[95] Again, it is a function that starts from 0 *and* 1, where 0 and 1 are *both* "truth-values."[96] More precisely, as a signifying articulation for which "0 has as much truth-value as 1," since 0 is the truth that 1 is missing, and that 1 thus fails to reach 2, truth amounts to a "double truth."[97] This level of structure, which Lacan calls a *monstration passive* of truth, is retroactively demonstrated in an active way through the sexed subject;[98] thanks to the One—which, as we have seen, sexuates both man and woman—the subject can half-say the truth, and he or she can do so in two different and irreconcilable ways: "There is something of the One," *Il y a de l'Un*, or "There are not two of them," *Il n'y en a pas deux*.[99]

The fact is, however, that in half-saying the truth as *not-two*—which man represses in fantasy through the reduction of the Other sex to another One, and which comes back at him only as the dissatisfaction of his desire—woman also confronts herself as *not-one*, as the real impossibility of representing her sex that initiated the process of sexuation. From this stance, truth and the real are *not* separated. Truth is not only secondary to the real. There is a "dimension" of truth, experienced as feminine *jouissance*, which supplements truth as a function through woman's subjectivation. We can speak here of *the truth of the real of the absence of the sexual relationship*: the impossible as the not-one of sheer indifference is now also the impossible as the infinity beyond actual infinity, to which woman, and sexual difference as such, are exposed. Both psychoanalysis and post-Cantorian mathematics are, according to Lacan, discourses that formalize this state of affairs. Philosophy, in turn, can no longer avoid them.

***

To sum up, the function of truth that proceeds solely from 0 *and* 1, as well as from the structural "equivocations" or error of counting they give rise to—whereby truth should be thought dialectically with semblance—should not be confused with the *real* as the impossibility of numbering. In other words, truth as a function—which, contra logical positivism, is *not* a true function, for both the 1 and 0 have truth-values—*writes the impossibility of writing the* sexual relationship; it therefore ultimately coalesces around $S(\bar{A})$,[100] and should consequently be distinguished from the real of the absence of the sexual relationship, $\bar{A}$, as that which "does not stop not writing itself." But strictly speaking there is no barred Other, or absence, without that which marks it; and vice versa, there is no marking without an absence, the lack of a symbol to represent woman's sex, which should, however, be thought as indifference prior to the emergence of the mark (unless we postulate a priori that the real—of nature—is as such barred, prior to the emergence of the symbolic, and accept the ontological consequences that follow from it).[101] For the same reason, it is only truth as a function that provides us with an access to the real of the absence of the sexual relationship, and it does so in the guise of infinity. On this level, that of "the love of truth in itself," truth is the "true truth" [vraie vérité],[102] Lacan says on more than one occasion.

Given Lacan's own premises, such a phrase is, as we have already noticed, very problematic. In fact, how does a "true truth" not propose again a "truth about truth"? How can Lacan's "knowledge of truth" not fall back into a "truth of knowledge," something he categorically rejects? Does such a "true truth" not suggest that the contingent in-differentiation of the indifferent not-one through the (sexual) difference of the not-two, culminating in woman's exposition to infinity, eventually returns to the not-one as an ultimate truth, a necessary ontological ground whereby the not-one—now subjectivized as incompleteness—is absolutized into One, the One (not-one)? In spite of many oscillations, I think Lacan senses this predicament; his warnings against identifying truth with the real,[103] which at times are themselves misleading (truth as a function as "nothing to do" with the real ...), should not only be taken as a critique of logical positivism, but also as a self-critique, against any final reification of the truth of incompleteness into being.

My own tentative solution, which I have sketched out in previous chapters and intend to develop in the near future, would be to propose that, thanks to Lacan's antiphilosophy, we can start to think a para-ontology for which the real indifference of the not-one, the impossibility of the sexual relationship that is accessible as infinity by means of the supplementary dimension of the function of truth, is not necessarily an ultimate "truth about truth," yet it is certainly the "true truth" of the speaking animal,[104] the in-itself-for-us, where we grasp ourselves and the nonsymbolic cosmos numerically, beyond the limits of logic. Para-ontology has to be developed out of a materialist agnosticism capable of preventing us from unintentionally clinging to the "one-being"—now masked as the One (not-one)—even after we have concluded that "the One is not Being."[105] The not-one is our true truth, but either the not-one is also an ultimate truth, or the not-One is One. In the latter case, the ultimate truth would anyway not be a knowledge of truth: it would know that it does not know itself and, concomitantly, not know that it knows itself. So there is no reason why we should not in the end practically opt for the not-one.

NOTES

PREFACE

1. Jacques Lacan, *Le séminaire. Livre XVIII. D'un discours qui ne serait pas du semblant* (Paris: Seuil, 2006) [henceforth SXVIII], 147. When unavailable in English, translations from French and other languages are mine.

2. Jacques Lacan, *Le séminaire. Livre XIX. ... ou pire* (Paris: Seuil, 2011) [henceforth SXIX], 186.

3. "Transcendental" should be understood in a loosely Kantian way. As early as Seminar II, Lacan acknowledges that we might "almost" qualify what he names the symbolic order as an a priori category that has a transcendental function (*The Seminar of Jacques Lacan. Book II. The Ego in Freud's Theory and in the Technique of Psychoanalysis* [London: Norton, 1991] [henceforth SII]), 36–38.

4. *The Seminar of Jacques Lacan. Book XX. Encore* (London: Norton, 1998) [henceforth SXX], 6.

5. Ibid., 45 (translation modified).

6. Jacques Lacan, *Le triomphe de la religion* (Paris: Seuil, 2005), 76.

7. SXX, 36.

8. Ibid., 68.

9. Jacques Lacan, *Le séminaire. Livre XVI. D'un Autre à l'autre* (Paris: Seuil, 2006) [henceforth SXVI], 30.

10. "The real is [the fact that] you bathe in signifierness, but you cannot catch all the signifiers at the same time; it is forbidden by structure itself" (SXIX, 30).

11. SXX, 56 (emphasis added).

12. See, for example, David J. Linden, *The Accidental Mind* (Cambridge, MA: Belknap Press of Harvard University Press, 2007), 221–234.

13. See SXX, 70.

14. Schreber believes that his psychic breakdown is due to God's opposing the "Order of the World" he has himself established. Following the orders of God which go against the "Order of the World," Schreber can nonetheless redeem it by "being transformed from a man into a woman," being impregnated by God, and giving birth to a new race of men (Daniel Paul Schreber, *Memoirs of My Nervous Illness* [New York: New York Review of Books, 2000], 41, 55).

15. See Jean-Claude Milner, *L'Œuvre claire* (Paris: Seuil, 1995).

16. "The simple fact that you live at this precise moment in the evolution of human thought does not exonerate you from what was openly and rigorously formulated in Descartes' meditation about God as incapable of deceiving us. [...] The notion that the real [...] is unable to play tricks on us [...] is, though no one really dwells on this, essential to the constitution of the world of science. [...] This step is not at all obvious. [...] The expression *act of faith* is not out of place, which consists in supposing that there is something absolutely nondeceptive" (*The Seminar of Jacques Lacan. Book III. The Psychoses* [London: Routledge, 1993] [henceforth SIII], 64–65).

17. René Descartes, *Meditations on First Philosophy* (Oxford: Oxford University Press, 2008), 16.

18. Quentin Meillassoux, *After Finitude* (London: Continuum, 2008), 92.

19. Ibid., 62.

20. SXX, 31.

21. Using Lacan's algebra beyond Lacan, for whom $S(\cancel{A})$—the signifier that structure amounts to the central flaw of structure—is the most conclusive phenomeno-logical formalization of structure, the either/or I am putting forward at a para-onto-theological level could also be rendered as: either $(S(\cancel{A})) = \cancel{A}$; or $(S(\cancel{A})) = \cancel{A} = A$.

22. See Lorenzo Chiesa, "Hyperstructuralism's Necessity of Contingency," S, volume 3 (2010): 159–177.

23. The deceiving God who is also a self-deceiving God would thereby render the outside-universe—the One, or $(S(\cancel{A})) = A$—truly indistinguishable from the inside-universe—the not-One, or $(S(\cancel{A})) = \cancel{A}$.

24. Jacques Lacan, Seminar XV (unpublished), lesson of June 19, 1968.

25. SXX, 98–99 (emphasis added). Although Lacan states that this God would know nothing of what is going on, it could be argued that the Yahweh of Job (and *mutatis mutandis* the evil genius of Descartes) amounts to a deceiving God who does *not* deceive himself but us (and perhaps the rest of creation?). In this sense, he stands for a less radical version of the il-logical absolute being I am trying to construct logically. His algebraic formula would be: $[(S(\cancel{A})) = \cancel{A}] = A$. That is, the phenomeno-logical oscillation between the One and the not-One is equal to the not-One, but all this is ultimately contained by the One.

26. *The Seminar of Jacques Lacan. The Other Side of Psychoanalysis. Book XVII* (New York: Norton, 2007) [henceforth SXVII], 136.

27. See Felix Ensslin, "Accesses to the Real," in Lorenzo Chiesa, ed., *Lacan and Philosophy: The New Generation*, European Journal of Psychoanalysis 32 (2011): 49–90.

28. Alenka Zupančič, "Realism in Psychoanalysis," in *Lacan and Philosophy*, 47. I have defined such a reassuring absolutization of the absent Cause as "*a* (not-One)" ("Editorial Introduction," in ibid., 15).

29. SXX, 44.

30. SXIX, 28.

31. See SXX, 31, 39; SXVII, 152.

32. SXVIII, 107.

33. SXI, 225–226.

34. SXIX, 110. This passage comes from *Le savoir du psychanalyste*, not ... *ou pire*. In 1971–1972, Lacan ran in parallel two different Seminars at distinct locations. Jacques-Alain Miller, the editor of the Seminars, has included some of the lessons of *Le savoir* in ... *ou pire*, while the others have been collected in *Je parle aux murs* (Paris: Seuil, 2011) [henceforth JPM]. The former are identifiable by the subtitle "talk" [*entretien*]. I will provide the page references of these published volumes but preserve the distinction between the two Seminars in the main text by calling them, respectively, Seminar XIX and Seminar XIXB.

35. SXX, 37.

36. Ibid., 99.

37. Ibid., 118.

38. Ibid., 120.

39. The author who has insisted on the ontological pregnancy of the nexus God–logic–love in Lacan is the philosopher-psychoanalyst François Balmès. I have discovered his work only late in the writing of this book. Balmès, however, by and large clings to Lacan's antiphilosophical pole. That is, he appears to be taking his metaphysical *boutades* as exclusively pertinent to a critical/deconstructive approach without considering them as the agnostic seeds of a much more constructive new atheistic para-ontology yet to be formulated. He cogently unpacks the way in which, according to Lacanian psychoanalysis and thanks to it, "atheism [...] implies a constant confrontation with the question of God" (*Dieu, le sexe, et la vérité* [Ramonville: Érès, 2007], 13). Yet he does not single out the hyperbolic doubt derivable from Lacan's parallel hesitations on this question, thus missing the meta-critical either/or horizon I have attempted to outline above, and, most crucially, the space for action it inaugurates. Conversely, the author who has developed the Lacanian junction being–logic–love in a very original and nondefeatist way, yet throwing God into the landfill of history, is of course Alain Badiou. Badiou has paid a heavy price for his obliteration of the divine by equivocally figuring as the inspirer of the utterly anti-Badiousian (a)theological proposal brought forward by Meillassoux.

40. SXIX, 188.

41. Badiou's stance on Lacan's antiphilosophy is more complex. His labeling Lacan an antiphilosopher is, to say the least, *philosophically* rich: "If Lacan is identifiable as a closure of contemporary antiphilosophy, this supposes [...] an antiphilosophical

relation to antiphilosophy itself. [...] What does Lacan's closure of contemporary antiphilosophy witness to with regard to that which is opened in philosophy?" (Alain Badiou, *Le Séminaire. Lacan* [Paris: Fayard, 2013], 12).

42. Jacques Lacan, *Le séminaire. Livre XXIII. Le sinthome* (Paris: Seuil, 2005) [henceforth SXXIII], 12.

43. SXIX, 30.

44. Seminar XVIII was published in 2006; Seminar XIX in 2011. Seminar XX, on the contrary, was published as early as 1975. Its intricacy cannot but have been enhanced by this disparity in publication dates.

45. Balmès, *Dieu, le sexe, et la vérité*, 81, 96.

46. Monique David-Ménard, *Les constructions de l'universel* (Paris: Presses Universitaires de France, 1997), 136.

47. Colette Soler, *Ce que Lacan disait des femmes* (Paris: Éditions du Champ lacanien, 2003) [henceforth CLDF], 275–276.

48. Geneviève Morel, *Ambiguïtés sexuelles* (Paris: Anthropos, 2000), 70–71, 285.

49. The most remarkable exception to this is the long chapter entitled "The Non-All" in his *Less Than Nothing* (London: Verso, 2012).

50. For an inventive but very convincing reading of the formulas of sexuation, see also Joan Copjec's by now classic "Sex and the Euthanasia of Reason," in *Supposing the Subject* (London: Verso, 1994).

51. In particular, I oppose David-Ménard's contention that, through the not-all, Lacan nonetheless ends up "reproducing the junction, carried out by Kant, between a masculine anthropology of desires and a logic of the universal" (*Les constructions de l'universel*, 24). The outcome of this logical conservatism—whose unfavorable appraisal provides, in the end, the main rationale of her book—would be that the formulas of sexuation "do not fully free themselves of totalization" (ibid., 151).

52. Seminar XVIII is discussed in Guy Le Gaufey's *Le pastout de Lacan* (Paris: Epel, 2006), but the way in which he interprets Lacan's subversion of Aristotelian logic differs widely from mine (see chapter 4 below).

53. SXIX, 30.

54. See SXX, 71. The *être de la signifiance* should be seen as the onto-logical face of the logical-numerical *pas-deux* introduced earlier.

55. SXIX, 36.

56. Animism is "the hypothesis that natural phenomena can and must be explained in the same manner, by the same 'laws,' as subjective human activity, conscious and projective. [...] It would be wrong to smile [...]. Do we imagine that modern culture has really given up the subjective interpretation of nature?" (Jacques Monod, *Chance and Necessity* [London: Collins, 1972], 38).

57. See Jacques Lacan, "Compte rendu du Séminaire 1964," in *Autres écrits* (Paris: Seuil, 2001), 187.

58. Adrian Johnston, "Preface," in Johnston and Catherine Malabou, *Self and Emotional Life* (New York: Columbia University Press, 2013), xvii. Over the last decade, Johnston has without doubt been the most convincing champion of a dialogue between the Freudian-Lacanian tradition and both biology and neuroscience. This is a great merit. I profoundly respect his work and very much benefited from our friendly exchanges. At the same time, I have the impression that his recent writings on "unconscious affects" (see ibid., 73–210) identify a Lacan in Lacan more than himself—following an original interpretive strategy, strongly supported by the texts, that is in many regards similar to mine—for the primary sake of making him acceptable to contemporary affective neuroscience, and only then enabling him positively to influence it. Needless to say, I would very much welcome a rebuttal.

59. Lacan uses the phrase "phallic function" to refer both to the transcendental logic of sexuation/subjectivation and to its formalization.

60. Philippe La Sagna, "Introduction au Séminaire XIX, ... ou pire," available at <http://www.causefreudienne.net/ou-pire>.

61. Jacques-Alain Miller, "Du symptôme au fantasme," unpublished seminar.

62. Paul Livingston, "Politics, Subjectivity, and Cosmological Antinomy," *Crisis and Critique* 1, no. 2 (2014), 33.

63. See Marie-Hélène Brousse, "God and the Jouissance of The Woman," available at <http://www.scribd.com/doc/59167097/God-and-the-Jouissance-of-the-Woman-Marie-Helene-Brousse>.

64. Lacan then eventually returns to "There is no sexual relationship" in 1979 after "the non-relationship—which had the ambition to positively say the absence of the relationship—lost its support," that is, the Borromean knot. In short, the latter's non-uniqueness proves incompatible with his thinking the sexual order as "rebellious to binarism" (Le Gaufey, *Le pastout de Lacan*, 166).

65. See, for instance, Morel, *Ambiguïtés sexuelles*, 11, 19–20. For an unsympathetic assessment of Lacan's alleged "shift away from the empirical world of biology to the metaphysical world of 'structures,'" see Dylan Evans, "From Lacan to Darwin," in Jonathan Gottschall and David Sloan Wilson, eds., *The Literary Animal* (Evanston: Northwestern University Press, 2005), 48.

66. SXIX, 95.

67. Ibid., 16.

68. See Jean Laplanche and Jean-Bertrand Pontalis, *The Language of Psychoanalysis* (London: Karnac, 1988), 239 (emphasis added; translation modified).

69. See JPM, 33.

CHAPTER 1

1. For an early and rightly cautious account of this nexus, see Jacqueline Rose, "Introduction—II," in Juliet Mitchell and Jacqueline Rose, eds., *Feminine Sexuality* (New York: Norton, 1982), 50–57. Of particular interest is Rose's critique of Luce Irigaray's

feminist appropriation of Lacan—which has been seminal for subsequent developments in gender studies—and of the fact that her "refusal of the phallic term brings with it an attempt to reconstitute a form of [feminine] subjectivity free of division [...] a concept of the feminine as pre-given," a notion that ultimately equates the maternal body with "an unmediated and unproblematic relation to origin" (ibid., 54–57).

2. SXX, 77.

3. The published version of this passage of Seminar XX edits and simplifies Lacan's spoken words to the point of completely changing their meaning: "And why not interpret one face of the Other, the God face, as based on feminine jouissance?" (ibid.). Other versions of Seminar XX read quite differently, and are consonant with my interpretation: "Et pourquoi ne pas interpréter une face de l'Autre, une face de Dieu, puisque c'était de ça, par là que j'ai abordé l'affaire tout à l'heure, une face de Dieu comme supportée par la jouissance féminine?" (unpublished GT version).

4. SXX, 74.

5. See ibid., 74, 77.

6. See ibid., 76.

7. Ibid., 77. Balmès has analyzed this formula in a couple of dense pages of *Dieu, le sexe et la vérité* (Ramonville: Érès, 2007, 40–45). The reading he proposes is very different from mine. Suffice it to notice here that (1) he takes for granted, following Miller, the idea that, for Lacan, feminine *jouissance* supports "one face of the Other, the God face" rather than "one face of the Other, one face of God"; (2) he unexpectedly associates the notion of ex-sistence with the masculine exception to the all rather than to the feminine not-all, which has no exception. This latter point will become clear in what follows.

8. Seminar XX starts precisely where Seminar XVIII ended, i.e., with the identification of the Freudian superego with the imperative "Enjoy!" (see SXX, 10; SXVIII, 178). What takes place between these two Seminars—in ... *ou pire* and *Le savoir du psychanalyste*—is the formalization of sexual difference through the four formulas of sexuation.

9. Jacques Lacan, *The Four Fundamental Concepts of Psycho-analysis* (London: Vintage, 1998) [henceforth SXI], 204.

10. SXX, 6–9.

11. See ibid., 11.

12. Ibid., 7 (translation modified).

13. Lacan's basic assumption is that woman's primary biological characteristic concerning sex, the vagina, is not as such symbolizable since, as it does not "stick out," it cannot imaginarily be associated with the differentiality of the signifier independently of the image of the male organ. This is a point he puts forward as early as Seminar III, and it is still valid in Seminar XX. I will return to it on various occasions.

14. SXX, 8.

15. Ibid.

16. Ibid., 7. "Jouissance, qua sexual, is phallic" (ibid., 9).

17. Ibid., 7.

18. Ibid.

19. Ibid., 8.

20. For a clear association of feminine nonphallic jouissance with ex-sistence, see ibid., 77.

21. Ibid., 73–74.

22. Ibid., 10.

23. See chapter 4 and the conclusion, below.

24. Ibid.

25. Ibid. Renata Salecl fails to make this point when she reduces the feminine myth of Don Juan to a fantasy that "proves that there is at least one man who has it from the outset, who *always has it and cannot lose it*" (Salecl, "Love Anxieties," in Suzanne Barnard and Bruce Fink, eds., *Reading Seminar XX* [Albany: SUNY Press, 2002], 96; emphasis added). Salecl is right in identifying Don Juan with the primal Father of the horde as seen by woman (rather than by his sons), as well as in associating him with the exception to the logic of castration, and to the hole of jouissance—as robbed by the Father—which sustains the phallic function. However, she confines the singularizing count of the one-by-one (the feminine phallic function) within the count of the One of universal fusion (the masculine phallic function), instead of evidencing them as the two sides of the same coin: for Lacan, Don Juan is, rather, the primal Father as *unable* to have all women at once. As Serge André observes, "in many versions of the myth, the character of Don Juan mocks the father" (*Que veut une femme?* [Paris: Seuil, 1995], 228–229).

26. SXX, 5–6.

27. Ibid., 4 (emphases added).

28. Speech conveys this ecstatic speechlessness in expressions such as "Oh my God!"

29. Ibid., 3.

30. Ibid., 6.

31. Ibid., 46 (translation modified; emphasis added).

32. See ibid., 4.

33. Ibid., 5.

34. Ibid.

35. See ibid., 4, 24, 83. When Lacan speaks of *la jouissance de l'Autre* in Seminar XX, he is referring to woman's nonphallic jouissance of the not-all. This phrase is, however, highly misleading, since Lacan had previously used it in Seminar XVII to designate knowledge, and, clinically, perversion—that is, the *phallic* jouissance of enjoying for the consistency of the Other, the ideological *j'ouïs-sens* as "I enjoy hearing the sense" of

the symbolic order, which thus corks the hole in structure (see Lorenzo Chiesa, *Subjectivity and Otherness* [Cambridge, MA: MIT Press, 2007], 185–186). The notion of the *jouissance* of the *barred* Other in Seminar XXIII seems to be trying to obviate this ambiguity (see ibid., 186–187).

36. Fink seems to be taking for granted the equation between "another satisfaction" and "Other *jouissance*" as a peculiarly feminine form of enjoyment. As he acknowledges, this leads him to an impasse, since the former is defined by Lacan as a "satisfaction of speech," while the latter is seen as unspeakable: "[Lacan] even says at one point in the seminar that [Other *jouissance*] is 'the satisfaction of speech.' How is that compatible with the notion that it is an *ineffable* experience where the bar between signifier and signified does not function, I do not profess to know." Shortly after, he opts to attribute this apparent contradiction to Lacan's own inconsistent arguments: "We need not assume that there is some sort of complete unity or consistency to his work, for he adds to and changes things as he goes along" ("Knowledge and Jouissance," in *Reading Seminar XX*, 40). The reading I propose, whereby the "other satisfaction" amounts to phallic *jouissance* as different from Other/feminine/nonphallic *jouissance*, shows that Lacan is far from contradicting himself.

37. See SXX, 51 (translation modified).

38. See ibid., 55.

39. Ibid., 33.

40. Ibid.

41. "In the end, if this *jouissance* comes to someone who speaks, and not by accident, it is because he is a premature child" (ibid., 61; translation modified).

42. Ibid., 24.

43. Ibid., 23.

44. Lacan is, however, cautious: what he has so far put forward in terms of *jouissance* "perhaps" involves a *substance jouissante* (ibid.).

45. Ibid.

46. See ibid., 59. I will expand on this in chapters 3 and 4.

47. Ibid. (emphasis added).

48. Ibid., 59, 79–80.

49. Ibid., 11, 23 (emphases added; translation modified).

50. He very briefly returns to it in Seminar XXI, lesson of March 12, 1974.

51. See SXX, 38 (translation modified).

52. See ibid., 64.

53. Ibid., 56.

54. Ibid., 81, 76 (translation modified).

55. See ibid., 24, 33.

56. Ibid., 74.

57. Ibid., 9.

58. Ibid., 81 (emphases added).

59. Ibid.

60. Ibid., 85 (translation modified). De Cock speaks of a "*hors-sexe*" in relation to feminine *jouissance*. This is confusing in light of Lacan's restricted application of the term to hysteria. It also lacks our explanation of the difference between feminine *jouissance*'s nonsexuality within sexuation as opposed to the angelic mirage of *a*sexuality that enchants the hysteric. Furthermore, De Cock states that Other *jouissance* "touches in equal measure man and woman, and can be located on both sides" of the graph of sexuation: this is a clear misunderstanding of Lacan's argument which, rather, contends that both biological females and males can symbolize themselves as "woman" (i.e., on the right-hand side of the graph) and, consequently, experience feminine *jouissance* (Édith De Cock, "Encore," in Moustapha Safouan, ed., *Lacaniana. Les séminaires de Jacques Lacan* [Paris: Fayard, 2005], 307).

61. On the hysteric as distinct from "a woman" yet indispensable for her emergence, see chapter 4 below.

62. SXX, 77. "The Other *jouissance* [is] unrelated to what is sexual [...] It is not a boudoir story; it is not Charcot's 'There is always something sexual'; it is not the 'G' spot" (Juan Pablo Lucchelli, *Le malentendu des sexes* [Rennes: Presses Universitaires de Rennes, 2011], 121).

63. "If she simply experienced it and knew nothing about it, that would allow us to cast myriad doubts on this notorious frigidity" (SXX, 75). Lacan does not specify whether the "frigid" woman is to be fully identified with the mystic *as seen by man*, or whether the fact that a mystic, after all, *speaks/writes* about her knowing nothing about feminine *jouissance* should induce us to consider the "frigid" per se as a failed mystic—a woman who, unlike the mystic, reduces to zero her active participation in the phallic function, but also fully preserves its empty form to the detriment of her *pas-toute*. Moreover, Lacan does not articulate the link between the frigid and the hysteric.

64. In this chapter I will not deal with the formulas of sexuation which appear above the diagram in Seminar XX.

65. SXX, 63.

66. Ibid., 9.

67. Ibid., 63.

68. Ibid.

69. Ibid., 35.

70. Ibid.

71. Insofar as man as $\bar{S}$ objectifies himself imaginarily in the void generated symbolically by the not-all of woman/Other, i.e., achieves identification, and a semblance of the One, only by seeing himself as that which sutures woman's desire—the *real* object-*cause* of his desire—he unconsciously repeats in the fantasy his Oedipal offering of himself as an imaginary phallus that would fully satisfy the mother.

72. On maternity as a *masculine* position in the context of Seminar XX—or, better, as a "masculine position" that is at the same time "a feminine solution to the use of fantasy"—see Marie-Hélène Brousse, "God and the Jouissance of The Woman," available at <http://www.scribd.com/doc/59167097/God-and-the-Jouissance-of-the-Woman-Marie-Helene-Brousse>. The tension in this definition is self-evident.

73. This is valid independently of the biological sex of the child in question: the baby girl also stands for the imaginary phallus of the mother before the resolution of the Oedipus complex.

74. "Analytic discourse [...] brings into play the fact that woman will never be taken up except *quoad matrem*" (SXX, 35).

75. "Negatively additional" since the *not* of the not-all is a *more* [*en plus*].

76. Jacques Lacan, *Le séminaire. Livre VIII. Le transfert* (Paris: Seuil, 2001) [henceforth SVIII], 298.

77. SXX, 75.

78. Ibid., 129.

79. Ibid., 128–129. This is the symbolic-real—or, better, symbolic *as* real—One of structure; of structure as the real. Or also, this is the One as "all alone" (i.e., without a partner) of *Y a d'l'Un* ("There's such a thing as One"). I will investigate it in chapter 4. Preliminarily, it is enough to stress that, in spite of its capital O, the One in question is obviously not the imaginary Plotinian One of wholeness and of what Lacan calls "onto-totology," but a linguistic thing ("There's such a thing as One").

80. Ibid., 83 (translation modified).

81. Ibid.

82. Ibid., 45 (translation modified).

83. See ibid., 82. See also Seminar XXIII: "There is no Other that would answer as partner. The absolute necessity for the human species was [then] that there should be an Other of the Other. It is that which we generally call God, but which psychoanalysis unveils as being quite simply *The* woman" (127–128).

84. SXX, 85. Man defames woman to the extent that as not-all she is regarded as soulless (diff-âme).

85. Ibid., 83.

86. "I wasn't making a strict use of the letter when I said that the locus of the Other was symbolized by the letter A. On the contrary, I marked it by redoubling it with the S that means signifier here, signifier of A insofar as the latter is barred: S($\cancel{A}$). I thereby added a dimension to A's locus, showing that qua locus it does not hold up, that there is a fault, hole, or loss therein. Object *a* comes to function with respect to that loss. That is something which is quite essential to the function of language" (ibid., 28).

87. See ibid., 83.

88. The notion of Y a d' l'Un stems from a complication of that of the big Other. Brousse seems to be suggesting something similar: "When Lacan says, 'There is something of One,' you can think precisely of that Other as the place of signifiers" ("God and the Jouissance of The Woman").

89. For the sake of simplification, we could refer to this further splitting as the distinction, and the connection, between the symbolic one and the imaginary One.

90. SXX, 6 (translation modified). Or also, "the Other cannot in any way be taken as a One" (ibid., 49).

91. Ibid., 57.

92. See ibid., 70.

93. See lessons XIII and XIV of Jacques Lacan, Le séminaire. Livre V. Les formations de l'inconscient (Paris: Seuil, 1998) [henceforth SV].

94. SXX, 72. In short, lovemaking qua perversion is thus the masculine universal in actu ...

95. Ibid., 47.

96. Thus, when religions preach that we should love God, what they really mean is that "by loving God, we love ourselves, and by first loving ourselves [...] we pay the appropriate homage to God" (ibid., 70–71).

97. See ibid., 81.

98. Ibid., 45–46.

99. Ibid., 20.

100. See Suzanne Barnard, "Tongues of Angels," in Reading Seminar XX, 179. Barnard goes so far as speaking of "the strange being of the angel."

101. Bernini's statue of an ecstatic Saint Teresa being pierced by an angel that figures on the cover of Seminar XX is therefore highly misleading. Jacqueline Rose insightfully notices that it makes Lacan's own question "And what is her jouissance, her coming from? [Et de quoi jouit-elle?]" (SXX, 76; Rose's translation) redundant (see "Introduction—II," 52).

102. Jelica Šumič Riha rightly observes that "Lacan opposes the reduction of mystical jouissance to a substitute of the phallic relation. What is aimed at is not the reduction of the Other to the One." However, a few pages later, she seems to equate the mystic with a nonphallic One: "What distinguishes the position of the mystic subject is being all [être tout(e)] in what makes woman not being all" ("L'écriture mystique," Filozofski vestnik 31, no. 2 [2010], 100–101, 109).

103. Jacques Lacan, "L'étourdit," in Autres écrits (Paris: Seuil, 2001), 466.

104. For woman as phallic, man remains part of the Don Juan myth even if she is the only woman he has (ever had). Man counts/matters for woman as long as her singularity is counted as part of a non-universal series.

CHAPTER 2

1. Jean-Claude Milner, *Clartés de tout* (Lagrasse: Verdier, 2011), 17.

2. See Lorenzo Chiesa, "The World of Desire," in *Filozofski Vestnik* 30, no. 2 (2009), 83–112.

3. SII, 41.

4. See Jared Diamond, *Why Is Sex Fun?* (London: Phoenix, 1997), who focuses on "unusual aspects of human sexuality" such as, among others, female menopause, having sex in private, and the expansion of women's breasts even before lactation. Of particular interest is Diamond's discussion of how "the size of the human penis [...] exceeds bare functional requirements, and that that excess size may serve as a *signal*" (ibid., 187; emphasis added).

5. *The Seminar of Jacques Lacan. Book I. Freud's Papers on Technique. 1953–1954* (New York/London: Norton, 1988) [henceforth SI], 145.

6. SXIX, 96–98. My stance is thus opposed to that of Evans, who claims that "the idea of a radical separation between humans and animals, the orthodoxy which Lacan had so boldly questioned in his comments on the mirror stage in 1936, was [...] beginning to creep into Lacan's own work" by the mid-1950s (Dylan Evans, "From Lacan to Darwin," in Jonathan Gottschall and David Sloan Wilson, eds., *The Literary Animal* [Evanston: Northwestern University Press, 2005], 49). Lacan's early work on the mirror stage, which indeed often refers to ethology, is overall aimed at neatly distinguishing man's alienation into his own *Gestalt* and accordingly laborious sexuality from the animal's supposedly smooth functioning of sexuality via the *Gestalt*.

7. SXIX, 110.

8. JPM, 36.

9. SXIX, 154.

10. JPM, 33.

11. Ibid., 69. The diagonal access to the real of sex as a symbolic impossibility that is also our nature requires, more precisely, *formalization*. "There is no sexual relationship" should therefore here be understood as both the intuitive enunciation of the absence of the sexual relationship (as experienced in everyday life and upon entrance into psychoanalytic treatment) and, as such, the axiomatic point of departure of a writing that captures this real as impossible (which in the clinic corresponds to the subject's "rewriting" of his libidinal history in the advancing of psychoanalytic treatment).

12. SXI, 72 (translation modified).

13. See JPM, 37.

14. SXIX, 13.

15. Ibid.

16. See JPM, 34; SXIX, 19.

17. SXIX, 13.

18. Ibid., 15.

19. Ibid. (emphasis added).

20. Ibid., 16.

21. Ibid.

22. Ibid.

23. Ibid., 17.

24. This is, first and foremost, the indifference of the child's own "little difference," independently of his anatomical sex, when he realizes the utter inadequacy of his organ before the differential Desire-of-the-Mother. "We should not forget that the phallus of the little boy is not much more valid than that of the girl" (*Le séminaire. Livre IV. La relation d'objet* [Paris: Seuil, 1994] [henceforth SIV], 193).

25. This, of course, immensely complicates the question of homosexuality. Homosexuality as a same-sex liaison should itself be rethought in symbolic terms. For Lacan, homosexuality always disavows the Other sex (i.e., woman as the *heteros*). It is therefore invariably a liaison between subjects symbolically sexed as men, independently of whether the anatomy involved is male or female. If we consistently think sexuality in symbolic terms, we should infer that not only is anatomy separated from sexuation, but, consequently, sexuation does not necessitate a choice of sexual object/orientation based on anatomy. We could then well speak, for instance, of anatomical females sexed as men who are not symbolically homosexual precisely by establishing a liaison with a subject of the same anatomical sex (sexed as woman). By the same token, anatomically heterosexual couples could easily be founded on symbolic homosexuality. These examples do *not* imply that there is a multiplicity of "genders": sexuation allows for only two sexual positions, out of which a multiplicity of *imaginary* identifications can arise. Lacan's treatment of homosexuality on its own would certainly deserve a systematic investigation of his teaching. This is complicated by the fact that when, even in his late work, he speaks of homosexuality, he tends mostly to refer to *anatomical* sex.

26. Transsexuals do not refute this. On the contrary, transsexuals exacerbate such a "common error" (SXIX, 17). What the transsexual really wants to get rid of by changing sex/organ is not, as he claims, his being positioned on the "wrong" side of anatomical difference, but the phallic signifier that decrees castration on both sides of sexuation. He mistakes the absence of the sexual relationship in language for an error of nature. Or, better, he psychotically mistakes the "common error" of transposing symbolic sexual difference onto the natural possession or lack of an organ for an error in the very order of nature that affects his body. For a clinical treatment of this issue, see Geneviève Morel, *Ambiguïtés sexuelles* (Paris: Anthropos, 2000), 197–225.

27. SXIX, 95.

28. Ibid., 15.

29. SV, 464.

30. Lacanian analysts tend to elide the natural dimension of this argument. They rightly stress that "language has in itself a real, that of number, which cannot be

accounted for by meaning" (Marco Focchi, "Number in Science and Psychoanalysis," *Psychoanalytical Notebooks* 27 [2013], 49). But language as in itself real, and thus number—the number two as not-two, I must stress—is also the in-itself of nature as such, for us at least. As Lacan puts it, "language is something. [...]. It is not us who have made it. It is there" (*Lacan in Italia* [Milan: La Salamandra, 1978], 65). Again, language is real, and thus unaccountable by means of meaning, as both "For logic, there is no sexual relationship, or measure, between the different sexes" *and* "There are two natural sexes."

31. SXIX, 141 (emphasis added).

32. Ibid., 154.

33. See ibid.

34. Ibid., 29.

35. Ibid., 95.

36. Ibid.

37. Ibid., 186.

38. SXX, 131 (translation modified). This juncture is also where one should start developing a dialogue between Lacanian onto-logy and serious gender studies. As Malabou observes, "the idea of 'gender' has never been taken back to its ontological source" (Catherine Malabou, *Changing Difference* [Cambridge: Polity Press, 2011], 1–2). Against Malabou, however, the most urgent problem to be tackled on this agenda would be the following: How can we avoid contradictorily claiming, as she inadvertently does, that "there are not just two genders; there is a multiplicity of genders. *Masculine and feminine* can refer to several of these gender identities at once"? (ibid., 6; emphasis added). If we maintain that the onto-logical "integrity of the concept of 'sexual difference,'" that is, of the primacy of the two—which, with Lacan, I strongly uphold—is by now untenable, where do the "masculine and feminine" needed for Malabou herself to understand the "multiplicity of genders" come from?

39. *Lacan in Italia*, 60.

40. See SXIX, 156.

41. Ibid.

42. Ibid., 156, 43.

43. Ibid., 156; JPM, 35–36.

44. SXX, 105.

45. SXIX, 34. On life as "the last god of modernity," and Darwinism as a "metaphysical paradigm," see Davide Tarizzo, *La vita, un'invenzione recente* (Rome: Laterza, 2010).

46. Mark S. Blumberg, *Freaks of Nature* (Oxford: Oxford University Press, 2009), 191.

47. "What determines sex in these species is the *temperature* at which the embryos are incubated" (ibid., 226).

48. Interestingly, this clitoris "can be erected and displayed during nonsexual interactions referred to as *meeting ceremonies*" (ibid., 232).

49. This is not to say that Freud does not problematically posit an a priori distinction between masculinity and femininity (which he never defines in detail)—where Lacan, rather, starts off from the empirical evidence of the absence of the sexual relationship—but that what, for Freud, falls under these two categories may have more intuitively been thought of as falling under the opposite category. For instance, the little girl's psychosexual development is masculine, while an adult man never completely loses a certain feminine disposition. It is also worth emphasizing that "a certain degree of anatomical hermaphroditism occurs normally" (Sigmund Freud, *Three Essays on the Theory of Sexuality*, in James Strachey, ed., *The Standard Edition of the Complete Psychological Works of Sigmund Freud*, Volume 7 [London: Vintage, 2001], 141) [references to the Standard Edition will henceforth be abbreviated as SE followed by the number of the volume].

50. Blumberg, *Freaks of Nature*, 198.

51. Let us remember that Hans takes a cow being milked as "milk coming out of its widdler" (Sigmund Freud, "Analysis of a Phobia," SE 10, 9). For Hans's attribution of a widdler to a lion, see ibid. Another entity that widdles, for Hans, is a steam engine: "He saw some water being let out of an engine. 'Oh, look,' he said, 'the engine's widdling. Where's it got its widdler?'" (ibid.). This more complex reference to the widdler points to the fact that not only is the penis as sex *organ* always-already a (symbolic-imaginary) phallus, but it can be identified as such even before we can materially locate it.

52. Blumberg, *Freaks of Nature*, 215.

53. SXIX, 43.

54. Ibid.

55. Mary Jane West-Eberhard, *Developmental Plasticity and Evolution* (Oxford: Oxford University Press, 2003), 157–158.

56. Eva Jablonka, "Introduction," in Snait B. Gissis and Eva Jablonka, eds., *Transformations of Lamarckism* (Cambridge, MA: MIT Press, 2011), 146 (emphasis added).

57. Ibid., 145.

58. SII, 48.

59. Stephen Jay Gould, *Life's Grandeur* (London: Vintage, 1997), 19–20.

60. Ibid., 33.

61. Ibid., 3 (emphases added).

62. Ibid., 16, 33 (emphasis added).

63. Consider the following sentence: "Darwin's revolution will be completed when we smash the pedestal of arrogance and own the plain implications of *evolution* for life's nonpredictable nondirectionality" (ibid., 29; emphasis added). This means either that (a) life is still seen as a (nondirectional qua nonunidirectional, and hence multidirectional?) movement that as such evolves—but why, if there is no "toward"?—or (b) if there is no real movement after all, evolution is to be acknowledged as a misleading term: independently of the idea of progress, life does not

evolve and, in turn, its supposed propulsive agency (taken for granted by Gould) needs itself to be tackled accordingly.

64. SXIX, 78.

65. Again, this is first and foremost Gould. See *Wonderful Life* (London: Vintage, 2000, 47), where his main argument revolves around "the largely random sources of survival or death, and the high overall probability of extinction." Not surprisingly, Gould is also a staunch opponent of continual adaptation, or phyletic gradualism.

66. SXX, 17.

67. Manfred Eigen, "What Will Endure of 20th Century Biology?," in Michael P. Murphy and Luke A. J. O'Neill, eds., *What Is Life? The Next Fifty Years* (Cambridge: Cambridge University Press, 1995), 10, 22.

68. Jacques-Alain Miller, "Lacanian Biology and the Event of the Body," *lacanian ink* 18 (2001), 7.

69. See the next two sections of this chapter.

70. SXX, 130.

71. See SXVIII, 90.

72. Milner, *Clartés de tout*, 18.

73. Consider also the political undertones of his condemnation: "The very principle of the idea of progress is that we believe in the imperative [...] 'Forward March!'" ("Conférence à Genève," *Le Bloc-notes de la psychanalyse* [1985, no. 5], 22). This should be counterbalanced with his contemporaneous suggestion, fully compatible with Milner's exhortation, according to which "we are only starting to have some idea of what is biology" ("Yale University, Kanzer Seminar," in *Scilicet* 6/7 [1975], 26).

74. See SXX, 36.

75. See ibid., 31.

76. "This world conceived of as the whole, with what this word implies in terms of limitation, *regardless of the openness we grant it*, remains a conception—a fitting term here—a view, gaze, or imaginary hold" (ibid., 43) (translation modified; emphases added).

77. Ibid., 105.

78. Ibid. (emphasis added).

79. Ibid.

80. Aristotle, *On the Soul*, 2.2.413a, 2.4.415b.

81. JPM, 36–37.

82. Ibid., 37.

83. Ibid.

84. Ibid., 30.

85. Ibid.

86. SXX, 63.

87. See JPM, 33.

88. See ibid.

89. SXX, 66.

90. SXIX, 126.

91. SXX, 67.

92. Ibid.

93. Ibid., 81.

94. Ibid., 82.

95. Ibid.

96. Ibid., 109.

97. Ibid., 110 (emphasis added).

98. Ibid. For Aristotle, the soul is indeed the form or essence of the living body, and that form here amounts precisely to that "in virtue of which individuality is directly attributed" (*On the Soul*, 2.1.412a–b).

99. SXX, 110.

100. SXIX, 40.

101. Ibid.

102. SXX, 84. See also Lacan's close association of the soul with the object a in man's $\$ - a$ fantasy (ibid., 82).

103. Ibid., 88. This in contrast to modern science, for which, "in order to explain the effects of gravitation, we don't need to assume that the stone knows where it must land" (ibid.).

104. Ibid., 78.

105. JPM, 24.

106. Ibid., 110 (translation modified).

107. SXI, 6.

108. See Jacques Lacan, "Science and Truth," in *Écrits* (London: Norton, 2006), 740–741. Lacan speaks of religion in general, but his arguments show that what he has primarily in mind is Christianity.

109. SXI, 8 (translation modified; emphasis added).

110. See Lacan, "Science and Truth," 742–743, 739–740.

111. See ibid., 741.

112. Lacan would have thus certainly disagreed with Gould's methodological precept of "non-overlapping magisteria," for which "the *lack of conflict* between science and religion arises from a *lack of overlap* between their respective domains of professional expertise" ("Non-overlapping Magisteria," in *The Richness of Life: The Essential Stephen Jay*

Gould, ed. Stephen Rose and Paul McGarr [London: Jonathan Cape, 2006], 592). Gould also concludes: "I also know that the subject of *souls* lies outside the magisterium of science" (ibid., 601; emphasis added).

113. SXI, 4, 7 (translation modified).

114. SXX, 107 (emphasis added).

115. See ibid., 84.

116. See SXI, 7–8.

117. Ibid.

118. See ibid.

119. Ibid., 7.

120. See ibid., 9; and Paolo Caruso, ed., *Conversaciones con Lévi-Strauss, Foucault y Lacan* (Barcelona: Anagrama, 1969), 111. The mysticism Lacan refers to here can only be understood as onto-totological phallic mysticism, not as feminine *jouissance*. This reinforces my suggestion in chapter 1 that there are for him two kinds of mysticism, and two faces of God.

121. Be they, in Lacan's times, developmental psychologies and genetic epistemologies à la Piaget or, nowadays, evolutionary psychologies and neuropsychologies hegemonized by cognitivism.

122. Lacan, "Science and Truth," 731.

123. SXI, 6.

124. Jacques Lacan, "Acte de fondation," in *Autres écrits* (Paris: Seuil, 2001), 229, 232.

125. SXI, 69.

126. Lacan, "Science and Truth," 738–741.

127. See ibid., 744.

128. See ibid., 729.

129. Ibid., 738.

130. "Nature provides [...] signifiers, and these signifiers organize in an inaugural manner human relations, giving them structures, and shaping them" (SXI, 20) (emphasis added; translation modified).

131. Lacan, "Science and Truth," 743.

132. Jacques Lacan, "Réponses à des étudiants en philosophie," in *Autres écrits*, 209.

133. SXI, 64 (translation modified).

134. Ibid., 63–64 (translation modified). The notion of *tuché* is adopted from Aristotle's *Physics*, where it designates chance in nature, as opposed to *telos*.

135. See ibid., 69.

136. See ibid., 64.

137. Seminar XI does not yet discuss the object *a* as the object of a specifically masculine fantasy.

138. SXI, 21.

139. Ibid.

140. Ibid., 24.

141. Ibid., 153.

142. Ibid., 154.

143. Ibid., 73 (translation modified; emphases added).

144. Ibid., 99, 73.

145. This applies to both the variegated eyespot of a butterfly with respect to the similar eye of another animal, itself dissimilar from that of a third animal (as both components of the variegated background), *and* the leaf-like appearance of a planthopper in a multicolored/variegated forest, beyond the distinction between attracting and avoiding detection used in evolutionary theory. I will soon return to the idea—in my view problematic—that the environmental background, as "an *itself* that is behind" (ibid., 99), is as such variegated.

146. Ibid., 101–102 (translation modified).

147. See especially Gould's notion of exaptation: the feathers of a bird initially functioned as a heat-regulating device, not as wings qua organ of flight. Gould importantly specifies that "the range of exaptive possibility must be set primarily by nonadaptation," since "nonadaptive sequelae are more numerous than adaptations themselves" ("Challenges to Neo-Darwinism," in *The Richness of Life*, 231).

148. SXI, 102.

149. Ibid.

150. Nature *could* as such correspond to univocal difference only in the case that, as a *whole*, it would be *different* from a transcendent principle, where the latter would prevent nature from partaking of its identity (and prevent localized differences, if present beyond *Homo sapiens*, from partaking of each other's species-specific difference). We will see how, by eventually positing the environmental background as in itself "variegated," in Seminar XI, Lacan is indeed advancing this last point, which I deem incompatible with his dialectical materialist premises.

151. Ibid., 153 (translation modified).

152. Ibid., 102 (translation modified).

153. Ibid. (translation modified).

154. Ibid., 196–198.

155. Lacan speaks in favor of a dialogue between psychoanalysis and an antivitalist biology that does "not simply call upon something real that is alive" in "On an Ex Post Facto Syllabary." The real of nature does not amount to the energetic reservoir of symbolic thought but, rather, to the latter's logical impasse qua its retroactive point of origin. At the same time, this real must be inscribed biologically in the corporeal imaginary of the speaking animal (*Écrits*, 607–608).

156. See SXI, 164–165.

157. Ibid., 162.

158. Ibid., 162–165 (translation modified).

159. Ibid., 187 (translation modified).

160. Ibid., 205.

161. As Lacan will have to admit in Seminar XIX, Freud's debt to nineteenth-century science does indeed, from *Project for a Scientific Psychology* (1895) up to *Beyond the Pleasure Principle* (1920), make him associate the libidinal drive with kinetic energy, a physical living force qua in the end onto-theological force of life.

162. SXI, 165.

163. To recapitulate: the drive does not partake of what biology normally defines as the register of the organic, yet it centers on bodily libidinal organs as revolving around a missing organ. The drive is not directed by a kinetic "shock force," yet it is initiated by the shocking absence of the sexual relationship.

164. One will recognize *jouissance* here. There are only five passing references to *jouissance* in the entirety of Seminar XI, just as the drive is fleetingly mentioned only three times in Seminar XX. Their articulation, however, is clear: in a nutshell, *jouissance* qua "other satisfaction," as treated in Seminar XX, is the paradoxical satisfaction of the drive, as analyzed in Seminar XI.

165. See SXI, 170–172.

166. Ibid., 169.

167. See ibid.

168. See ibid., 176–177.

169. Ibid., 188.

170. Ibid., 183, 177 (emphases added).

171. Ibid., 166.

172. See ibid., 168.

173. See ibid., 177–179.

174. See Jean Laplanche and Jean-Bertrand Pontalis, *The Language of Psychoanalysis* (London: Karnac, 1988), 214.

175. SXI, 179.

176. *Jouissance* thus stands as a third aspect of the partiality of the drive: (1) the drive merely represents sexuality; (2) it does so only in part by representing exclusively the dimension of enjoyment, and not the reproductive function of sexuality (see ibid., 203–204); (3) enjoyment is never absolute.

177. Slavoj Žižek, *Looking Awry* (Cambridge, MA: MIT Press, 1992) 5. Lacan seems to further complicate this in the last sentence of the passage in question, which is usually ignored by commentators. Not only is the goal unattainable (qua "full satisfaction," as Žižek says), and as such negatively subsumed under the circuit of the drive as aim, as I have just explained (what Žižek calls "the path to and from the goal" as

missed), but irrelevant: as in archery, where it is on the other hand possible to attain the goal, the purpose of the drive is not to shoot down a bird, but to score a hit [*avoir marqué le coup*] (see SXI, 179), i.e., making a favorable impression (on the other who is gazing at me). Let us also note that the image of the bow and arrow is somehow deceiving when it comes to illustrate the *circuit* of the drive, one which, moreover, does not involve any kinetic energy.

178. SXI, 180.

179. See ibid., 189.

180. Ibid.

181. SXX, 80.

182. SXI, 196; Jacques Lacan, *Le séminaire. Livre X. L'angoisse* (Paris: Seuil, 2004) [henceforth SX], 50–51.

183. Or also, as "the *object* as absence" (SXI, 182; emphasis added).

184. Ibid., 103.

185. See ibid.

186. An *ex*-aptive homomorphism, we could add.

187. See SXI, 197. It is Miller who speaks of sexuality as "isomorphic" with the "stream of signifiers" (see <http://staferla.free.fr/S11/S11%20FONDEMENTS.pdf>). This part of the discussion, following the lesson of May 27, 1964, has—strangely—not been included in the book version of Seminar XI.

188. SXI, 176–177.

189. See SX, 51.

190. Again, this is a partial enjoyment not only because one cannot reach, or incorporate, the blank object *a* qua squaring of the phallus, but, more importantly, because the goal is fundamentally indifferent for *jouissance*. Paradoxically, what is de facto incorporated procures, in the end, dissatisfaction. For instance, in the oral drive's circling around the breast without ever incorporating it and thus enjoying it, the assumption of food (maternal milk and its "adult" surrogates) always points in the direction of a lack of satisfaction (this is most clearly visible in so-called "eating disorders"): what food lacks in satisfaction (for desire, as we will see) is instead enjoyed by the drive. See also Mladen Dolar, "The Enjoying Machine," UMBR(*a*) (2001), 131–132.

191. SXI, 181.

192. Ibid., 189.

193. Ibid., 191 (emphasis added).

194. See ibid., 186.

195. Lacan makes explicit the link between the object and the soul in ibid., 196.

196. See ibid., 194.

197. Ibid., 196 (emphasis added).

198. See Lorenzo Chiesa, "Le ressort de l'amour," *Angelaki* 11, no. 3 (2006), 61–81.

199. SXI, 186.

200. SV, 443.

201. For instance, Fink adopts this approach in the last chapter of his *A Critical Introduction to Lacanian Psychoanalysis* (Cambridge MA: Harvard University Press, 1997).

202. SXI, 186 (emphasis added).

203. In this sense, in Seminar VIII, Lacan speaks of the phallus as both "the real presence" of desire and, as such, a "shadow of nothingness" (291; emphasis added).

204. Adrian Johnston, *Time Driven* (Evanston: Northwestern University Press, 2005), 195.

205. See SXI, 184–186. Desire would otherwise extinguish itself instantly as a tragic desire for the void.

206. Jamet is right in suggesting that the ideal ego (and ultimately the ego-ideal) provides a unification of the partial drives. I also agree with his contiguous claim that in love, "partial drives have been unified," for they have passed through "the imaginary filter" (see Jean-Richard Freymann and Pierrot Jamet, "Les pulsions I—Les apports de Lacan," available at <http://www.fedepsy.org/pageArticle.php?id=13>).

207. SX, 210. Here we cannot tackle the precise role of sublimation, which is mostly ignored in Seminars X and XI.

208. SX, 51.

209. SXI, 189.

210. This last point is never really articulated by Lacan in Seminar XI. One would need here to patiently read his theory of the drive from Seminar XI, together with his theory of the Oedipus complex—and, in particular, its resolution in castration and the passage from the symbolic phallus to the penis as "real phallus"—from Seminars IV and V.

211. "Everything that is defined [...] at the level of the *Ich* assumes sexual value [...] only in terms of [...] its seizure by one of the partial drives" (SXI, 191). More precisely, what the gaze and the voice carry out by symbolizing the phallus as lacking is a symbolization of the image of the penis as *synthesis* of presence and absence, the *repression* of which is what makes the genitalia appear as *discrete* objects. As for the breast and the feces, Lacan considers them as part-objects related to the insistence of demand during the Oedipus complex (this is explored in his work of the late 1950s, and by and large avoided later). We are left to assume that they are filtered through the gaze and the voice once the full dialectic between the drive and desire is established in fantasy after castration. The strict connection between the breast and the gaze seems self-evident: what fascinates us about the breast is its being all the more hidden as it is increasingly displayed.

212. See Jacques Lacan, *Television* (New York: Norton, 1990), 24.

213. Marie-Hélène Brousse, "The Drive (II)," in Richard Feldstein, Bruce Fink, and Maire Jaanus, eds., *Reading Seminar XI* (Albany: SUNY Press, 1995), 112.

214. SXI, 163 (emphasis added).

215. Ibid., 181.

216. Ibid., 165. On how—in spite of Lacan's exegetical contortionism—a thrust that is thus conceived is something "much more stable" than Freud's notion of *Drang*, which does clearly partake of movement, see Mathieu Bidard, "La pulsion en psychanalyse" (<http://www.apjl.org/IMG/pdf/la_pulsion.pdf>). Bidard is one of the few commentators who rightly emphasizes this point.

217. SXI, 162. It is unclear to me on what textual grounds Brodsky can claim that "what characterizes the drive is its thrust." Her interpretation becomes even more problematic when she argues that the drive qua thrust should be conceived in terms of the "will" (Graciela Brodsky, *L'argument* [Paris: Navarin/Seuil, 2006], 186, 188). All this misses Lacan's main point, namely, separating the drive as a partial representational circuit from any supposed idea of natural-voluntaristic sexual energy.

218. SXI, 171.

219. Ibid.

220. See ibid., 170–171.

221. SII, 95.

222. See "On Freud's 'Trieb,'" in *Écrits*, 722.

223. Johnston, *Time Driven*, 197.

224. See SIV, 46.

225. Johnston, *Time Driven*, 197.

226. SIV, 32.

227. SXI, 171. Or also, as explained, the circuit of the drive has no head or tail, yet it closes onto itself through a gap.

228. Ibid., 169. Lacan says that the pretty woman in question "is lying there for the beauty of the thing." This cannot be a random reference: woman stands here for the *Ziel*, or unachievable goal of the drive, which is barely tickled by the feather/phallus qua missing *Objekt*, enjoyed as such by the circuit/aim of the drive.

229. See also *Television*. We can detect in this later text a minor but noteworthy change of orientation. The objective is still dissipating any idea of "natural energy"—Lacan returns to the image of the dam—insofar as it presupposes that of a substantial "force of life." But here Lacan stresses that the libido/*jouissance* of the drive can never be conceived in energetic terms, *not even as potential/constant energy*: it cannot be numbered, since it is that which un-counts itself (18–19). While Seminar XI attempted to integrate psychosomatically the drive-thrust into the drive-source as a *symbolic* One of potential/constant energy (to be opposed as such to the presumed imaginary One of whole kinetic cycles), *Television* evidences the "difference" between the symbolic One of constant energy and the reliance of the drive-thrust on the not-One of bodily rims (24–25).

230. Brousse, "The Drive (II)," 105. This oversimplification is refuted even more evidently in Lacan, "On Freud's 'Trieb'" (723).

231. SXI, 163.

232. Ibid., 198.

233. Ibid., 197, 200.

234. Ibid., 197–198.

235. Ibid.

236. Ibid.

237. Ibid., 205 (emphasis added).

238. Ibid., 26.

239. Ibid., 197–198.

240. Ibid., 199.

241. Ibid., 205. The unreal is "in direct contact with the real" ("Position of the Unconscious," in Écrits, 718).

242. SXXI, lesson of April 23, 1974.

243. Ibid.

244. SXVI, 33.

245. SXI, 206.

246. SXVI, 33.

247. I owe this reference to Alenka Zupančič.

248. SXVI, 33.

249. Ibid., 34.

250. Ibid., 32.

251. Ibid., 30.

252. SII, 38.

253. Ibid. (translation modified).

254. See JPM, 73–74.

255. "If we are nominalists, we must completely renounce dialectical materialism, so that, in short, the nominalist tradition, which is strictly speaking the only danger of idealism that can occur in a discourse like mine, is quite obviously ruled out" (SXVIII, 28).

256. SXVI, 32.

257. Ibid., 33.

258. Ibid., 35.

259. Ibid., 214.

260. Ibid., 229–230.

261. Ibid., 31.

262. Ibid., 211.

263. I will take Žižek's recent magnum opus *Less Than Nothing* (London: Verso, 2013) as a privileged point of reference, although much of what will be discussed also concerns his earlier books.

264. Ibid., 4, 619, 544.

265. Ibid., 13.

266. Jacques Lacan, *The Ethics of Psychoanalysis* (London: Routledge, 1992) [henceforth SVII], 127.

267. Žižek, *Less Than Nothing*, 8, 15, 16.

268. Ibid., 496–497.

269. Ibid., 547.

270. Ibid., 603, 582.

271. Ibid., 486.

272. Ibid., 4.

273. Ibid.

274. Ibid., 639.

275. Ibid., 498.

276. Ibid., 499 (emphasis added); 4.

277. Ibid., 535.

278. Ibid., 540.

279. Ibid.

280. Ibid., 602.

281. Ibid., 4.

282. Ibid., 596, 498.

283. Ibid., 502, 18.

284. Ibid., 619.

285. Gilles Deleuze, *Cinema 1* (Minneapolis: University of Minnesota Press, 1986), 122.

286. Žižek, *Less Than Nothing*, 608.

287. Ibid., 620.

288. Ibid., 619–620.

289. Ibid., 608–609.

290. Ibid., 499–500.

291. More precisely, as an indispensable weapon against accusations of "idealinguistery."

292. Or also, in Frank Ruda's convincing formulation, we need to think the dialectic between dialectic and nondialectic (phone conversations with the author).

293. Adrian Johnston, "Naturalism or Anti-naturalism?," *Revue Internationale de Philosophie* (2012, no. 3), 326, 332.

294. Ibid., 322, 326.

295. Ibid., 327 (emphasis added).

296. Ibid., 331–332.

297. Ibid., 333.

298. Slavoj Žižek, "A Reply," *Revue Internationale de Philosophie* (2012, no. 3), 440–441.

299. Ibid., 441.

300. Johnston, "Naturalism or Anti-naturalism?," 329–330.

301. Ibid., 333.

302. Ibid., 330.

303. Ibid.

304. Ibid.

305. I owe this expression to Frank Ruda.

306. More specifically, this sublation would correspond to the subjective assumption of the *repetition* of difference *as* identity.

307. Žižek, *Less Than Nothing*, 498, 523.

308. Johnston, "Naturalism or Anti-Naturalism?," 330.

309. Ibid.

310. Ibid., 333.

311. Adrian Johnston, "The Weakness of Nature," in Slavoj Žižek, Clayton Crockett, and Creston Davis, eds., *Hegel and the Infinite* (New York: Columbia University Press, 2011), 174.

312. See Johnston, "Naturalism or Anti-Naturalism?," 340.

313. Ibid., 338 (emphasis added).

314. Ibid.

315. Johnston, "The Weakness of Nature" (draft).

316. According to Johnston, this question could be solved in the near future by an unholy alliance between dialectical materialism, psychoanalysis, and the neurosciences.

317. This proviso should specifically be kept in mind when considering Lacan's anthropogenetic considerations about so-called "prematurity of birth." In brief, for Lacan, the basic species-specific traits of humans, such as an initial lack of motor coordination entwined with an enhancement of the sense of sight, would stem from our (scientifically accountable) premature birth, the fact that, during the first months

of his life, the human baby continues to develop as an embryo extra-utero. This "helplessness" is what in turn would immanently give rise to a high dependency on adult members of the species, thus paving the way for the establishment of symbolic/linguistic "complexes" that partly compensate for our natural "deficiency" by providing us with an ersatz pseudo-environment. More to the point, according to what could be seen as a physiological explanation for the "absence of the sexual relationship," prematurity of birth would be followed by a prematurity of sexual maturation (infantile sexuality as premature with regard to the development of our organism and its ability to reproduce) which would eventually coalesce in our—primarily sexual—neoteny, i.e., our retention of infantile traits as adults. In my view, the mistake to be avoided here is to posit prematurity of birth as a primal onto-logical difference, which not only inevitably introduces the problem of the (phylogenetic) "moment" of anthropogenesis, but also, if we exclude any preestablished norm of nature, poses the question of the parameters with respect to which *Homo sapiens* would be "premature." To complicate things further, as evolutionary theorists have contended, prematurity of birth could itself be an *adaptive* response to difficulty in parturition due to the *excessive* dimension of man's encephalon. According to Gould, "at birth, our brains are still growing at fetal rates [...] if this increase continued in utero, heads would soon become too big for successful parturition" (*Ontogeny and Phylogeny* [Cambridge MA: Harvard University Press, 1977], 370). Again, one should ask here the blunt question: what sense does it make to talk of man's encephalon as such as "too big"? The ontological implications that go with these arguments about a supposedly primal difference of *Homo sapiens* are, to say the least, confusing for a materialist understanding of anthropogenesis. This does not mean that I am denying the relevance of a life-sciences-inspired genetic approach to psychoanalysis's theory of sexuation/subjectivation. It means, rather, that the biological processes described above should always be considered from the standpoint of *empirical* difference, that is, of the absence of the sexual relationship we experience in everyday life, as itself thinkable qua onto-logically in-different.

318. Paul Livingston, "Politics, Subjectivity, and Cosmological Antinomy," *Crisis and Critique* 1, no. 2 (2014), 43–44 (emphasis added).

319. Livingston's proposal is more subtle, in that he identifies the crux of any discussion about the barred real in the alternative between what he calls "inconsistent completeness" and "consistent incompleteness," of which he favors the former. I aim at tackling this in a forthcoming work. Let me just mention that our *differend* ultimately rests on whether, in my view, this alternative is really such, or better, whether "'the world' could not be [thought of as] both inconsistent and incomplete while producing the semblance of consistency and completeness." Livingston argues that one "could maintain 'incompleteness and inconsistency,' but only at the cost of severing the link between them that is shown by the paradoxes [of formal logic] (and Gödel, etc.)." Livingston, however, agrees with my suggestion—which will be tentatively introduced in what follows—that the barred real should also be investigated in relation to the "idea of noumenal causation as 'homogeneous' with the antinomies," i.e., of the equation between One and not-One (personal communications, December 19–20, 2013).

320. Again, Žižek's One *as* not-One, the identity of the Whole with the not-Whole ("totality is by definition 'self-contradictory,' antagonistic, inconsistent," *Less Than Nothing*, 523), becomes also *the two*—because it always-already was it—the (deadlocked) differential movement of the drive.

321. In Seminar XI, Lacan identifies Descartes's *"good"* God, as the God who alone can "reassure" him *against* the hypothesis of the deceiving God, with his *voluntarism*: "Whatever he might have *wanted* to say, would always be *the* truth—even if he had said that two and two make five, it would have been true" (36, translation modified; emphasis added). This "elegant solution" allows Descartes to "get rid of" the subject-supposed-to-know, thus paving the way for the establishment of the knowledge of modern science as detached from truth: "The eternal truths are eternal because God wishes them to be," hence they are simply "his business" (ibid., 225). But here Lacan fails to grasp that, according to this reading, in so doing Descartes would save us from a willingly evil genius only at the cost of implicitly acknowledging that the eternal truth might be that two and two make five; the evil genius that enjoys deceiving us is exorcized only by contaminating the "good" God with the possibility of a God who deceives himself, a God whose *very will would be the indifference of what he wants as eternal truth* (unless we take for granted that two and two must necessarily be willed by God as making four). We could suggest that, from this stance, Descartes already anticipates what Lacan says, in the same context, of psychoanalysis: "The correlative of the subject is henceforth no longer the deceiving Other, but the *deceived* Other" (ibid., 37; emphasis added).

322. I cannot dwell here on how incompleteness, inconsistency, and indifference should be more precisely articulated in para-ontology.

CHAPTER 3

1. SXIX, 31 (emphasis added).

2. Ibid.

3. See SXVIII, 107.

4. See ibid.; see also SXX, 12–13, 69.

5. See SXVIII, 131.

6. Ibid.

7. "What is essential in a relationship is an application, a applied onto b: $a \rightarrow b$. If you do not write it a and b you do not have a relationship as such. […] Something as simple as this would already suffice to make conceivable that there is no sexual relationship" (ibid., 65).

8. Ibid., 83.

9. Ibid., 75.

10. Ibid., 132; JPM, 61.

11. See SXVIII, 132.

12. "The notion of relationship does not quite coincide with the metaphorical use that is made of this simple word 'relationship.' 'They have had a relationship.' It is not at all like that" (JPM, 33). Jean-Luc Nancy captures well the complexity of the term *rapport* as the impossibility of a ratio that goes together with a nonrelational "relation," which eventually rests on what I call the "not-two" (the oscillation between One and an Other that is not another One): "Lacan's axiom uses the resources provided by the double meaning of the word *rapport* [...]; *rapport-bilan* (*report* in English) and relation understood as an activity that goes from one to the other, or, rather, the act of between-two that is neither the one nor the other (neither of the two, nor their presumed unity, nor their simply disjunctive duality). There is no report, no account to be given, no result or product or accomplishment—*achievement* in English—of the sexual relation, and it is precisely according to this measure that there is, indeed, 'sexual relation'" (*Corpus II* [New York: Fordham University Press, 2013], 98). Nancy, however—strangely—seems to play this excellent explanation of the core of Lacan's argument *against* Lacan (ibid., 1–2).

13. "To speak of love is in itself a *jouissance*" (SXX, 83).

14. See SXVIII, 132, 67.

15. Ibid., 67.

16. Ibid., 66.

17. Ibid., 97.

18. JPM, 34. "Sexuality is at the center of everything that happens in the unconscious. But it is at the center in that it is a lack. That is to say that, at the place of whatever would write itself of the sexual relationship as such, we find the impasses that engender the [phallic] function of sexual *jouissance*" (ibid., 34–35).

19. See SXVIII, 105.

20. Ibid., 132.

21. Ibid., 31.

22. Ibid., 32.

23. Ibid., 34.

24. Ibid., 32 (emphasis added).

25. Ibid.

26. Ibid., 142; JPM, 61.

27. SXVIII, 34.

28. Ibid., 142.

29. Ibid., 34–35.

30. See ibid., 35.

31. Ibid., 65. Knowledge indeed occupies the so-called position of truth in the matrix of the discourse of the analyst in Seminar XVII.

32. See SXVIII, 166, 153.

33. Ibid., 166.

34. SXIX, 19.

35. Ibid., 20.

36. SXVIII, 143.

37. See ibid., 15. See also 146, 165.

38. Ibid., 166 (emphasis added).

39. Ibid.

40. Ibid., 27, 13, 26.

41. See ibid., 13.

42. Ibid.

43. Ibid., 165. We can thus sense why logicism and hysteria are basically contiguous ways of inhabiting language (157). The hysteric's denunciation of discourse as mere semblance paves the way for the logician's search for a discourse that would not be a semblance of discourse.

44. See ibid., 15.

45. SXIX, 33.

46. SXVIII, 133.

47. Ibid., 14.

48. Ibid.

49. See ibid., 12, 14.

50. Ibid., 19 (emphases added).

51. Ibid., 13.

52. Ibid., 64. See also 78, 80, 89. This is colorfully confirmed in Seminar XIX (25): "On this function of writing, which is on the agenda thanks to some little smartass, I was not too keen to take sides, but my hand has been forced." The way in which Lacan quickly dismisses arche-writing as a "myth" (SXVIII, 78) is open to debate. Lacan acknowledges that Derrida has good reasons to denounce "a certain blind spot" (ibid.) in everything that has been cogitated philosophically about writing. Overall, what is at stake for Lacan in Derrida is the missing Thing (l'achose) as that which "is absent there where it holds its place" (77). Derrida rightly attempts not to "embody" l'achose, for instance by means of bracketing it or barring it in writing, yet he does not fully realize that in speaking of the missing Thing, all we can do is nonetheless to *speak* of other things (78). In short, Derrida's mistake is to associate l'achose with a critique of logocentrism: logocentrism (or semblance, in Lacan's jargon) remains unsurpassable, for "speech always exceeds the speaker" (ibid.). Likewise, the risk for the "astute" partisans of arche-writing is in the end that of dissociating writing (l'écriture) from what is concretely written (l'écrit) and commented on (89, 80), i.e., of reifying the very bracketing/barring they have successfully accomplished. Michael Lewis comes close to this Lacanian conclusion: arche-writing means that "if

the signifier is actual [...] 'in the real' [...] what must necessarily and continuously characterize the real [...] is that the real must write. It must contain a heterogeneity or two orders, one of which is capable of leaving a trace in the other. From our standpoint, within the signifier, one way in which we may speak of the capacity to trace is in terms of a 'primitive' form of writing." In Lacan's jargon: for deconstruction, la Chose must write itself as l'achose, must write itself as its trace. But, Lewis continues, should this be the case, "what if, in deconstruction [...] there was [...] a substantive thesis on the nature of language and its relation to the real?" (*Derrida and Lacan. Another Writing* [Edinburgh: Edinburgh University Press, 2008], 4–5).

53. SXVIII, 89, 64–65.

54. Ibid., 91, 10–11. In this sense Lacan also defines what is written [l'écrit] as "the return of the repressed" (SXIX, 26).

55. SXVIII, 65.

56. Ibid., 92 (emphasis added).

57. See ibid., 81.

58. Tom Eyers conveys this well: "Lacan forms his concept of the letter by emphasizing its 'material' dimension. The use of the letter as a putatively separate concept is [...] meant to highlight the duality of the signifier. The signifier qua letter, defined as it is through its persistence in the Real, is constructed by Lacan as a material unit that underlies, and undermines, the temporary epistemological sedimentation of meaning via the 'Imaginary effects' of the signifier-in-relation" (*Lacan and the Concept of the "Real"* [Basingstoke: Palgrave, 2012], 53).

59. SXVIII, 81.

60. Ibid., 82.

61. SXIX, 12 (emphasis added).

62. SXVIII, 139 (emphasis added).

63. In the next section I will expand on this point.

64. SXVIII, 72.

65. Ibid., 90.

66. Ibid., 151.

67. Ibid., 77.

68. See ibid., 79.

69. Ibid., 28.

70. Ibid.

71. Ibid.

72. Ibid., 133.

73. Ibid.

74. Ibid., 134.

75. See ibid., 42–43.

76. See ibid., 43, 28.

77. Ibid., 134.

78. Ibid., 99.

79. Ibid., 99–100.

80. We should just mention in passing that this positive acceptation of intuition as real should be linked with Lacan's appreciation of intuitionism when he thinks the not-all. As Russell Grigg has shown, Lacan shares with intuitionist logic the view that the negation of a universal is not equivalent to the affirmation of a negative existential (a view which, we will soon see, in turn follows from his critique of the way in which Aristotle understands the universal negative proposition). This, however, does not mean that he accepts the other strictures of intuitionism—such as the rejection of the idea of the actual infinite ("Lacan and Badiou," Filozofski Vestnik 26, no. 2 [2005], 55–61). On how Lacan's not-all refuses the existence of something (i.e., an exception) that results from a negation of the universally quantified proposition but, rather, involves "'an indeterminate existence,' an existence which must be understood in the intuitionistic sense as an element to be constructed," see Darian Leader's succinct but fascinating article "The Not-All," Jcfar, 4, 1994.

81. "It is a writing, where the metrically superimposable can be talked about" (SXVIII, 82).

82. Ibid., 81–82.

83. SXIX, 130–131.

84. JPM, 61–62 (emphases added).

85. See SXVIII, 65.

86. As Žižek argues, this is witnessed by the recent success of New Age wisdom.

87. JPM, 63–65.

88. SXIX, 71.

89. Ibid., 78.

90. SXVIII, 132.

91. Ibid., 68.

92. Ibid., 148.

93. Ibid.

94. "It is certain that human sexual behavior easily finds its reference in this display as it is defined at the animal level. It is certain that human sexual behavior consists in a certain maintenance of this animal semblance. The only thing that differentiates it from it is that this semblance is conveyed in discourse" (ibid., 32).

95. Ibid., 168 (emphasis added).

96. Ibid.

97. See ibid., 83–84.

98. JPM, 35 (emphasis added).

99. These dystopic passages from the 1970s should be read together with the many instances in which, as early as the 1940s, Lacan harshly attacks social and genetic engineering, particularly with regard to its possible implications for sexuality. For instance, in "Aggressiveness in Psychoanalysis" (1948), he speaks of the "correlation" between the demise of traditional forms of sexuation and "the service of the machine." On the one hand, "in abolishing the cosmic polarity of the male and female principles, our society is experiencing the full psychological impact of the modern phenomenon known as the 'battle of the sexes.'" On the other, "we are engaged in a technological enterprise on the scale of the entire *species*" (Écrits, 99; emphasis added). The two issues must be understood dialectically.

100. SXVIII, 84 (emphasis added).

101. Lacan was heavily indebted to both Koyré (for his understanding of modern science) and Kojève (for the way in which he treats desire and sexuality at large in terms of an intersubjective dialectic of recognition—desire is the desire of/for the other). We might be tempted to attribute Lacan's conflicting stances on the historical dimension of the absence of the sexual relationship to their respective influences: on the one hand, Koyré's take on the scientific revolution of the seventeenth century as a radical epistemic break that nonetheless should be understood according to Kuhn's later idea of periodic "paradigm shifts" in the plural. On the other hand, Kojève's "end of history" scenario, for which, following the advance of twentieth-century capitalism as a homogenizing and globalizing force that fully subdues nature and fulfills human needs, "Man remains alive as animal in *harmony* with Nature or given Being. What disappears is Man properly so called—that is, Action negating the given, and Error, or, in general, the Subject *opposed* to the Object" (*Introduction to the Reading of Hegel* [Ithaca: Cornell University Press, 1980], 158). However, a close reading of Koyré problematizes this alleged dichotomy; he in fact speaks of the modern scientific revolution as a transformation of "not only [man's] fundamental concepts and attributes, but even the very framework of his thought" (*From the Closed World to the Infinite Universe* [London: Forgotten Books, 2008], 4). The extent to which this could be said to have impacted on *Homo sapiens'* transcendental logic as such is not openly tackled by Koyré.

102. To put it simply, the absence of the sexual relationship and the phallic function are, respectively, the real and symbolic aspects of the transcendental: again, structure is the real.

103. See SXX, 12–13.

104. These considerations intersect with what Milner says about Lacan's understanding of the persistence of ancient science in modernity and beyond. To sum up Milner's argument: (1) "The *episteme* [of ancient science] from which modern science separates itself is more a structural figure than a properly historical entity"; (2) "It is therefore true that *episteme* as a historical figure has disappeared, but some of its defining traits remain, because the Ego [or '*dispositif* of Sameness'] remains, independently of periodizations"; (3) Lacan's theory of discourses thus amounts to an

"anti-history," which nonetheless allows us to think periodizations as "a non-chronological and, more generally, non-successive articulation of the concept of cut" (Jean-Claude Milner, L'Œuvre claire [Paris: Seuil, 1995], 54–59).

105. SXVIII, 13. It is fair to admit preemptively that Lacan does not engage closely with Frege's texts, which, however, we have good reason to believe he knew quite well. For a tentative list of the logicians Lacan is likely to have read (including Russell and Peirce, whom he often discusses) see Miller's notes in SXIX, 246–247. In what follows, the signifiers "Frege" and "logical positivism" are to be referred more generally to the various theories of sense and reference initiated by Frege's distinction between Sinn and Bedeutung, and to the modern predicate logic inaugurated by his invention of quantified variables. Here it is not our aim to establish whether Lacan's interpretation of Frege (and logical positivism in general) is exegetically tenable. What matters is the way in which he distinguishes modern—i.e., late-nineteenth- and early-twentieth-century—logic from Aristotle's in order to further develop and subvert them in his own logic of sexuation.

106. SXVIII, 13.

107. Ibid., 73.

108. More precisely, logical positivism takes truth as an ultimate extralinguistic referent without questioning the genesis of language/structure, i.e., without moving from critique to meta-critique.

109. Ibid., 74 (emphasis added).

110. Ibid., 59.

111. Ibid., 45.

112. Ibid.

113. Ibid., 46.

114. Ibid.

115. Ibid., 170. The fact that the objective referent of language is both the real as what is impossible to designate and the phallus is captured well in Seminar XIV, where Lacan equates Frege's Bedeutung with "*structure insofar as it is real*," i.e., not-all (see lesson of February 1, 1967). This means that while there is a real Bedeutung the latter is, however, nothing other than the Bedeutung of the inexistence of the big Other (ibid.). Balmès comments on this important passage, and rightly emphasizes that "Bedeutung is to be understood in the Fregean sense of reference, not of signification" (*Structure, logique, alienation* [Toulouse: Érès, 2011], 56–59); given the inexistence of the big Other, or meta-language, structure as real is the *object* to which language refers. For Lacan, the problem with Frege and logical positivism in general is then that it ends up privileging true reference over metaphorical meaning, instead of dialecticizing them.

116. In the next chapter and the conclusion, it will become clear how this condemnation does not involve only logical positivism's premodern belief in the possibility of expressing a meta-linguistic truth about truth, but also, and in strict relation to this, its attempt at obliterating the *extralogical* status of *number*, which is instead central to Lacan's logic.

117. SXVIII, 135.

118. Ibid., 170.

119. Geneviève Morel, *Ambiguïtés sexuelles* (Paris: Anthropos, 2000), 118 (emphasis added).

120. See SXX, 31, 118.

121. SXVIII, 140.

122. Ibid., 109. As we will see, Lacan's ultimate argument is that all the propositions of Aristotelian logic rest on the presupposition of the universal affirmative as essence. His formulation of the negative propositions in the form of "There are ..." already evokes this. Miller's decision to render the universal negative treated in the passage in question as *Il n'y en a pas qui* ... ("There is not any that ..."), which is supported only by some of the available transcriptions of the Seminar, loses such subtlety and makes it harder to follow Lacan's reasoning.

123. Ibid., 140. As we saw in chapter 2, throughout Lacan's oeuvre the phrase "it is what it is" refers to the *real*. Thus a function, structure as a function, is real. This should be further explored elsewhere in terms of in-difference, that is, in terms of how the being of the structure that is real, in being "what it is," i.e., a metaphoric operator of language as difference, is also literally "that which it is," i.e., an indifferent "idizwadidiz." It is no coincidence that Lacan opposes the idizwadidiz precisely to the use of the copula made by Aristotelian logic (see SXX, 31).

124. SXVIII, 140.

125. Ibid. (emphasis added).

126. Ibid., 111.

127. Ibid., 109.

128. Ibid., 19.

129. This is just a brief anticipation of what I will analyze in detail in the rest of the book.

130. SXVIII, 109.

131. See SXIX, 45. See also ibid., 21: "Everyone knows what emerges, if I can say so, naively from the proposition Aristotle calls particular, namely, that there exists something that would answer to it. When you use *some*, it seems that this goes without saying. However this does not go without saying."

132. Ibid., 44.

133. Ibid., 44–45.

134. See SIX, lesson of January 17, 1962.

135. Aristotle, *On Interpretation*, Ch. 10 (20a 5).

136. *Ambiguïtés sexuelles*, 160.

137. Ibid.

138. In order to better grasp what is at stake, I think we should render such logic of the universal as at work even in the particular negative as follows: "Not *all men are* doing well."

139. SIX, lesson of January 17, 1962.

140. Morel fails to elucidate this. Although she acknowledges that Lacan's turning of the phallus into a propositional function adopts a logic of quantification that is different from Frege's, her presupposition remains nonetheless that the formalization of the real of "There is no sexual relationship" is "parallel" to logicism's reductivist attempt at "constructing the real of number" (Morel, *Ambiguïtés sexuelles*, 119). This is certainly not the case, for the formulas of sexuation aim, on the contrary, at logically circumscribing the incommensurability of the numerical character of sexual difference (the two as *pas-deux*) with logic.

141. SXIX, 14. We should understand these definitions of the Aristotelian universal negative as follows: the universal negative does not strictly speaking *negate* the universal affirmative as *essence*. Rather, it negativizes it by predicating an opposite universal essence: the universal nil of "No man is mortal" turns "All men are mortal" into "All men are immortal."

142. SXVIII, 111.

143. Ibid., 141.

144. Ibid., 111 (emphasis added).

145. See SXIX, 22.

146. SXVIII, 141.

147. Ibid.

148. Ibid.

149. Ibid.

150. Ibid. We have explained how, on the contrary, according to Lacan's critique of logical positivism, for the latter, $F(x)$ can be written only if all x satisfy $F(\forall x . Fx)$, $\underline{\text{or}}$, if some existent x satisfies it ($\exists x . Fx$), although $\exists x . Fx$ does ultimately entail $\forall x . \overline{Fx}$, a nonwriting of the function (about which we do not want to know anything) as universal negative in the Aristotelian sense, unless it is supported by $\forall x . Fx$. For Lacan, $\overline{Fx}$ *becomes instead inherent to the very writing of the function*. It is in this sense that we should understand his claim that "it is not insofar as $\forall x$ or $\exists x$ is given that I can write or not write the function."

151. See SXIX, 22.

152. SXVIII, 141.

153. Morel, *Ambiguïtés sexuelles*, 160.

154. See SXVIII, 109–110.

155. From now on I will try to refrain from using "Universal Affirmative," "Universal Negative," "Particular Affirmative," "Particular Negative," as, evidently, Lacan's rethinking of the four propositions makes these very concepts inadequate for

expressing what is logically at stake in the phallic function. The universal affirmative ("all men are phallic") is preserved only at the cost of making it rely on a particular that *contradicts* it ("there exists a man, the Father, who is not phallic"). Moreover, given Lacan's new way of conceiving negation as a negation of the quantifier, the Father as an *existing* negation of the phallic function could be rendered at best, as an approximation, as a particular *affirmative*, the affirmation of an exception to the phallic function. Nonetheless, at times Lacan also refers to it as a traditional particular *negative* (see SXIX, 207), since after all it still negates the function, which complicates things further. In parallel, a novel approach to the particular negative could be recovered in the proposition for which "there does not exist a woman who is not phallic." This would at first sight seem to point at a traditional universal affirmative (i.e., all women are phallic) or at an equivalent universal negative (i.e., no woman is not-phallic). We will see how this is not the case. Given that, again, negation applies primarily to the quantifier, what Lacan intends to express here is the *nonexistence* of a particular that negates the function. Finally, with regard to the universal negative, it could be associated with the proposition "not-all woman is phallic" in its twofold declination as "not-'all women' is phallic" and "no woman as singular is all phallic." But what such a universal negative loses is precisely *universality*.

CHAPTER 4

1. See Guy Le Gaufey, *Le pastout de Lacan* (Paris: Epel, 2006), 66.

2. One could thus argue that the speaking animal *remains* an unknown in spite of sexuation. Given that "all men are phallic," it would seem that the speaking animal can be known at least as man. But the universality of man rests on the not-all of woman, which is as such unknowable. It is also in this sense that the phallic function sutures the absence of the sexual relationship without superseding it. In other words, both man and woman ultimately preserve their indetermination; psychoanalysis attests to the fact that "What does it mean to be a father?" and "What does a woman want?" are the unanswered questions of the speaking animal.

3. In Seminar XX, the four formulas accompany the so-called diagram of sexuation (78), whose objective is to schematically show how the two sexes are both divided by a vertical bar (representing the absence of the sexual relationship) and interacting with each other. Most readers limit themselves to interpreting Seminar XX, leaving aside even Seminars XIX and XIXB.

4. Lacan starts to formalize his logic in Seminar XVIII. However, important elements of it can be traced back to Seminar IX (see lessons of January 17, 1962 and May 23, 1962).

5. SXVIII, 146.

6. Ibid., 106.

7. Ibid., 143.

8. SXX, 7.

9. This common knowledge is marked at its extremes by the experience, but also the fear or fantasy, of, respectively, impotence and frigidity.

10. SXVIII, 173. It is in this precise sense that "it is not insofar as there exists some man that I *can* write Φx as negated." A particular man's embodiment of the Father, and thus bearing of the phallus, would equate with his being *non*castrated, with the suspension of the very writing of the phallic function as written (affirmed) *and* not written (negated). The function is, rather, negated—but, at the same time, founded—through a *disembodied* Father. Ultimately, the phallic function is nothing other than a logical way of rendering the Freudian "anecdote" of castration (SXIX, 40).

11. SXVIII, 142.

12. Ibid.

13. See SXIX, 21.

14. SXVIII, 142.

15. Ibid. This is close to a naive understanding of psychoanalysis: man is defined as phallophore, woman as not having the phallus (and hence determined by penis envy). In this reading, the notion of negation is limited to the copula "is not." Furthermore, note that in stating "every man is phallic; every woman is not phallic," only to denounce the fact that this statement is untenable, Lacan turns the meaning of the adjective "phallic," which for him means "castrated," into its opposite, that is, "noncastrated."

16. Ibid.

17. Ibid.

18. Ibid., 136.

19. Ibid., 143.

20. Ibid.

21. See ibid., 68.

22. SXIX, 105.

23. Ibid., 136. See also SXVIII, 109.

24. SXVIII, 146.

25. Ibid. (emphasis added).

26. Ibid., 106. I.e., the whole man exists as "some man" only if we understand the "some" as "not-more-than-one." We will return to the *pas-plus-d'un* later in this chapter.

27. See ibid., 142.

28. "There does not exist an x that satisfies the phallic function" seems far less compatible with my reading—aimed at showing that particular existence is in the end postulated retroactively—than "It is not insofar as *there exists some man* that I can write or not write Φx," unless we change the former into "There does not exist an x that *alone* satisfies the phallic function."

29. Monique David-Ménard, *Les constructions de l'universel* (Paris: Presses Universitaires de France, 1997), 148–149.

30. I thus concur with Lemoine's suggestion that "the phallic function is already contradictory in its very principle, as it defines itself by its own limit." However, I find it more problematic to state that "the universal cannot be limited from the outside, by omnitude, the closed whole, but can only be negated from within by the absence of the trait in question" (Gennie Lemoine, "A Reading of the Formulae of Sexuation," available at <http://www.jcfar.org/jcfar_vol_3.html>). No doubt the closed whole is, for man, a semblance, given that universality is contradictory. But Lemoine's claim already takes it for granted that such contradiction, and the oscillation between the masculine all and the feminine not-all without which there would be no contradiction, could not as such have as an outcome their limitation from the outside or an identity of all and not-all. Even leaving aside these para-ontological considerations, Lemoine does not account for the fact that the universal that is—perhaps—ultimately not a closed whole nonetheless appears to man as a closed whole, as the World. One must indeed "not confuse" logically "universality and omnitude" (ibid.); yet this confusion is precisely what defines *phenomeno*-logically man as man. ...

31. I therefore agree with Simmoney in saying that "existence is here only of the domain of the *possible*," which amounts exactly to the logical modality through which Lacan thinks the universal masculine. However, I find it problematic to state that "the universal *every man* does not ensure existence for man" (Dominique Simmoney, "... ou pire," in Moustapha Safouan, ed., *Lacaniana. Les séminaires de Jacques Lacan* [Paris: Fayard, 2005], 260). It *does* ensure it in the sense that it is possible for particular men to exist as phallic after the instauration of the phallic universal, which itself relies on the nonphallic exception. I also disagree with Simmoney's assertion that the existence of man "will thus be taken through the one by one" (ibid., 261): for Lacan, it is women who in-exist, and ex-sist—as we shall see—as singular "one by one" in relation to the phallic exception. On the contrary, once again, men have the retroactive possibility to exist only as particular—split—elements of the phallic universal qua logic of exception. Particular xs finally exist as men as long as they are subsumed by a universal essence initially deprived of existence, which the universal essence nonetheless "passes on" to the particulars via the (nonessential) existing exception—and thus acquires itself through the particulars. The eventual existence of "all men are phallic" is nothing other than the semblance of the World, of a men's World.

32. SXVIII, 74. *La femme n'existe pas* does not appear verbatim in Seminar XX. After Seminar XVIII, Lacan uses this expression in *Television* (38), Seminar XXI (lessons of February 12, 1974 and June 11, 1974), and Seminar XXII (lessons of February 11, 1975 and February 18, 1975).

33. SXVIII, 143.

34. See ibid., 65–66.

35. Yet every brother continues to desire the "all women," so that the establishment of a sexual liaison with one or more women is still under the aegis of the absence of the sexual relationship. Particular men always take themselves a little for the Father of the horde.

36. See SXVII, 113.

37. Freud would thus remain a thinker of the One, of the solidarity between the original Father, Being, and Life.

38. Seminar XVIII's overall task is spelled out by Lacan as "interrogat[ing] a bit further, from the stance of logic, of writing [...] the myth [...] of the primordial father" (ibid., 68–69).

39. Ibid., 69.

40. The negated "all women" are thus conceived as a segregated harem; or also, as an *orgiastic* fantasy particular men indulge in (see SXIX, 98). The retroactive emergence of universality is already implicit in Freud's own story: "One day the brothers who had been driven out *came together*, killed and devoured their father" (*Totem and Taboo*, SE 18: 141; emphasis added). The communal coming-together of men, universal brotherhood, can be thought only against the background of the killing of the Father, which turns him into a symbol, namely, the disembodied phallus.

41. SXVIII, 97.

42. See Freud, "Analysis Terminable and Interminable," SE 23: 250–253.

43. Finally, Freud would then put forward the function $\Phi(x,y)$. It is in this sense that we should understand Lacan's reproach to Freud in "L'étourdit" (in *Autres écrits* [Paris: Seuil, 2001], 463) that he ended up measuring the two sexes with the same "yardstick" [*toise*]. Of course, as Morel reminds us, this does not in the least mean that Lacan does not "preserve the reference to the phallus for both sexes" (Geneviève Morel, *Ambiguïtés sexuelles* [Paris: Anthropos, 2000], 154).

44. SXVIII, 106 (emphasis added).

45. Ibid., 74–75.

46. Ibid., 106.

47. Obviously, this existence negating the phallic function could not be the phallus, i.e., the symbolic Father's negation of Φx, but an alternative symbol (possibly derived from the vagina) that would found a different feminine sexual function Ωx, valid for "every woman." However, Ωx would instantaneously cause the collapse of Φx, and the symbolic order with it, since man becomes a man only by "making the man" in the presence of woman qua not-"*every woman.*"

48. SXVIII, 106.

49. See ibid.

50. See SXIX, 46; SXVIII, 33. The myth of the Father of the horde would ultimately conceal nothing other than the *Ablehnung der Weiblichkeit* as a symptomatic "neurotic product" of Freud's "own impasses," of his obsessional inability to fully confront the desire of the hysteric (see ibid., 158, 161).

51. Ibid., 143.

52. In this sense, all women *are* hysterics for Freud, to the extent that, as Lacan spells out, "the hysteric is not *a* woman" (ibid., 155).

53. In other words, man is a barred subject that exists only through the contradictory essence provided by castration.

54. David-Ménard, Les constructions de l'universel, 139.

55. See Le Gaufey, Le pastout de Lacan, 47–101.

56. See SXIX, 109–110.

57. Ibid., 46.

58. Ibid. (emphasis added).

59. Dylan Evans, An Introductory Dictionary of Lacanian Psychoanalysis (London: Routledge, 1996), 220–221.

60. SXX, 72.

61. "There is no such thing as The woman, where the definite article designates the universal. There is no such thing as The woman because, in her essence [...] she is not-all" (ibid., 72–73) (translation modified).

62. See SXIX, 47. Transcripts of this tricky passage widely differ, and there is no doubt it can be interpreted in various ways. I think Miller's decision to render Lacan's argument as $\overline{\exists x} . \Phi x$ makes perfect sense. On the other hand, I disagree with Miller when he writes the formula that follows on the same page as $\overline{\exists x} . \Phi x$. In this case, Lacan is in fact speaking of the Father, as is clear from the context.

63. This is the problem with Ragland's conclusion that "one of the paradoxical consequences of all women's lacking the totalized phallic injunction is that all are not all under the sway of its requisites" (Ellie Ragland, The Logic of Sexuation [Albany: SUNY Press, 2004], 183).

64. SXIX, 47.

65. Ibid.

66. Ibid.

67. Ibid. (emphasis added).

68. Lemoine summarizes this well: "It is thus proposed that woman, like any x, cannot say no to the phallic function. But not no only; nor yes only. [...] They say yes and no" ("A Reading of the Formulae of Sexuation"). As we will see, Lacan thinks this in terms of undecidability.

69. Or clitoral, or extragenital, for that matter. ...

70. See especially SXXI, lesson of June 11, 1974.

71. SXVIII, 34.

72. See ibid.

73. Ibid., 155.

74. Ibid., 156. See also 170.

75. Ibid., 147.

76. Ibid., 155.

77. Ibid., 143.

78. Ibid.

79. See Seminar VI, lesson of February 11, 1959. I do not refer to the recently released book version, since the lesson in question presents the reader with numerous editorial problems.

80. "'Not being without' [...] puts into question the logic of attribution through a negation that lightens the ontological weight of the verb 'to be,' indicating that what defines sexuation skirts around any ontological determination, and thus no doubt a logic of the Aristotelian kind" (David-Ménard, Les constructions de l'universel, 141).

81. SIII, 176. As I write in Subjectivity and Otherness, quoting Lacan's early Seminars, "this is due to the fact that, in the case of the female sex, 'the imaginary furnishes only an absence where elsewhere there is a highly prevalent symbol [...] the phallic Gestalt.' In other words, [...] the girl has 'to take the image of the other sex as the basis for her [symbolic] identification.' She cannot assume her sex at the symbolic level in a direct way" (Lorenzo Chiesa, Subjectivity and Otherness [Cambridge, MA: MIT Press, 2007], 84–85).

82. SIV, 153.

83. See Chiesa, Subjectivity and Otherness, 87–88.

84. In what follows, we should refrain from associating this distinction with that between the imaginary phallus φ and the symbolic phallus Φ as presented in the late 1950s and early 1960s. Lacan himself drops it. In the 1970s, the Phallus as an exceptional symbolic existence that does not abide by the phallic function, which is written as Φ, clearly brings with it imaginary aspects, i.e., the phantasy of absolute jouissance. Conversely, the phallus can no longer simply be seen as that which both sexes renounce during the Oedipus complex in terms of the imaginary being in relation to the Mother: as Lacan knew as early as the 1950s, this "relation" is always-already symbolically mediated. After the resolution of the Oedipus complex, the phallus is, moreover, that which circulates between man and woman—in their approaches to the Phallus—as their very sexual difference. These complications are proximate to Lacan's overlapping, in the same years, of (symbolic) desire with (imaginary) love, as discussed in chapter 1. Last but not least, the real phallus is here far from being reducible to the penis as an organ. The Phallus as an exceptional symbolic existence clearly also partakes of the register of the real: "There exists an x that does not abide by the phallic function," i.e., Il y a de l'Un, is a logical necessity only insofar as it marks a logical impossibility, that is, the absence of the sexual relationship. Or, also, the symbolic One (imaginarily phantasized as having all women) is structurally "all alone," without a partner, and thus real.

85. David-Ménard, Les constructions de l'universel, 149.

86. Again, this relation is (1) indirect, since the phallus is needed as a third term; (2) asymmetrical, since there is no feminine alternative to the phallus; (3) unmediated, since the phallus as a third term does not function as a middle term between

the sexes (or we can equally speak of an indirect mediation, whereby man does not relate to woman via the phallus, but only insofar as she refers to it while he also refers to it, and vice versa).

87. Colette Soler, *Ce que Lacan disait de femmes* (Paris: Éditions du Champ lacanien, 2003) [henceforth CLDF], 27.

88. SXVIII, 68 (emphasis added).

89. The expression "not-at-all" is mine, while "*parenthèse vide*" comes from Soler (CLDF, 26). I propose to read the latter especially with reference to the formal writing of the phallic function. The "()" of hysteria is required for the speaking animal x to be inscribed as man or woman in $\Phi(x)$. Later on it will also become clear that such empty parenthesis should also be understood numerically as a zero.

90. CLDF, 61.

91. Conversely, for man, being phallic by having the phallus entails not being the Phallus, i.e., being castrated. In order to be the uncastrated Phallus, man should have *The* woman. Since *The* woman does not exist, man has access only to *a* woman, or better, to the insignificant little nothing through which *a* woman is herself phallic (which is far from exhausting her being also "beyond the phallus"). Even more limitedly, man has phantasmatic access only to that part of *a* phallic woman that is passively captured as the object *a* (as his phallus). The active dimension of *a* woman's being in the phallic function as the one-by-one itself escapes man, or also, is presented to him as the impasse of constructing *The* woman out of the object *a*.

92. CLDF, 61.

93. Ibid.

94. See SXVIII, 106, 155.

95. See ibid., 144, 153.

96. In Seminar XVIII, Lacan conveys such a hysterical deadlock—whereby the hysteric "reserves to [her man] a deliberate castration"—precisely when he first advances his two formulas of sexuation: "In the impossible solution to her problem," namely, finding a man who is a whole man, "it is by measuring the cause [of this problem] in the most accurate way," i.e., by being fully aware that man's embodying the phallic + is a semblance, "that, among those she feigns to be the bearers of this semblance, the hysteric gives herself at least one conforming to the bone her *jouissance* needs for her to gnaw on it" (153).

97. SXX, p. 85.

98. See SXVIII, 144. See also <http://staferla.free.fr/S18/S18%20D'UN%20DISCOURS ...pdf> for a transcription that seems to me more accurate.

99. SXVIII, 143.

100. Ibid., 144.

101. Ibid.

102. Ibid. (emphases added).

103. Miller fails at times to differentiate *tout homme* from *touthomme*. For example, the passage we have just analyzed becomes in my view unintelligible if we transcribe it as "*Ce que l'hystérique articule, c'est bien sûr que, pour ce qui est de faire le touthomme, elle en est aussi capable que le touthomme lui-même.*" Given the context, the second *touthomme* should read *tout homme*, i.e., "every man."

104. Lacan, "L'étourdit," 464.

105. "Potentially," since out of "every man" some particular really existing men are more inclined than others to fall in love with the hysteric. This is due to their own problematic coming to terms with castration and the fact that they cannot be the Father. "You must not believe that [the hysteric's] success passes by way of one of these men, virile men, who are rather embarrassed by semblance," i.e., by embodying the phallic +. "Those that I am designating in this way [as 'at least one'/*hommoinzin*] are the wise men, the masochists" (SXVIII, 153).

106. Ibid., 143.

107. Ibid., 156, 170.

108. Ibid., 154.

109. Ibid., 155.

110. Ibid., 156.

111. Ibid., 155.

112. Ibid., 156.

113. Ibid., 147.

114. JPM, 35.

115. CLDF, 7, 65.

116. I am by no means exaggerating Lacan's critique of Freud. Although he tends to stress the continuities between Freud's and Lacan's take on hysteria (and woman more in general), and does not always share the way in which Lacan reads Freud, Verhaege comes to a conclusion very similar to mine. Quoting Seminar XVIII, he suggests that "with his answer, that is, his Oedipal theory"—where, more specifically, "this answer is *Totem and Taboo*, according to Lacan"—"*Freud followed in the footsteps of the hysterical subject. His Oedipal theory*"—whereby woman is defined through penis envy as a "biological bedrock"—"'*was dictated by hysterics*'" (Paul Verhaege, *Does The Woman Exist?* [London: Rebus Press, 1997], 206–207, 229; emphasis added). Verhaege also concludes that, for Lacan, "the hysteric opts for a masculine line of development and can only inscribe herself phallically in a *negative way*" (245; emphasis added), a point which I am trying to unravel here, in all its logical complexity. André's considerations on Lacan's "veritable solution to the Freudian impasse" concerning hysteria and femininity at large are also consonant with my interpretation. He admits that "the problem of feminine penis envy [...] should be considered, in Freud's oeuvre, as the attempt to seize the key to a univocal desire, which would allow for the uniting of women in a set. It is precisely this notion of a 'set of women' that Lacan puts fundamentally into question; this is why we will emphasize the term *a* woman [*une femme*]" (Serge André, *Que veut une femme?* [Paris: Seuil, 1995], 29, 19).

117. SXVIII, 147.

118. SXIX, 176 (emphasis added).

119. Lacan claims that "in any relation of man with a woman [...] it is from the perspective of the One-missing that she must be taken up" (SXX, 129; emphasis added). As Fink observes, the French expression *l'Une en moins* can be rendered as both "the One-missing" and "the One-less." I would specify only that the capital "One" stresses the absence of the feminine universal, while the lower-case "one" seems more appropriate when focusing on woman's singularity. In the latter case, "the one-*less*" better emphasizes the counting of the "one-by-one" than "the one-missing." These two dimensions (that of "the One-missing" and that of "the one-less") are, however, entwined, and cannot be conceived correctly in isolation.

120. I.e., the vectors $\$ \rightarrow a$ and $\cancel{L\!a} \rightarrow S(\cancel{A})$. It will become clear that these result from $\forall x . \Phi x \rightarrow \overline{\forall x} . \Phi x$ and $\overline{\forall x} . \Phi x \rightarrow \overline{\exists x} . \overline{\Phi x}$. Similarly, the vector $\cancel{L\!a} \rightarrow \Phi$ from Seminar XX, that is, woman's active involvement in the phallic function, results from $\overline{\forall x} . \Phi x \rightarrow \exists x . \overline{\Phi x}$ as discussed in Seminars XIX and XIXB.

121. SXIX, 39–40.

122. Ibid., 222.

123. Ibid., 210.

124. And vice versa: woman accesses man only insofar as he relates to the Phallus in a way that is logically different to the one in which she relates to it. As I have argued, such logically different relating to the Phallus also involves differently (mis-)taking the other sex for the phallus.

125. SXIX, 69, 207.

126. Ibid., 14.

127. See JPM, 16.

128. Ibid., 21; SXIX, 195, 11.

129. I have decided to translate "sur" as "of," although it should be clear by now that "knowledge of truth" does not at all mean "knowing the truth," in the sense of "owning the truth." The literal translation "over" would be misleading, as it seems to suggest a primacy of knowledge over truth. Maybe the most straightforward way to capture *savoir sur la vérité* is to refer to the matrix of the discourse of the analyst, where S_2, i.e., knowledge, occupies the position of truth, but does not exhaust it.

130. See SXIX, 12. The title of Seminar XIX, ... *ou pire*, should therefore be read as "Say the void (the aptly called "suspension points") or say worse." This also gives us a key with which to interpret the title of Seminar XIXB, *Le savoir du psychanalyste*. The psychoanalyst should know that either one says the void or one says worse.

131. See SXIX, 173–174.

132. JPM, 83. In two schemas of Seminar XIX, Lacan indeed writes the object *a* in between $\forall x . \Phi x$ and $\overline{\forall x} . \Phi x$ (see 202, 207).

133. JPM, 83–84.

134. SXIX, 182.

135. See SXX, 112, 126; SXVIII, 34.

136. SXIX, 203.

137. See JPM, 67–68.

138. SXIX, 183–184. I will return to this in the next section.

139. Ibid., 21.

140. Ibid., 35.

141. Ibid., 36, 27.

142. Ibid., 21.

143. This precedes his three accounts of the "circulation" among the formulas, and should be seen as propaedeutic to them.

144. Ibid., 22. Lacan does not call the "to be able not to" "contingency" (although this is implicit) and, rather intriguingly, asks—without answering—whether this is contingency or possibility. Why? Because, for reasons that will become apparent, in spite of dethroning Aristotle's notion of possibility (as *there exist some*), he nevertheless stresses possibility's mutual dependence as universality with contingency as the not-all. He calls this a "discord," and characterizes it as the only realm where "the opposition between the sexes is *founded*," and the phallic function (which also encompasses necessity and impossibility) functions (ibid., 107, 105).

145. Ibid., 22.

146. As we have seen in previous chapters, para-ontologically, we can only know that we do not know whether this in-itself-for-us is in itself illogical.

147. Hence the return to impossibility as impotence does *not* entail a resigned acceptance of impotence. The same move in fact involves "raising impotence (that which accounts for phantasy) to the level of logical impossibility (that which embodies the real)" ("Compte rendu du Séminaire XIX," in SXIX, 243). As Badiou nicely puts it: "This could well be the definition, which I have sought for a long time, and which Lacan had found long ago for a completely different use, of … philosophy" (Alain Badiou, *Le Séminaire. Lacan.* [Paris: Fayard, 2013], 10).

148. Monique David-Ménard, *Éloge des hazards dans la vie sexuelle* (Paris: Hermann, 2011), 62.

149. Ibid., 63.

150. Ibid., 63–64. A close consideration of the return to impossibility as active assumption of castration, or better, of the extent to which this assumption is *possible*, would also give us an appropriate logical context in which to test the viability of *true* love in Lacanian theory.

151. SXIX, 48.

152. See ibid., 47.

153. "There is no status of the *all*, that is, of the universal, except from the level of the possible" (ibid., 45). This possibility is more precisely that of a "limited" sexual (i.e., phallic) *jouissance* granted by castration (ibid., 47).

154. Here I disagree with Žižek's contention that "contradiction only occurs within each of the sexes, between the universal and the particular of each sexual position" (Slavoj Žižek, *Less Than Nothing* [London: Verso, 2013], 760). Lacan states that the two propositions of both sexual positions should be read in terms of an intrasexual "opposition," but *contradiction* applies exclusively to the *masculine* opposition.

155. SXIX, 48.

156. Ibid., 47.

157. We have investigated this by means of the hysteric's and Freud's similar mistake in considering sexuation. Such a mistake eventually turns impossibility as "There does not exist a woman for whom the phallic function cannot be written" into *necessity* as "It is impossible for woman not to know the phallic function." In this way, one returns to the marginalization of impossibility for the benefit of the equation between necessity and universality that characterizes classical onto-logy.

158. SXIX, 47.

159. See ibid.

160. Ibid. The latter is a good general description of the object a—as the way in which man approaches woman in $\barred{S} \rightarrow a$. The "approach" in question is less than an "access," an access which would anyway be confined to the phallic function (as is woman's access to man qua "every man" in contradiction with the One) and would thus anyway preclude the Other sex as such. This is the case because man does not relate to woman as *a* singular woman—that is, to the way in which woman not-all gives herself to man—but in a vain orgiastic attempt to possess *every* woman. This point will become clearer as we progress in our analysis of the logical circulation between the four formulas.

161. SXIX, 47.

162. Ibid., 48 (emphases added).

163. These variations on the one correspond, respectively, to $\overline{\exists x}.\overline{\Phi x}$, $\exists x.\overline{\Phi x}$, $\forall x.\Phi x$, and $\overline{\forall x}.\Phi x$.

164. SXIX, 99.

165. Ibid.

166. Ibid.

167. Ibid., 103.

168. Ibid., 100.

169. Once again, x itself is not masculine or feminine: it refers to "speaking being."

170. "Inasmuch as it is a matter of the phallic function, from whatever side you look at it, […] something prompts us to ask then how the two partners are different. […] If it proves that from the fact of equally dominating the two partners the phallic function does not make them different, it nonetheless remains that we should search for difference elsewhere" (ibid., 101); that is, in the real not-two of sexual difference, in the gap between the fact that there are two sexes but there is not a second sex, represented as such.

171. Ibid.

172. Ibid.

173. Ibid.

174. Ibid.

175. We will return to the phrasing of this argument. Given Lacan's own premises, it is quite problematic to refer to the absence of the sexual relationship as the "true truth." One in fact needs to clarify how this would not amount to a "truth of knowledge," or a "saying the truth about truth," which Lacan rejects.

176. Ibid., 102 (emphasis added).

177. See ibid.

178. The last passages remain implicit in Lacan.

179. Ibid., 103.

180. See ibid., 102–103.

181. Here we should bear in mind that $\overline{\exists x}.\overline{\Phi x}$ does not imply that there exist some particular women, or even a particular woman, who is phallic, since singular women in-exist as not-all phallic only through an insignificant little nothing. As for particular phallic men, we have seen how they are derived only through the contradiction between $\exists x.\overline{\Phi x}$ and $\forall x.\Phi x$: strictly speaking, the formulas of sexuation do not allow us to put forward the proposition "there exist some men who are phallic" (or even "there exists a man who is phallic").

182. See ibid., 103.

183. Ibid.

184. "We find on the one side only *one* [...] and, on the other, non-existence, that is, *the relation of one to zero*" (ibid.; emphasis added).

185. Ibid.

186. See ibid., 104.

187. Ibid., 102, 105.

188. Ibid., 107 (emphasis added).

189. Ibid., 105.

190. Ibid., 106. As we will see in the conclusion, the passage from 0 and 1 as 2 qua not-two to 2 as a natural number is what, for Lacan, is problematic in Frege's logical account of number, and has for him distinctively ontological repercussions. This passage is also crucial for any attempt at distinguishing between imaginary ordinary love—the semblance of 2 as *one* natural number—and true love—the not-two. With regard to the latter, the question then arises as to whether the not-two is, to put it simply, phenomeno-logically subjectivizable as such.

191. Ibid., 107.

192. Ibid.

193. Ibid., 163.

194. Ibid., 107.

195. Which is, as a syncope, the true nature of "the One happens" as all alone. See the conclusion.

196. That is, $\forall x . \Phi x \leftrightarrow \exists x . \overline{\Phi x}$; $\overline{\forall x} . \Phi x \leftrightarrow \exists x . \overline{\Phi x}$.

197. Woman's relation to her inexistence—$\overline{\forall x} . \Phi x \rightarrow \overline{\exists x} . \overline{\Phi x}$ or $\cancel{L\!a} \rightarrow S(\cancel{A})$—which makes her ex-sist beyond the phallus, is ultimately the reason why sexuation is obtained only as "discordant."

198. SXIX, 105 (emphases added).

199. Ibid., 107–108.

200. The first adheres to Lacan's customary association of necessity with one of the four formulas of sexuation, i.e., with the One that necessarily exists as an exception; the second extends logical necessity to the two formulas of man, but unlike the passage commented on earlier, in this case logical necessity as the contradictory relation between the possibility that all men are phallic and the necessity of the one man who is not phallic relies on *contingency*; the third also encompasses woman, and thus refers to the necessity of the phallic function taken in its entirety (the four formulas) as a necessity of *discourse*, which is a semblance.

201. SXX, 94 (emphasis added).

202. See ibid., 93–94. See also Seminar XVIII, where Lacan speaks of "favorable anatomic contingencies" (33).

203. Or, better, into the necessity of the contingency of necessity.

204. The absolute necessity of the deceiving God can be thought of as the necessity of *contradiction*, the contradiction between our universal, and unredeemable, contingency and God's necessity: God deceives us through his logic of exception, which now closes onto itself as an ultimate truth. But also, more boldly, it can be thought of as the *equation between absolute necessity and absolute contingency*, i.e., as the inconsistency of a God who deceives us because, first and foremost, he deceives himself.

205. SXIX, 109.

206. Ibid., 110. Although Lacan does not yet define it in such a way, this opposite of a limit is infinity as constructible through the empty set.

207. Ibid.

208. Ibid., 107.

209. That is, $\forall x . \Phi x$ is true and $\overline{\forall x} . \Phi x$ is also true. One should of course bear in mind here that, for propositional logic, disjunction is obtained when one of the two terms is true, and the other false, but also when *both* terms are true.

210. This is also a good definition of the two faces of God as treated in chapter 1.

211. For the following general points, I partly rely on Recalcati's clear compendium in "Per una introduzione alla logica dei discorsi" (*La Psicoanalisi* 18 [1995], 24–39).

212. The series is interrupted here as, for Lacan, there cannot be communication between the place of production and that of truth. He predictably calls this interruption "impotence." Here, let us simply note that if this dynamic could continue indefinitely, feeding back into itself in a circular manner, discourse would *complete* itself.

213. These are therefore obtained by a "quarter turn," that can be either clockwise or counterclockwise, of the unvarying clockwise order of the elements (i.e., the university discourse arises from a counterclockwise turn of the master's discourse; the hysteric discourse from a clockwise turn of the master's discourse; the analyst's discourse from a clockwise turn of the hysteric's discourse, or two clockwise turns of the master's discourse). I will leave aside any consideration regarding such an approach to structural change, which limits the number of possible discourses to four, and the proximate question of the role of history in this context. This matter should obviously be assessed together with my previous treatment of Lacan's—unresolved—evaluation of the import of history for the phallic function as a transcendental logic.

214. Recalcati, "Per una introduzione alla logica dei discorsi," 36 (emphasis added).

215. Ibid.

216. Oliver Feltham, "Enjoy Your Stay," in Justin Clemens and Russell Grigg, eds., *Jacques Lacan and the Other Side of Psychoanalysis* (Durham: Duke University Press, 2006), 183 (emphasis added).

217. "It is fairly curious that what [the analyst's discourse] produces is nothing other than the master's discourse, since it's S_1 that comes to occupy the place of production. [...] Perhaps it's from the analyst's discourse that there can emerge another style of master-signifier" (SXVII, 176).

218. Algebraically, the lower level of the matrix of the discourse of the master ($\$//a$) is then to be read along with the $\$ \to a$ by means of which man (fails to) relate(s) to woman in Seminar XX's diagram of sexuation (or, more precisely, $\$ \to a$ summarizes the dynamics of the discourse of the master as $\$ \to S_1 \to S_2 \to a$). In turn, both adopt and complicate the basic formula of fantasy $\$ \lozenge a$. On the other hand, through the feminine formulas of sexuation, psychoanalysis unveils $\cancel{La}$ and $S(\cancel{A})$ beneath the object a.

219. Recalcati, "Per una introduzione alla logica dei discorsi," 32. However, Recalcati does not attach any relevance to the noncoincidence between the extraneousness of object a as an element and the loss of production as a place in the university and hysterical discourses.

220. This is also "the gap there is between the signifier and its denotation" (SXIX, 45).

221. SXVII, 203.

222. The "other style" of S_1 to which Lacan alludes in Seminar XVII has therefore to do with contingency, the contingency of its logical necessity.

223. See JPM, 44–45.

224. SXIX, 40 (emphasis added).

225. Ibid., 50.

226. This is discourse as the big Other.

227. This second aspect of logic is indeed what is stressed in Lacan's definition: logic is "l'art de produire une nécessité de discours" (SXIX, 50).

228. Ibid., 40.

229. Ibid., 41.

230. More specifically, this ideal One would amount to the correspondence between the logician's formal logic *and* the one-to-one correspondence between discourse's own synchronic logic and the universe, which formal logic takes for granted.

231. Ibid., 41 (emphases added).

232. Ibid.

233. Dominiek Hoens, "Toward a New Perversion: Psychoanalysis," in Clemens and Grigg, *Jacques Lacan and the Other Side of Psychoanalysis*, 97 (emphasis added).

234. See Chiesa, *Subjectivity and Otherness*, 94.

235. SXIX, 41 (emphasis added).

236. Ibid., 42.

237. Barbara Cassin has extensively discussed the proximity between Lacan's psychoanalytic theory and a constructive understanding, and updating, of Ancient sophistry. See *Jacques le sophiste* (Paris: Epel, 2012).

238. SXIX, 42.

239. Ibid.

240. Ibid.

241. Furthermore, *whatever we say*, we cannot but half-say the truth of incompleteness, independently of whether we engage in common discourse or in formal logic, and whether, as logicians, we accept incompleteness or not. Yet this is not to say that all the ways of half-saying it—and all kinds of logic—are the same. "There is no meta-language" half-says it less badly; one can say "There is no meta-language" or worse ... (see SXIX, 12).

242. Lacan also drops any mention of the object *a* in this context, preferring to convey its status of object-*cause* (when put in the position of the agent of discourse) through the notion of *inexistence*.

243. SXIX, 51.

244. Ibid.

245. SII, 5 (emphasis added).

246. This is, again, the circulation among the "gaps" between the four formulas of sexuation as sustained by the One of the nonphallic exception. To the extent that discourse appears to us to extend itself into perpetuity, the "gaps" of contradiction and indetermination/undecidability are subsumed by necessity.

247. See the conclusion.

248. SXIX, 50 (emphasis added).

249. Ibid.

250. Ibid. This reinforces the idea that the university and hysterical discourses are just variations of the discourse of the master, and that the space for a truly new discourse with regard to that of the master is opened (if not yet inhabited) only by the discourse of the analyst.

251. Ibid.

252. Ibid., 51.

253. Ibid.

254. "When another structural order emerges, well then, it creates its own perspective within the past, and we say—*This can never not have been there, this has existed from the beginning*" (SII, 5).

255. SXIX, 52.

256. Ibid., 51.

257. Ibid., 53.

258. Creation *ex nihilo* is the quintessence of purely dogmatic belief and of a rejection of logic (ibid., 52–53). Lacan's earlier pro-creationist pronouncements (such as those of Seminar VII) should be reassessed in light of what we call here creation ex-inexistence. In short, such creation corresponds to what we discussed in chapter 2 in terms of the "point of in-difference."

259. Ibid., 52.

260. Ibid.

261. Ibid.

262. Ibid., 53.

263. Ibid., 52, 144. In the conclusion, we will then have to detail the logical-numerical passage from impossibility to inexistence, to in-*existence*, or, from the non-numerable to the zero as the one missing, to the zero as the one missing as itself counted as one. Lacan tends to conflate these different levels here.

264. Ibid., 52.

265. Ibid., 53.

266. Ibid., 54.

267. Ibid., 53.

268. Ibid. (emphasis added).

269. Again, these would correspond to the deceiving God and the self-deceiving God.

270. *Lacan in Italia* (Milan: La Salamandra, 1978), 35 (emphasis added). "One says as a fact"—although this fact "remains forgotten behind what is said / in what is

understood" (SXIX, 221). Lacan's suggestion that "the signifier is matter that transcends itself into language" also points in the same direction.

271. Yet again, "it *seems* that nothing appears that can be properly speaking called *ananke* elsewhere than in the speaking being" (SXIX, 50). Similarly, the "need for belief" that, as a semblance or retroactive "necessity of always," accompanies what seems to the (psychoanalytic) logician the foundation of logical necessity on the contingent emergence of the transcendental parallelism between the existence of the One and the inexistence of the zero, cannot exclude that "it is God"—a deceiving God—"who has created whole numbers": "Nothing is sure in things of this order" (ibid., 55).

CONCLUSION

1. SXIX, 35.

2. Ibid., 106.

3. Ibid., 134. "Bifidity" is a term normally used in botany; it refers to something that is divided into two lobes by a median cleft.

4. Ibid., 106, 35.

5. Ibid., 126, 132 (emphasis added).

6. Ibid., 101.

7. Ibid., 133.

8. Ibid., 52–53.

9. Ibid., 144 (emphasis added).

10. Ibid., 176.

11. Ibid., 56. More precisely, for Frege, the 1 is the number that belongs to the concept "identical to zero."

12. We could argue more accurately that Lacan preserves the concept "not identical with itself": he in fact refers to the impossibility of numbering also as the "not-one." But the latter should be thought ontologically as *indifference*, not nothingness. This is not far from Badiou's own notion of the pure multiple. The exploration of such proximity would deserve a book in itself.

13. SXIX, 58.

14. Gottlob Frege, *The Foundations of Arithmetic* (New York: Harper, 1960), 88.

15. "Zero-concept" and "zero-object" are Miller's expressions (see "Suture," *Screen* 18, no. 4).

16. SXIX, 61.

17. Ibid., 59 (emphasis added).

18. Guillaume Collett, "The Subject of Logic: The Object," in Lorenzo Chiesa, ed., *Lacan and Philosophy: The New Generation, European Journal of Psychoanalysis* 32 (2011), 202 (emphasis added).

19. This is equally rendered as S(A̶).

20. SXIX, 132.

21. Ibid., 135.

22. "Existence, from its first emergence, right away enunciates itself through its correlative inexistence. There is no existence except on a foundation of inexistence, and reciprocally. [...] This is indeed what is involved in the One" (ibid.).

23. Ibid., 134.

24. Ibid., 146–147.

25. Ibid., 142.

26. Ibid., 144.

27. Ibid., 82.

28. "Ex-sistere: to only have one's support from an outside which is not" (ibid., 135). As we have seen, this is woman's feminine *jouissance* beyond the phallus.

29. Ibid., 177.

30. SXVIII, 74. This confirms that the phallic fantasy of having all women (*toutes les femmes*) as *The* woman, her essence, is concurrently also the fantasy of having woman as the exceptional existence of the *whole woman* (*toutefemme*) that would negate the phallic function.

31. $\cancel{L\!a} \to S(\cancel{A})$.

32. SXIX, 190.

33. Ibid., 165.

34. Ibid., 164–165.

35. In this sense, "the One of a lack, of an empty set [...] suggests itself as being *at the source* of repetition" (ibid., 162; emphasis added).

36. $\cancel{L\!a} \to S(\cancel{A})$.

37. See ibid., 165.

38. The bifidity of the real one is thus "the One inasmuch as whatever may be any difference that exists, all the differences that exist and are *all the same* [*toutes se valent*], there is only one of them, that is *the* difference" (ibid.; emphases added).

39. Again, Lacan writes this as (o → 1) → 1. We could also render it as the gap between $\exists x . \overline{\Phi x}$ and $\overline{\exists x} . \overline{\Phi x}$.

40. Ibid., 176.

41. Ibid., 177.

42. Ibid., 147.

43. Ibid., 177.

44. Ibid.

45. Ibid.

46. See chapter 3.

47. SXIX, 178.

48. Ibid., 179.

49. See Robin Mackay, "Translator's Preface," in Alain Badiou, *Number and Numbers* (Cambridge: Polity Press, 2008), vii.

50. It continuously reemerges for man as the impossibility of fully reducing the object *a* to *one* object: the object *a* remains also real.

51. "The eleven thousand virgins, as it is said in the *Legenda aurea*, is a way to express the uncountable [*non-dénombrable*]. Because eleven thousand, you understand, is an enormous figure, above all for virgins, and not simply nowadays!" (SXIX, 204). On the crowds [*foules*] of women, see ibid., 167. These eleven thousand virgins thus stand as the uncountable side of the countable—but only one by one—one thousand and three women who give themselves to Don Juan.

52. See ibid., 204.

53. If woman tries to be a virgin, i.e., nonphallic, she hysterically falls back into the imaginary angel of man (see chapter 1).

54. Ibid., 205.

55. Ibid., 106.

56. Ibid., 204.

57. We have tackled this in chapter 3: Freud misleadingly identifies woman with the hysteric through the *Ablehnung der Wieblickeit*, that is, with the reduction of woman to the zero as *One* qua the partner of the Father.

58. SXIX, 204.

59. Ibid.

60. Ibid.

61. Ibid., 200.

62. Ibid.

63. That is, the "one being" exists only insofar as it draws its existence from the "One alone," from which it is constructed. But if it is thus seen as existing, it ceases to be "one being": the Father exists only as himself without a partner.

64. SXIX, 200.

65. Ibid.

66. Ibid.

67. Ibid., 209.

68. Ibid., 207, 202.

69. Ibid., 207.

70. Ibid.

71. Ibid. (emphasis added).

72. Ibid.

73. Ibid., 209.

74. Ibid.

75. Ibid.

76. See ibid., 227.

77. This complex "circulation" is conveyed by the graph in ibid., 207 (see below), of which there exist several other versions. I am not specifically commenting on it, since it does not carefully reflect all of Lacan's passages. The earliest transcripts of Seminar XIX warn the reader that it should be taken as approximate.

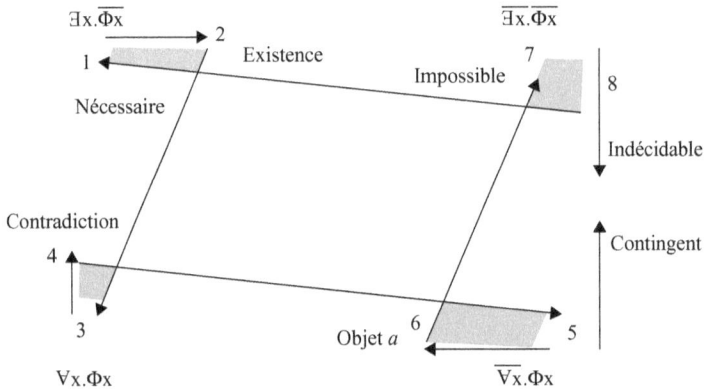

78. "It is not a matter of genesis, or of history. [...] It is not a matter of event, but of structure" (ibid., 203). One should bear in mind here that in these pages Lacan's objective is primarily polemical: what he categorically refuses is Freud's Father of the horde as a historical event.

79. See ibid., 210.

80. Ibid., 119.

81. Ibid., 231. One could of course argue that Lacan is speaking here about the origin of a specific discourse, that of psychoanalysis. But if it seems likely that the phallic function formalized by psychoanalysis, as its *savoir sur la vérité*, constitutes for him the transcendental invariant of the human species—in spite of the oscillations we have discussed in chapter 3—what is ultimately at stake in the origin of the discourse of psychoanalysis is strictly linked with the origin of discourse *tout court*.

82. Lacan states this, a clear reference to arguments he anticipated in Seminar XVIII, less than one month after he gave his allegedly purely synchronic account of the circulation between the formulas (ibid., 222; emphases added).

83. Jacques Lacan, "L'étourdit," in *Autres écrits* (Paris: Seuil, 2001), 466.

84. SXIX, 205.

85. "What is important, what constitutes the Real is that, through logic, something happens that demonstrates not that in turn p and not-p are false, but that neither of them can be verified logically in any way" (SXXI, lesson of 19 February 1974).

86. The mystic could thus also take herself for an illusory angelical figure.

87. SXIX, 175.

88. Ibid., 200 (emphasis added).

89. Ibid. (emphasis added).

90. JPM, 59 (emphases added).

91. Ibid., 56–58.

92. SXIX, 184.

93. Ibid.

94. Ibid.

95. Ibid.

96. Ibid., 199.

97. Ibid., 176.

98. See ibid., 175.

99. Ibid., 185–186.

100. See SXX, 90.

101. See the last section of chapter 2.

102. SXIX, 69, 101, 103.

103. See also SXX, 91–93.

104. See ibid., 12.

105. SXIX, 222.

INDEX

agnosticism, xiii, xv, 59, 64, 74, 179
angel, 3, 10–11, 16, 17, 19, 21
animal, 18, 23–25, 29–30, 46–47, 48, 59–60, 63, 92
  human, 24, 27, 46, 55, 73, 146, 150
  linguistic, 54, 146, 147
  One and the, xvi, 24, 59
  speaking, xii, 24, 25, 45, 50, 89, 93, 94, 105–106, 108, 121, 123, 127, 144, 159, 175, 179
animism, xix, 39–40, 55, 59, 60, 66, 72, 79, 80
  Jung and, 45–46
  and science, 33, 38, 41
antiphilosophy, xvi–xvii, 179
Aristotle, xvii, 16, 36–39, 85, 89, 97–103, 108, 110, 113, 114, 116, 117, 120, 129, 130, 133, 172
atheism, xii, xiii, xiv, xv, 74

Badiou, Alain, xxiii
Balmès, François, xvii–xviii
Beauvoir, Simone de, 28
behaviorism, 35–37, 40
being, xii–xiii, xiv–xvi, xvii, xviii–xix, 2–3, 6, 8–9, 11, 16, 19, 20, 36, 38, 39–40, 42, 58–59, 60, 65, 69, 70, 71, 72, 74, 79, 92, 97, 106, 109, 111, 113, 117, 120–123, 125, 130, 145, 156, 162, 163, 169–171, 172, 173, 174, 175, 176, 179

  of language, 2–3, 5, 12, 64, 70–71, 73, 80, 130, 132, 143, 145, 146
  speaking, xx, 2, 7, 19, 25, 78–79, 83, 90, 91, 92–93, 106, 148, 156
biology, xvii, xxi–xxii, 28–40, 45–46, 47–48, 58, 65, 78, 80, 92–93, 108, 116
  animistic, 23, 33, 35–37, 40–41, 47, 54, 92
bio-logy, 27–28, 33, 38
Blumberg, Mark, 29–30
brother(s), 111, 112, 167, 170
Brouwer, Luitzen Egbertus Jan, 88

Caillois, Roger, 46
castration, xx, 25, 80, 81, 86, 90, 91, 92, 99, 105, 109, 116, 117, 119–120, 122–124, 125, 127, 128, 132, 134, 136, 172, 173, 175
Christianity, 78, 92, 93
Collett, Guillaume, 163
contingency
  absolute, xiv, 144
  of discourse, 143, 156
  in evolution, 32
  and the hysteric, 124
  of man, 142–143
  modality of, 130, 133–134, 171–172
  of necessity, 142–144, 150–151, 155, 157, 159

contingency (cont.)
  of the phallic function, 90, 138, 143, 176
  of woman, 118, 130, 134–137, 141–142, 150, 155, 171–173, 174, 176
  in Žižek, 65, 67
contradiction, 15–16, 87, 88, 99, 109, 110, 119, 120, 125, 129, 130, 134, 135, 136, 137, 138, 139, 141, 143, 165, 169, 171, 172, 173, 175, 176
  in Aristotle, 97–98, 99, 100–101, 103
  energetic, 55
  law of non-, 90, 95, 103
copulation, 24–25, 29, 49, 50, 54, 57, 63, 78, 90, 91, 92, 93, 125
critique, xiii, xvii, xviii, xix, 64, 67, 94–95, 161

Darwinism, 24, 29, 31, 34, 35, 36, 40, 46, 47
David-Ménard, Monique, xvii–xviii, 110, 114, 120, 134
Deleuze, Gilles, 66, 67–68, 91
Derrida, Jacques, 84
Descartes, René, xiv, 88
desire, 7, 11, 12, 14, 23, 40–41, 48, 56, 58, 69, 119, 146, 172
  in Deleuze, 68
  and drive, 52–54, 65, 71
  feminine, 122
  hysteric's, 122, 125, 126
  masculine, 121–122, 178
  not to know, 36
  to be one, 20, 176
  to be One, xii, 5–6, 16, 17–18, 20, 45, 52, 54, 77, 121, 123, 146
  of the Other, 18
  to be the Phallus, 121, 122, 123, 124, 125, 128, 175
difference
  anatomical, 25–26
  discursive, 63
  empirical, 73
  identity and, 71
  imaginary, 65
  little, xxi, 25–27, 30, 56

natural, 25, 30, 60, 61–62
onto-logical, 73–74
ontology of, 60–61
phallic, 47
pure, 65–67, 70, 74, 164, 166, 170, 174
real, 27, 30, 63, 70, 73, 166
sameness of, 166–167, 170
sexed life as, 59
sexual, xi, xviii, xix, xxi, xxii, 1, 3, 10–11, 13, 14, 17, 25–29, 30, 35, 37, 56, 60, 93, 127, 137, 138, 154–155, 161, 164, 168, 174, 175, 176, 178, 179
symbolic, 26, 30, 73
univocal, 47
discourse(s), xvi, 2, 25, 29, 79, 134, 137, 141, 143, 145–148, 152–159, 174
  of the analyst, 78, 147, 148–153
  of ethology, 24
  of history, 18
  of the hysteric, 82–83, 94, 147, 149
  limit of, 82–83
  of the master, 147–150, 154
  mythical, 17
  and nature, 62–64, 70
  psychoanalytic, 2, 7, 8, 77–78, 79, 82–84, 87–88, 89, 90, 91, 132, 133–134, 148, 157, 176–178
  religious, 41–42
  of science, 86–88, 90, 91
  and semblance, 82–84, 95, 132, 148
  of the university, 87, 147, 149
DNA, 34, 40, 159
Don Juan, 4, 14, 15, 20
drive(s), xxii, 23, 40–41, 47–55, 56–59, 63–64
  in Žižek, 64–66, 67–69, 71

energetics, 33, 54, 56, 57, 62, 63
energy
  as a function, 55–56, 62
  kinetic, 47–48, 55, 57, 58
  living, xxii, 47–48, 58, 146
  negative, 65
  potential, 47–48, 54–58, 60, 63, 64, 68
  psychic, 45

240

Ensslin, Felix, xv
environment, 18, 23, 30, 31, 46, 61, 146
Eros, xxii, 38, 40, 52, 55
essence
    divine, xii, xiii, xv, 74
    without existence, 109–110
    and logic, 85, 97, 98, 99–100, 101, 102
    and the One, 2, 8–9
    and sexuation, xviii, 7, 80, 106, 108–113, 115–119, 121, 122, 123–124, 127–128, 133, 138
    of the signifier, 6
Euclid, 88, 89
Evans, Dylan, 115, 117
Evo-Devo, 31–32, 35
evolution, xix, xxi, 23, 29, 31–33, 34–35, 36, 37, 40
existence, xix, 8, 12, 15, 99–103, 106–113, 117, 119, 121, 123, 124, 126, 127, 128, 132, 133, 137, 140, 141, 144, 158, 162, 163, 165, 169, 170, 171–172, 173, 174, 176
    without essence, 109, 110, 119, 152
    ex-sistence, xix, 3, 4, 16, 99, 117, 122, 128–129, 135, 136, 148, 150, 164–165, 168, 169, 171, 173, 176, 177
    of God, xii–xiii, xv, 6, 9, 16

fantasy, xx, 3, 4, 11, 12–13, 16–17, 18, 20, 24, 28, 38–39, 54, 121, 131–132, 164, 178
Father
    exceptional existence of the, 8, 99, 103
    of the horde, 8, 11, 84, 108, 110, 111–112, 113, 130, 170
    and the hysteric, 118–119, 120, 121, 122–123, 125, 126, 127, 128–129, 131
    and man, 119, 123, 124, 126, 132, 170
    as name, 118
    Name-of-the, 153
    as number, 118
    as One, 8, 141
    as Phallus, 15, 107, 112, 116, 118, 119, 141
    as whole man, 108–109, 117, 118
    and woman, 119, 126, 128
Feltham, Oliver, 148
formalization, xi, xvii, xviii, xix, xx–xxi, xxii, 8, 16, 34, 35–36, 77, 78, 80, 83–84, 85, 96, 103, 105, 121, 129, 149, 151, 161, 176–177, 178
Frege, Gottlob, xviii, xx, xxiii, 85, 89, 95, 96–97, 98, 99, 100, 101, 106, 136, 138, 161–163, 169
Freud, Sigmund, xiii, xviii, xix, xxii, 11, 25, 26, 30, 33, 38, 43, 47, 48, 49, 52, 57, 58, 63, 73, 79, 80, 90, 99, 108, 111–114, 116, 118, 126, 128, 138, 146, 147, 169
Freudianism, xvii, 41, 43
function
    alternative feminine, 106, 111, 116
    binary, 106
    biological, 6, 46, 49
    in Frege, xx, 85–86, 96–97, 98, 100–101, 138
    if-, 94–95
    "is what it is," 98, 101, 103
    logical, 78–79
    and mother, 12–14, 15
    phallic, xi, xvii, xviii, xix, xx, xxii–xxiii, 2, 4, 8, 9, 11, 13, 14, 15, 16, 19, 20, 23, 25, 26, 28, 29, 37, 46, 77, 79, 80, 84, 86, 89, 90, 93, 94, 99, 102–103, 105–125, 128–131, 133–143, 145, 148, 149, 150, 153, 154–155, 156, 159, 161, 163–166, 168, 171–174, 176–177
    and truth, 94–95, 98, 138–140, 177–179

Galileo, 86, 92
    Galilean discourse, 36
    Galileanism of the living, 34
    Galilean revolution, 38, 41, 89
    Galilean science, 33, 34, 95
genitality, 18, 45, 50, 53–54, 57–58, 112
Gestalt
    of man's sexual organ, 131, 143
    theory, 34

God
  as absolute being, xii, xiv, xv, 16, 19, 39
  of atheists, xv, 74–75
  classical, xx
  death of, xii, xv
  deceiving, xiii–xv, 74–75, 94–95, 137, 144
  existence of, xii, xv, 6
  and feminine *jouissance*, 1, 10, 16–17, 19
  hypothesis, xii–xv, xix, xxi, 1, 2, 8, 9, 16, 23, 74
  ignorant, xv
  and love, 18–19, 20
  as name, xiii, 16
  neither one nor two, 1–2, 6, 17–18, 20–21
  particle, 87
  self-deceiving, xiii–xv, 74–75, 94–95, 137, 144
  and truth, xii, xiv, 88
  vicious, xv
Gödel, Kurt, 154
Gould, Stephen Jay, 31–32, 34
Green, André, 48, 56
Guattari, Félix, 67–68, 91

Hadewijch of Antwerp, 1
Hegel, Georg Wilhelm Friedrich, 62, 65, 66–67, 68, 70, 71, 72
Heidegger, Martin, 46–47
Hoens, Dominiek, 153
Homo sapiens, xi, xiii, xxi, xxii, xxiii, 7, 12, 24, 27, 29, 32, 41, 44, 49, 51, 57, 58, 60, 64, 73, 81, 89, 93, 129, 130, 146, 175, 176
hysteric
  and angel, 10–11
  and "at least one," 122, 123–126, 130, 131, 141, 142, 175
  difference from woman, 118–119, 120–122, 126, 128–129, 139
  discourse of the, 82–83, 94, 147, 148, 149, 157
  and Father, 118–119, 120, 121, 122–123, 125, 126, 127, 128–129, 131
  and Freud, 43, 90, 112, 128
  and in-existence, 128–129
  as "man-sexual," 11, 20, 21, 122–123, 131
  and "no one," 125
  as not-at-all, 121, 128–129
  and ontogenesis, 126–127, 174–176
  as "outside sex," 11, 20, 122, 125, 128
  and "there is no sexual relationship," 77, 123

Il y a de l'Un, 6, 21, 126, 129–130, 134, 136–137, 145, 152, 155, 163, 166, 170, 178
imaginary, 17, 23, 41, 164, 165
impossibility
  and contingency, 134–136, 142, 172–173, 174
  and impotence, 133–134
  and indifference, 164, 174, 175, 176, 178
  and inexistence, 155–156, 157–158, 159, 164, 171
  logical, 2, 26, 30, 78, 80, 105, 117, 145, 154–156, 158, 159, 161
  and man, 176–177
  modality of, 130, 133–134, 171–172
  and necessity, 8, 84, 117, 130
  of numbering, xxiii, 159, 162, 163, 164, 165, 166, 169, 171, 173, 174, 175, 177, 178
  and the real, 23, 27, 30, 66, 68, 84, 86, 96, 113, 130, 132, 144, 145, 154, 174, 177, 178
  of sexual relationship, xi, 2, 5, 18, 24–25, 29, 59, 78, 79, 90, 91, 111–112, 113, 123, 133, 136, 138, 143, 150, 154–156, 161, 179
  and undecidability, 172–173, 174, 176
  and woman, 113–115, 124, 134, 150, 176–177
impotence, 133–134, 149, 175, 177

incompleteness, xi, xii–xiii, xiv–xv,
   xviii, xix, 17, 40, 42, 44, 49, 51, 59,
   75, 77, 79, 81–82, 83, 84–86, 87,
   88–89, 93–95, 96, 99, 102, 120, 121,
   125, 129, 135, 137, 145, 150–151, 154,
   176, 179
inconsistency, xiv–xv, 71, 73, 74, 75
indifference, xxi, 26–27, 30, 37, 46–47,
   56, 61–64, 66–67, 70, 72, 73–75,
   144, 159, 164, 166, 174–175, 176, 178,
   179
   as in-difference, xxi, 56, 60, 62–64,
      66–67, 68, 69, 70, 71–72, 73–74, 161,
      179
   and point of in-difference, 70, 144,
      174
inexistence, xxi, 102, 130, 133, 140–141,
   145, 155–156, 157–159, 162–163, 164,
   165, 166, 167, 168–169, 171, 173, 174,
   176, 177
   as in-existence, xviii, xix, 117, 122, 126,
      128–129, 135, 136, 137, 140, 148, 150,
      161, 164, 168, 169, 171, 172, 173, 176
infinity, xxiii, 4, 163, 165, 167–171, 176,
   177, 178, 179
instinct, 5, 23, 30, 40, 46, 48, 50, 56, 146
   death, 58

Jablonka, Eva, 31
Jacob, François, 33, 61
John of the Cross, Saint, 1
Johnston, Adrian, xxii, 34, 53, 69–75
jouissance
   absolute, 7, 8, 80, 106, 119, 132, 143,
      148
   angelical, 4, 6
   animal and, 63
   asexual, 3, 4, 9, 16
   of bacteria, 61
   of the body, xix, 7
   clitoral and vaginal, 11
   and drive, 49, 50, 52, 53, 63
   feminine nonphallic, xx, 1, 4, 5, 6,
      9–11, 13–14, 15, 16, 17, 19–20, 21,
      106, 122, 171, 178

   feminine phallic, 3, 4, 10, 19–20, 21,
      106, 122, 171
   inexistence of, 158, 159
   and language, 7, 148
   masculine, 4, 5, 17–18, 21, 77, 106, 122,
      123
   of the mother, 12
   Other, 3, 6, 9, 115, 117, 129, 141, 168
   as other satisfaction, 6–7
   phallic, 1, 3, 5, 6, 9, 11, 49, 52, 81, 86,
      91, 106, 119, 146, 147, 148, 149, 150
   and semblance, 81, 82
   sexual, xviii, 2, 3, 5, 6, 7, 11, 80, 81, 92,
      93, 106
   strange, 3–4, 10, 19
   and substance, 7–9
   that would be, 2, 80, 119, 132
Jung, Carl, 45–46

Kant, Immanuel, 65
knowledge, 41, 81, 107, 111, 147
   of the analyst, 149, 151, 157
   animistic, 35–36, 79, 134
   non-, 131, 177
   and psychoanalysis, 36, 43–44, 77,
      81–82, 87–88, 131–132, 134
   and religion, 41
   and science, 34–36, 38–40, 41, 43–44,
      86–88, 90
   sexual, 38–39
   theory of, 39, 40, 79, 91
   of truth, 29, 36, 77, 131, 137, 144, 149,
      161, 177, 179
   truth of, 131, 137, 177, 179

Lamarckianism, 35
lamella, xxii, 58–61, 63, 64
language, xii, xiii, xiv–xv, xvi, xix, xxi,
   xxii, 2, 3, 5, 6–7, 9, 12, 13, 17, 19, 24,
   25, 33, 38, 44, 50, 51, 54, 57–58, 59,
   60, 62–64, 68, 69, 70, 71, 72, 73,
   78–79, 81, 82, 84–86, 89, 91, 94,
   95–97, 105, 130, 131, 132, 137, 141,
   142, 143, 145–147, 154, 156, 159, 162,
   175, 177, 178

Le Gaufey, Guy, xx, 106, 114
letter, 28, 33, 34, 62, 85, 86, 88, 89, 96, 152
libido, xxii, 40, 45–48, 49, 50, 51, 52, 54, 58, 59, 63, 68
life, xix, xxii, 5, 27, 28, 29, 31–32, 33, 35, 36–37, 38, 55, 57, 58–61, 63, 66, 69, 159
  instinct, 55, 58
Little Hans, 25, 30
Livingston, Paul, 73–74
logic, xi, xii, xviii, 47, 85, 88, 93, 131, 133, 137, 145, 154–155
  Aristotelian, xviii, 19, 84, 85, 89, 96–103, 107, 108, 110, 113, 114, 116, 117, 120, 129, 130, 133, 136, 172
  commencement of, 62
  formal, 19, 82, 84, 98, 102, 134, 152, 154
  Fregean, xviii, xxiii, 85, 89, 95, 96–97, 98, 99, 100, 101, 138–139
  as il-logical, 27, 30, 43, 133, 150, 151, 156, 158, 161, 164
  impasse of, 23, 25–29, 37, 77, 82, 88, 93, 96, 103, 152, 159
  of incompleteness, 84, 135, 137
  of life, xix, xxii, 27, 28, 38, 47, 159
  limit of, 81–83, 88, 90, 179
  of logical positivism, xxiii, 83, 87, 95–97, 98–99, 100, 101, 102, 110, 136, 154, 178, 179
  and necessity of discourse, 145–159
  nonlogical element of, 146, 149, 150
  and number, xxiii, 26–29, 153–154, 161–162, 179
  object of, 151–152
  phallic, 45, 57, 70, 99, 131, 132
  psychoanalytic, 77, 83, 152, 153, 157
  of sexuation, xii, xvii, xviii, xix, xx, xxi, xxii, xxiii, 23, 37, 44, 70, 77, 89, 90, 94, 98, 99, 102, 103, 106, 108, 126, 128, 134, 137, 141, 142, 145, 148, 149, 152, 154, 161, 163
  of the signifier, 44, 57

transcendental, xi–xii, xvi, xvii, xix, xxi, xxii, xxiii, 23, 44, 77, 106, 134, 137, 141, 142, 145, 148–149, 152, 154, 161, 163, 176
  and writing, 77, 79, 80, 82–87, 88–89, 90–91, 93
logicism, 82–83, 162
Lorenz, Konrad, 56
love
  as desire to be One, xii, 5–7, 17–18, 23, 52, 54, 77, 121, 123, 146
  and drive, 48, 52–54
  everyday experience of, xi–xii, xiii, 146
  and fantasy, 39, 53–54, 58, 165, 167
  feminine, 20, 125, 169, 176
  and God, xiii, 18–19
  and hysteric, 118, 121, 123, 129
  masculine, xix, 18–19, 123, 169
  as metaphor, 29, 38
  phallic, 17–19, 129
  soul-, 39–40, 134
  true, xii
  for truth, 177, 179

man
  as barred subject, 11–13, 110, 114, 121, 123, 126, 132
  and contingency, 142–143
  and contradiction, 15, 16, 99, 109–110, 117, 119, 120, 123, 124, 125, 129, 130, 134, 136, 137, 138, 139, 141, 142, 143, 165, 169, 170, 171–172, 173, 175, 176
  in diagram of sexuation, 11–13, 14, 15, 17, 18, 126
  and essence, 8, 80, 99, 108–110, 111, 113, 119, 123, 133, 138
  and exception, 8, 15, 99, 103, 109–110, 113, 117, 118, 119, 123, 124, 125, 126, 127, 129, 130, 135, 138, 141, 142, 163, 166, 167, 169, 170, 175, 176
  and existence, 8, 12, 99, 103, 108–110, 111, 115, 117, 119, 123, 124, 127, 133, 139–140, 152, 163, 169, 171–172, 173

and fantasy, xx, 3, 4, 11–13, 17, 18, 19, 20, 122, 132, 148–149, 164–165, 172, 173, 175, 178
and formula(s) of sexuation, 8, 105–110, 115, 126–127, 129–131, 134, 137–145, 148–149, 165–166, 167–168, 169–170, 171–173, 174–176
and God, 2, 17–18, 21
and hysteric, 11, 20, 40, 121–125, 131, 174–175
and *jouissance*, 2–5, 6–8, 11–13, 17–18, 21, 77, 92, 106, 121–122, 123, 143, 146, 147, 148
and love, xix, 17–18, 40, 123, 125, 129, 165, 167, 169
and mother, 13, 15, 17
and necessity, 8, 117–118, 123, 130, 133, 134, 136–137, 142–143, 155–156, 170, 171, 172, 173
and the One, xi, 16, 17–18, 40, 77, 123, 134, 141, 142–143, 144, 154–155, 170, 173, 175, 178
as particular, 107–110, 111, 113, 115, 117, 123, 126, 132, 167–168, 170, 175–176
and phallus, 2, 13–14, 15, 80–81, 106, 108–110, 112, 119–125, 126, 127, 130–131, 141, 142, 143, 166, 175
and possibility, 118, 122–123, 134, 136, 137, 142–143, 165, 172, 173, 175, 176
and sexuation, 14–15, 78–81, 106–110, 118, 119–122, 126–127, 130, 136, 164–166, 176–177, 178
as signifier, 7, 25, 26, 122, 171
as universal, xxii, 26, 108–110, 111–113, 117, 118, 123, 124, 125, 126, 129, 130, 132, 134, 136, 137–138, 139, 140, 141, 142, 143, 144, 165, 167–168, 169–170, 172, 173, 175, 176
as whole man, 108–110, 113, 117, 118, 122, 123–124, 126, 127, 136
as x, 106, 108, 138
materialism, xii, xiii, xiv–xv, xvi, xix, 34, 44–45, 47, 48, 58–59, 60, 62, 64, 67–68, 152, 159, 179

dialectical, 63, 66, 69, 70, 71, 72, 74, 75
transcendental, 70–71, 73, 74
meaning, xii, xv, xix, 2, 18, 19, 27, 32, 40, 41, 43, 44, 78, 83, 85–86, 95–96, 100, 127, 132, 139, 152, 153, 156–157, 178
Meillassoux, Quentin, xiv–xv, 67, 74–75
Mendelianism, 31, 35
metacritique, xiii–xiv, xviii–xix, 94–95, 142
metalanguage, xii, 44, 82, 85, 87, 101, 154, 162
Miller, Jacques-Alain, xx, 33, 52
Milner, Jean-Claude, 23, 29, 34
Monod, Jacques, xix
Morel, Geneviève, xviii, 97, 100–101
mother, 12–13, 14, 15, 20, 21, 30

naturalism, 25, 27, 47, 63, 64, 66, 69, 70
nature
  approach to, xvii, 37
  chant of, 42
  and culture, 25, 37, 65, 69, 73–74
  as difference, 47, 59–61, 95, 179
  idea of, 24, 37, 83
  as in-difference, xxi, 27, 30, 37, 46–47, 56, 60–74, 159, 174
  and number, 27–29, 30, 37
  philosophy of, xxii, 62
  as real, 27–29, 37, 179
  and sensible substance, 33, 39, 88
  and sex, xxi, xxii, 24, 25–29, 30, 37, 44, 48, 59, 78, 143–144, 150, 174
necessity
  absolute, xv, 144
  of always, 155–156, 157–159
  and contingency, 133, 141, 176
  of contingency, 143–144
  contingency of, 142–144, 150, 151, 157, 159
  of contradiction, 142–144
  of discourse, 145, 151–159
  of exception, 118, 123, 142
  and God hypothesis, xii
  and impossibility, 8, 130, 133, 136, 150, 155–156

necessity (cont.)
    and inexistence, 133
    logical, 2, 7–8, 117–118, 123, 142, 143, 150, 153, 155–159
    and love, 5
    modality of, 130, 133–134, 171–172
    mythical, 84
    of non-necessity, xiv
    of the One, 130, 133, 134, 136, 137, 143, 145, 153, 154–155, 170, 171–173, 176
    in ontology, xvii, 39
    and possibility, 134, 176
need, 6–7, 9, 41, 78, 159
negation, 20, 97, 99, 100–103, 109, 111–113, 115–117, 119, 120–121, 126–128, 129, 130, 135–136, 138–139, 169, 172
    absolute, 127–128
    discordant, 102–103, 107, 110
    of femininity, 90, 112, 116, 118, 128
    foreclosing, 102
Newton, Isaac, 86, 89
not-all, xviii, xx, xxii, 3, 9, 12, 13, 14, 16, 19, 20, 26, 28, 42, 58, 60, 61, 66, 72, 84, 89, 90, 96, 98, 99, 100–103, 110, 113, 114–115, 116–117, 118, 119, 120–121, 122, 123, 124, 125, 126, 127, 128, 129, 134, 135, 137, 138, 139, 140, 141, 142, 144–145, 148, 150, 164, 165, 166, 168, 170, 171–173, 175, 176
not-two, xi, xxi, 2, 21, 28, 38, 43, 48, 56, 72, 73, 75, 125, 137, 140, 144, 161–162, 163–164, 167, 172, 177, 178, 179
number
    in Frege and Lacan, xxiii, 153–154, 161–163
    of God, 1–2, 16–21
    as real, xxi, 27–29, 37–38, 43, 133, 159, 161–162, 163–164, 166, 167, 174, 177, 178
    and science, 28, 33, 34, 88
    and sexuation, 27–29, 118, 129–130, 131, 133, 158–159, 161–179

object a, 11–15, 17, 18, 21, 45, 50–54, 56, 122, 132, 140, 146–152, 164–165, 167, 170, 171, 172, 173
Oedipus complex, 13, 25, 26, 50, 54, 80, 105, 112, 128, 143
one, 1–2, 17, 20–21, 103, 110, 133, 137, 141, 147, 150, 161–179
    all alone, 132, 149, 156, 162, 163, 167
    -being, 169–171, 172, 173, 174, 175–176, 179
    bifidity of the, xxiii, 161, 163, 166, 167, 177
    as concept, 162–163, 166
    imaginary, 164, 165
    of inexistence, 162–163, 164, 165, 166, 167, 168, 169, 174, 177
    at-least-, 122–126, 130, 131, 141–142, 144, 175
    -less, 28, 129, 165
    as missing, 156, 161, 163, 178
    -more, 4, 124, 125, 126, 127, 130, 141, 142, 154, 165–166
    no more than, 109, 122, 124–126, 130, 144, 154, 170–171, 173, 175
    not-, 71, 73–75, 144, 161–162, 172, 176, 177, 178, 179
    as number, 161–163, 166, 167
    as object, 163–164, 166, 169, 170, 173
    -by-one, 4–5, 10, 14, 15, 20, 124–126, 129, 164–165, 166, 168, 170, 175
    and One, 8–9, 10, 17, 21, 23, 137, 141
    -and-only, 20, 125, 176
    real, 161, 162, 164, 166
    of repetition, 166
    symbolic, 164, 166
    and zero, xxiii, 126, 129, 140–141, 144, 155, 156, 161–169, 170, 172, 174, 177
One, xi, xiii–xiv, xix, 7, 8, 12, 15, 16, 17, 18, 21, 23, 28, 38, 58–59, 60–61, 62, 63, 64, 94–95, 124, 125, 129, 130, 140, 141, 143, 144, 145, 150, 166, 169–170, 172
    /All, 2, 72, 137, 163, 165, 168, 169
    all alone, 137, 145, 152, 166, 167, 168, 169–170, 172
    and animal, xvi, 24, 59

another, 2, 136, 167, 173, 178
and Being, xvii, xviii–xix, 16, 19, 20, 38, 39, 65, 121, 125, 130, 137, 162, 163, 174, 175, 179
bifidity of the, 163, 166, 170, 171, 172, 174, 177
of the body, 2–3, 6, 8–9, 10–11, 28, 39–40, 125
desire to be, xii, 5–6, 16, 17–18, 20, 45, 52, 54, 77, 121, 123, 146
and equation with not-One, xiv, xv, 59, 72, 74–75, 137, 179
as exception, 118, 121, 126, 135, 141, 163, 166, 170, 175
of fusion, xi, xix, 4, 6, 15, 17, 18, 20, 38, 121, 175–176
ideal, 141–143, 145, 152, 165, 169–170, 171, 173, 174, 175
imaginary, 8, 9, 17, 145, 153, 165, 167
impossibility of the, xi, 2, 5, 18, 26, 80, 130, 137
-missing, 15, 129, 137, 140, 161, 164, 166, 178
-more, 167–168, 170, 173, 175
necessity of the, 2, 5, 64, 130, 133, 134, 136–137, 142–143, 145, 151, 152, 153, 154–155, 166, 172–173, 176, 179
not-, xi, xiii–xiv, xv, xix, xxi, 2, 8, 9, 10, 16, 17, 19, 21, 23, 28, 58, 59, 61, 66, 71–72, 74–75, 137, 151, 152, 153, 179
One (not-One), 17, 61, 74, 179
and oscillation with not-One, xiii–xiv, xix, 2, 8, 9, 10, 16, 17, 23, 58, 59, 66, 72, 137, 153, 155
Other as, xii, xiii, xix, 52, 135, 137, 140, 146, 175
Other than, 2, 72, 81
Phallus as, 121, 130, 135, 141, 142, 143, 163, 166, 172, 174–176
production of the, 143, 145, 151–156
requirement of the, 4–5, 142
semblance of the, xi–xii, xxi, 6, 12, 48, 58, 77, 153, 155
two-as-, xi, xix, xxi, 2, 18, 21, 28, 35, 132, 164, 165

universe as, xiii, xvi, 33, 87, 132, 152
in Žižek, 71, 74
ontology, xii, xvi, xvii, xix, xxi, xxii, xxiii, 2, 23, 33, 38, 59, 60–75, 89, 94, 97, 98, 115, 116, 117, 118, 120, 126, 137, 161, 179
onto-totology, 10, 38, 39–40, 41
other, 52, 53, 146–147, 149
satisfaction, 6–7, 9, 49
sex, 4, 20, 78, 80–81, 106, 119, 130, 131
Other, 9, 52, 54, 57, 146
as barred, xiii, 10, 16, 17, 19, 21, 166, 179
big, 17
body of the, 5, 7
feminine, xix–xx, 14, 129, 136, 137
and God, xii, xiii, 1, 16, 20–21
jouissance, 3, 6, 117, 129, 141, 168
most radical, 10, 15, 16, 128
as One, xii, xiii, 135, 137, 167, 178
than One, 2, 9, 28, 81, 166
sex, xx, xxi, 2, 9, 11, 15, 26, 28, 38–40, 49, 77, 81, 132, 137, 140, 141, 144, 161, 175, 178
there is no Other of the, xiii, 10, 19

para-ontology, xii–xvii, xviii–xix, xx, xxii, 8–9, 24, 42, 64, 74, 137, 142, 144, 145, 177, 179
particular(s), 96, 107, 140
in Aristotle, 97–103, 114
and man, 107–110, 111, 113, 115, 123, 132, 167, 170, 175–176
and woman, 113–116, 117, 172, 176
Pascal, Blaise, xv, 72
Paul, Saint, 93
penis, 26, 29–30, 46, 50–51, 53, 81, 143
envy, 112, 128
phallus, xx, 2, 3, 20, 26, 46, 50, 99
beyond the, xx, 1, 3, 4, 5, 6, 9–10, 13, 115, 117, 128, 129, 141, 148, 150, 165, 171, 176
and Father, 99, 107, 112, 116, 118, 120, 121, 122, 123, 126, 141
and hysteric, 120–125, 128, 135, 174–175, 176

phallus (cont.)
  imaginary, 13
  and man, 108–109, 119–120, 123, 126, 127, 142, 143, 175
  as missing organ, 47, 50–52, 53–54
  other sex as, 80
  as Phallus, 119–125, 126, 128, 130, 131, 141, 142, 143, 163, 166, 175, 176
  and the real, 96, 132, 166, 172
  symbolic, 14–15
  as third term, 80–81, 106, 130
  and woman, 4, 108, 113, 117, 118, 119–126, 173, 175
Plato, 39, 89, 93
possibility
  of man, 117–118, 122–123, 130, 134, 136, 142–143, 165, 170, 175, 176
  modality of, 130, 133–134, 149, 154, 171–172
  of the universal, 134, 136, 137, 142–143, 165, 170, 173, 175, 176
psycho-erotology, xxi, 38, 40

real
  absence of the sexual relationship as, 26, 79, 85, 90, 91, 113, 130, 131, 155, 178–179
  barred, 66, 70–73, 74, 179
  and impossibility, 23, 30, 84, 86–87, 96, 112, 113, 130, 136, 144, 145, 154, 159, 162–164, 174, 177–179
  and intuition, 89–90
  and *jouissance*, 146, 148, 149
  and lack, 59–60, 62
  and logic, 26–29, 30, 37–38, 43–44, 62–64, 65, 82, 85, 86–90, 93, 99, 130, 131, 150, 151–153
  missing partner as, 11–12, 18, 49
  as natural, 26–29, 30, 37–38, 43–44, 62–64, 65, 71–73
  and number, xxi, 27–29, 38, 43, 133, 161–164, 166–167, 168, 169–170, 174, 177–179
  phallus as, 132, 166, 172
  and praxis, 41, 43

  and science, 34–37, 38–39, 62–64, 87–90
  of sex, xxi, 24–29, 37, 47, 80
  and structure, xiii, xxi, xxiii, 44, 62, 73, 161–164, 168, 169–170
  and truth, 177–179
  void as, 41, 44, 131–132
  and woman, 99, 117, 136
  in Žižek, 66–67
realism, xiv, 34, 47, 64, 66
reality, 7, 8, 9, 25, 27, 32, 42, 45, 52, 62, 65, 68, 146, 152, 178
Recalcati, Massimo, 147, 148
reproduction, xxii, 5, 6, 14, 18, 23, 29, 35, 37, 41, 45, 48, 49, 50, 55, 57, 58–59, 60, 78, 90, 92–93, 159

Schreber, Daniel Paul, xiv
science(s)
  ancient, 23, 35–36, 39–40, 86, 87, 88, 92
  life, xiii, xix, xxi–xxii, 24, 28, 29, 30–34, 37, 40, 46, 92–93
  modern, xiv, xxi, 23, 28, 33–34, 36–38, 41–44, 62, 82, 86–93, 95
  and psychoanalysis, xix, 23, 34–40, 41–44, 82, 86–93
semblance, xi–xii, xiii, xxi, 4, 6, 12, 16, 19, 48, 57, 58, 62, 77, 79–85, 86, 87, 89, 90, 92, 93, 95, 96, 99, 103, 109, 111, 117, 121, 132–133, 134, 136, 145, 148, 150, 153, 155, 159, 162, 164, 165, 169–170, 172, 173, 178
sex(es)
  an-other, 2, 26, 38, 161
  and biology, xxi–xxii, 3, 23–24, 27–31, 35, 37–38, 49–50, 78, 80, 92–93
  as illogical, 25–27, 30, 38, 43, 44, 161
  misadventures of, xi, 45, 78, 107
  as natural, xxi–xxii, 24, 25–29, 30, 37, 48, 59, 78, 143–144, 150, 174
  and organ(s), 3, 18, 20, 26–27, 30, 46, 47, 49, 50–51, 143, 175
  other, 4, 20, 78, 80–81, 106, 119, 130, 131

Other, xx, xxi, 2, 9, 11, 15, 26, 28, 38–40, 49, 77, 81, 132, 137, 140, 141, 144, 161, 175, 178
  outside, 11, 20, 122, 125, 128
  as real, xxi, 24–29, 37, 47, 80
  and representation, 2, 5, 28, 48–49, 51, 54, 58, 59, 78, 90, 92, 106, 119, 137, 142, 154–155, 172, 173, 174–175, 177, 178, 179
  second, xxi, 27–28, 80, 140, 150, 161
  two, xi, xxi, 2, 18, 25–29, 30, 37, 48, 58–59, 80, 90, 123, 126, 140, 161
sexuation, xi, xii, xxii, 23, 25, 26, 28, 43, 44, 77–81, 86, 94, 119–121, 123, 125, 127–129, 141, 144–145, 163, 164, 167, 169, 172, 173, 174, 176, 177, 178
  asymmetry of, xxi, 3, 15, 28, 45, 81, 106, 120, 130–131, 136, 164
  diagram of, 11–21, 122, 126, 128, 164, 168, 173
  formulas of, xvii, xviii, xxiii, 8, 77, 78, 84, 102–103, 105–118, 120, 125–128, 129–145, 148–149, 150–151, 171–176
signifier, xvi, xix, 2–3, 6, 7, 10, 15, 16, 17, 19, 44, 50, 51, 56, 57, 62, 63, 64, 65, 66, 67, 68, 70, 71, 72, 80, 81, 83, 96, 97, 108, 119, 122, 131, 133, 143, 147–148, 149, 150, 152, 153, 163, 166, 171, 172
signifierness, xix, xxi, 17, 64, 70, 83, 147
Silesius, Angelus, 1
singular, xx, 3, 4, 14–15, 16, 20, 108, 113–114, 116, 117, 118–120, 122, 124–125, 126–129, 130, 131, 135, 137, 140, 141, 164–165, 166, 167, 168, 170, 175–176
Soler, Colette, xviii, 120, 121, 122, 127
soul, 23, 41–42
  in Aristotle, 36–37
  soul-love, 38–40, 41, 52, 134
speech, xiii, 9, 19, 53, 78, 84–86, 89–90, 146
structure, xii–xiii, xix, xx, xxi, xxiii, 1, 2, 17, 19, 21, 28, 41, 42, 43, 44, 51, 52, 53, 54, 59, 62, 63, 70, 73, 79, 81, 83, 84, 86, 88, 89, 91–92, 94, 95, 143, 145, 146, 148, 149–150, 159, 161–162, 163–164, 168, 169–170, 172, 177, 178
subject, xi, 2, 18, 20, 26, 41, 50, 51, 58, 59, 63, 73–74, 84, 105, 116, 119, 123, 125, 130, 134, 146, 150, 153, 158, 161, 164, 166, 168, 178
  in Aristotle, 97, 100, 101
  barred, 11–12, 13, 15, 43–44, 52–53, 110, 121, 132, 146–148, 149, 153, 172
  of psychoanalysis, xiv, 43–44
  of science, xiv, 36–37, 40, 41, 43–44
  in Žižek, 66, 69, 71, 72
subjectivation, xii, xvi, xvii, xix, xxii, xxiii, 23, 26, 44, 53, 70, 77, 90, 106, 125, 126, 127, 129, 130, 134, 137, 141, 142, 145, 161, 163, 164, 166, 167, 168, 169, 172, 173, 176–177, 178
substance, xviii, xx, 2, 6, 7–9, 10, 24, 25, 27, 28, 29, 33, 37, 39, 47, 48, 55, 58, 60, 66, 69, 71, 79, 86, 98, 99, 138, 159
symbolic, xii, xiii, xxi, 9, 10, 13, 14, 16, 17, 21, 23, 27, 36, 41, 43, 48, 49, 58, 66, 67, 72–73, 77, 91, 117, 146, 148, 153, 164, 170, 179

Teresa, Saint, 1, 20
"There is no sexual relationship," xi, xiv, xvii, xix, xx, xxi, xxiii, 2, 7, 8, 12, 24, 25, 27, 28–29, 38, 40, 45, 48, 56, 59, 70, 77–78, 81–82, 89–94, 102, 103, 107, 117, 118, 123, 130, 133, 171
  and sexed liaisons, xi, xiii, xviii, xxii, 2, 10, 25, 29, 58, 78, 90, 113, 115, 117–118, 121, 124–125, 133, 138, 171, 174
Thing, 49–50, 51–52, 53, 66–67
transcendental, 70, 73, 89, 93–94
truth
  and absence of sexual relationship, 44, 81, 85, 86, 91, 94, 119, 132, 178
  conditional, 85, 93–95
  in discourse, 146–149, 153
  as function, 94–95, 177–179
  half-said, xiv, 67, 131, 133, 154, 178

truth (cont.)
  and hysteric, 121, 125, 129
  of incompleteness, xi–xii, xiv–xv, 44, 77, 81, 83–85, 86, 87, 89, 93–95, 129, 151, 154, 179
  inexistence of, 158–159
  and intuition, 88
  and knowledge, 41–42, 43, 81–82, 88
  of knowledge, 131, 137, 177, 179
  knowledge of, 29, 77, 82, 131, 137, 144, 149, 151, 157, 161, 177, 179
  and logical positivism, 95, 136, 138
  as material cause, 44
  as meaningless, xiv–xv, 156
  and the real, 177–179
  and science, 87, 90
  and semblance, 81, 82–84, 86, 89, 92, 95, 178
  true, 138–139, 179
  truth about, xii, xiv, 77, 82, 93–94, 95, 131, 179
  as void, 41, 43–44
  whole, xiv, 131
two
  "gap of the," 161
  and God, xix, xxi, 1–2, 6, 17–18, 20–21
  as inaccessible, 145, 162, 167, 169
  and number, xxiii, 27–29, 38, 43, 48, 59, 129, 140, 161, 163–164, 165, 166–168, 170
  -as-One, xi, xix, xxi, 2, 18, 21, 28, 35, 132, 164, 165
  ones, 21
  sexes, xi, xxi, 2, 18, 25–29, 30, 37, 43, 48, 58–59, 80, 90, 123, 126, 140, 161
  them-, 18, 178
  in Žižek, 71

unconscious, xiv, xxi, 13, 43, 44, 45, 47, 53, 55, 58, 59, 60, 78, 90, 95, 127, 132, 146, 158
undecidability, xv, xxiii, 74, 94–95, 117, 134, 143–144, 145, 171–173, 174, 176, 177
universal(s), xviii, 137–138, 139, 140, 144, 148

  in Aristotle, 97–102
  man as a, 108–110, 111, 118, 123, 126, 129, 130, 132, 134, 136, 137–138, 139, 140, 141, 142–143, 144, 165, 167, 169–170, 172, 173, 175, 176
  negation of the, 102–103, 107
  woman and, 3, 4, 14, 15, 111–117, 119, 120, 121, 124, 126, 127–129, 134, 135, 136, 137–138, 139, 140, 141, 144, 166, 168, 172, 173, 175

vagina, 30, 53, 116
virgin, 168–169, 170, 173
void, xix, 41, 43, 44, 50, 51, 64, 65–67, 68, 69, 70, 71, 100, 116, 131–132, 141, 144, 177

Weismann, Friedrich Leopold August, 30–31
Weltanschauung, xiv, 35, 36, 44, 93
West-Eberhard, Mary-Jane, 31
Wollman, Elie, 61
woman
  and contingency, 134–136, 137, 142–143, 150, 171, 172, 173, 176
  in diagram of sexuation, 11–16, 19–21, 122, 126, 128, 164, 168, 173
  "does not exist," xiii, 3, 110–111, 115–117, 120, 155, 164, 168, 171–172, 173
  ex-sistence of, 3, 4, 16, 99, 117, 122, 128–129, 135, 136, 148, 150, 164, 168, 169, 171, 173, 176, 177
  and formula(s) of sexuation, 105–108, 111, 112, 113–117, 126, 128, 129–130, 134–135, 138–140, 144, 166, 168, 171–173, 176, 177
  and God, 1, 16–17, 19–21
  and hysteric, 118–119, 120–129, 131, 139, 175–176
  and impossibility, xxiii, 26, 106, 108, 112–113, 114, 117, 124, 130, 134–136, 137, 142, 144, 150, 161, 164, 165, 166, 169, 171, 172, 173, 174, 175, 176–177, 178

inexistence of, xviii, xxi, 117, 122, 126,
128–129, 130, 133, 135, 136, 140–141,
148, 150, 155, 161, 164–166, 168–169,
171, 172, 173, 174, 176
and infinity, xxiii, 4, 168, 169, 170, 171,
176, 177, 178, 179
and *jouissance*, xx, 1, 2–5, 9–21, 92, 115,
129, 141, 143, 168, 171, 178
and love, 20, 176
as mother, 12–14, 15, 20
and negation of the exception, 129,
135, 166
as not-all, xi, xviii, xix, xx, xxii, xxiii,
19, 26, 28, 99, 102, 107, 111–117,
120–128, 129, 135, 137–138, 139, 140,
141, 148, 150, 164–165, 168, 170, 171,
172, 173, 175–176
objectification of, 15, 132, 141,
148–149, 150, 164–165, 167–168,
173
as Other sex, 9, 10, 15, 26–27, 28, 40,
77, 132, 137, 144
and phallus, 119–128, 130, 143,
170–171
and sexuation, 78–81, 103, 106, 108,
118
as signifier, 7, 25
as singular, xx, 3, 4, 14–15, 16, 20, 108,
113–114, 116, 117, 118–120, 122,
124–125, 126–129, 130, 131, 135, 137,
140, 141, 164–165, 166, 167, 168, 170,
175–176
undecidability and, xxiii, 134, 171, 172,
173, 174, 176, 177
as x, 106, 138
world, xii–xiii, xix, 23, 28, 31, 32, 33, 35,
36, 40, 41, 42, 45, 71, 73, 79, 84, 88,
132, 146, 162, 165
writing
arche-, 84
and impossibility, xii–xiii, 78–84, 88,
90, 92–93, 102, 138, 139–140, 143,
178–179
and letter, 85
logical, 84–86, 88–89, 96, 98–102
of mystics, 9, 16

and phallic function, xii, 77–83, 86,
88, 90, 102–103, 105–107, 109–117,
120, 128–129, 131, 134–135, 138,
178–179
scientific, xxi, 86–91

zero, xxiii, 161–169
-concept, 162–163, 169
duality of, 162, 169
dyad one/, 161, 167, 172
gap between one and, 140, 141, 163,
168, 169
and hysteric, 135, 175
and impossibility of numbering, 162,
169
of inexistence, 129, 137, 140, 145,
155–156, 158, 162, 163, 165, 168–169,
177
as limitless, 144
as missing one/One, 140, 141, 156,
161–162, 164
-object, 162–163, 169
as one, 126, 144, 162–164, 165, 166
as One, 140, 144, 163–164, 165, 166,
167–168, 170
Žižek, Slavoj, xviii, xxii, 49, 64–72, 74–75
Zupančič, Alenka, xv

www.ingramcontent.com/pod-product-compliance
Lightning Source LLC
Chambersburg PA
CBHW021350300426
44114CB00012B/1160